Postcolonial Images

ROY ARMES

Postcolonial Images

Studies in North African Film

INDIANA UNIVERSITY PRESS
Bloomington and Indianapolis

This book is a publication of

Indiana University Press
601 North Morton Street
Bloomington, IN 47404-3797 USA

http://iupress.indiana.edu

Telephone orders   800-842-6796
Fax orders   812-855-7931
Orders by e-mail   iuporder@indiana.edu

Library of Congress Cataloging-in-Publication Data

Armes, Roy.
  Postcolonial images : studies in North African film / Roy Armes.
    p. cm.
  Includes bibliographical references and index.
  ISBN 0-253-34444-1 (cloth : alk. paper) — ISBN 0-253-21744-X (pbk. : alk. paper)
  1. Motion pictures—Africa, North. I. Title.
  PN1993.5.A35A76 2004
  791.43'0961—dc22

                                        2004007896

1 2 3 4 5   10 09 08 07 06 05

For Jayne and Sarah

The post-colonial highlights a political condition characterising certain forms of cultural production, i.e. the legacy of colonial domination out of or against which cultural practices are seen to emerge. . . . [T]o speak of a post-colonial condition is to affirm the right to political and cultural self-determination.

—Alec G. Hargreaves & Mark McKinney, eds.,
Postcolonial Cultures in France

By taking hold of the means of representation, colonized peoples through-out the world have appropriated and transformed those processes into culturally appropriate vehicles. It is this struggle over representation which articulates most clearly the material basis, the constructiveness and dialogic energy of the "post-colonial imagination."

—Bill Ashcroft, *Post-Colonial Transformation*

Contents

Acknowledgments   xi
List of Acronyms   xiii

Introduction   1

PART ONE: HISTORIES

1. Beginnings in the 1960s   15

2. The 1970s   23

3. The 1980s   39

4. The 1990s   55

5. Into the Present   74

PART TWO: THEMES AND STYLES

6. An Indigenous Film Culture: *El Chergui* (1975)   87

7. History as Myth: *Chronicle of the Years of Embers* (1975)   96

8. A Fragile Masculinity: *Omar Gatlato* (1976)   105

9. Memory Is a Woman's Voice: *La Nouba* (1978)   114

10. Imag(in)ing Europe: *Miss Mona* (1987)   123

11. Defeat as Destiny: *Golden Horseshoes* (1989)   132

12. Sexuality and Gendered Space: *Halfaouine* (1990)   141

13. A Timeless World: *Looking for My Wife's Husband* (1993)   150

14. A New Future Begins: *Silences of the Palace* (1994)   159

15. A New Realism? *Ali Zaoua* (1999)   169

Conclusion   178

Appendix A. Dictionary of Feature Filmmakers   189
Appendix B. List of Films   213
Notes   229
Bibliography   255
Index   267

Acknowledgments

During my years of research into African—and particularly North African—cinemas, I have received help and support from a wide range of individuals and organizations. Among those deserving especial thanks for material help or intellectual stimulus are Hédi Abdeljaoud, Olivier Barlet, Mourad Bouchichi, Ahmed Boughaba, Sandra Carter, Isabelle Debien, Zineb Derbal, Kevin Dwyer, Yulia Egorova, Sabry Hafez, Philippe Jalladeau, Ida Kummer, R. Kevin Lacey, Oliver Leaman, Martine Leroy, Tudor Parfitt, Marta Sanchez, John Simmo, Dominique Santhiles, Andrej Sprah, Geil Teicher, N. Frank Ukadike, Magda Wassef, and Abdellah Zaakour. I owe particular thanks to Matthew Stevens for his early support for this project, even though we were not able to continue our collaboration through to publication.

Some of the material presented here has been published in an earlier form in the various publications listed in the bibliography, in my regular annual articles on Maghrebian cinemas for *International Film Guide,* or in papers prepared for conferences in locations as diverse as Llubjana, Taba, Punkaharhu, and Binghamton, New York.

For help with the illustrations I am grateful to various film festivals and distributors: the Journées Cinématographiques de Carthage, the Festival International de Montpellier, the Festival des Trois Mondes at Nantes, the Festival Cinema Africano Milano, the Biennale des Cinémas Arabes at the Institut du Monde Arabe, Women Make Movies, and the Médiathèque des Trois Mondes in Paris.

I must in particular thank Middlesex University, the British Academy, and the Arts and Humanities Research Board for their consistent financial support for my research over the years and the Leverhulme Trust for the Emeritus Fellowship which made the book's completion possible.

List of Acronyms

ACCT	Agence de Coopération Culturelle et Technique	France
ACE	Atelier du Cinéma Européen	France
ACT	Association des Cinéastes Tunisiens	Tunisia
AJCT	Association des Jeunes Cinéastes Tunisiens	Tunisia
ALN	Armée de Libération Nationale	Algeria
ANAF	Agence Nationale des Actualités Filmées	Algeria
CAAIC	Centre Algérien pour l'Art et Industrie Cinématographiques	Algeria
CAC	Centre Algérien de la Cinématographie	Algeria
CAV	Centre Audio-Visuel	Algeria
CCM	Centre Cinématographique Marocain	Morocco
CDC	Centre de Diffusion Cinématographique	Algeria
CLCF	Conservatoire Libre du Cinéma Français	France
CNC	Centre National de la Cinématographie	France
CNCA	Centre National du Cinéma Algérien	Algeria
CNSAD	Conservatoire National Supérieur d'Art Dramatique	France
DEA	Diplôme d'Etudes Approfondies	France
DEFA	Deutsche Film-AG	Germany
EC	European Community	
ENADEC	Entreprise Nationale de Distribution et d'Exploitation Cinématographiques	Algeria
ENAPROC	Entreprise Nationale de Production Cinématographique	Algeria
ENPA	Entreprise Nationale de Productions Audiovisuelles	Algeria
ENTV	Entreprise Nationale de Télévision	Algeria
ERTT	Etablissements Radio-Télévision Tunisiens	Tunisia
ESEC	Ecole Supérieure des Etudes Cinématographiques	France
ESRA	Ecole Supérieure de Réalistion Audiovisuelle	France

FACC	Fédération Algériennne des Ciné-Clubs	Algeria
FAMU	Filmov Akademie Múzikých Uměni (Film and Television Faculty of the Academy of Performing Arts)	Czechoslovakia
FAS	Fonds d'Action Sociale	France
FEMIS	Fondation Européenne des Métiers de l'Image et du Son	France
FEPACI	Fédération Panafricaine des Cinéastes	Africa
FESPACO	Festival Panafricain du Cinéma de Ougadougou	Burkina Faso
FIFAK	Festival International du Film Amateur de Kélibia	Tunisia
FLN	Front de Libération Nationale	Algeria
FNCCM	Fédération Nationale des Ciné-Clubs au Maroc	Morocco
FTCA	Fédération Tunisienne des Cinéastes Amateurs	Tunisia
GATT	General Agreement on Tariffs and Trade	
GDR	German Democratic Republic	Germany
GPRA	Gouvernement Provisoire de la République Algérienne	Algeria
ICADI	Institut Communal des Arts Décoratifs et Industriels de Liège	Belgium
IDHEC	Institut des Hautes Études Cinématographiques	France
IFC	Institut Français de Cinéma	France
INC	Institut National de Cinéma	Algeria
INSAS	Institut National des Arts du Spectacle et Techniques de Diffusion	Belgium
INSIC	Institut National des Sciences de l'Information et de la Communication	Algeria
ISADAC	Insitut Supérieur d'Art Dramatique et d'Animation Culturelle	Morocco
JCC	Journées Cinématographiques de Carthage	Tunisia
MNA	Mouvement National Algérien	Algeria
NCO	Nationale Commissie Voorlichting Bewustworging Ontwikkelingssamenwerking	Holland
NFTVA	National Film and Television Academy	Holland
NOS	Nederlandse Omroepstichting	Holland

OAA	Office des Actualités Algériennes	Algeria
ONCIC	Office National du Commerce et de l'Industre Cinématographiques	Algeria
ORTF	Office de Radiodiffusion et de Télévision Française	France
RAI	Radio-televisione italiana	Italy
RTA	Radiodiffusion Télévision Algérienne	Algeria
RTM	Radio-Télévision Marocaine	Morocco
RTT	Radio-Télévision Tunisienne	Tunisia
SAC	Service Algérien du Cinéma	Algeria
SATPEC	Société Anonyme Tunisienne de Production et d'Expansion Cinématographiques	Tunisia
SDC	Service de Diffusion Cinématographique	Algeria
SEACI	Secrétariat d'Etat aux Affaires Culturelles et à l'Information	Tunisia
SNED	Société Nationale d'Edition et de Diffusion	Algeria
TNP	Théâtre National Populaire	France
UCLA	University of California at Los Angelesm	USA
VGIK	Vsesoyuznyi gosudarstvennyi institut kinematografii (All-Union State Cinema Institute)	Russia

Postcolonial Images

Introduction

> Perhaps it belongs to film makers of societies which weren't in at the origins of cinema's invention to question the structures and types of construction of films inherited from classical cinema. It seems to me that cinema can be a form of writing capable of regenerating a mode of thought.
>
> —Moumen Smihi[1]

Novel, Film, and Imperialism

In *Culture and Imperialism* Edward Said posits that the European nineteenth-century novel and contemporary European imperialism are closely related. It is not that the novel can be said to have "caused" imperialism, but that "the novel, as a cultural artifact of bourgeois society, and imperialism are unthinkable without each other." Said further argues that "imperialism and the novel fortified each other to such a degree that it is impossible . . . to read one without in some way dealing with the other." For Said, there are parallels at every level. Firstly, in the nature of the protagonist:

> The novelistic hero and heroine exhibit the restlessness and energy characteristic of the enterprising bourgeoisie, and they are permitted adventures in which their experiences reveal to them the limits of what they can aspire to, where they can go, what they can become. Novels therefore end either with the death of the hero or heroine . . . or with the protagonists' accession to stability (usually in the form of marriage or confirmed identity . . .).[2]

In a situation where, in Said's view, "without empire . . . there is no European novel as we know it," a similar parallel between narration and imperialism can be found in the narrative stance adopted by European writers. This is evident in "the far from accidental convergence between the pattern of narrative authority constitutive of the novel on the one hand, and, on the other, a complex ideological configuration underlying the tendency to imperialism."[3] Where plot is concerned, Said even goes so far as to toy with the idea that the novelist Samuel Richardson's minute constructions of bourgeois seduction and rapacity

> actually relate to British military moves against the French in India occurring at the same time. Quite clearly they do not in a literal sense; but in both realms we find common values about contest, surmounting odds and obstacles, and patience in establishing authority through the art of connecting principle with profit over time.[4]

And for Said there is a similar significance to be attached to the eighteenth- or nineteenth-century novel's reticences and exclusions. In his reading of Jane

Austen's novel *Mansfield Park* there is absolutely no doubt that "we are to conclude that no matter how isolated and insulated the English place (e.g., Mansfield Park), it requires overseas sustenance."[5] Yet the references in the novel to the Park's overseas source of support—Sir Thomas's sugar plantation in Antigua (which at this period would have been worked by slave labor)—are casual, external, and barely half a dozen in number. Jane Austen—like other European writers of the time—does not offer to the non-white Caribbean "any status imaginatively, discursively, aesthetically, geographically, economically other than that of sugar producer in a permanently subordinate position to the English. This, of course, is the concrete meaning of domination whose other side is productivity."[6]

Though Edward Said make no mention of film, a connection remarkably similar to that linking the novel and European colonialism can be posited between the Hollywood movie and U.S. twentieth-century imperialism. Moreover, though the novel was never overtly promoted by European governments in the nineteenth century as an expression of imperial values, the Hollywood movie has consistently and consciously been given direct support by successive U.S. governments, in the 1930s, during the cold war, and subsequently, as an expression of U.S. ideology. To quote Richard Maltby,

> The [U.S.] government's principal interest in promoting American film exports was derived from their value in the ideological war it was itself waging under Truman and Eisenhower. . . . The American film industry, because of its propaganda value, found itself a covert beneficiary of the Marshall Plan.[7]

Ironically the former European colonial powers have now come to suffer foreign dominance themselves, as exemplified by the Byrnes-Blum agreements between the U.S. and French governments of 1948, in which U.S. aid was promised to French industry on conditions which threatened to destroy the French film industry. More recently, as the stalled General Agreement on Tariffs and Trade (GATT) talks of 1993 show, the United States continues to seek hegemony, to open up markets totally for U.S. films, though Hollywood's current market dominance is staggering: "81% of European Community (EC) screenings in 1991, over 70% of European box-office takings, and 54% of all dramas and comedies broadcast on television," according to David W. Ellwood and Rob Kroes in their study of *Hollywood in Europe: Experiences of Cultural Hegemony.*[8] As the American analyst Thomas H. Guback put it as long ago as 1969:

> The American presence in Europe has been assisted by the American government. Our diplomatic corps and our trade specialists lend their help to the film industry in dealing with import restrictions, negotiations for film agreements, and in alleviating currency problems. Our government recognizes that film is not only a commodity which brings dollars to the United States, but it is useful in a propaganda sense. It tells our story.[9]

This sentiment is echoed by Ellwood and Kroes, who agree that "throughout Hollywood's history the world-wide power of the industry has been deliberately and effectively amplified by the nature of its connections with the Federal government. . . . There have rarely been times when the U.S. government has not been involved to some degree in the defence or promotion of the American industry's position in the world."[10]

Just as the continuity of imperial dominance from nineteenth to twentieth century (though now with a new dominating power and an added range of victims) is undeniable, so too is the Hollywood film's role as successor to the European novel as purveyor of the kind of narratives we so crave. In his study of *Reading for the Plot,* Peter Brooks notes that "from sometime in the mid-eighteenth century through to the mid-twentieth century, Western societies appear to have felt an extraordinary need or desire for plots, whether in fiction, history, philosophy, or any of the social sciences."[11] What Brooks does not add is that since that date, as serious literature has shown an ever greater distrust of plot, the need for strongly plotted narratives has been met by that most Aristotelian of forms, the Hollywood movie. There are crucial distinctions between novel and film (which are glossed over by the conventional notion that both are "texts to be read" and which I have tried to bring out clearly elsewhere),[12] but there can be little doubt that film's photographic images have that very same power of ambiguity which Brooks sees as characteristic of the novel's use of the preterite tense. He notes that many analysts of narrative have argued that "the preterite used classically in the novel is decoded by the reader as a kind of present, that of an action and a significance being forged before his eyes, in his hands so to speak."[13] Brooks's own comments on this novelistic usage can be applied word for word to the similar ambiguity of photographic images, which, by definition, must belong to the past (since they have been recorded) but unfold in an ongoing present tenseness as the film is projected before us: "If the past is to be read as present, it is a curious present that we know to be past in relation to a future we know to be already in place, already in wait for us to reach it. Perhaps we would do best to speak of the *anticipation of retrospection* as our chief tool in making sense of narrative, the master trope of its strange logic."[14]

If we look at the overall structure of Hollywood movies, a number of striking continuities with the nineteenth-century novel can be posited. In Brooks's definitions of how a novel starts, and what the role of the protagonist is, as in his estimation of the novel's underlying ethos and of the motive force which keeps the action moving forward, we find views echoed in virtually every Hollywood screenwriting manual from the 1920s onward (though most of these avoid his specifically psychoanalytic terminology). As an instance, David Mamet's set of three basic questions which, in his view, underlie the logic of screenwriting— "What does the hero want? What hinders him from getting it? What happens if he does not get it?"[15]—finds an echo in Brooks's concept of desire: "Desire is always there at the start of the narrative, often in a state of initial arousal, often having reached a state of intensity such that movement must be created, action undertaken, change begun."[16] The screenwriting manuals' active heroes, taking conscious decisions and then acting decisively and individualistically in the face of obstacles, are no more than a twentieth-century continuation of those "desiring machines," "whose presence in the text creates and sustains narrative movement through the forward march of desire, projecting the self onto the world through scenarios of desire imagined and then acted upon,"[17] whom Brooks defines as the typical protagonists of the nineteenth-century novel. Here Brooks anticipates Said in explicitly linking the nineteenth-century novel and the bourgeois society which produced it, in that at this period the novel for the first time in literature "takes aspiration, getting ahead, seriously, rather than as the object of satire":

> Ambition provides not only a typical novelistic theme, but also a dominant dynamics of plot: a force that drives the protagonist forward, assuming that no incident or action is final or closed in itself until such a moment as the ends of ambition have been clarified through success or renunciation.[18]

In similar vein Brooks argues that the essence of Balzac, a key figure in his formulation of the nineteenth-century novel, lies in the fact that "the concentration of desire projected onto the world as will constitutes the *primum mobile* of plot, leverage on circumstance, movement forward and upward."[19]

Brooks is very much concerned with positive dynamics and his basic definition of how plot might best be conceived is an erudite expression of the need to combine logic and surprise which the Hollywood manuals urge on aspirant screenwriters. In Brooks's view, the essence of plot is best conceived as the combination of two codes postulated by Roland Barthes, the proairetic (or code of actions) and the hermeneutic (the code of enigmas and answers), or, more precisely, the overcoding of the former by the latter. His elegant definitions of these two codes are as relevant to the Hollywood movie as to the nineteenth-century novel, since the former too combines a code of action ("the logic of actions, how the completion of an action can be seen as a complete and nameable unit, which then enters the combination with other actions, to form sequences") and a code of enigmas ("the questions and answers that structure a story, their suspense, partial unveiling, temporary blockage, eventual resolution, with the resultant creation of a 'retarding structure' or 'dilatory space' which we work through towards what is felt, in classical narrative, to be meaning revealed").[20]

Brooks, in his analysis of the novel, deals more with what is included (and how it functions) rather than with the search for significant exclusions. But if we look properly, we can find in Hollywood and other forms of Western cinema during the twentieth century the very kind of omissions which, for Edward Said, are so significant in the eighteenth- or nineteenth-century novel. In the case of those Western films (mostly French) which have been shot on location in North Africa we find very clear equivalents to the exclusion of direct reference to Antigua in *Mansfield Park*. In an analysis of the Algerian people as seen in the mirror of colonial cinema, Abdelghani Megherbi, for example, finds "the explicit world vision of the colonisers" in the films shot by foreign outsiders in Algeria under colonialism:

> As far as these films are concerned (about fifty in total), colonial society had no need of certain conscious or subconscious interpretations to make everyday lived

reality coincide with the fictional image. The correspondence between the two is harsh, brutal, continuous, total. In accordance with the implacable logic of colonization, the Algerian is more or less absent everywhere. Whether this is in the cinema audience or in the profession of film making itself. Everywhere, if you happen to see him, it is in a phantasmagoric, fleeting form, represented by a two-dimensional silhouette, without weight, like a picture postcard palm tree or a threatening shadow wielding a cutlass or a gun.[21]

This conclusion is echoed by David Henry Slavin in his recent study of French colonial cinema in the period 1919–1939. As he notes, the films produced in the Maghreb inevitably had a very close relationship with the colonial authorities:

Because they were made on location in North Africa, the task of attracting a mass audience and financial backing was complicated by an equally urgent need for logistical support. French authorities in the Maghreb provided such support but extracted a price, influencing content and manipulating the message.[22]

A gap therefore opens up between the ambitions of the filmmakers and the actual meanings of the works produced:

While film makers declared their commitment to verisimilitude in portraying colonised peoples, their depictions of native life, accurate or not, were incidental to stories that reflected the worldview and mind-set of Europeans, colonial and metropolitan.[23]

By the late 1920s, according to Slavin,

Films respectful of Islamic culture were going out of style. Directors began shifting locales to settler-dominated Algeria, focusing scripts exclusively on Europeans and rendering North Africans invisible.[24]

A typical example is the most celebrated of the colonial films, *Pépé le Moko* (1937), in which director Julien Duvivier offered no roles to Algerian actors: "in that sense," Slavin notes, "no 'natives' inhabit Duvivier's Casbah."[25] In her analysis of the film, Ginette Vincendeau notes that, in the opening montage sequence, "Arabs" are not listed among the ten or so nationalities said to inhabit the Casbah:

Just as Arabs are erased from the list of ethnic groups in the Casbah, their voices are hardly heard in the rest of the film. . . . The silencing of Arab voices is particularly acute by contrast with the volubility of the actors speaking Jeanson's sparkling dialogue.[26]

The Colonial Heritage

Today it is clear that nationalism and colonialism are not simply antagonistic opposites, since, as Wimal Dissanayake points out in his study of Indian cinema, their relationship is riddled with paradoxes and is "complex, ambiguous, and multifaceted." Nationalism "extends the range and depth of colonialism, offers the most palpable resistance to it, subverts its imperatives and determi-

nations, and serves to reproduce it in subtle and not so subtle ways."[27] Maghreb
cinemas illustrate this point with particular clarity.

There had been film making in North Africa since the days of Lumière,
whose operatives shot a number of little scenes in Algeria and Tunisia and just
one scene, it seems, in Morocco. The 1895–1905 Lumière catalogue of 1,800
views lists around sixty little films shot in North Africa.[28] One of Lumière's best-
known cameramen, Félix Mesguich, who was born in Algeria, returned to work
there in 1905, and two years later traveled to Morocco with Western newspaper
reporters to film the aftermath of the French shelling of Casablanca, part of the
French involvement in Morocco which would lead to the establishment of the
Protectorate in 1912. In the period up to independence there is just one pioneer
figure in Maghreb film making, the Tunisian Albert Samama, also known as
Chikly (1872–1934), who made a pioneering short, *Zohra* (1922), and a longer
fictional piece, *Aïn al-ghazal* (*La fille de Carthage/The Girl from Carthage*, 1924),
both starring his daughter Haydée Chikly.[29] Apart from the work of Chikly, all
North African film production activity in the period before independence was
financed by foreign capital, used foreign players, and was destined for foreign
markets. Pierre Boulanger has admirably chronicled the 210 feature films he
has identified as being shot in North Africa between 1911 and 1962. Over fifty
fictional feature films were shot in Algeria, for example, during the period between the end of the First World War and the beginning of the war of liberation.
But these films were unknown to Algerians. As Merzak Allouache has observed,

> When people talk about this colonial cinema, we don't know what it's all about. We
> know that important directors came to film in Algeria. That there were all sorts of
> films, from the most racist to the most elaborate, the most paternalistic. . . . The
> problem is, we haven't seen these films. Or, at best, very few of them.[30]

The use of the Maghreb as a location for the shooting of U.S. and European
films has, of course, continued since independence. The only independent production company in 1960s Algeria, Casbah Films, co-produced a number of European films of very varying quality, among them Gillo Pontecorvo's *La bataille
d'Alger* (*The Battle of Algiers*, 1965) and Luchino Visconti's adaptation of Albert
Camus's novel *L'étranger* (*The Outsider*, 1967). The Algerian state film organization (Office National du Commerce et de l'Industrie Cinématographiques—
ONCIC) also adopted a policy for co-funding expensive works that had little
or no connection with the realities of Maghrebian life (and returned remarkably little to their backers). The best known and most respected of these co-
productions was Costa-Gavras's *Z* (1968). The use of Morocco and Tunisia as
locations for American and European productions emphasizes the disparity between Maghrebian film making and that of the West. Far more foreign films,
with infinitely larger resources, are shot in the Maghreb by outsiders than are
produced by Maghrebian directors. The figures for Morocco in 1996–1997 speak
for themselves: nine local features with a total budget of 21.5 million dirhams
(around $2.4 million), twenty-three foreign features with a budget (for local
shooting) of 885.5 million dirhams (i.e., $98 million).[31]

In the period between the end of World War II and independence, the French colonial state also set up its own production and distribution structures in the Maghreb. Abdelkader Benali, in *Le cinéma colonial au Maghreb*, argues that these structures were motivated mainly by a desire to act "against the growing influence of Egyptian cinema in the countries of the Maghreb": "in trying to create a Maghrebian cinema they were trying to preserve the countries of the Maghreb from the influence of an Arab-Islamic nationalism aiming at independence."[32]

The physical infrastructure of 560 or so 35mm cinemas inherited from the colonial state at independence was predominantly urban, reflecting the location of the settler communities for whose entertainment needs these cinemas had been built. This was a capitalist infrastructure which demanded—in order to be profitable—around three hundred feature films a year to circulate in each of the three countries. But barely three hundred features in total have been made in the Maghreb over the last thirty-five years and, since overall production in the Maghreb averages at about eight features a year, there is a huge demand for imported films (American, European, Egyptian, or Hindi). These have created an audience with a taste for the consumption of foreign movies with alien structures and values, which local production (however worthwhile) will never be able to match in terms of production values. Basically, every single Maghrebian film has to compete with thirty or forty imported films, virtually all of which will have had larger production budgets and have already recovered their costs elsewhere.

It is true that future Maghreb filmmakers could learn from working in various production roles on films which were exclusively foreign funded. But for the filmmakers who were to create a true indigenous film production in the Maghreb, this was not the model of production to be adopted. Many, like the Algerian Merzak Allouache, saw their task as to tell stories in a simple way, to avoid the "heavy machinery" of big international production and to sweep away the "classical structures of cinema." Their ideal was "a crew operating freely, with a hand-held camera if need be, with, of course, freedom for the expression of a point of view."[33] But this is a battle that can, of course, never simply be won. At the Fourth Moroccan National Film Festival at Tangier in December 1995 delegates were still noting that authorizations were given annually to five hundred foreign productions (features, publicity films, documentaries, and television programs), but that the feedback for Moroccan national production was minimal. For the filmmaker Abdelkader Lagtaâ, the question still to be addressed was, "Why is it that our film making has not been capable as yet, after existing for decades, of communicating with foreign audiences and arousing their interest?"[34]

The Filmmaker after Colonialism

The national cinemas born in the late 1960s, in the aftermath of independence in the Maghreb, are clearly very much part of the new sense of national identity which is seeking new forms of expression. But the particular approach adopted did not, in most cases, follow the pattern of stylistic innovation proposed by some of the Moroccan filmmakers, such as Moumen Smihi, in the early 1970s. Instead there was generally recourse to a variety of basically realist devices, such as the choice of the local variant of Arabic as the films' language and the production of compilation films documenting in conventional ways the evils of colonialism (pioneered by Ahmed Rachedi in his excellent *L'aube des damnés* [*Dawn of the Damned*, 1965]). Most early films adopt a predominantly realist style to chronicle the national struggle, seen as unifying the mass of the people against the colonizers and the wealthy landowners who were their collaborators (as in Mohamed Lakhdar Hamina's Algerian *Le vent des Aurès* [*The Wind from the Aurès*, 1966] and Omar Khlifi's Tunisian trilogy on the liberation, beginning with *L'aube* [*The Dawn*, 1966]). The filmmakers' overriding ambition continued to be that of expressing reality as seen from a specifically Algerian, Moroccan, or Tunisian perspective. In this spirit, Moumen Smihi describes his debut film, *El Chergui* (1975), as "the history of the Moroccan people on the eve of independence,"[35] while Abdellatif Ben Ammar sought in *Sejnane* (1974) to offer "a global analysis of Tunisian society during the events leading up to its independence."[36]

The personal aspirations of the individual filmmakers, however, could only be realized within the context provided by the state, without whose active support a film was unlikely to be realized. While all three countries set up national film corporations, the most extreme instance of state control occurred in Algeria. In this connection it is instructive to compare the output of the state monopoly, ONCIC, with that of the Deutsche Film-AG (DEFA), which occupied a similar position in the German Democratic Republic (GDR). In both cases we find the filmmaker occupying an ambiguous representative role, "a middle ground where originality is compromised by speaking on behalf of others," to quote Thomas Elsaesser's verdict on the "subsidised artist."[37] Censorship is ever present (whether this is self-censorship, a bureaucratic choice of subjects to receive funding, or the cuts demanded after shooting). In addition, there is, in both instances, a paucity of women filmmakers combined with a constant recourse to female protagonists, and an increasing distance from popular taste, as filmmakers are pressured to conform to what, over time, becomes an outdated state rhetoric.[38]

If the dominant Egyptian commercial cinema was widely seen as an enemy, all the new Maghrebian filmmakers—like their contemporaries elsewhere in the Arab world—could draw positive inspiration for their work from the pioneering efforts in Egypt of Youssef Chahine and Chadi Abdel Salem. In broad terms we have in North Africa a corpus of about 312 feature films made over thirty-eight years by 141 directors. In addition there are some fifty features made over thirty-three years by twenty-eight filmmakers of Maghrebian origin working in Europe. It is difficult to give exact figures. Conventional listings include feature-length compilation films, some (but not all) feature-length documentaries, a handful of films shorter than seventy-five minutes, some features made up of episodes directed by different filmmakers (usually newcomers), and a few privately funded 16mm films made with little hope of commercial cinema release. This figure ignores television films, unless these were given a cinema release or shown at film festivals. It is equally difficult to give exact dates for the films themselves, since a number of them have received no showing at all, others have been seen only abroad or at festivals, and some have had their release delayed because of censorship or distribution difficulties. Kevin Dwyer notes, for example, that between 1988 and 1996—a period in which some Moroccan films were finding a real audience at home—twelve of the thirty-three films produced were never distributed.[39] The situation is also complicated by the fact that so many filmmakers previously resident in North Africa now live abroad.

Of the 362 fictional features produced in all, 46 percent (169) are first features, and of the 169 filmmakers, under half (83) have gone on to produce a further feature. This abundance of first features may seem surprising but, thanks to the patterns of state funding and the policies of the television companies, the same phenomenon has occurred in France with a rise from just 9 percent first features in 1954 (on the eve of the New Wave) to 42 percent (62 features out of 150) in 1992.[40] For many of those Maghrebian filmmakers who have made a second film, the gap between productions has been enormous: twenty-one years (1972–1993) for the Algerian Djafar Damardjji, twenty-two years (1980–2002) for the Tunisian Abdellatif Ben Ammar, twenty-five years (1970–1995) for the Moroccan Hamid Benani. Moreover, the difficulties caused by low national outputs and the scarcity of production finance mean that only a handful of filmmakers have directed as many as half a dozen fictional feature films for cinema release, Merzak Allouache, Mostafa Derkaoui, and Hakim Noury being the most prolific (with eight features each).

The Maghrebian filmmakers are members of a Westernized bilingual elite of the kind found throughout the postcolonial world. They can probably claim to be the best-educated group of filmmakers in the world, with qualifications which many academics might envy.[41] In addition there has been a long tradition of film school training for filmmakers from the Maghreb, and of the 139 filmmakers who have completed a feature, around 56 percent (seventy-nine in all) are film school graduates. The first Maghrebian student at the French film school (Institut des Hautes Études Cinématographiques—IDHEC) in Paris seems to have been the Moroccan Ahmed Belhachmi, who, after graduating in 1951, returned to become the first Moroccan director of the national film organization (Centre Cinématographique Marocain—CCM), before seeking his further career outside cinema. Since it shaped so many Maghrebian filmmakers, it is interesting to consider Moumen Smihi's comment on the French film school in the mid-1960s:

> The IDHEC courses were very bookish at the time, and it can't be said there was a great openness to what is called the Third World. No one was really interested

in that except for Georges Sadoul. Then, cinema was only considered from two angles: the Hollywood angle and the angle of French cinema, old or new wave. In fact the teaching was essentially technicist, and kept to that.[42]

From a 2002 perspective, the 139 Maghrebian filmmakers form, to a remarkable extent, a homogeneous group. They are almost all men. Only ten women have directed a conventional feature film—the Tunisians Selma Baccar, Nejia Ben Mabrouk, Moufida Tlatli, Kalthoum Bornaz, Nadia El Fani, and Raja Amari; the Moroccans Farida Bourquia and Farida Benlyazid; and the Algerians Yamina Bachir-Chouikh and Hafsa Zinaï Koudil (the latter working in Super 16)—while the Algerian novelist Assia Djebar has made two feature-length reflective pieces for the Radiodiffusion Télévision Algérienne (RTA), which have received film festival showings abroad. If we consider their age, the 133 filmmakers whose dates are available were born between 1927 and 1971. At first sight, the spread seems wide, but with just three exceptions, all of them were born after 1930, and only six were born after 1960. If we contract the time scale slightly, over 70 percent were born between 1940 and 1959 and indeed over half were born in the 1940s. With only one director born in the 1970s, the dearth of younger filmmakers is even more striking than the paucity of women directors.

Even in the 1990s some of the newcomers are much the same age as those whose feature film careers began twenty or more years earlier, and it is reasonable to see the bulk of this group as forming a single generation of filmmakers. In Tunisia, for example, Ferid Boughedir (b. 1944), whose first co-directed feature was released in 1970, is virtually the same age as Ridha Behi (b. 1947), whose career began in 1977; Mahmoud Ben Mahmoud (b. 1947), who began in 1982; Nouri Bouzid (b. 1945), whose first feature dates from 1986; and Kalthoum Bornaz (b. 1947), who made her debut in 1998. In Morocco, the pioneer Souheil Benbarka (b. 1942), whose striking first feature appeared in 1972, is the same generation as Jillali Ferhati (b. 1948), whose first work dates from 1977; Mohamed Aboulouakar (b. 1946), who began in 1984; Farida Benlyazid (b. 1948), who directed her first feature in 1988; Nour Eddine Gounajjar (b. 1946), whose initial 16mm feature was first shown in 1991; and the documentarist Abdelmajid Rchich (b. 1942), whose first fictional feature appeared in 2000. In Algeria, Mohamed Bouamari (b. 1941), whose first feature began the cycle of agrarian films in 1972, belongs in age terms alongside Merzak Allouache (b. 1944), who began in 1976; Brahim Tsaki (b. 1946), who put together his first feature in 1981; the film editor Rachid Benallal (b. 1946), who made his directing debut in 1993, and the documentary maker Azzedine Meddour (b. 1947), whose first fictional feature was released in 1997. By contrast, the twenty-six filmmakers of Maghrebian origin located in Europe tend to be on average some ten years younger (almost 80 percent were born in the 1950s and 1960s), and just over a quarter of them (27 percent) are film school trained.

As far as those based in the Maghreb are concerned, we can talk of a fairly coherent group in terms of shared experiences, typically a childhood under colonialism, followed by the heady excitement of independence (and in Algeria a possible firsthand acquaintance with the liberation struggle). They mostly studied abroad in the 1960s, a time of excitement in student politics (the May 1968 movement) and a golden age of film making, with the emergence on the international scene not just of the French New Wave but also of Antonioni and Fellini, Jancsó and Pasolini, and many more innovative filmmakers. To succeed in their studies they had to cope with tuition in a foreign language, whether they were studying academic subjects, drama, or film making. Most lived for at least three years away from North Africa, and several lived for much longer—up to ten years in some cases—in Paris, Brussels, Moscow, or some other major European city. A number of them are now permanently resident in France, Italy, or Belgium. On their initial return to the Maghreb, there were real problems to face, as Nouri Bouzid has recorded: "When they returned home, they were full of hopes and dreams. But harsh reality hit them in the face: no resources, no market, no freedom of expression—in addition to an array of defeats."[43]

When these filmmakers were very young, cinema in the Maghreb was an entertainment largely reserved for the French colonizers, though they may well have been first introduced to the classics of French cinema through screenings arranged in schools by the French authorities. By the time they became filmmakers themselves, North African screens were colonized by the same mixture of films found everywhere in Africa: cheap U.S., French, and Italian films, supplemented by Hindi and Egyptian melodramas and Hong Kong karate films. In setting out to tell stories of their own peoples they could hardly fail to be influenced by the European cinema they absorbed in their formative years, and those who studied in Paris could hardly fail to be affected by the cultural importance accorded to cinema by the French. But at the same time the new professional structures—the African Filmmakers' Association (Fédération Panafricaine des Cinéastes—FEPACI) and the festivals at Tunis (Journées Cinématographiques de Carthage—JCC) and Ouagadougou (Festival Panafricain du Cinéma de Ouagadougou—FESPACO), which came into being in the 1960s and 1970s—served to introduce them to the work of their colleagues elsewhere in the African and Arab worlds and to remind them of their shared cultural identity.

Part One   *Histories*

Culture in the Maghreb emphasises the role of popular national culture and
the relationship of cultural processes to the forces and relations inherent in
the prevailing mode of production, and pays considerable attention to the
structures of the social totality in which culture functions. This has given the
quest for independence and for national identity in its films a distinct flavour
and enabled them to probe its complex and constantly shifting nature.

—Sabry Hafez[1]

1   Beginnings in the 1960s

The question of national identity is central to the new cinemas which emerged in the Maghreb after independence and it is reasonable to see the gradual development of cinema as part of the wider search to restore an Arab identity in a world of rapid transition. In the case of cinema, this search was, of course, strengthened by the fact that the state has, since the mid-1960s, had a crucial role in deciding which films get made and which, having been made, get shown. Moreover, in addition to overt censorship, self-censorship, the adoption of the official line, and the avoidance of so-called taboo subjects are factors which have shaped overall development and the background against which the truly major Maghrebian films made since 1966 need to be judged. But the beginnings of cinema after independence in the three countries of the Maghreb could hardly have been more different.

Algeria

In Algeria film was seen to form a vital part of the liberation struggle by the Front de Libération Nationale (FLN), the army, and the Algerian provisional government in exile (Gouvernement Provisoire de la République Algérienne—GPRA). The first production unit, the Groupe Farid, was set up in 1957 by a group of filmmakers led by the French FLN activist René Vautier (b. 1928), who went on to make the major film of the period *Algérie en flammes* (*Algeria in Flames*, 1959).[2] A film school was set up, but Vautier was to see four of his pupils die in battle. As Mouny Berrah notes, "from 1957–1962, Algerian cinema was a site of solidarity, exchange and expression between members of the Algerian maquis and French intellectuals who sympathised with the liberation movement."[3] Among those involved were some of the key figures of the future Algerian cinema, including Mohamed Lakhdar Hamina and Ahmed Rachedi. The first post-independence feature, *Une si jeune paix* (*Such a Young Peace*, 1965), was directed by the French FLN activist, Jacques Charby.

Subsequent Algerian-directed features were produced by a variety of state production organizations, initially the Centre National du Cinéma Algérien (CNCA), which produced three features, including that of Jacques Charby, between 1965 and 1966, and the newsreel company the Office des Actualités Algériennes (OAA), which was gradually transformed into a feature film production organization by its director Lakhdar Hamina, who made two features there between 1966 and 1967 (and produced two more in the 1970s). Another important production context was the Algerian television organization RTA, which co-produced the first Algerian feature and nurtured the careers of many who would go on to contribute to the international reputation of Algerian film making. The sole private company, active in 1965–1967, was Casbah Films, which specialized in foreign co-productions (with foreign directors). Its founder was the former FLN activist Yacef Saadi (b. 1928), whose own story formed the basis of the company's best-known film, Gillo Pontecorvo's *The Battle of Algiers* (1966). In addition, the CNCA co-produced a film with France, Denys de la Patellière's *Soleil noir* (*Black Sun*, 1967)—a policy which was continued, after the reorganization of production, when Algeria co-produced, among other features, Costa-Gavras's internationally celebrated film *Z* (1968).

The 1967 reorganization led to a new monopolistic state company, ONCIC, which focused specifically on production. ONCIC was to produce virtually all the Algerian features up to 1984, when it was dissolved. A unique feature of ONCIC was that filmmakers became state employees, receiving a monthly salary. As a further part of the reorganization new administrative organizations were set up. The Centre de Diffusion Cinématographique (CDC) was established to take over the ciné-bus role initially run by the colonial Service de Diffusion Cinématographique (SDC), and the Centre Algérien de la Cinématographie (CAC) took on administrative roles such as controlling access to the profession, supervising film theatres, running the Cinémathèque Algérienne, and so forth. This state-controlled film making monopoly had many paradoxes, as the director Merzak Allouache explains:

> Film makers functioned as civil servants. I worked in this way, and my first film was produced under this system. At one level, this system of state film production protected film makers from harsh market realities. But on the other hand it posed the problem of state censorship and self-censure. It also meant that even if a film maker were unable to produce a film, or could only make one every five years because of lack of funds, he would still receive a salary. There was inevitably a lot of corruption and a lot of bureaucratic waste.[4]

Inactivity was inevitable for some filmmakers, given that there were dozens of salaried film directors, but—on average—only two or three features could be made in Algeria each year. There have been severe criticisms of this system, for example by the emigré filmmaker Ali Akika.[5] Despite the fact that it was recovering from a savage war, Algeria produced more films than its neighbors (a situation which would continue until toward the end of the 1990s). As Mouny Berrah observes, the films "were all built upon idealistic nationalism, featuring heroes with no weaknesses and unity and cohesion against all obstacles."[6] Two films by Algerian directors were made at the CNCA. Ahmed Rachedi (b. 1938) made his first feature, *L'aube des damnés* (*Dawn of the Damned*, 1965), a compilation film which put the Algerian war of liberation within the context of contemporary Third World struggles. Writing thirty years later, Berrah notes that this powerful analysis of colonialism and the liberation movements in Africa remains "a classic of the genre."[7] Mustapha Badie (b. 1928) made the first Algerian fiction feature, co-produced with RTA, the ambitious but flawed *La nuit a peur du soleil*

(*The Night Is Afraid of the Sun*, 1966), a three-hour epic study of the origins, unfolding, and outcome of the war. Rachid Boudjedra is particularly harsh on the film, describing it as "the example of a bad film, melodramatic and superficial" and as revealing "an insidious influence, that of the Egyptian style in its most questionable form and with the most hackneyed folklore."[8] Mohamed Lakhdar Hamina (b. 1934) used the OAA as his production base for his two 1960s features, the masterly *Le vent des Aurès* (*The Wind from the Aurès*, 1966), a powerful if conventionally structured dramatic tale of a family destroyed by war, which established its director as Algeria's leading filmmaker. The symbolic figure of the mother, "though somewhat stereotyped, crystallises the common cause and brings forward a reality completely travestied by colonial cinema."[9] By contrast, *Hassan Terro* (1968) is the comic tale of a "little man" who becomes a hero by accident, adapted from his own play by the actor Rouiched, who plays the lead. Writing from a 1971 perspective, Boudjedra views the film very positively: "Algeria goes very far in its anti-militarism and already has its popular anti-hero who became almost legendary: *Hassan Terro*."[10]

At ONCIC after 1968 the thematic focus remained initially unchanged, with the war remaining the dominant topic for treatment for at least four more years, though the approaches to the subject were many and varied. The first film produced by ONCIC, *La voie* (*The Way*, 1968), directed by Mohamed Slim Riad (b. 1932), was based on the director's own experiences as a detainee in France and shows the deterioration of life for Algerian prisoners in French prison camps between 1958 and 1961 and the prisoners' struggle to retain their dignity. Other features were more conventional in inspiration. For his first feature Tewfik Fares (b. 1937), who had scripted Lakhdar Hamina's *The Wind from the Aurès*, made the Hollywood-style *Les hors-la-loi* (*The Outlaws*, 1969), a tale of three young men drawn into the liberation struggle. Rachedi adopted a blockbuster approach to his first fictional feature, *L'opium et le bâton* (*Opium and the Stick*, 1969), the adaptation of a novel by Mouloud Mammeri. Set in Kabylia, the film has a strong narrative structure but is marred both by a certain schematism in the definition of the characters and (for Arab speakers) by a distinct artificiality in the dialogue, caused by the government's ban on the use of the Berber language which would have been appropriate here. ONCIC's two collectively realized films used an episodic format: *L'enfer à dix ans* (*Hell for a 10 Year Old*, 1968) offered six stories dealing with children's experiences of the war and *Histoires de la révolution* (*Stories of the Revolution*, 1969) contained three stories of the resistance in action. These films offered initial 35mm production experience to a number of future directors but brought little that was new. These 1960s films, particularly *The Wind from the Aurès* and *Dawn of the Damned*, set the pattern for the future development of Algerian cinema:

> It became a militant cinema, a cinema with a cause and an educative mission, brimming with metaphors of change, rebirth and the forces of nature. It equates revolution and change with the sweeping winds that cleanse and refresh or the glowing fire that purifies and forges new reality.[11]

Fig. 1. *Dawn of the Damned* (1965), Ahmed Rachedi, Algeria

Morocco

In Morocco after independence, by contrast, the state took no powers to control film import, distribution, or exhibition, and Morocco's 350 35mm cinemas, mostly situated in urban areas, were left in the private sector. For the first twelve years after independence in 1956, almost all film making took place

Fig. 2. *The Wind from the Aurès* (1966), Mohamed Lakhdar Hamina, Algeria

within the secure context of the CCM, founded by the colonial authorities in 1944. At the CCM the focus was on the production of short films dealing with the sectors deemed to be state priorities, such as information, education, agriculture, and health. As Moulay Driss Jaïdi observes, "The films made responded to the demands of the different ministries which also commissioned newsreels designed for state propaganda."[12]

The first Moroccan feature films were produced by the CCM, twelve years after independence had been achieved. All three 1960s films were directed by CCM employees who had a considerable experience of producing short documentaries, and the Moroccan critic Jaïdi notes that "the feature films (co-)produced by the CCM and directed by its technicians were intended to extend that 'folklore' tendency which was appropriate to the commercial tourist short."[13] Two films were made in 1968. Mohamed B. A. Tazi (b. 1936) and Ahmed Mesnaoui (b. 1926) co-directed *Vaincre pour vivre* (*Conquer to Live*), which told of the social rise of a young carpenter who becomes a popular singer in the capital. Abdelaziz Ramdani (b. 1937) and Larbi Bennani (b. 1930) were joint authors of *Quand murissent les dattes* (*When the Dates Ripen*), which looked at the clash of tradition and modernity in a South Moroccan village. As Jaïdi has pointed out, these two films continued many of the tendencies of the short film output, combining propaganda and the conflict of tradition and modernity, with an added touch of melodrama.[14] The third Moroccan feature film, *Soleil de printemps* (*Spring Sunshine*, 1969) by Latif Lahlou (b. 1939), was much more indicative of the future of Moroccan cinema, being a seriously intended, if only partially successful, social study, dealing with the problems of an office worker from a rural background who finds it difficult to adjust to life in the city.

Tunisia

In Tunisia a state-owned organization, Société Anonyme Tunisienne de Production et d'Expansion Cinématographiques (SATPEC), was set up in 1957 to manage import, distribution, and exhibition of films. In the early 1960s SATPEC attempted to confront the multinational distribution companies whose films dominated the Tunisian domestic market, but a boycott by the foreign majors led to eventual capitulation by the Tunisian government in 1965. Undeterred, SATPEC established a film production context at Gammarth, an ambitious development which unfortunately was always slightly behind the times. Built to process film newsreels, it found these replaced by television news within two years of its opening. Moreover it was equipped to handle black-and-white film at just the moment when color was taking over. Needless to say it incurred losses which were eventually to lead to the virtual bankruptcy of the company.[15] The film division of Secrétariat d'Etat aux Affaires Culturelles et à l'Information (SEACI), the government department set up to supervise culture and information, was headed for most of the 1960s by the critic Tahar Cheriaa, a key influence on Maghrebian cinema. It produced two films by foreign directors, Mario Ruspoli's documentary *Renaissance* (1963) and Jean Michaud-Mailland's fictional feature, *H'mida* (1968). Tunisia was also the location of Jacques Baratier's internationally distributed feature *Goha* (1958), which introduced Omar Sharif to worldwide audiences. In addition, Tunisia—despite its limited number of cinemas (about one hundred fifty at the time of independence)—had a vibrant film culture, with a ciné-club movement which dated back to 1950. The strong amateur film making movement was reinforced by the creation of an organization which could act as its focus and spokesperson, the Association des Jeunes Cinéastes Tunisiens (AJCT), in 1961. Similar groupings of amateur filmmakers did not occur in Algeria, the Fédération Algérienne des Ciné-Clubs (FACC), or in Morocco, the Fédération Nationale des Ciné-Clubs au Maroc (FNCCM), until ten years later. The first amateur film festival, Festival International du Film Amateur de Kélibia (FIFAK), was set up at Kélibia in 1964, closely followed by the establishment of the JCC in Tunis, in 1966. Both these festivals continue into the new century, as does the film revue *SeptièmArt,* established as *Goha* in 1964. For the Tunisian critic Tahar Chikhaoui, "the 1960s were the years when things were constructed, put into place. What was most important was to unite Tunisia with the image."[16]

Omar Khlifi (b. 1934), who had already produced about a dozen short films within the context of the flourishing Tunisian amateur film movement in the 1960s, completed the first Tunisian feature. Like his Algerian colleagues, Khlifi chose the liberation struggle as his subject matter for a trilogy to be completed in 1970. All these films were independently produced or co-produced by the director's own company, Les Films Omar Khlifi. *L'aube* (*The Dawn,* 1966), set in 1954, was the story of three young men who give their lives in the struggle. It ends with an epilogue: the return from enforced exile of the future president, Habib Bourguiba, on 1 June 1955. Khlifi's second film, *Le rebelle* (*The Rebel,* 1968), looks back to an earlier Tunisian struggle in the 1860s under the rule of the beys and deals with a young man who is impelled into revolt by the murder of his father and brother. Another independently produced feature is *Mokhtar* (1968). While Khlifi's narratives are straightforwardly structured, this work by Sadok Ben Aicha (b. 1936), who was to edit several features in the 1970s, is a deliberately experimental tale, beginning with the funeral of a young writer who has committed suicide and mixing scenes from his life with fictional scenes from his novel.

SATPEC began its first involvement with feature production (like the corresponding Algerian organization CNCA) in collaboration with the national television service. *Khlifa le teigneux* (*Khlifa Ringworm,* 1968), adapted from a story by Béchir Khraief and directed by Hamouda Ben Halima (b. 1935), tells of a young man who makes good use of the baldness caused by his illness, since it allows him unique access to women. As Tijani Zalila has noted, "Tunisian national production is rather complex. It is too diversified to allow anyone to unravel its principal tendencies."[17] Yet, as Victor Bachy notes, it cannot be denied that "Tunisian films offer an image of a Tunisia which is independent but not yet free from the aftereffects of colonialism and confronted with all the problems of economic and cultural development."[18]

Though the production structures in the three countries of the Maghreb varied sharply, the filmmakers had things in common that cut across national boundaries. In terms of age, they were all born in the 1920s and 1930s and were thus about ten years older than the new generation of filmmakers, born in the 1940s, who began to dominate Maghrebian cinema from the 1970s. The Algerian directors are set apart by their close personal links with the liberation struggle. Vautier and Charby were both FLN activists. Rachedi had worked with Vautier in the army film unit and then followed him to the production collective, the Centre Audio-Visuel (CAV), where the documentary *Peuple en marche* (*A People on the March*, 1963) was made. Lakhdar Hamina had worked in the provisional government's film unit in exile in Tunis, while Riad had been interned in France for his political views. Though he had no combat experience, the Tunisian Khlifi relates to this group through his concern with the liberation struggle—the subject of his first three films and a clear thematic link between Algeria and Morocco.

As far as training is concerned, we find two groupings which cross national barriers. All five Algerians lack formal film school training, and to this group we may add the Tunisian Khlifi, who came from the Tunisian amateur film movement, and the Moroccan Mesnaoui, who began his involvement with cinema not at film school but through a correspondence course.[19] By contrast, the other six members of the group—four from Morocco (Lahlou, Ramdani, Tazi, and Bennani) and two from Tunisia (Ben Aicha and Ben Halima)—had received a formal three-year training at the French film school, IDHEC, graduating between 1954 and 1965. All except Bennani were in France to witness the birth of the New Wave and the striking stylistic innovations in cinema at that time.

2 The 1970s

Two welcome new expansions of North African cinema occurred in the 1970s. At the end of the decade, the first two films directed by women were completed by Selma Baccar and Assia Djebar respectively. Both films were to some extent marginalized, but they do signify a real breakthrough: each woman was able to make a further feature in the 1980s or 1990s, and each of the three subsequent decades would see at least three new women filmmakers emerge. The second development was the beginning of film making by Algerians living in France or Belgium, a process which would grow steadily over the following decades. Otherwise, for all three Maghreb countries, the 1970s were largely a period of consolidation.

Algeria

At the beginning of the 1970s there was considerable criticism in Algeria of ONCIC's continuing policy of funding expensive co-productions with France and Italy. Later in the 1970s—perhaps in response to this criticism and the commercial failure of most of these co-productions—ONCIC's co-production policy shifted toward the establishment of a new Arab identity and support for more meaningful films. Among the films co-produced in the mid-1970s were three films by the great Egyptian filmmaker Youssef Chahine—*Le moineau* (*The Sparrow*, 1973), *Le retour du fils prodigue* (*Return of the Prodigal Son*, 1975), and *Alexandrie pourquoi* (*Alexandria Why?*, 1978). This policy was continued in 1980 when ONCIC co-produced *Aziza* (1980), a major production by the Tunisian director Abdellatif Ben Ammar. The 1970s were the only decade in which Algerian film production was not disrupted by administrative changes. Perhaps as a result, the number of productions rose to thirty-five features in the decade. Four of the five directors who had made their debuts in the 1960s continued in the 1970s, with Mohamed Slim Riad making three further features, and Mohamed Lakhdar Hamina and Ahmed Rachedi each completing two. In addition, fifteen newcomers made their appearance and seven of these were able to establish themselves with more than one feature in the decade. By the end of the 1970s, Algeria had maintained its position of having produced more films than Tunisia and Morocco combined.

The last two films produced by Lakhdar Hamina at OAA were released in the early 1970s. His own feature *Décembre* (*December*, 1972), a tale of torture seen through the eyes and mind of a French officer who practices it, completed a loose and very diverse trio of films on the liberation struggle. Mouny Berrah links the film's Hollywood-style approach to Rachedi's 1969 film, *Opium and the Stick:* the two films share many of "the same qualities and flaws," and "illustrate the official version of history."[1] In a lighter vein, *El-Ghoula* (1972), directed by the actor Mustapha Kateb, is a tale of rural corruption (the title is slang for profiteering) ending with the discomfiture of the crooks (a fate which did not befall many of those who indulged in real profiteering and corruption in post-independence Algeria). Otherwise, with just a couple of exceptions, ONCIC maintained its monopoly and continued initially to foster films dealing with the liberation struggle. *Patrouille à l'est* (*Patrol in the East,* 1972), directed by Amar Laskri (b. 1942), recounts the misadventures of a patrol from the liberation army which is charged with delivering a French prisoner to the Tunisian border. It succeeds in its task, but only after heavy losses. In *Zone interdite* (*Forbidden Zone,* 1974), Ahmed Lallem (b. 1940) uses fictional footage and archive material to help show the growth of political awareness and activity in a village previously oppressed by the colonial forces and their local allies. In a similar vein, *Sueur noire* (*Black Sweat,* 1972), made by Sid Ali Mazif (b. 1943), shows a group of miners driven to political awareness by the repression of a strike in 1954. A film to some extent aside from the dominant 1970s trend of treating almost exclusively national subjects, though still a story of armed conflict, is Riad's tale of the Palestinian struggle *Sana'oud* (1972), which focuses on a young man recruited into the anti-Zionist movement and charged with an attack on a military camp in occupied territory.

But the two compilation films made in the 1970s followed the dominant trend. *La guerre de libération* (*The War of Liberation,* collective, 1973) retold the story of the war through archive footage and in a way acceptable to the authorities (an earlier personal version by Farouk Beloufa had been rejected). *Morte la longue nuit* (*Dead the Long Night,* 1979), co-directed by Riad and Ghaouti Bendeddouche (b. 1936), dealt with the worldwide struggle against neocolonialism. In a comic vein, Mustapha Badie's ONCIC feature, *L'évasion de Hassan Terro* (*Hassan Terro's Escape,* 1974), and the six-part television serial for RTA directed by Moussa Haddad (b. 1937), *Hassan Terro au maquis* (*Hassan Terro in the Resistance,* 1978), continued the adventures of Rouiched's comic hero previously chronicled by Lakhdar Hamina. It was Lakhdar Hamina who outshone all other tales of resistance and rebellion with his own epic account of fifteen years of struggle, *Chronique des années de braise* (*Chronicle of the Years of Embers,* 1975), which was the first African or Arab film to win the Palme d'or at the Cannes Film Festival. Shot in color, in a wide-screen format and with stereophonic sound, the film showed considerable visual imagination and was a remarkable technical achievement, with its three-hour narrative tracing the main events of Algerian history from 1939 to 1954. In a retrospective look at the ideology of the Algerian war film, Sabry Hafez finds

> The prevalence of a strong, and often simplistic, binary opposition between the positive hero, the *mujahid* (revolutionary or freedom fighter), the peasant and/or the intellectual, and his counterpart, the antagonist who is either a French soldier

or an Algerian collaborator. The *mujahid* is always noble, generous, proud, ready to sacrifice everything for the revolution.[2]

Given that ONCIC was a state organization, it is hardly surprising that the agrarian revolution of the early 1970s found an immediate reflection in the cinema and formed the second collective focus for Algerian cinema. Two 1972 features set the pattern of a whole series of films with rural themes and are key examples of the double approach adopted: looking at progress in contemporary rural society and documenting the abuses of the colonial past. *Le charbonnier* (*The Charcoal Burner*, 1972), the feature debut of Mohamed Bouamari (b. 1941), is a contemporary tale about a charcoal burner who loses his livelihood with the introduction of gas to the countryside and who also has to come to terms with his wife, who sides with the new order because of the opportunities it offers women. Bouamari's second feature, *L'héritage* (*The Inheritance*, 1974), also followed the trend for depictions of rural postcolonial society and is a harrowing picture of the heritage of colonialism, focusing on a man driven mad by torture but saved by his wife, who restores his sanity and leads the progressive forces to rebuild the village. Bouamari's third film, *Premier pas* (*First Step*, 1979) was a more overtly experimental work, a complexly structured tale about women's emancipation which received a muted reception.

Riad's *Vent du sud* (*Wind from the South*, 1975) is a look at the situation of women whose fathers refuse them the right to choose their own husbands, telling of an educated young woman who rebels, runs away, and finds happiness with a young peasant. Mazif's *Les nomades* (*The Nomads*, 1975) is the story of three sons who, on the death of their father, each choose a different way of proceeding—one leaving for the city, one keeping to the old ways, and the third joining one of the new farming collectives. A further hymn to the virtues of collective action was Haddad's *Auprès du peuplier* (*Beside the Poplar Tree*, 1972): the whole village rallies around old Slimane when he gets into trouble while digging a well which is financed by money sent from abroad by his son. Bendeddouche's *Les pêcheurs* (*The Fishermen*, 1976) follows the same line, depicting a group of fishermen who gradually develop the political awareness needed to succeed in the struggle with the boss who owns all the resources they need to make a living. Lallem's *Barrières* (*Barriers*, 1977) tells the story of Tahar, son of a wealthy family, who tries to keep control of his estates in the face of the social change brought about by the revolution, while Laskri's *El moufid* (*The Benevolent*, 1978) raises issues concerning the agrarian revolution through the story of the members of a documentary film crew who gradually become directly involved in the villagers' problems. Another film which belongs broadly to this trend, though adopting a very distinctive approach, is *L'olivier de Boul'Hilet* (*The Olive Tree of Boul'Hilet*, 1978), directed by Mohamed Nadir Azizi (b. 1941). Here, drawing on the wisdom of a dying old man, the hero succeeds in finding the water his village desperately needs, but he cannot find a place in the community and is forced to take on the old man's identity and continue his wanderings.

Fig. 3. *The Inheritance* (1974), Mohamed Bouamari, Algeria

The colonial period was also explored by two new filmmakers in the 1970s. *Noua* (1972), the sole feature made by Abdelaziz Tolbi (b. 1938), gives an explicit picture of the sufferings endured by the peasantry under French rule—high taxation, land seizure, eviction, forcible enlistment for military service in Indochina—but ends with the emergence of *mujahin* who give the people fresh hope and kill their principal oppressors. Two features directed by Mohamed Lamine Merbah (b. 1946), who had studied sociology, looked at the same subject of the colonial past from a more analytic perspective. *Les spoliateurs* (*The Plunderers*, 1972) plots the way in which a ruthless landlord totally destroys a hapless peasant by seizing his land, while *Les déracinés* (*The Uprooted*, 1976), a second and more profound exploration of the same theme, shows the lives of peasants uprooted from their land under colonialism, driven to a life of poverty in the slums of the big cities or exploited as underpaid labor in foreign-owned enterprises. The collectively made *Pour que vive l'Algérie* (*So That Algeria May Live*, 1972) drew attention to a whole range of government programs and achievements, of which rural reform was one. Berrah points to an interesting contrast:

> While the war films insisted on re-establishing, more often unconsciously than deliberately, a proud national image that had been tarnished by the French, rural films wanted to build a national image independent of the eyes of foreigners, the colonialists.[3]

The sense of conformity to a centrally determined set of themes was strong in the 1970s. When Rachedi wanted to deal with emigration in collaboration with the novelist and screenwriter Rachid Boudjedra, he first made an independent low-budget 16mm film, *Le doigt dans l'engrenage* (*A Finger in the Works*, 1974), for l'Amicale des Travailleurs Algériens en France. This film combines documentary and interview footage with fictional sequences depicting an emigrant who arrives in Paris and promptly gets lost in the métro. Subsequently Rachedi and Boudjedra were able to explore the same subject for ONCIC in a 35mm feature, *Ali au pays des mirages* (*Ali in Wonderland*, 1979), which offers a caustic picture of the situation confronting emigrants in France: Ali is a crane driver who uses a pair of binoculars to study the world below, into which he can never be assimilated. *Les bonnes familles* (*The Good Families*, 1972), a deliberately propagandistic feature made independently on behalf of the FLN by a collective headed by Djafar Damardjji (b. 1934), attacks the tendency to restore feudal privileges and other moves against the spirit of the revolution and contrary to the interests of the workers in 1970s Algeria. The film was completed, but apparently it was never distributed by ONCIC. Other features away from mainstream concern with war and agrarian reform include Riad's *Autopsie d'un complot* (*Autopsy of a Plot*, 1978), a political thriller in the mode of Costa-Gavras or Yves Boisset which traces the progress of a young journalist investigating an attack on his country's consulate in a Western country, and Mazif's *Leïla et les autres* (*Leïla and the Others*, 1978), a study of women's lives, this time in an urban context. In the film, the stories of two women, Myriem, a student who refuses an arranged marriage, and Leila, who struggles for respect and recognition at the workplace, are interwoven.

All the films outlined above fit comfortably with the dominant ideology of the period. But as Berrah observes, the real Algerian cinema "is composed of thematic and aesthetic exceptions."[4] Throughout the 1970s isolated works of distinctive quality, aside from the prevailing style and mood, were made and distributed, and it is these which have best stood the test of time. *Alger insolite* (*Tahia ya Didou*, 1971), a portrait of Algiers made by Mohamed Zinet (1932–1995), is a loosely shaped narrative about the wanderings of two French tourists. The film begins lightly but takes on a quite new coloring when the Frenchman, an ex-serviceman, finds himself unable to endure the apparent stare of an

Algerian he once tortured but who is in fact now blind. *Omar Gatlato* (1976), a picture of Algerian youth, was the feature debut of Merzak Allouache (b. 1944). A key date in the history of Algerian cinema, *Omar Gatlato* marked an end to the eternal stream of earnest tales of the liberation struggle and agrarian revolution, offering instead an amusing and very unofficial view of the post-revolutionary generation growing up in Algiers. Allouache's second feature, *Les aventures d'un héros* (*The Adventures of a Hero*, 1978), is equally original, a philosophic fable, the tale of a young peasant, Mehdi, who is given the role of confronting twentieth-century oppression and injustice and who roams though time and space, reality and legend.

Another isolated but striking work is *Nahla* (1979), directed by Farouk Beloufa (b. 1947). Set in Lebanon in 1975, the film follows the relationships between an Algerian journalist and three women, the singer Nahla, the journalist Maha, and the Palestinian activist Hind. Deftly shot and elliptically narrated, the film captures graphically the confusions of civil conflict. Equally unclassifiable is *La nouba des femmes du Mont Chenoua* (*The Nouba of the Women of Mount Chenoua*, 1978), which was directed by the novelist Assia Djebar (b. 1936). The fictional story of Lila—an architect who returns to her home region to investigate the circumstances of her brother's death—is interwoven with the documentary accounts of six old women who recall the events of the war and a section devoted to the legends and battles of the distant past (such as the 1871 revolt in the area of Mount Chenoua).

These are films that stand out in the 1970s. Unfortunately neither Zinet nor Beloufa was given the resources to make a second feature. Nor was Djebar able to make a 35mm feature for cinema release, though she did make one further 16mm film for RTA. But Allouache did pursue his distinctive path with a succession of further remarkable films in the following decades. The 1970s were also a period of cross-fertilization between ONCIC and RTA. A number of RTA films were given cinema release, including Tolbi's *Noua*, Merbah's *The Plunderers*, and Beloufa's *Nahla*. RTA participated in a number of co-productions of films destined for cinema release by ONCIC, including Allouache's *The Adventures of a Hero*, Riad's *Autopsy of a Plot*, and Mazif's *Leila and the Others*. Several directors established at RTA were able to direct films for the cinema. Moussa Haddad, for example, made *Les vacances de l'inspecteur Tahar* (*Inspector Tahar's Holiday*, 1973), the comic tale of Inspector Tahar's holiday in Tunisia, which involves him in a complicated murder. Djebar's two films of 1978–1982 were shown at international festivals, and films by television directors helped shape foreign perceptions of Algerian filmic identity but did not, however, create institutional unity between film and television production at home.

Morocco

In Morocco in the 1970s there was no sense of continuity with the previous decade, since all ten filmmakers who completed a feature in the 1970s were newcomers. Though the CCM had funded or co-funded the first three Moroccan feature films in the 1960s, it did not immediately continue this support in the new decade. There was little state support for the crucial experiments with narrative in the early 1970s, as it was not until 1977 that CCM's policy of involvement in feature film production was resumed. Between 1977 and 1979 CCM acted as co-producer of seven features (including Abdallah Zerouali's *Le tourbillon* [*The Whirlpool*], which remained incomplete until 1995) with contributions of between 19 percent and 63 percent. CCM also contributed 100 percent financing for Ahmed Bouanani's key experimental narrative *Mirage* (*Mirage*) and co-financed a Moroccan-Roumanian co-production, *Les bras d'Aphrodite* (*The Arms of Aphrodite*, 1975), directed by Mircea Dragan. This latter venture proved as ill judged as those embarked upon in the early 1970s by ONCIC in Algeria and was a total commercial disaster.[5]

The limited state involvement in film making led to a paucity of films in the 1970s, just fifteen in the decade, though during this period two filmmakers, Souheil Benbarka (b. 1942) and Abdellah Mesbahi (b. 1936), managed to establish themselves with three and four feature films, respectively. In some respects they occupy the two opposing poles of Moroccan cinema. Mesbahi followed the pathway opened up by Mohamed B. A. Tazi and Ahmed Mesnaoui in their first Moroccan feature, *Conquer to Live,* and adopted the model of the Egyptian musical melodrama in his first feature-length film, *Silence, sens interdit* (*Silence, No Entry,* 1973), a story illustrating the clash of generations: a young man refuses to lead the same kind of life as his parents. Subsequently in the 1970s Mesbahi made other commercial efforts. In *Demain la terre ne changera pas* (*Tomorrow the Land Will Not Change,* 1975) the struggle is that of a group of fishermen against the encroaching town which threatens their village, with the story focused on one of their number, Abbas, who refuses the possibility of defeat. *Où cachez-vous le soleil?* (*Where Are You Hiding the Sun?,* 1979) is a film which looks afresh at religion and offers a cry of protest against modern life. Mesbahi's third film, *Feu vert* (*Green Fire,* 1976), was an Egyptian-style musical melodrama, filmed in co-production with the Libyan state organization the General Organisation Al Khayala. Mesbahi also worked for a time in the Egyptian studios.

Similarly, the purely commercial route followed by Abdelaziz Ramdani and Larbi Bennani in *When the Dates Ripen* was followed by the veteran amateur filmmaker Mohamed Osfour (b. 1927) in his sole full-length feature film *Le trésor infernal* (*The Devil's Treasure,* 1970), which is a tale of the abduction (and subsequent rescue) of a princess traveling in a camel train, treated in a mixture of popular styles: "westerns, Zorro, Robin Hood, Karate, Hindu and Egyptian melodramas," according to Ferid Boughedir.[6] Another, very different, commercial piece was offered by the dramatist-turned-filmmaker Nabyl Lahlou (b. 1945), who began a series of theatrically inspired satirical dramas with *Al Kanfoudi* (1978), in which an unknown musician dreams that he wins a lottery, but the transformation makes his life no better in a world full of greed and ruthless moneymaking.

Benbarka, in contrast, represents a more intellectual strand which runs through the whole history of Moroccan film making. Trained in film making at the Centro sperimentale di cinematografia in Rome and in sociology at the University of Rome, he worked for five years in Italy as assistant to, among others, Pier Paolo Pasolini. His first feature, *Mille et une mains* (*A Thousand and One Hands*, 1972), made with some backing from abroad and widely acclaimed on the international festival circuit, was set in Marrakesh and contrasts the lives of rich and poor, looking at the exploitation and misery that goes into the manufacture of exquisite Moroccan carpets. The film got virtually no distribution in Morocco, and though is it highly regarded by most critics, Benbarka now rejects it (and its successor). When asked by interviewers in 1990 why his early films were not a success with audiences, he replied, "For several reasons: first our films are rather mediocre. *A Thousand and One Hands* or *The Oil War Will Not Happen*, if you've seen them, are, I think, execrably bad and they are considered as being among the best in Morocco."[7] Despite this retrospective view, Benbarka's second and third films are ambitious features in which a strong European influence is very apparent. *La guerre du pétrole n'aura pas lieu* (*The Oil War Will Not Happen*, 1974), a political tract in the contemporary manner of Elio Petri or Francesco Rosi and starring European actors, is a fictional account of the struggles of various social levels in an (unnamed) Third World country against the multinational oil companies. This was followed by an adaptation of the play by Garcia Lorca, *Noces de sang* (*Blood Wedding*, 1977), again using European actors (Irene Pappas and Laurent Terzieff) and transposed to a setting in Southern Morocco. The story of two lovers kept apart by family hatreds, it tells of Amrouch, a young peasant who is prevented from marrying the girl he loves because she is the daughter of a rich man from the next village.

Other directors equally concerned with society but without Benbarka's polemicism include Ahmed El Maânouni (b. 1944), who made *O les jours* (*The Days, The Days*, 1978), a close, perceptive, and realistic look at everyday life in a Moroccan village, filmed without any trace of folklore or exoticism. It focuses on Abdelwahab, a young man who sees emigration as his only hope. But his mother Halima, an admirable and forceful woman, tries to hold him back as he is, after the death of her husband, the head of the family. In a similar vein, Jillali Ferhati (b. 1948), who had studied literature and sociology in France, began a career devoted to social realism with *Une brèche dans le mur* (*A Hole in the Wall*, 1978), a study of life on the margins in Tangier, as seen through the eyes of a deaf-mute.

A highly intellectual approach and a self-conscious play with narrative form are also apparent in the work of three Moroccan film school graduates from IDHEC in Paris and from Lodz whose careers also began in the 1970s. The debut film of Hamid Benani (b. 1940) was the highly impressive *Wechma* (*Traces*, 1970), which tells the story of an orphan who is stifled by his upbringing and who grows from awkward child to delinquent adolescent following a path that can only lead to death. The film was the only work produced by a short-lived collective, Sigma 3, involving the future directors Mohamed Abderrahman Tazi and Ahmed Bouanani, as well as Med Seqqat (b. 1940), who went on to specialize in the production of advertising shorts. Moumen Smihi (b. 1945) wrote and

Fig. 4. *The Days, The Days* (1978), Ahmed El Maânouni, Morocco

directed *El chergui ou le silence violent* (*El Chergui,* 1975), the story of a woman, Aïcha, whose efforts to prevent her husband from taking a second wife lead only to her own death. *De quelques événements sans signification* (*About Some Meaningless Events,* 1974), the first feature of Mostapha Derkaoui (b. 1941), is a film which weaves together reflections on the inner life of a film director with his investigations into a crime he uncovers by chance. It is the first part of a loose trilogy of films which reflect on the nature of film making.

Ironically—as with Benbarka's *A Thousand and One Hands*—these films, which critics in both the Maghreb and Europe regard as one of Morocco's major contributions to world cinema, received no showings at home. *Wechma* was first shown ten years later in a single art cinema in Rabat, *El Chergui* was rejected "for the simple reason that it was not in color and didn't contain any action,"[8] while *About Some Meaningless Events* never received a visa, apparently simply because it dealt with unemployment.[9] Derkaoui followed this unreleased debut work with work on a second, collectively made feature, *Les cendres du clos* (*Cinders of the Vineyard,* 1979), made with a group of young filmmakers, all of whom eventually directed solo feature films of their own: his brother the cinematographer Mohamed Abdelkrim Derkaoui, Mohamed Reggab, Nour Eddine Gounajjar, Abdellatif Lagtaâ, and Saâd Chraïbi. At the end of the decade this loose grouping was joined by Ahmed Bouanani (b. 1938), who followed a series of noted short films with a CCM-funded experimental work, *Mirage* (1979), a black vision of the ensnarements of city life set in the 1940s: a young man sets out, full of hope, for the city, but his early wonder and awe leads only to disillusionment. Ferid Boughedir's view of these experimental works is one which most critics would share:

> These films protest against the blockage of a society stuck in its rites and dogmas by adopting an extremely innovative form, with a great power of expression but at times hardly accessible to the non-initiated.[10]

With just fifteen films produced and a total gap between filmmakers and audiences, the 1970s were the lowest point for Moroccan cinema in terms of its popular appeal.

Tunisia

In Tunisia, the participation of SATPEC in foreign co-productions was, as elsewhere in the Maghreb, at best questionable, as with Francisco Arrabal's 1970 production of *Viva la muerte,* which was funded but which could not be screened in Tunisia for foreseeable censorship reasons. In 1974 there was pressure to close SATPEC and destroy its monopoly, a move which was opposed by all concerned with film culture, led by the filmmakers' association, the Association des Cinéastes Tunisiens (ACT), which had been set up in 1970. SATPEC (and its monopoly) survived, and indeed it embarked on a campaign to buy up U.S. distribution agencies, United Artists and Cinema International Corporation in 1975 and Warner Bros. and Columbia in 1979. But in general, the overall level of Tunisian feature film production—under two films a year from the mid-1960s through to the year 2000—has allowed few opportunities for sustained individual output. This was certainly the case in the 1970s, when twenty features were made by fourteen filmmakers, twelve of them making their debuts. Summing up the role of the Tunisian cinema at this time, Tahar Chikhaoui argues that "the gaze became distinctly more critical in the 1970s, with the accent put on the social problems of the period; at the same time the cinema acquired greater technical maturity."[11] This judgment can be extended to cover developments in the 1970s throughout the Maghreb.

At the beginning of the 1970s, Omar Khlifi reaffirmed his status as Tunisia's most forceful director with two features. *Les fellagas* (*The Fellagas,* 1970), co-produced with Bulgaria, depicts the struggle in the 1950s against the French, who continue to threaten Tunisian independence. It tells the story of two cousins who love the same woman but are on opposite sides of the conflict. Ali, however, changes his allegiance to the Tunisian cause and they die together, driving the French from their village. After his war trilogy, Khlifi turned to the problems of women in Tunisian society and produced *Hurlements* (*Screams,* 1972), perhaps his finest and most personal feature. The film focuses on two women, one of whom is raped, then disowned and eventually killed by her family, while the other, her sister, is married against her will. Khlifi is an unsophisticated director, but his output, marked by the release of four features in just six years, was virtually unique at the time in North Africa. The late 1970s also show some continuity with the earlier years through the work of Ben Aïcha, who released his second feature, *Le mannequin* (*The Mannequin,* 1978), a look at the status of women in Tunisia under the rule of President Bourguiba.

Other directors of the same generation as Khlifi and who, like him, had no formal training in film were seldom able to complete more than a single feature. Ahmed Khéchine (b. 1940), for example, made just *Sous la pluie d'automne* (*Under the Autumn Rain,* 1970), a realist tale of a mother who tries to hold together her family after her husband has been imprisoned for drunkenness. Two directors trained in theatre also made a single film. Ali Abdelwahab (b. 1938) made *Om Abbes* (1970), the tale of a mother who avenges the death of her son, set in Southern Tunisia before independence, and Abderrazak Hammami (b. 1935) completed *Omi Traki* (1973), in which an indefatigable old woman arranges the affairs of her family and the neighbors in the quarter where she lives. Then, in each case, silence or a shift to a different career. The exception to this pattern is Ridha Behi (b. 1947), a product of the amateur film movement who had also studied social science in Paris. He began a career which was to extend into the 2000s with the widely praised indictment of tourism, *Soleil des Hyènes* (*Hyenas' Sun,* 1977). While in no way presenting traditional life as an idyll, this film is a savage denunciation of the impact of foreign visitors. The 1970s also saw the appearance of the first female Tunisian film director when Selma Baccar (b. 1945) completed her feature-length documentary, *Fatma 75* (1978), a series of portraits of major Tunisian women from the days of Carthage onward, but found its release blocked by the authorities.

The career of another filmmaker active in the 1970s, the critic and documentarist Ferid Boughedir (b. 1944), is more complex and long lasting. During the 1970s he co-directed just one feature, *La mort trouble* (*Murky Death,* with the Frenchman Claude d'Anna, 1970), a complex allegory involving three girls who kill an old man and fall under the sway of a servant on an imaginary island, and contributed a single episode, *Le Pique-nique* (*Picnic*), to another feature, the collectively made *Au pays de Tararani* (*In the Land of Tararani,* 1972). Boughedir remained influential through his work as a critic and his documentaries on Arab and African cinemas, and twenty years later he returned to the forefront of Tunisian feature film making. The other episodes of *In the Land of the Tararani* were contributed by two filmmakers who had received a formal film training, Hamouda Ben Halima (b. 1935) and Hedy Ben Khalifa (1937–1979). Neither, however, was able to sustain a career in film making.

But other newcomers were able to make a stronger impact. In the 1970s Abdellatif Ben Ammar (b. 1943) made two striking and successful features. In *Une si simple histoire* (*Such a Simple Story,* 1970) the clash of cultures, as experienced by a young Tunisian who returns from training in France, is embodied in the stories of two mixed couples, both of which end in failure. *Sejnane* (1973) traces the growth in political awareness of Kemal, who abandons his studies to take up a struggle which culminates in his death, setting this story against that of Anissa, the girl he loves who is married against her will to a rich neighbor. Both films give precise and detailed portrayals of Tunisian society. Another member of the forceful new generation of 1940s-born filmmakers was Naceur

Fig. 5. *Sejnane* (1973), Abdellatif Ben Ammar, Tunisia

Ktari (b. 1943) who made a most striking debut with one of the most successful films on emigration to France, *Les ambassadeurs* (*The Ambassadors*, 1975), in which the protagonists move from individuality to friendship and from being victims of violence to a realization of the need for unity.

Other graduates from European film schools include Mohamed Ali El Okbi (b. 1948), who began his career with *Un ballon et des rêves* (*A Ball and Some Dreams*, 1978), a semi-documentary which combines a study of the training of the 1978 Tunisian football team with the fictional tale of two young fans. Brahim Babaï (b. 1936) contributed the widely seen fictional feature *Et demain?*

(*And Tomorrow?* 1972), which follows the experiences of a young man who leaves his drought-stricken village to seek work in Tunis but whose fate remains very much in doubt at the end of the film. He subsequently completed a feature-length documentary survey of Tunisian history, *Victoire d'un peuple (A People's Victory,* 1975). Rachid Ferchiou (b. 1941), who had studied film in Berlin, made *Yusra* (1972), in which a painter leaves his girlfriend for a new model— a reincarnation of Aphrodite who emerges from the sea—then discovers, when she abandons him, that the two women are one and the same. He followed this with *Les enfants de l'ennui (The Children of Boredom,* 1975), chronicling the struggle of women in a Tunisian village to improve their lives in response to new ideas brought back by their children who have studied in the city. Later in the decade Mohammed Hammami (b. 1951), a graduate of the Vsesoyuznyi gosudarstvennyi institut kinematografii (All-Union State Cinema Institute—VGIK) film school in Moscow, made his sole feature, *Mon village (My Village,* 1979), which is one of the rare Maghrebian films set abroad and shows how group of guerrillas liberate their village from Israeli occupation.

A work which is quite unclassifiable but clearly a major experiment in cinematic narration is *La noce (The Wedding,* 1978). This is a tale of unhappy sexual relationships, based loosely on a play by Brecht but set in a bleak and crumbling Tunisian mansion. The film is a transposition to the screen of one of the stage productions of a theatrical collective, the Nouveau Théâtre de Tunis, led by Fadhel Jaïbi (b. 1945) and Fadhel Jaziri (b. 1948), both of whom were to be involved in future film productions.

Immigrant Cinema

A fresh note is struck in the 1970s by the first work in France and Belgium by North African-born filmmakers treating social or political subject matter relating to the Algerian community in France. The French-made works of the 1970s include the early films of Ali Ghalem (b. 1943 in Constantine): *Mektoub?* (1970), which deals with the day-to-day misadventures of an Algerian emigrant who works and saves so as to be able to send home money to his family, and *L'autre France (The Other France,* 1975), which depicts the slow progression of a Maghrebian worker toward militancy and working-class solidarity. Ali Akika (b. 1945 in Gigel), working with Anne-Marie Autissier, dealt with the problems of Algerian emigration in *Voyage en capital (Journey to the Capital,* 1977). In Belgium, as part of his studies at Institut National des Arts du Spectacle et Techniques de Diffusion (INSAS), Mohamed Ben Salah (b. 1945 in Oran) made a very low budget feature-length film, *Les uns, les autres (Some People and Others,* 1972). These works, like the films shot in France by Naceur Ktari (*The Ambassadors,* 1975) and Rachedi (*Ali in Wonderland,* 1979), were firsthand accounts of the problems and pressures of emigrant life. They were generally considered in relation to the work of contemporary French filmmakers, such as Michel Drach and Yves Boisset, whose films contain images of Maghrebian immigrants living in France and for whom a social message is the vital aspect. Aside from this concern with social issues are the three films of Mohamed Benayat (b. 1944 in Algeria)—*Le masque d'une éclaircie* (*The Mask of an Enlightened Woman*, 1974), *Barricades sauvages* (*Savage Barricades*, 1975), and *Les nouveaux romantiques* (*The New Romantics*, 1979)—which anticipate 1980s developments by their lack of concern with emigrant issues. Benayat's aim is rather a cinema that fuses gangster and western genres.[12]

Considerable progress in film making was made in the 1970s, as new film-makers made their debuts. Four Algerian directors from the 1960s (Riad, Lakhdar Hamina, Badie, and Rachedi) and two Tunisians (Khlifi and Ben Aicha) continued to be active, and thirty-seven newcomers made their debuts. These 1970s filmmakers are broadly similar to their 1960s predecessors, but there is a significant shift, which increased in the 1980s, toward youth and formal training. Of the thirty-seven new directors, twenty-three were born in the 1940s and nineteen had a formal film school education.

Like the Algerian directors of the 1960s, the Moroccan Osfour and the Algerians Bouamari, Nadir Aziri, and Haddad had no formal film training, though the latter was a trainee in French television and assistant on foreign co-productions in Algeria. Also without formal film training were three Tunisians (Boughedir, Ahmed Khéchine, and Behi) who came, like Khlifi, from the amateur film movement. Selma Baccar made her first short in this context too, but went on to study at the Institut Français de Cinéma (IFC) in Paris before embarking on feature production. No less than eight of the newcomers came, like Kateb in the 1960s, from the theatre. Zinet and Damardjji, both of whom had studied drama—if only briefly—in Berlin, were associated with the beginnings of the Algerian national theatre. The Moroccan dramatist Nabyl Lahlou and the Tunisians Ferhati, Abdelwahab, and Abderrazak Hammami all studied drama in France (for ten years in Ferhati's case). Of the two founders of the Nouveau Théâtre de Tunis, Jaziri received no formal training in theatre or film, but Jaïbi studied for five years at the Institut des Etudes Théâtrales in Paris. There was one figure from literature: the Algerian French-language novelist Assia Djebar, who had studied in France, where she has subsequently lived.

There is also an increase in the number of new directors—like Ben Aicha, Ben Halima and Latif Lahlou in the 1960s—who had at least some formal film school training, particularly those born in the 1940s. Merbah and Mazif were graduates of Algeria's own short-lived film school, Institut National de Cinéma (INC), as were Allouache and Beloufa, who both also completed further studies at IDHEC in Paris. Other directors who studied at IDHEC included two Algerians (Bendeddouche and Lallem—though the latter was there for just eight months), four Moroccans (Benani, Smihi, Derkaoui, and Bouanani), and three Tunisians (Ben Ammar, El Okbi, and Babaï). Otherwise the net was cast wide. Among the Moroccans, Mesbahi studied at Ecole Supérieure des Etudes Cinématographiques (ESEC) in Paris, El Maânouni at INSAS in Brussels, and Benbarka at the Centro sperimentale di cinematografia in Rome. Abdelaziz Tolbi from Algeria studied film in Cologne and also worked as a trainee in German television, while the Tunisian Ferchiou studied in Berlin and worked as a trainee in both French and Italian studios. Eastern Europe was a favored location for some. Among the Algerians, Amar Laskri spent many years studying theatre, radio, television, and film making in Belgrade, while the Tunisian Mohamed Hammami spent six years completing his courses at VGIK in Moscow.

With the increase in the number of films produced in the Maghreb—in all, eighty-six films made by fifty directors in the course of the 1970s—it becomes possible to define the common stylistic approaches and to uncover the themes that engage filmmakers across the three countries at this period. The first aspect of note is the fact that only a handful of films are concerned with the situation outside the Maghreb—Riad's *Sana'oud*, Beloufa's *Nahla*, and Mohamed Hammami's *My Village* are among the rare examples. Maghrebian cinemas deal almost exclusively with national problems and even a neighboring North African state shown as a very foreign land, as is the case with Tunisia in Haddad's *Inspector Tahar's Holiday*. Just as most films present the official version of events (their makers arguing, with some justification, that otherwise their work will be censored), so too most adopt a conventional realist style, with Riad in *Opium and the Stick* and Lakhdar Hamina in *Chronicle of the Years of Embers* showing positively Hollywoodian aspirations. But a handful of experimental narratives offer a critique of this style. This type of experimentation is notable in Morocco in the early 1970s with films such as Benani's *Wechma* and Smihi's *El Chergui*, supplemented at the end of the decade by Bouanani's *Mirage* (the least "official" of films despite its 100 percent state funding). In Algeria, there are Bouamari's *The First Step* and Beloufa's *Nahla*, and in Tunisia toward the end of the decade, the collectively made Brechtian adaptation *The Wedding*. This experimentation continues in the 1980s.

The cinemas of the Maghreb, however diverse their origins, emerge as socially and politically involved in the 1970s. Of course, in Algeria at this time there are subjects (the war of independence and the agrarian revolution) that cannot be critiqued. But a real social involvement can be sensed, with the films on rural subjects in particular offering careful analysis of the impact of colonialism and of some of the difficulties (such as vestiges of a semi-feudal tradition) that the post-independence campaign faces. The limit of what can be achieved in Algeria is represented by Damardjji's *The Good Families*, which was independently produced by the FLN. Claude Michel Cluny writes of the film, "It's less a matter of a protest film than of using fictional film just to provoke a precise awareness of social data, and hence a political reflection."[13]

Elsewhere filmmakers could be more outspoken. Mohamed Jibril, less willing than most critics to separate the 1970s from the 1980s, sees, as the common features of both decades in Morocco, three major themes: the search for identity, social injustice (particularly with regard to the status of women), and the suffocation of the individual.[14] Benbarka's *A Thousand and One Hands* and Behi's *Hyenas' Sun* are fine examples of the combination of social insight and political confrontation. The rural issues which are predominant in Algerian cinema in the wake of Bouamari's *The Charcoal Burner* also raise concern elsewhere, as in the work of Babaï (*And Tomorrow?*) and El Maânouni (*The Days, The Days*). Though Maghrebian cinema is almost entirely male, the issue of women's status and rights provokes a concern which will increase in the 1980s. Key films include Mazif's *Leïla and the Others,* Khlifi's *Screams,* Ben Ammar's *Sejnane,* and Smihi's *El Chergui.* In 1978 women's voices (those of Baccar and Djebar) offer a female perspective on these issues for the first time (though the release of Baccar's film was delayed by the authorities for six years). The concern about emigration expressed by Rachedi in Algeria (*Ali in Wonderland*) and Ktari in Tunisia (*The Ambassadors*) finds its answer in the films made in France and Belgium by Ghalem, Akika, and Ben Salah.

3   The 1980s

The 1980s were a period of some development, with film production more or less maintained in Algeria and Tunisia and soaring in Morocco. The first representatives of a new and younger generation of filmmakers of Maghrebian origin emerged in France, a trio of talented new foreign-trained women directors (Farida Bourquia, Farida Benlyazid, and Nejia Ben Mabrouk) made their first appearances in the Maghreb, and Assia Djebar completed a further feature-length piece. As before, developments in production structures and funding varied widely in the three Maghreb countries.

Algeria

In Algeria the 1980s saw further disrupting reorganizations of production. ONCIC was dissolved in 1984 and its functions split between two separate organizations, with the Entreprise Nationale de Production Cinématographique (ENAPROC) being responsible for production and the Entreprise Nationale de Distribution et d'Exploitation Cinématographiques (ENADEC) for distribution. But the state monopoly of film production was abolished, so that filmmakers could now set up their own production companies. In November 1987 there was another decisive reorganization, with the setting up of the Centre Algérien pour l'Art et l'Industrie Cinématographiques (CAAIC) to replace both ENAPROC and ENADEC and to take over all the activities previously undertaken by ONCIC. A parallel step was taken with respect to television production when RTA resources were regrouped in the same year (1987) to form the Entreprise Nationale de Productions Audiovisuelles (ENPA). The new organization offered support for a wide range of filmmakers and participated in numerous co-productions with CAAIC, so that the boundaries which had separated television from cinema at the time of RTA and ONCIC became blurred.

In the 1980s the veterans of Algerian cinema continued their careers despite this disruption. There were two Hassan Terro sequels: Riad's *Hassan-Taxi* (1981), in which Hassan is down on his luck and reduced to driving a taxi, and Ghaouti Bendeddouche's *Hassan niya* (1989), where he is now working in his sister's restaurant. Both are minor works but offer vivid pictures of life and aspirations in contemporary Algeria. Bendeddouche's earlier 1980s feature, *Moissons d'acier* (*Harvests of Steel*, 1982), is a more substantial work, a positive tale of peasant resistance, as villagers rebuild their lives despite the "harvests of steel" of the title: the mines laid during the war and still threatening life and limb. Ahmed Rachedi's *Le moulin de Monsieur Fabre* (*Monsieur Fabre's Mill*, 1984) was a work showing all the director's communicative vigor, in what is a clear satire on the government and petty-minded bureaucrats. The film pits Monsieur Fabre, a Polish immigrant who is known for his support of the FLN, against local politicians who want to take possession of his mill so as to have something for a visiting dignitary from the capital to nationalize. Mohamed Bouamari's *Le refus* (*The Denial*, 1982), like his previous film *First Step*, is a complexly narrated film, the flashback account of the death of a former resistance fighter who has lived in France since independence, which allows a portrait of the immigrant community to emerge. An esoteric effort, it found a little audience response in Algeria. Amar Laskri, after a ten-year silence, completed *Les portes du silence* (*The Gates of Silence*, 1987), the story of Amar, a deaf-mute, who witnesses the destruction of his village in 1955 and who, seeking ways to avenge himself, joins the French army as a stable lad. Assia Djebar, Algeria's sole woman filmmaker at this period, made her second 16mm piece for RTA: *La zerda ou les chants de l'oubli* (*La Zerda*, 1980), a personal and meditative piece, giving a view of women's place in history and society, and focusing on music as a unifying factor of Maghreb life.

Several other veterans were able to make two films in the decade. Sid Ali Mazif first made *J'existe* (*I Exist*, 1982), co-produced with the Arab League, a three-part compilation film looking at a range of issues concerning women's roles in society: women's own aspirations, the role of the state, and the contribution of organizations which had been created during the struggle for emancipation. He then returned to fiction with *Houria* (1986), which is set in Constantine and tells the story of the unhappy love affair of two young students whose relationship meets with parental disapproval. Merzak Allouache's third film was *L'homme qui regardait les fenêtres* (*The Man Who Looked at Windows*, 1982), a brooding view of contemporary Algeria, which comprised the dark visions of a middle-aged bureaucrat whose life is turned upside down when he is transferred to the film book section of the library where he works, and whose path leads him eventually to murder. Allouache left Algeria for France to make *Un amour à Paris* (*A Parisian Love Story*, 1986), a French-language production shot in Paris, which tells the doomed love story of a young French Jewish woman from Algiers and an Algerian youth born in Clichy in Paris. It contrasts their dreams (becoming a model, training as an astronaut) with the bleak reality of their lives. Mohamed Lakhdar Hamina's two 1980s films show the continued pull of Europe and international audiences for Algeria's leading director. *Vent de sable* (*Sand Storm*, 1982) is the study of an isolated rural community battered by the violence of nature and by the more private conflict between men and the women who bear the brunt of their anger. *La dernière image* (*The Last Image*, 1986) is, according to Lakhdar Hamina, an autobiographical piece, an evocation of his own childhood experience. Set in an Algerian village in 1939, on the eve of the outbreak of World War II, it shows the disruption caused in the village by the arrival of a new teacher from the metropolis, Mademoiselle Boyer.

Among the newcomers, Rabah Laradji (b. 1943) made *Un toit, une famille* (*A Roof, a Family*, 1982), the story of Selim, the oldest of a large family living in cramped conditions, whose dreams of marriage can be realized—but only if he can find an apartment for himself and his future wife. Sid Ali Fettar (b. 1943) made a family drama, *Rai* (1988), the story of Rachid, who emerges from prison to find his parents divorced and who is therefore compelled to review the image of the mother he adored. Mohamed Meziane Yala (b. 1946) made *Chant d'automne* (*Autumn Song*, 1983), the unhappy love story of Catherine, daughter of a French farmer, and Abdelmalek, son of the local blacksmith, during the early years of the liberation struggle. Jean-Pierre Lledo (b. 1947) made his debut with *L'empire des rêves* (*The Empire of Dreams*, 1982), which looked at the lives of an eccentric body of actors and would-be actors at the moment when they find themselves invited to take part in a film.

Okacha Touita (b. 1943) made *Les sacrifiés* (*The Sacrificed*, 1982) in which Mahmoud, deported from Algeria by the French colonial authorities, becomes involved in the events of 1955 in the slums of Nanterre, when two Algerian nationalist groups come into conflict. Touita's second feature looked at the figure of *Le rescapé* (*The Survivor*, 1986), a *harki*, one of the thousands of Algerians who fought for the French in the war of liberation. Though he survived having his throat cut after the end of the war, he is helpless as his son turns to crime and drug dealing. The film seems not to have been released. From his base in Paris, Mahmoud Zemmouri (b. 1946) directed the comedy *Prends dix mille balles et casses-toi* (*Take a Thousand Quid and Get Lost*, 1981), in which two young Algerians, brought up in France and unable to speak Arabic, take up the French government's offer of 10,000 francs to return "home," but find it impossible to adjust to life in Algeria. Zemmouri then went on to make the first of his three Algerian features, *Les folles années du twist* (*The Crazy Years of the Twist*, 1983), which brought a quite new tone to the depiction of the liberation struggle and of contemporary Algeria. The film demystifies all the familiar tales of heroism and selfless commitment with the story of a community torn between the demands of the FLN and those of the French army. Abderrahmane Bouguermouh (b. 1936) contributed *Cri de pierre* (*Cry of Stone*, 1986), in which a group from Constantine, led by disillusioned architect Douadi, returns to the land, where a young boy offers them mature words of wisdom, remembered from his dead grandfather.

Brahim Tsaki (b. 1946) made two highly original studies of children. *Les enfants du vent* (*Children of the Wind*, 1981) comprises three episodes. "Les oeufs cuits" (Boiled Eggs) is about the disillusionment with the world about him experienced by a boy whose job is to sell eggs in the bars of Algiers. In "Djamel au pays des images" (Djamel in the Land of Images) a boy struggles to come to terms with the world offered to him daily by the television, while "La boîte dans le désert" (The Box in the Desert) shows the creative ingenuity of children building fantastic toys for themselves from scraps of wire and metal. Tsaki's second feature, *Histoire d'une rencontre* (*Story of a Meeting*, 1983), deals with the relationship of two deaf-mute children. For a while they are able to communicate across the cultural barriers that separate the daughter of an American oil

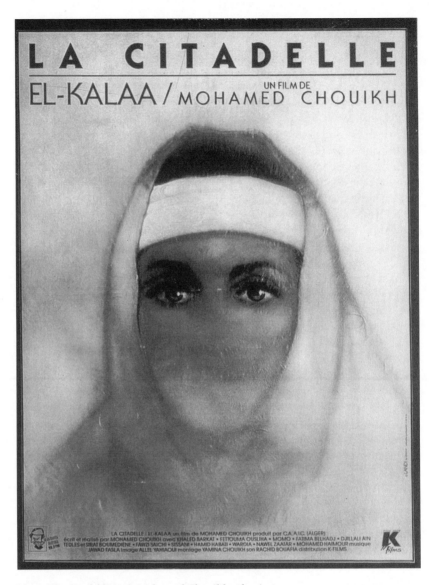

LA CITADELLE
EL-KALAA / MOHAMED CHOUIKH
UN FILM DE

LA CITADELLE / EL-KALAA un film de MOHAMED CHOUIKH produit par C.A.A.I.C. (ALGER)
écrit et réalisé par MOHAMED CHOUIKH avec KHALED BARKAT • FETTOUMA OUSLIHA • MOMO • FATIMA BELHADJ • DJILLALI AIN
TEDLES et SIRAT BOUMEDIENE • FAWZI SAICHI • SISSANI • HAMID HABATI • WARDIA • NAWEL ZAAIAR • MOHAMED HAIMOUR musique
JAWAD FASLA image ALLEL YAHIAOUI montage YAMINA CHOUIKH son RACHID BOUAFIA distribution K-FILMS

Fig. 6. *The Citadel* (1988), Mohamed Chouikh, Algeria

engineer from the son of an Algerian peasant, but eventually they are separated as the girl's father moves on.

Mohamed Rachid Benhadj (b. 1949), who had worked for RTA, made his feature film debut with *Rose des sables* (*Desert Rose,* 1989), which received wide acclaim. This is the story of Moussa, a crippled youth who lives with his sister and struggles to overcome his handicaps, only to lose the girl he loves. Another director previously active with RTA also turned to films for cinema release in the 1980s. Mohamed Chouikh (b. 1943) first made *La rupture* (*Breakdown*, 1982), in which the protagonist, Amar, escapes from prison with his friend the poet Bendris and continues the struggle. He abducts the woman he loves, Aïcha, but eventually the colonial system closes in on him. In Chouikh's second feature, *La citadelle* (*The Citadel*, 1988), the love of Kaddour for the shoemaker's wife creates tensions in a village community where men and women keep to their traditional roles; his passion can lead only to disaster.

Otherwise the ranks of directors were reinforced in the 1980s by self-taught filmmakers. Ali Ghalem (b. 1943) returned from film work in exile in France to make a rather muted version of his own novel, *Une femme pour mon fils* (*A Wife for My Son*, 1982), which is an exposé of the difficult relations between wife and mother-in-law in a claustrophobic setting after an arranged marriage. Tayeb Mefti (b. 1942) directed *Le mariage de Moussa* (*Moussa's Wedding*, 1982), in which a young emigrant returns to Algeria only to find himself an outsider in his community. Compelled to stay to do his military service, he falls in love with his cousin Nacira. In addition to these full-length feature narratives, two young directors, Mustapha Mengouchi and Rabah Bouchemha, compiled the episodes of a film on children's roles in the liberation struggle, *Nous irons sur la montagne* (*We Shall Go onto the Mountain*, 1987).

Morocco

In Morocco radical steps were taken to enhance production as early as 1980, when the government introduced a system of assistance for production (the so-called "fonds de soutien"), funded by a special tax on cinema admissions and administered through the CCM. This support was offered to both short and feature films and had the effect of greatly stimulating production activity in Morocco. Initially the 1980 scheme paid little attention to quality, being focused essentially on the development of a *Moroccan* cinema (filmmakers resident in Morocco, Moroccan technicians, and Moroccan locations). The immediate effect was the intended upsurge in production, but no limitations were placed on who could apply for funding and, as Souiba and El Alaoui note, concern about "fund chasers" soon developed.[1] After eight years of operation and the funding of thirty-four features (over four a year), the system was changed in 1987 to become the aid fund ("fonds d'aide"). A further seven features were funded in 1988–1989 under this new scheme, though some of these did not appear until the 1990s. The "fonds d'aide" offered two types of funding: preproduction funding on the basis of an initial script or completion money after shooting. From 1980 onward virtually all Moroccan feature films were state aided, with all the constraints that this implies. As a result of these new arrangements, production rose in the 1980s to thirty-eight feature films, twenty-one of them made by new directors. The plan was undoubtedly well intentioned, but though production rose, there was no corresponding surge in audience numbers, which actually fell from forty-five million in 1980 to about twenty-five million in 1992. Moreover the scheme was not supported by any system to control imports or to organize distribution, so that a number of films were produced for which there was virtually no audience, either inside Morocco or abroad.

The increase in production had a sharply differing impact on experienced Moroccan filmmakers. Abdallah Mesbahi and Souheil Benbarka, who had been the two most prolific Moroccan filmmakers of the 1970s, directed just one feature each in the 1980s. Mesbahi made *La terre du défi* (*Land of Challenge*, 1989), a film which traces some sixty years of Moroccan history, emphasizing acts of courage and solidarity. Benbarka produced *Amok* (1982), an ambitious anti-apartheid drama, made with funding from Senegal and Guinea as well as Morocco. Inspired by (if not adapted from) Alan Paton's novel *Cry the Beloved Country*, it concerns a black village schoolteacher summoned to Johannesburg by news of his sister's illness and confronted there with all the violence, terror, and corruption of South African urban life.

Other established directors had more production opportunities. Nabyl Lahlou directed four distinctive features in the 1980s. *Le gouverneur-général de Chakerbakerbane* (*The Governor-General of Chakerbakerbane*, 1980) was a satire on the demagogy of a pseudo-democratic Third World administration in which a newspaper worker takes the place of the missing governor of the island of Chakerbakerben. *Brahim qui?* (*Brahim Who?*, 1984), his third feature and the first to make full use of the resources of cinema, is a sardonic fable of a man robbed of his pension by the misspelling of his name in his papers, who finds that even after his death bureaucracy continues to defeat him. His fate is paralleled by that of a director, Jalil, who is frustrated by producers in this world and equally blocked in the afterlife. In *L'âme qui brait* (*The Soul That Brays*, 1984) the unhappy fate of a former resistance fighter is contrasted bitterly with the situation of those who collaborated with colonialism and still remain rich and powerful. In *Komany* (1989), an actor is chosen to play the role of the dictator in films made by a religious sect which wishes to depict the leader indulging in sex, violence, and killing. Nabyl Lahlou's films are unclassifiable, made on tiny budgets, often weighed down by theatrical devices but bristling with (often contradictory) ideas. Another prolific director in the 1980s is Mohamed B. A. Tazi, co-director of the first Moroccan feature, who made three solo features. *Amina* (1980) is the story of a student who has to face the consequences of becoming pregnant while still unmarried. *Lalla chafia* (*Medicine Woman*, 1982) is a further tale of female problems, set this time in the countryside, while the apparently insignificant Jouha in *Abbas ou Jouha n'est pas mort* (*Abbas or Jouha Is Not Dead*, 1986) can, the director tells us, teach us to look afresh at ourselves.

For most directors the maximum possible was just two features in the decade. Mostafa Derkaoui directed one of his most striking films, *Les beaux jours de Chahrazade* (*The Beautiful Days of Sheherazade*, 1982). This is partly a tale about a woman singer, partly the story of a man who becomes rich, partly the account of a filmmaker who fails to make his film. It is a work that constantly shifts registers of time and reality, mixing actuality and fiction in ways that deny the viewer the pleasure of a single extractable meaning. Derkaoui's third successive film about the processes of film making and the situation of the filmmaker is *Titre provisoire* (*Provisional Title*, 1984). Here again fiction and reality are intertwined and the focus is on a film crew engaged on a film shoot that seems to have no end. As Souiba and El Alaoui note, "This autobiography combined with a self-portrait shows convincingly the Moroccan film maker's permanent and constant search for his identity and for his socio-cultural role."[2] Moumen Smihi had to wait six years after his first feature before he could make *Quarante-quatre, ou les récits de la nuit* (*Forty-Four, or Tales of the Night*, 1981) The forty-four of the title denotes the number of years of Franco-Spanish occupation of Morocco, and the fragmented story chronicles the fate, over a long period, of two families, one living under French occupation, the other under Spanish rule. Smihi then waited a further six years before completing *Caftan d'amour* (*Caftan of Love*, 1987), about a man who marries the woman of his dreams, only to find that their life together turns into a nightmare.

Other filmmakers who had previously shown promise could complete only one further feature in the new decade. Sixteen years after his debut with *Spring Sunshine*, Latif Lahlou made his second feature, *La compromission* (*The Compromise*, 1986): Mehdi and Leïla are drawn to each other by their shared love of art and decide to live together, but the relationship is destroyed by Mehdi's weakness and taste for money. Ahmed El Maânouni quickly followed his widely seen first feature *The Days, The Days* with *Transes* (*Trances*, 1981), a study of the music group Nass el-Ghiwane, whose music, based on traditional Arab and African sources, is extremely popular in Morocco. But subsequently El Maânouni was reduced to silence (apart from a few shorts and videos). Jillali Ferhati's second film is one of his best. *Poupées de roseau* (*Reed Dolls*, 1981) is the story of Aïcha, a young woman who, while little more than an adolescent, is married, widowed, and then rejected by her family when it is discovered that she is pregnant. Deprived of her children and her home, she has nowhere to turn but to prostitution. This study of female oppression sets the tone for Ferhati's mature style, but he had to wait a further ten years before he worked again.

Only three of the twenty-one new filmmakers of the 1980s were able to make two features in the decade. Ahmed Kacem Akdi (b. 1942) made *Le drame des 40,000* (*The Drama of the 40,000*, 1982), which showed the brutal aftermath for ordinary Moroccan citizens of a police raid in Oran in December 1975, followed by *Ce que les vents ont emportés* (*What the Winds Have Carried Away*, 1984), in which an anti-drug campaign is led by a boy of twelve whose brother has become a drug victim. Abdallah Zerouali (b. 1939) began a first feature, *Le tourbillon* (*The Whirlpool*, 1980), which was left uncompleted until 1995, when it emerged as *Moi l'artiste* (*I'm the Artist*). Zeroualli's second 1980s film, *Les copains du jour* (*Pals for the Day*, 1984) was completed but failed to be released. In it, Jamal promises to look after Zohra, his friend Paul's protégée, but has to cope with the intervention of his father. By far the most important of the newcomers to make two features in the 1980s is Mohamed Abderrahman Tazi (b. 1942). *Le grand voyage* (*The Big Trip*, 1981) is the story of a journey under-

Fig. 7. *Badis* (1988), Mohamed Abderrahman Tazi, Morocco

taken by a lorry driver from the South to Casablanca. Everywhere he is cheated and robbed, but when he decides to emigrate he realizes too late—when already at sea—that he is about to be cheated again. Tazi's second film, *Badis* (1988), deals with the tragic friendship between two women, one oppressed in her domestic life, the other a peasant girl persecuted because of her love for a Spanish soldier. Together the pair plan to flee but are caught and stoned to death for their actions. Tazi continued his career successfully into the 1990s.

Newcomers with a single 1980s film who eventually went on to make a further feature are comparatively few in number. Lodz-trained cinematographer Mohamed Abdelkrim Derkaoui (b. 1945) and ex-actor Driss Kettani (b. 1947) co-directed *Le jour du forain* (*The Travelling Showman's Day*, 1984), which deals with the adventures of Moulay Yacoub, an enigmatic travelling showman who takes his wheel of fortune from souk to souk. Najib Sefrioui (b. 1948) directed *Chams* (1985), an allegorical tale of a young intellectual's return from Europe to confront his feudally minded father and to meet Shams, the beautiful young woman his father has taken into his "protection." Saïd Souda (b. 1957), a martial arts specialist, made the action drama *L'ombre du gardien* (*Shadow of the Guardian*, 1985), involving a secret society formed to fight the smuggling of Arab treasures, with settings ranging from New York to Fez. Mohamed Abbazi (b. 1938) directed *De l'autre côté du fleuve* (*From the Other Side of the River*, 1982), which traces the adventures of a boy who is sent to fetch his mother's caftan, has it stolen, and seeks help from his aunt on the other side of the river in Rabat. Hakim Noury (b. 1952), who was to become a major and prolific director in the 1990s, had to wait ten years after *Le facteur* (*The Postman*, 1980) before he could make another film. His debut film shows the tribulations of a marginalized young postman, a dreamer whose dreams are seldom realized—and then only fleetingly. Ahmed Yachfine (b. 1948) made *Cauchemar* (*Nightmare*, 1984), a troubling nightmare vision of the Moroccan past in which a Moroccan businessman dreams that he is back in the French Protectorate during last century, where he is guilty of several crimes—and wakes up to find that he has the key of his dream home in his pocket.

The difficulty of making more than one film in the decade was also a feature of the careers of the two new women filmmakers who made their first films as part of this upsurge of Moroccan cinema. Farida Bourquia (b. 1948) made what proved to be her only feature, *La braise* (*The Embers*, 1982), a somber tale of three children who are orphaned when their parents die in an accident. Instead of receiving help from villagers, they are rejected and persecuted as bringers of bad luck. Farida Benlyazid (b. 1948), who had written the scripts of two films by her then husband Jillali Ferhati (*A Hole in the Wall* and *Reed Dolls*), made her directing debut with *Une porte sur le ciel* (*A Gateway to Heaven*, 1987), the story of a young woman who, returning home from France for her father's funeral, discards her French boyfriend and rediscovers her Islamic identity as a woman working with women in Morocco.

With film-directing debuts coming at a rate of two or three a year, we find solitary debut films of very variable quality with strikingly differing themes and subjects. Mohamed Reggab (1942–1990) is widely regarded as one of Morocco's leading filmmakers. He had participated in the collectively made *Cinders of the Vineyard* and made, as his sole feature film, the widely praised *Le coiffeur du quartier des pauvres* (*The Barber of the Poor Quarter*, 1982). This is the story of a poor barber deprived of everything, including his shop and his wife, by the rich man—an ex-collaborator with the French—who now controls the area. Reggab, ruined by the film's commercial failure, died in debt in 1990. Mohamed Aboulouakar (b. 1946) made, as his sole but critically well-received feature, *Hadda* (1984), a slow but visually resplendent and poetic evocation of a drought-stricken village. The young man returning from Europe, to whom the villagers look for an answer to the drought, turns out to have been alienated by his stay abroad. Instead of helping them, he rapes a young village girl, Hadda. One of Morocco's major dramatists, Tayeb Saddiki (b. 1937), adapted one of his own plays to produce a quite unclassifiable fantasy, *Zeft* (1984). This is the comic tale of a poor peasant whose existence is threatened both by the past (a holy man who installs himself on his land and builds a shrine there) and by the future (the new motorway built by the modernizers).

Beyond this there are half-a-dozen isolated features which have attracted very little critical attention. Abdou Achouba (b. 1950) made *Tarounja* (*Taghounja*, 1980), a black vision of the ensnarements of city life, following two characters wandering through a traditional Moroccan landscape. Hamid Bensaïd (b. 1948) directed *L'oiseau du paradis* (*The Bird of Paradise*, 1981), in which the present is colored by memories and by the looks, murmurs, and whispers of two intertwined childhoods. Hamid Benchrif (b. 1940–1986) directed his sole feature, *Des pas dans le brouillard* (*Steps in the Mist*, 1982), in which a young man, Mehdi, attempts to take his Parisian girlfriend on a journey across Morocco but runs into financial problems and ends up in prison. Hassan Moufti (b. 1935) made the musical *Les larmes du regret* (*Tears of Regret,* 1983), in which Karim, a young taxi driver, achieves success as a singer thanks to the support of his neighbor, Latifa, and arouses the envy of his uncle. Driss Mrini (b. 1950) made *Bamou* (1983), a love story of a couple whose life is impeded by the difficulties of the struggle against foreign occupation. Mustapha Khayat (b. 1944) directed *L'impasse* (*Dead End,* 1984), in which the fascination which Casablanca exercises over people from the surrounding countryside is illustrated by the tale of a man's first visit to the city.

Tunisia

In Tunisia, two key developments occurred in 1981. SATPEC's monopoly of import and distribution was abolished, allowing private companies to begin to take over the distribution sector. In addition, a system for helping to fund production ("fonds d'aide"), similar to that in Morocco and based on 6 percent of gross box office receipts and aimed to support short films as well as features, was introduced. The result was less spectacular, however, and production levels actually fell in Tunisia from twenty-one features in the 1970s to seventeen in the 1980s. Initially SATPEC was active. In 1981 it produced four features and the following year it continued its foreign co-production policy by supporting Borhan Alawiya's Lebanese feature *Beyrouth la rencontre* (*Beirut the Meeting,* 1982). In 1983 a color film facility was finally inaugurated at the Gammarth studios and two further features were produced. But SATPEC's days were numbered, and since the mid-1980s there has been a new and marked emphasis on international co-production and the role of independent producers in Tunisian film making. Key developments have been the opening of the new studios of Carthago Films by Tarak Ben Ammar at Sousse in 1985 ("the most important studios built in Africa since independence," according to Boughedir[3]) and the emergence of Ahmed Attia as a major Tunisian film producer with his company Cinétéléfilms. It was Attia who produced the films that constitute the "golden age" of innovative Tunisian film making in the late 1980s and early 1990s. Tahar Chikhaoui offers a useful overview of Tunisian cinema in the decade: "In the course of the 1980s the individual takes over, with a tendency toward autobiography and a remarkable recourse to the places of memory."[4] Interestingly this remark is echoed with regard to Algerian cinema by Mouny Berrah, who concludes her survey of "Algerian Cinema and National Identity" with the 1988 uprising and the words "Many films were dedicated to history. With the exception that the characters will from now on say 'I.'"[5]

The 1980s began well with Abdellatif Ben Ammar's finest film, the masterly *Aziza* (1980), which offers a view of contemporary society seen through the eyes of a young orphan, Aziza, who lives with a family which moves from the old Arab quarter of Tunis to a new housing development on the outskirts. Ben Ammar subsequently abandoned direction for twenty years and turned to production activities through his company Tanit Productions, which produced, among others, Nacer Khemir's *The Searchers of the Desert* and Fitouri Belhiba's *Wandering Heart.* Ferid Boughedir was finally able to complete his long-term documentary project on film making south of the Sahara, *Caméra d'Afrique* (*African Camera,* 1983), and then a second documentary, this time on Arab film making, *Caméra arabe* (*Arab Camera,* 1987). Ridha Behi contributed a melodrama in the Egyptian style, *Les anges* (*The Angels,* 1984), the story of a group of young actors and their relationship with a rich businessman, set in Tunisia but using Egyptian stars. Behi subsequently made a feature with French players in the leading roles, *Champagne amer* (*Bitter Champagne,* 1988), the story of Pierre, a settler forced to break his ties with the past on the eve of independence in 1955, and Mariam, the mistress he abandons. Fadhel Jaïbi and Fadhel Jaziri followed *The Wedding* by completing their second masterly theatrical adaptation, *Arab* (1988), a complex fable dealing, on one level, with an air hostess from Beirut transported into a world of legend and, on another, with fundamental questions of Arab history and contemporary experience.

Omar Khlifi returned after fourteen years to direct the kind of story of violent action with which he had made his reputation, but *Le défi* (*The Challenge,* 1986), depicting a rising by Tunisian resistance fighters in 1952 which provokes mass arrests and the assassination of political leaders, showed how far Tunisian cinema had developed during his absence. A further filmmaker with a highly personal style who emerged in the early 1980s is the sculptor, writer, and performing storyteller Nacer Khemir (b. 1948), whose first feature, *Les baliseurs du désert* (*The Searchers of the Desert*), was widely shown and praised at international festivals when it appeared in 1984. A young schoolteacher who is sent to a remote village in the desert experiences a succession of events which successively come into view and then fade from sight.

The 1980s also saw the production of a first feature by a second woman director, but again her progress was thwarted by the authorities. Nejia Ben Mabrouk (b. 1949) had to wait six years for the release in 1988 of her fictional feature, *La trace* (*The Trace*), completed in 1982, but delayed because of a dispute with the state production organization, SATPEC. The film depicts the efforts made by a young girl, Sabra, in a remote South Tunisian village to keep an independent identity, efforts which eventually drive her into exile, to study in Europe. By contrast, two highly talented male newcomers of the 1980s with similar film school backgrounds to that of Ben Mabrouk found an immediate enthusiastic international audience for their films. *Traversées* (*Crossing Over,* 1982), directed by Mahmoud Ben Mahmoud (b. 1947), is one of the most expressive films made on the subject of immigration. The film plots the parallel fates of two refugees, a Polish dissident and a middle-class Arab, who are trapped on a cross-channel ferry between London and Brussels on New Year's Day because their passport documents have expired. In contrast to the precise

placing in time and place of *Crossing Over, L'ombre de la terre* (*The Shadow of the Earth*, 1982), made by Taïeb Louhichi (b. 1948), has a timeless setting. It is the tale of an isolated rural family community torn apart by natural forces and, to a lesser extent, by the impact of the modern world. Both directors went on to complete a second feature, though Ben Mahmoud had to wait until the 1990s. Louhichi meanwhile made his new fictional feature, *Layla ma raison* (*Leïla My Reason*), in 1989. Set in a mythical past and adapted from André Miquel's re-telling of the traditional Arab tale, it chronicles the tragic love of the young poet Qays, whose love for the beautiful Layla meets with opposition from her father.

The dominant figure of the decade is undoubtedly a newcomer whose first feature appeared in 1986. Nourid Bouzid (b. 1945), a former political detainee, brought a new range of subject matter to Arab film making and established himself as one of North Africa's major filmmakers. *L'homme de cendres* (*Man of Ashes*, 1986) deals with Hachemi, a young carpenter, whose imminent marriage, arranged by his parents, makes him recall his childhood. In particular he remembers the male rape of which he was the victim as a child of 12, an event he is unable to discuss with anyone within his own family circle. Bouzid's second film, *Les Sabots en or* (*Golden Horseshoes*, 1989), is the story of a man who emerges from years in prison but is unable either to recognize the society in which he finds himself or to re-establish relationships with his family. The film ends in suicide.

Otherwise most of the films of the 1980s were first features by newcomers who failed to get subsequent backing, though most had studied at one of Europe's film schools. The range of background and approach is wide. Ali Mansour (b. 1944) made a low-budget comedy, *Deux larrons en folie* (*Two Thieves in Madness*, 1980), tracing the adventures of two naive peasants on their way to the capital. Abdelhafidh Bouassida (b. 1947) made a lavish period drama, *La ballade de Mamelouk* (*The Ballad of Mamelouk*, 1981), in which a young peasant saves the king's life, but instead of receiving a simple reward, he is plunged into a nightmare journey: he can have all the land he can cover between dawn and sunset. Lotfi Essid (b. 1952) completed *Que fait-on ce dimanche?* (*What Are We Doing This Sunday?* 1983), in which two North African émigrés, one Algerian and one Tunisian, spend a summer Sunday in Paris, wandering between the Goutte d'or and the smarter districts. Mohamed Damak (b. 1952) made a comedy about football, *La coupe* (*The Cup*, 1986), showing a football fan who sacrifices everything, even his family, in his passion for following his favorite team. Habib Mselmani contributed Tunisia's first film for children, *Sabra et le monstre de la forêt* (*Sabra and the Monster from the Forest*, 1986). While all the village is scared of the monster, little Sabra is fearless; she knows the monster is nothing but a harmless doll.

Immigrant Cinema

In France, two of the film pioneers of the 1970s continued their careers much as before. Ali Akika (again with Anne-Marie Autissier) probed the silence

Fig. 8. *The Trace* (1988), Nejia Ben Mabrouk, Tunisia

and isolation characteristic of the lives of many emigrant women in *Larmes de sang* (*Tears of Blood,* 1980), while Mohamed Benayat made two further features that resolutely turned their back on specifically Maghrebian problems, *L'enfant des étoiles* (*Child of the Stars,* 1985) and *Arizona Stallion* (1988). By contrast, three new directors, who had either been born in France or had reached France as children and had grown up there, brought a new approach, shifting the perspective from issues resulting from emigration to the problems of the immigrant community settled in France. The customary term adopted for films by filmmakers with Maghreb connections is *beur* cinema, the product of a slang inversion of the consonants RB in "Arab" to give BR. A surprising number of films have been made by this group since the 1980s and their range of subject matter is wide.

Abdelkrim Bahloul, born in 1950 in Algeria and an Algerian citizen who arrived in France at the age of 20, made, as his first film, *Le thé à la menthe* (*Mint Tea*, 1984), in which a young immigrant's fantasies about life in Paris—as conveyed in his letters home—are exposed when his mother arrives to take him back to marry his cousin. Rachid Bouchareb, born in 1953 in France and a French citizen, began his career in television in 1986. In his first film, *Bâton Rouge* (1985), three young people, frustrated by their dead-end jobs, set off for new life in the United States (the Bâton Rouge of the title), but only one is allowed to stay. Mehdi Charef, born in 1952 in Algeria and living in France since the age of 10, though still an Algerian citizen, made three features. Charef is also a French-language novelist and he adapted his own first novel as the basis for his debut feature. *Le thé au harem d'Archimède* (*Tea at Archimedes' Harem,* 1985) looks at the life of an immigrant family in a Nanterre housing estate and all the problems to be faced: unemployment, racism, boredom. Charef's second feature, *Miss Mona* (1987), widened the focus by taking as its protagonist an aging transvestite who can no longer make a living on the streets. His meeting with a young illegal immigrant and their friendship reveals the truth about two worlds of poverty and exclusion. *Camoumille* (*Camomile,* 1988) charts the relationship between a young man passionate about the old Panhard car he has rebuilt and a young middle-class drug addict who is attracted by the idea of suicide. These five films set the particular pattern for work produced in France by filmmakers with links to the Maghreb, which continues into the new century. Charef in particular initiates a move toward new subject matter and issues outside those raised by the immigrant community.

In the 1980s production declined slightly in Algeria and Tunisia, but the profile of new filmmakers directing their first films (twelve in Algeria and ten in Tunisia) fits the pattern we have seen through the 1960s and 1970s: a trend toward younger filmmakers who have formal qualifications in film making. Of the twenty-two new filmmakers, all were born in the 1940s except for one Algerian (Bouguermouh) born in the 1930s and two Tunisians (Essid and Damak) born in the early 1950s. Fifteen have formal film school training in Europe. In Morocco, on the other hand, where 21 new directors emerged in response to the fresh possibilities of state funding, the profile is inevitably more blurred, since the principal requirement for obtaining funding was Moroccan nationality, not relevant training or experience. In Morocco the dates of birth range from 1935 to 1957 (though only four were born before the 1940s), and the range of training is exceptionally wide: two U.S. universities, the Cairo Institute of Cinema, the Hong Kong film studios, and a Hamburg course in audiovisual communication. But if we leave the five filmmakers with these backgrounds (Yachfine,

Abbazi, Moufti, Souda, and Mrini respectively) to one side, the pattern is much the same as in Algeria and Tunisia.

Looking at the Maghreb as a whole, twenty-nine of the forty-five newcomers had formal film training and most of the major European film schools are represented: the Film and Television Faculty of the Academy of Performing Arts (Filmov Akademie Múzickych Umění [FAMU]) in Prague (Bouassida), Lodz in Poland (Yala, Bensaïd, Mohamed Abdelkrim Derkaoui), VGIK in Moscow (Lledo, Aboulouakar, Reggab), INSAS in Brussels (Ben Mabrouk, Ben Mahmoud, Tsaki, Bouzid), IDHEC (Zemmouri, Bouguermouh, Zerouali, Mohamed Abderrahman Tazi), IFC (Louhichi, Touita), and other Parisian film courses (Benlyazid, Sefraoui, Achouba, Benhadj, Mansour). Two further graduates of the Algerian film school INC also made a belated appearance as feature directors (Laradji and Fettar), the latter having completed his studies in Lodz. Of those without formal film training, eight new directors came from acting and/or drama training (Chouikh, Saddiki, Essid, Kettani, Bourquia, Noury, Jaïbi, and Jaziri), and two from work in television (Mselmani and Khayat). Of the rest, one (Damak) was a late recruit from the Tunisian amateur film movement and two were French-language novelists (Khemir and Ghalem), while the others (Mefti, Benchrif, and Akdi) seem to have had little relevant formal training.

In all, some eighty-four films were made in the Maghreb, supplemented with eight more produced by filmmakers resident in France. The thematic concerns of the 1980s are largely a continuation of those apparent in the previous decade, but there is now a sharper and more critical approach to social issues and a greater inwardness on the part of filmmakers. There is even room for humor. Again the focus is largely on the domestic situation—Benbarka's anti-apartheid epic *Amok* is one of the few films set outside the Maghreb. It is noticeable that in Algeria there was a softening of the rigid system which imposed cycles of films, first on the war and then on the agrarian revolution. A few worthy films still explore the war years (Laskri's *The Gates of Silence,* Touita's *The Sacrificed,* or the collectively made *We Shall Go onto the Mountain*) and the war's aftermath (Bendeddouche's *Harvests of Steel*), but the old official line can now be treated with derision (Zemmouri's *The Crazy Years of the Twist*) or satire (Rachedi's *Monsieur Fabre's Mill*). A few filmmakers even offer simple love stories: Fettar's *Houria,* Yala's *Autumn Song,* and Allouache's *A Parisian Love Story.* Mouny Berrah notes a similar new tone in Meddour's documentaries: "Azzedine Meddour, breaking with the droning commentaries of the war film, undeniably inaugurates a new documentary school and reconciles the audience with a genre which had fallen into disgrace because of its triumphalist appearance."[6]

There are still a few filmmakers experimenting with narrative in all three countries: Khemir with *The Searchers of the Desert* and Jaïbi and Jaziri with *Arab* in Tunisia, Bouamari with *The Denial* in Algeria, Mostafa Derkaoui with his self-conscious explorations of film making in *The Beautiful Days of Sheherazade* and *Provisional Title* in Morocco. But for most, the chosen social themes are largely unchanged: rural issues (Louhichi's *The Shadow of the Earth,* Lakhdar Hamina's *Sand Storm,* Chouikh's *The Citadel*) or urban social problems (Noury,

Tazi, and Ferhati in Morocco, Laradji in Algeria, Ben Ammar in Tunisia). The distinctive female concerns raised by the voices of the four women directors active in the decade (Djebar, Ben Mabrouk, Bourquia, and Benlyazid) are complemented by such male-directed films as Ben Ammar's *Aziza*, Ferhati's *Reed Dolls,* and Ghalem's *A Wife for My Son.* A new tone is even brought to the examination of emigration. If Ben Mahmoud's *Crossing Over* is a masterly exploration of a Kafkaesque loss of identity, other filmmakers (Bahloul in *Mint Tea* and Zemmouri in *Take A Thousand Quid and Get Lost,* for example) treat the subject as a source of comedy. There are also signs of a kind of interiority quite missing in the 1970s: Djebar's *La Zerda*, Lakhdar Hamina's evocation of his own childhood (*The Last Image*), Mostapha Derkaoui's concern with the artist's personal identity and role, Tsaki's two totally personal studies of children (*The Children of the Wind* and *Story of a Meeting*) and, above all, Bouzid's emotionally powerful depictions of personal crises, *Man of Ashes* and *Golden Horseshoes.* If the 1970s are the years of social concern, the 1980s are increasingly those of the individual.

4 The 1990s

In simple statistical terms, film production rose in all three countries of the Maghreb in the 1990s, from seventy-eight features in the 1980s to a hundred in the new decade. While the small increases in Morocco (up from thirty-eight to forty-one) and Tunisia (up from nineteen to twenty-three) give an adequate picture of developments there, the overall figure for Algeria disguises the fact that after a very bright start in the early 1990s, production was virtually extinguished by the latter years of the decade: only one Algerian-made feature was released in 1998 and 1999. This was the Algerian-Vietnamese co-production, *Fleur de lotus* (*Lotus Flower*), with which Amar Laskri had been concerned for much of the decade. In the late 1990s, with most of its principal directors driven abroad, Algerian cinema became again what it had been in 1957: a cinema in exile. Meanwhile, film making by directors from the immigrant communities in France and the Netherlands experienced a sharp upsurge in the 1990s (twenty-one new films by thirteen filmmakers). There were also some real developments in film making by women during the 1990s. In addition to three women (Rachida Krim, Zaïda Ghorab-Volta, and Fatima Jebli Ouazzani) making their debuts in Europe, five women (three of them newcomers) each made a feature film in the Maghreb: Selma Baccar, Moufida Tlatli, and Kalthoum Bornaz in Tunisia; Farida Benlyazid in Morocco; and the novelist Hafsa Zinaï-Koudil in Algeria.

Algeria

October 1993 saw another radical reorganization of the Algerian film sector, when production was privatized and film directors were given three year's salary and invited to set up their own companies. CAAIC continued in existence to offer production support and to administer a new system whereby filmmakers could receive state support for specific projects on the basis of scripts read by a commission chaired initially by the writer Rachid Mimouni. This reorganization, coinciding with widespread political upheaval, seriously threatened Algerian film output. But worse was to come in 1998 when the government closed down CAAIC, ENPA (the television production organization), and the newsreel organization Agence Nationale des Actualités Filmées (ANAF), without any indication of what new structures—if any—would be put in place. Four feature films—Sid Ali Fettar's *Meriem*, Ghaouti Bendeddouche's *La voisine* (*The Neighbor*), Sid Ali Mazif's *Mimouna,* and newcomer Abderrahim Laloui's *Hurlement* (*Scream*)—were left uncompleted, though *The Neighbor* was finally completed and released in 2002. CAAIC's 217 employees—the backbone of the

Algerian film industry—found themselves unemployed. At the same time a report indicated that cinema audiences had declined from nine million in 1980 to just half a million in 1992, while the number of cinemas (now mostly converted to video halls) had declined from 458 at the time of independence to a bare dozen in 1999.[1] The new privatization, combined with the increasing political turmoil and waves of mass killings, seriously disrupted Algerian cinema and its links with the outside world. Only five Algerian features were seen abroad in 1995–1999 and many leading filmmakers, actors, and technicians were forced into exile.

Initially the 1987 reforms had seemed to favor Algerian production and nineteen features were released in 1990–1993, an average of almost five a year. The early 1990s saw new films from a number of established 1980s directors, and ENPA co-produced two features. *Les enfants des néons* (*The Neon Children*, 1990), was made by Brahim Tsaki in France after two features shot in Algeria. It is a characteristic story of two boys (one of them a deaf-mute) and the older French girl with whom the other boy falls unhappily in love. *Le cri des hommes* (*The Cry of Men*, 1990), a new film by Okacha Touita (after a first feature made in France), explored the friendship of two policemen—one a "pied noir" (settler), the other an Arab—who find themselves on opposite sides in the increasingly savage conflict in Mostaganem between the FLN and the French in 1959. Mahmoud Zemmouri, who had also begun his career in France, made his third feature, a further fictional satire, *De Hollywood à Tamanrasset* (*From Hollywood to Tamanrasset*, 1990), this time dealing amusingly with the alienating influence of foreign television on the community in rural Algeria, where the director was born and grew up. Jean-Pierre Lledo completed his second idiosyncratic feature, *Lumières* (*Lights*, 1992), which deals with a 40-year-old filmmaker whose enthusiasm for cinema is rekindled when an old projectionist makes him realize his debts to Hollywood and Soviet cinema. Fettar's sole 1990s feature, *Amour interdit* (*Forbidden Love*, 1993), is set in 1955 and tells of the doomed love of Azzedine, a young Algerian student, and Francine, a French girl born in Algiers. Such a film would have been deemed conventional anywhere but in Algeria, where instead it represents a move away from the socially and politically committed mainstream.

Veterans from the 1970s also made their reappearance. The new head of ENPA, Mohamed Lamine Merbah, made a 16mm feature, *Radhia* (1992), the story of a fragmented family: the family land has been sold; the son has settled in the United States, where he had been sent to study; and the daughter leads her own life as a schoolteacher. Djafar Damardjji, whose first film dates from 1972, finally completed a second, *Errances* (*Wanderings*), also known as *Terre en cendres* (*Land in Ashes*, 1993), based on the travels of the European woman explorer Isabelle Eberhardt. Another isolated achievement by a veteran was the completion by Amar Laskri—head of CAAIC from 1996—of the Algerian-Vietnamese co-production *Lotus Flower*, which had occupied him through much of the 1990s. This ambitious Algerian-Vietnamese co-production (co-directed by Trân Dàc) chronicles some of the less expected outcomes of colonial occupations and wars through the tale of a Vietnamese woman journalist, Houria, who arrives in Algiers to seek out her Algerian father. The latter had been sent to Vietnam as part of the French expeditionary forces in the 1940s, but had shifted his sympathies to the Vietnamese cause (in which Houria's mother was also active) as a result of French massacres back home, before returning to Algeria to fight in the final liberation struggle.

A new generation emerged, quite literally, with the feature debut of Mohamed Lakhdar Hamina's son, Malik Lakhdar Hamina (b. 1962), with *Automne— Octobre à Alger* (*Autumn—October in Algiers*, 1991). This is a vivid portrayal of a family caught up in the tumultuous events of October 1988, when young Algerians took to the streets in protest and were confronted by inexperienced and frightened soldiers. Other early 1990s debuts include those of journalist Saïd Ould Khelifa with *Ombres blanches* (*White Shadows*, 1991): a close friend seeks out Youssef, a young man who disappeared two days earlier. Youssef, who is in love with a girl in Paris, has been studying by day and doing odd jobs at night, becoming a friend of those who roam the streets at night. Rabie Ben Mokhtar (b. 1944) made *Marathon Tam* (1992), the story of a young runner who trains in the rugged landscape of the mountains of Southern Algeria, and the editor-turned-director Rachid Benallal (b. 1946) directed *Ya ouled* (1993), which is very much an echo of the 1960s and early 1970s, the tale of the events of July 1962 as seen through the eyes of children growing up in an Algiers cut in two by the struggle: on one side the colonizers, on the other the Algerians.

Many of the others who made their first films for cinema release in the 1990s came—often with considerable experience—from television, the old RTA which was reshaped in 1987 to become Entreprise Nationale de Télévision (ENTV) and then ENPA. The veteran Mohamed Hilmi (b. 1931) wrote and directed *El ouelf essaib* (1990), in which a composer and his friends live a hectic and eventful life in a comedy of everyday life. Another veteran, Hadj Rahim, made *Le portrait* (*The Portrait*, 1994), the story of a taxi driver and his family in the popular quarter of Algiers. Abderrazak Hellal (b. 1951) directed *Question d'honneur* (*Question of Honor*, 1997) and Benamar Bakhti (b. 1941) made the highly successful *Le clandestin* (*Moonlighting*, 1991), in which a vivid comic portrait of contemporary Algiers forms the background for the tale of a resourceful man, Si Abdellah, who supports his large family by working illegally as a taxi driver. Rabah Bouberras (b. 1950), who, like Bakhti, had made a number of RTA television features, directed *Sahara Blues* (1991), the story of a woman who reassesses her past and takes stock of her present as she travels to Southern Algeria with her son and second husband. Rachid Ben Brahim (b. 1951) directed *Le troisième acte* (*The Third Act*, 1991), a theatrical drama, showing the backstage rivalries which lead to violence and death. Yahia Debboub (b. 1940) made a first feature for ENPA, *La vieille dame et l'enfant* (*The Old Lady and the Child*), about the problem of abandoned children, in 1991, but because of technical difficulties it was not released until 1997. The same year saw the appearance of his second feature, *Les résistants* (*The Resistance Fighters*, 1997), a tale about the 1870 invasion and the crushing of El Mokrani's army of resistance. In the aftermath, some return to the land, while others continue the struggle. ENPA also initially supported the female novelist Hafsa Zinaï-Koudil (b. 1951), whose controversial *Le démon au féminin* (*The Female Demon*, 1993) led to a dispute with the producers. It is the story of a woman whose husband becomes persuaded that she is possessed by the devil and who puts her at the mercy of charlatans who torture her under the guise of carrying out an exorcism.

The confusions within the film industry and the chaos within society at large, as Islamic fundamentalists continued their war on politicians, intellectuals, and foreigners, find clear reflection in a number of films of 1993–1994. In Mohamed Rachid Benhadj's second film, *Touchia* (1993), a woman trapped in her flat by pro-Islamic Republic demonstrators in 1991 recalls a parallel disillusionment when her 1950s childhood dreams of independence ended in the brutal reality of rape and the death of her closest friend. Mahmoud Zemmouri's *L'honneur de la tribu* (*The Honor of the Tribe*, 1993) is a bleak—if often farcical —look at the impact of twenty-five years of FLN rule, which reflects the confused situation of Algeria in the early 1990s. It begins as an apologia for the new Islamic force for change, but ends with a caption that contradicts the whole logic of the narrative: "Djamel and his friends have now shown their true faces. People die every day in Algeria." In Mohamed Chouikh's *Youcef: la légende du septième dormant* (*Youssef: The Legend of the Seventh Sleeper*, 1993) an amnesiac travels through the country struggling to understand and failing to find in contemporary Algeria any of the ideals for which he and his colleagues fought during the liberation struggle. Perhaps the clearest depiction of the Algerian predicament is Merzak Allouache's *Bab el-oued City* (1994), which marks a return to the quarter of Algiers which had formed the setting of *Omar Gatlato*, but which is now totally transformed by the new and violent force of Islamic fundamentalism. With a plot built around the unexpected outcomes of the removal of an intrusive mosque loudspeaker, it depicts unemployed young men who find a sense of direction in the new rigid Islamic attitudes and young women whose lives are stifled in the new environment. The film constitutes a major statement about contemporary Algeria. In his study of what he terms Algeria's "invisible war" in the 1990s, Benjamin Stora draws attention to the importance of the handful of films which looked at contemporary society: "what is particularly striking about these few films, made in such a somber period, is the will to survive. It is as if the filmmakers had taken the collective decision to confront a world which, visibly, was no longer expecting them."[2]

Since 1995 production in Algeria has been reduced to a mere trickle of one or two films a year, most of them French co-productions exploring the strengths and contradictions of traditional attitudes. They mark a retreat from the urban environment and a shift from realistic narratives to fables and allegories. Some filmmakers have turned to the Atlas Mountains. The first of three films in the Berber language released in 1995–1997 was *Machaho* (*Once Upon a Time*, 1995) directed by Belkacem Hadjadj (b. 1950). In this Hadjadj offers a critical examination of traditional attitudes and beliefs, particularly the male concept of honor, in a simple narrative leading inexorably to confrontation and death.

Fig. 9. *Machaho* (1995), Belkacem Hadjadj, Algeria

Abderrahmane Bouguermouh followed with his long-delayed *La colline oubliée* (*The Forgotten Hillside,* 1996), based on the novel by Mouloud Mammeri, which tells of an isolated mountain community shaken by the forces of colonialism and by its own inner passions. Another film to depict a mountain community and to use the Berber language was *La montagne de Baya* (*Baya's Mountain,* 1997), a first fictional film by the documentarist Azzedine Meddour (1947–2000). Set at the beginning of the century, this is the story of a woman, Baya, who is torn between love and the resistance struggle and who incarnates the spirit of the Berber villagers' opposition to the French forces after they have been driven up into the mountains. Mohamed Chouikh, in another allegory, *L'arche du désert* (*The Desert Ark,* 1997), looked instead at a remote desert community, exploring and questioning the validity of its values and traditions.

But for many other filmmakers the only choice was exile. Merzak Allouache made two feature films in France. *Salut cousin!* (*Hello Cousin!,* 1996) shows the adventures of a young Algerian, Alilo, who is introduced to Parisian life by his very Frenchified second-generation *beur* cousin, Mok. The film ends with Alilo settled with the beautiful Guinean Fatoumata and the hapless Mok sent "back"

The 1990s 59

to an Algeria he has never seen. In *Alger-Beyrouth, pour mémoire* (*Algiers-Beirut: In Remembrance,* 1998), which has a French heroine, Laurence returns to Beirut, which she left as a child. There she meets Rachid, whom she had previously known in Algiers. They fall in love and she tries to persuade him to seek asylum in France, but instead he goes back to face death in Algiers. Mahmoud Zemmouri directed his musical film, *100% Arabica* (1997), in France. The film combines a satiric portrayal of a poor Parisian neighborhood with the *raï* music of Khaled and Cheb Mami. From his base in Italy, Mohamed Rachid Benhadj produced *L'albero dei destini sospesi* (*The Tree of Suspended Fates,* 1997), which shows two young people—Samir, a Moroccan youth, and Maria, a young Italian woman—who meet up and travel South in what becomes a voyage of initiation. Their love is real but is destroyed. Another particularly interesting initiative by the Paris-based Internews Europe group was the documentary *L'autre Algérie: Regards intérieurs* (*The Other Algeria: Views from Within,* 1998), containing five episodes directed in Algeria by Meddour, Ben Brahim, the documentary filmmaker Boualem Kamel (b. 1953), and two journalists, Abdelkader Ensaad (b. 1973) and Abed Charef (b. 1957). This was Meddour's last project before his death in 2000.

Morocco

In Morocco, the level of funding under the "fonds d'aide" scheme increased in the early 1990s and new tax concessions were offered to film producers. Moreover, for the first time, Moroccan films began to attract substantial local audiences. The 1990s saw the flow of productions continue at a rate of about four films a year, with most contributed by established directors (who nevertheless often experienced long gaps in output), but with new directors making their impact increasingly felt as the decade unfolded. The CCM also developed an enlightened co-production policy in the 1990s, helping to fund serious productions from other African countries, such as Mali, the Ivory Coast, and Tunisia.

In 1990, after a gap of ten years and in the same realist vein that characterized his first feature, Hakim Noury resumed his career with *Le marteau et l'enclume* (*The Hammer and the Anvil*), the story of a civil servant whose forced early retirement disrupts his ordered existence and causes him psychological as well as material problems. Noury subsequently became the most prolific Moroccan filmmaker of the decade with four further features. *L'enfance volée* (*Stolen Childhood,* 1993) is the story of Rkia, a girl of 10 sent to work as a maid in Casablanca, whose world is shattered when she finds herself pregnant and abandoned. *Le voleur de rêves* (*The Dream Thief,* 1995) explores the friendship of two men—Mehdi, a man released from prison after five years, and Driss, a young dropout—who share their fears and dreams. In *Un simple fait-divers* (*A Simple News Item,* 1997), an old journalist tells the story of a young colleague who, in the 1970s, tries to pursue a state official on grounds of corruption. When attempts to stop him fail, the death of the young journalist—at the hands

Fig. 10. *Stolen Childhood* (1993), Hakim Noury, Morocco

of a burglar—is announced in the newspapers. *Destin de femme (A Woman's Fate,* 1998) shows what happens when a woman who thinks she is happily married finds, to her horror, that her husband cannot tolerate her success and even wants to take control of her inheritance. Only proof of his adultery can save her. With this succession of features, Noury became, as Ahmed Araib notes, the "leading figure" in the consolidation of a social cinema in Morocco.[3]

Another filmmaker enabled to make a succession of films in the decade was Mostafa Derkaoui, who had also experienced a long gap since his last film. He began the 1990s with *Fiction première (First Fiction,* 1992), about two young people, Hilma, a factory worker, and Larbi, a book salesman, who meet and fall in love but still have many problems to face. In *Je(u) au passé ((Ga)me in the Past,* 1994), Natalia sets off to find a man her mother had once known who is remarkably like the Moscow student she herself has just fallen in love with. *Les sept portes de la nuit (The Seven Gates of the Night,* 1994) depicts the adventures of a man, Brahim, who sets out in search of his son and encounters his friend Kamal. Derkaoui's final film in the decade was a sixty-minute piece, *La grande allégorie (The Great Allegory,* 1995), in which a young woman writer constructs a story in which she evokes the memory of a young man who died in the war.

But others were markedly less successful in making more than a single film. Mostapha Derkaoui's brother, the cinematographer and director Mohamed Abdelkrim Derkaoui, who had co-directed *The Travelling Showman's Day* with Driss Kettani in 1984, had to wait fourteen years for his solo directing debut, *Rue le Caire (Cairo Street,* 1998), which traces the difficult struggle for a new society in the years immediately after independence in Casablanca. Nabyl Lah-lou, who had made four films in succession in the 1980s, quickly followed up with a new feature, *La nuit du crime* (*The Night of the Crime,* 1992), the story of a chauffeur, Miloud, who is driven to murder his boss, the newspaper reporter Salim, when he falls in love with the latter's wife. But after this film, Lahlou was reduced to silence. Ahmed Yachfine too made only one film, *Khafaya* (1995), his second film, which explores the role of women in contemporary society through the confrontation of two contrasting models of feminine behavior. One of Morocco's few women directors, Farida Benlyazid, had to wait a dozen years till the end of the decade to complete her second feature, *Keid Ensa* (*Women's Wiles,* 1999). A fairy tale about male violence, this charming film shows how, after many tribulations, the daughter of a rich merchant finally wins the love of the handsome prince who tries in vain to make her admit male superiority.

Four other experienced but totally diverse directors were able to make two features in the decade. Moumen Smihi completed *La dame du Caire* (*The Lady from Cairo,* 1991), which he filmed in Egypt. Following the conventions of the Egyptian musical, it is the story of Jawhara, a peasant woman who goes to Cairo to seek her brother and who stays on to become a famous singer. Smihi is one of the few Moroccan directors to make a feature without CCM funding, either at the scripting stage or for competition. His 16mm feature *Chroniques marocaines* (*Moroccan Chronicles,* 1999), a European co-production, contains three tales of contemporary Morocco: boys misbehaving in the Jemma el Fna square in Marrakesh, lovers meeting and flirting on the walls of Essaouira, and a grandfather's madness and a family torn apart by emigration in Tangier. While Smihi has found himself marginalized, Souheil Benbarka, head of CCM and successful producer/director/distributor/exhibitor, remains the dominating figure in Moroccan cinema. His work—comprising expensive co-productions dealing with epic historical subjects—is quite unlike any other Moroccan production. In the 1990s he first made the historical drama *Les tambours du feu* (*Drums of Fire*) in 1991 and later received funding from the CCM which allowed him to do a complete re-edit. The film emerged as *Les Cavaliers de la gloire* (*Horsemen of Glory,* 1993), in which the Moroccan prince Abdelmalek sacrifices everything to recover his father's throne but dies, poisoned, on the battlefield at his moment of triumph. Benbarka followed this in 1996 with another ambitious superproduction, *L'ombre du pharaon* (*Shadow of the Pharaoh*). Here the Pharaoh's son, Anhur, overcomes the opposition of the fanatics so as to succeed his father, but only after the death of his twin brother, the recognized heir.

Mohamed Abderrahman Tazi achieved new prominence with his comedy, *A la recherche du mari de ma femme* (*Looking for My Wife's Husband,* 1993), the most successful film ever in Morocco, with audience figures of around a million spectators (more than double its nearest rival). Hadj Ben Moussa, a wealthy jeweler, repeatedly repudiates (and then reconciles himself with) his beautiful young third wife, Houda, until he discovers—on the third occasion—that he can only take her back if she has been married meanwhile to another husband. Tazi followed this with a (more serious) sequel, *Lalla Hobby* (1997), tracing the further misadventures of Hadj Ben Moussa in Belgium in search of his third wife's husband, while his first wife, Lalla Hobby, runs the household in his absence. Another key figure in the socially committed realist stream of Moroccan cinema is Jillali Ferhati, who made *La plage des enfants perdus* (*The Beach of Lost Children*, 1991). Mina discovers that she is pregnant when she is alone after the death of her lover, but finds the force to defy both her repressive father and his antagonistic second wife. Ferhati's second film of the decade was *Chevaux de fortune* (*Make-Believe Horses*, 1995), in which a group of characters who meet up in Tangier all nurse hopeless dreams which involve crossing into Europe, visible on the horizon. Their efforts end in death.

In 1989, the 53-year-old Abdellah Mesbahi had been funded to complete *J'écrirai ton nom dans le sable* (*I Shall Write Your Name in the Sand*), which had been shot in 1980 and which emerged as *Terre du défi* (*Land of Challenge*, 1989). Similarly, in the 1990s, Abdallah Zerouali (b. 1939) was given money to re-edit the footage of *The Whirlpool*, which had also been left incomplete in 1980, and the result was *Moi l'artiste* (*I'm the Artist*, 1995), the story of an ambitious artist who dreams of becoming an international star but is forced by his family to take up a more lucrative career. After fifteen years of inactivity as a feature filmmaker, Mohamed Abbazi received funding to make his second film, *Les trésors de l'Atlas* (*The Treasures of the Atlas*, 1997), a historical drama, in which a spoiled elder son, who has been disinherited, unsuccessfully seeks to use the treasures of the Atlas to regain his lost power. No less that twenty-five years separate Hamid Benani's debut film, *Traces*, from his second feature, an adaptation of Tahar Ben Jelloun's novel, *La prière de l'absent* (*A Prayer for the Absent*, 1995), in which Mokhtar, who has become amnesiac, undertakes a journey across Morocco to recover his past and his memory. In addition, Larbi Bennani, co-director of the second Moroccan film in 1968, returned to film making twenty-seven years later with *Le résistant inconnu* (*The Unknown Resistance Fighter*, 1995). The film deals with an episode in the history of Moroccan national resistance after the exile of King Mohammed V. At the age of 58 the experienced producer Mohamed Lotfi (b. 1939) made his directing debut with *Rhésus ou le sang de l'autre* (*Rhesus or Another Person's Blood*, 1996), in which a young filmmaker neglects his fiancée for an affair with a Canadian director, until an accident to his mother brings him to his senses.

Another characteristic feature of the early 1990s was the debut as directors of the members of the collective—led by Derkaoui and Mohamed Reggab—which had produced *Cinders of the Vineyard* in 1979. The most striking 1990s debut was that of Abdelkader Lagtaâ (b. 1948), who had trained in Lodz and who sees his role as "questioning society, questioning social practices, questioning how people behave and the kinds of relationships they have with one another."[4] Lagtaâ attracted considerable attention with his first feature, *Un amour à Casablanca* (*A Love Affair in Casablanca*, 1991): Saloua, an 18-year-old schoolgirl feeling oppressed at home, runs off with her 50-year-old seducer, then abandons him for her true love, who turns out to be the older man's son. Lagtaâ then made *La porte close* (*The Closed Door*, 1995), the story of a young man who frees himself from his oppressive stepmother and sets out in search of an independent life, but this film's release was delayed for years by financial problems and censorship difficulties. His next film, *Les Casablancais* (*The Casablancans*, 1998), interweaves three stories about Casablanca today: a man terrified of the police, a teacher harassed because of her beauty, and a boy corrupted by his fundamentalist teacher. As Mohamed Jibril notes, "Confronting subjects which are still largely taboo, Lagtaâ draws attention to the troubled effects of 'traditional' ways of life, which now find expression only in a coercive or castrating force exercised by parents or other moral authorities discredited by their own incoherence."[5]

Another member of the collective, Saâd Chraïbi (b. 1952) made *Chronique d'une vie normale* (*Chronicle of a Normal Life*, 1991), which traces the effects of a chance meeting, after a dozen or so years, of two old school friends whose lives have taken them in very different directions. He followed this with *Femmes . . . et femmes* (*Women . . . and Women*, 1998), featuring Zakia, a television presenter dismissed for her feminist views, and her three friends who share mutual commitment in a hostile world of male prejudice and violence. A third member of the collective, Nour Eddine Gounajjar (b. 1946), directed a video, *La mémoire bleue* (*Blue Memory*, 1991) and a 16mm feature *La salle d'attente* (*The Waiting Room*, 1991) in which, waiting his turn in a doctor's reception room, a patient looks back over his life.

Another 16mm feature, *Ymer ou les chardons florifères* (*Ymer or The Flowering Thistles*, 1991), is perhaps the ultimate experimental film in that its author, Tijani Chrigui (b. 1949), a painter who had earlier co-scripted Mohamed Aboulouakar's *Hadda* (1984), described it in the film's publicity material as featuring "a series of situations in which it is difficult to know what the characters do or say."[6] It proved to be Chrigui's only film. Another outsider (not listed in the CCM documentation) is Naguib Ktiri Idrissa, who was born in Casablanca but had no connections with film making in Morocco when he returned from teaching at the University of California at Los Angeles (UCLA) in the United States to show *Aziz et Itto: Un mariage marocain* (*Aziz and Itto: A Moroccan Wedding*, 1991) at the 1992 JCC. This 16mm production features Aziz, a young shoemaker, who marries Itto, a young Berber girl, on impulse at the Imilishil Wedding Festival and, despite the negative efforts of one of his ex-girlfriends, manages to win over his conservative parents. The most prolific newcomer was Hassan Benjelloun (b. 1950), who made his debut with *La fête des autres* (*Other People's Celebrations*, 1990), a study of three families living in close proximity in a poor district of Casablanca. He followed this with two further films in quick succession. *Yarit* (1993) deals with the problems of Said, who is preparing his thesis in psychiatry and is concerned with his mentally troubled sister and, at the same time, falls in love and becomes seriously ill. *Les amis d'hier* (*Yesterday's Friends*, 1997) shows a young girl, forced to work to pay for her brother's medical treatment, who gets a job reading to a rich blind man. Listening to his memories, she realizes he is her embittered father's childhood friend: a happy reunion ensues. With these films Benjelloun has become a central figure in Moroccan cinema, following the path of social commitment mapped out by Noury, Ferhati, and Lagtaâ.

In 1997, a truly new generation finally emerged with *Mektoub,* the first feature of Nabil Ayouch (b. 1969), who had previously made three fictional shorts. This thriller, about a young woman attending a conference in Tunis with her husband, where she is kidnapped and raped, but recovers her relationship with her husband through a trip to the South, was a great commercial success in Morocco and opened the way for other young directors. Ayouch himself went on to make the outstanding study of street children *Ali Zaoua* (1999). Reminiscent at times of Buñuel in its combination of violence and surreal images, it offers an uncompromising portrait of life in the slums of Casablanca. The debut films of three other young directors quickly followed. *Aouchtam* (1998), which was made by producer Mohamed Ismaîl (b. 1951), is a Berber melodrama concerning an autocratic, blind old man and his two sons, set against the background of the 1940s Spanish occupation. *Adieu forain* (*Bye-Bye Souirty,* 1998), the debut film of Daoud Aoulad Syad (b. 1953), who had made several remarkable short documentaries, is a portrait of Kacem, a veteran showman traveling with his wheel of fortune, who makes a last trip to the South, accompanied by his aggressive and unsympathetic son Larbi and Rabii, a young transvestite dancer. *Mabrouk* (1999), made by Driss Chouika (b. 1953), who had a background in television, was the lighthearted story of the encounter between Miloud, with his donkey Mabrouk, and a wealthy European tourist, Lycénia.

Tunisia

If the 1980s had been a period of renewal for Tunisian film making, the early 1990s were largely time for consolidation, with the bulk of the films being made by those with a prior experience of feature production. Toward the end of the decade newcomers made their appearance but failed, in most cases, to make a significant impact. The key figure of the late 1980s and early 1990s is Ahmed Attia (b. 1946), producer of the first fictional features of Bouzid, Boughedir, Tlatli, and Moncef Dhouib and of the collectively made *La guerre du Golfe . . . et après?* (*After the Gulf?,* 1992), which allowed five Arab filmmakers to offer short meditations, mixing documentary and fiction, on the aftermath of the Gulf War. In all, nineteen Tunisian filmmakers, nine of them newcomers, made twenty-three films in the 1990s.

The greatest successes of Tunisian cinema in the early 1990s (continuing from Attia's work with Bouzid in the late 1980s) were a series of films made in quick succession by directors of Attia's own generation (i.e., born in the 1940s). The first success of the new decade came with Ferid Boughedir's dazzling first feature, the wonderfully humorous fictional evocation of childhood, *Halfaouine —l'enfant des terrasses* (*Halfaouine,* 1990), in which a young boy growing up in Tunis displays an increasingly intense interest in the goings-on in the women's bath house to which his unsuspecting mother takes him. Boughedir's subsequent feature, *Un été à la Goulette* (*One Summer at La Goulette,* 1995), which he produced himself, was a complex story tracing the interactions of three families of friends—especially the three daughters—on holiday at the resort of La Goulette. The distinctive quality of this mutual friendship was the way in which it crossed racial and religious barriers: one family was European, one Arab, and one Jewish. The film is a passionate plea for tolerance and has many fine comic moments but lacks the very special qualities that made *Halfaouine* such an international success. Central to the success of the new decade was Nouri Bouzid, who made *Bezness* (1992), which probes the contradictions in the life of Roufa, who sells himself to tourists while remaining totally repressive with his sister and his girlfriend and who loves his country but dreams of Europe. Five years later Bouzid made his fourth feature, concentrating this time on women's problems and issues. *Tunisiennes* (*Bent familia/Girls from a Good Family*, 1997) shows three women—Amina, a woman suffering violence at home, Aida, a divorcee, and Fatiha, an Algerian refugee—who come together to offer each other love and comfort until their lives drive them apart again.

The third member of the group was Moncef Dhouib (b. 1952), who was already well known for his distinctive short films.[7] But he achieved less success with his initial feature, *Soltane el Madina!* (*The Sultan of the Medina*, 1993), the story of a young bride who dreams of escaping from the medina with the aid the her future brother-in-law, the holy fool, Fraj, but who finds that their explorations of the limits of freedom lead only to disaster. Attia and his production team returned to their very best form with the remarkable feature debut of the former editor Moufida Tlatli (b. 1947). In *Les silences du palais* (*Silences of the Palace*, 1994) the 25-year-old Alya remembers her upbringing in the bey's palace where her mother was servant. As she probes her memories a vibrant portrait of women's suffering and resistance is built up. Tlatli's contemporary, Kalthoum Bornaz (b. 1945), followed several short fiction films with an independently produced first feature, *Keswa—le fil perdu* (*Keswa—The Lost Thread*, 1997). In it, Nozha returns home from France for her brother's wedding, but finds herself left behind when the party leaves for the ceremony. Looking for her family, she wanders through Tunis at night wearing her expensive traditional wedding dress (*keswa*), which gradually unravels.

For several key figures of Tunisian cinema, the early 1990s were a time when their reputations were consolidated. One such filmmaker was the third member of the trio of Tunisian women active in production in the 1990s, Selma Baccar, who had waited seventeen years to complete a new feature. *La danse du feu* (*The Fire Dance*, 1995), a fictional story based on a real character, tells the story of Habiba M'sika, a singer and dancer who created her own band of devoted admirers but also scandalized Tunisian audiences in the 1920s. The film creates a powerful female figure set against a well-delineated historical setting. Nacer Khemir, who had achieved wide success at international festivals with *The Searchers of the Desert*, made a new exploration of the richness of the oral narrative tradition, *Le collier perdu de la colombe* (*The Dove's Lost Necklace*, 1990). Set in the eleventh century, at the height of Andalusian civilization, the

Fig. 11. *The Dove's Lost Necklace* (1990), Nacer Khemir, Tunisia

film tells of the mysterious events which issue from a young calligrapher's quest for love and knowledge. Two other 1980s filmmakers, Mahmoud Ben Mahmoud and Fadhel Jaïbi, combined to make *Poussière de diamants* (*The Dust of Diamonds*, 1992), a darkly brooding tale of family secrets and rivalry, focused on a stolen bracelet (the Chichkhân of the Arab title) and treating the doomed love of an aging aristocrat for a young girl. Independently, Ben Mahmoud later made a further feature, *Les siestes grenadine* (*The Pomegranate Siesta*, 1999), an ambitious examination of tensions between the Arab world and Black Africa. In it, a young woman, brought back home from Senegal by her father, who wants to make her a true Tunisian citizen, finds the transition difficult and the separation of her parents (her mother is French) painful. It is the father's unspoken prejudices, silences, and past lies which lead directly to the film's unhappy outcome. In a very different mood, Mohamed Ali El Okbi directed a second, highly successful comedy, *Les zazous de la vague* (*The Teddy Boys*, 1992), the lighthearted tale of four young people who become emotionally involved when they visit a nightclub, La Vague. Toward the end of the decade, Taîeb Louhichi made his third feature, *Noces de lune* (*Moon Wedding*, 1998), in which five young people in Tunis enjoy a sense of freedom and superiority until the accidental death of one of their number brings the idyll to an end.

Otherwise the results have been mixed, particularly for those who made their initial impact in the 1970s. Among those who made welcome reappearances, but without adding substantially to their reputations, was Rachid Ferchiou with two features in the decade. In *Automne '86* (*Autumn '86*, 1991) the inquiries undertaken by a journalist bring him into conflict with the authorities, while *Echec et mat* (*Check and Mate*, 1995) looks at a deposed African head of state who contemplates his fate and the attitude of his wife and supporters as he is sheltered in a remote and isolated castle. Brahim Babaï, author of *And Tomorrow?* gave a similar realistic treatment to *La nuit de la décennie* (*The Night of the Decade*, 1991), the story of two former lovers who meet up after ten years which have seen their lives go in very different directions. Ridha Behi's continued search for international success led him to choose a French lead for his dramatic study of the Palestinian struggle, *Les hirondelles ne meurent pas à Jérusalem* (*Swallows Don't Die in Jerusalem*, 1994). The film, which is one of the few works made in North Africa dealing with situations outside the Maghreb, deals lucidly with the problems of a French journalist in Israeli-occupied Palestine.

In the early 1990s a number of new filmmakers born in the 1950s emerged, many of them having their work previewed at the Tunisian film festival, the JCC, but few achieved a national let alone an international reputation. These new filmmakers include Ali Abidi (b. 1950), whose debut film, *Eclair nocturne* (*Barg Ellil*, 1990), was adapted from a novel by Bhéchir Khraief, whose work had also formed the basis of Ben Halima's first feature, *Khlifa Ringworm*, back in the 1960s. In *Barg Ellil*, a sixteenth-century emperor's appeal for help in the struggle against the Ottomans forms the background for a pair of love stories, one involving the slave Barg Ellil and the other his master Chaachou. Abidi followed this later in the decade with a very different kind of film. *Redeyef 54* (1997) depicts two diverse characters (a Frenchman, François, and a Tunisian, Brahim), who arrive in Redeyef having traveled on the same boat from Marseilles and find that their lives become entangled in the 1954 Tunisian struggle for independence. Fitouri Belhiba (b. 1950) made *Coeur nomade* (*Wandering Heart*, 1990), a film about women's issues depicting a woman who fights for her independence—and refuses remarriage—after the death of her husband.

Ahmed Djemaï made his appearance at the JCC in 1994 with *Le vent des destins* (*Wind of Destinies*, 1993), the story of a young man who has great difficulties with the two women in his life, his mother and his wife. At the same festival, Ezzedine Fazaî Mellitti (b. 1957) made his debut with *Le magique* (*The Magic Box*, 1994). This is the story of a 10-year-old boy from a rural background who finds himself alone at home when his parents leave to seek work in France. He is free to do as he pleases and one day he makes a magic box he considers to be his cinema. At the end of the decade a further newcomer to make his debut was the actor Mohamed Ben Smaïl (b. 1953), with *Demain je brûle* (*Tomorrow I Burn*, 1998). The film charts the final days of Lotfi, who returns to Tunis exhausted after twenty years of seeking success in Europe and seeks out the places and people of his childhood. The most successful of this new generation was in fact the youngest, Mohamed Zran (b. 1959), with *Essaïda* (1996), the story of a painter who becomes involved with the inhabitants of the poor Tunisian district of Essaïda and whose trajectory allows keen insights into the divisions of modern-day Tunis.

Immigrant Cinema

The films by filmmakers of Maghrebian origin in Europe serve as examples of the extremely fruitful situation for a filmmaker of being astride two cultures, but labels such as "*beur*" or even "immigrant" cinema help little, since they tend to blur the very significant differences between those thus grouped. Certainly, in the 1990s, the work produced in France by filmmakers with links to the Maghreb far surpasses the simple treatment of the theme of immigration and extends to embrace the fictional expression of a great many of the forms of alienation found in modern urban society.

The three new French-based filmmakers of the 1980s continued their careers prolifically in the 1990s. Mehdi Charef made *Au pays des Juliets* (*In the Land of the Juliets,* 1992), in which three women who have never met before are stranded by a railway strike and, as they become acquainted, reveal details of their lives. Abdelkrim Bahloul made three features, the first a tongue-in-cheek comedy, *Un vampire au paradis* (*A Vampire in Paradise,* 1991), in which a well-brought-up young lady in Paris suddenly begins to speak Arabic, apparently thanks to the powers of Nosfer, an Arab living in Clichy. Bahloul's subsequent two films were more realistic studies of immigrant life. In *Les soeurs Hamlet* (*The Hamlet Sisters,* 1996) two adolescents rediscover something of their Algerian heritage through a chance meeting when they are stranded in Paris overnight, while *La nuit du destin* (*The Night of Destiny,* 1997) deals with the aftermath of an immigrant witnessing a murder and realizing who is responsible. Rachid Bouchareb made five features in the 1990s. In the first of these films, *Cheb* (a Franco-Algerian co-production, 1990), Marouan, a young *beur* who has lived all his life in France but kept his Algerian nationality, is expelled to Algeria and enrolled in the Algerian army. There he falls in love with a woman with whom he tries to escape. This was followed by *Segou* (1992) and *Des années déchirées* (*Shattered Years,* 1992), a study of post-revolutionary Algeria, which had to be shot in Tunisia, in which two former combatants returning home in 1945 after fighting against the Germans experience the events which will change the face of Algeria. After a study of Vietnam orphans, *Poussières de vie* (*Life Dust,* 1994), based on the book *La colline de Fanta* by Duyen Anh, in which three Amerasian children are in custody in a re-education camp after the fall of Saigon, Bouchareb returned to the subject of the immigrant community in France with *L'honneur de ma famille* (*My Family's Honor,* 1997), the story of a liberated young second-generation immigrant, Nora, who goes through a conventional arranged marriage after she finds herself pregnant by her French lover. But things do not turn out as she hopes.

New directors of the 1990s include Amor Hakkar, born in 1958 in Algeria and brought up in Besançon, who is the director of *Sale temps pour un voyou* (*Bad Weather for a Crook,* 1992), in which a 30-year-old man's life is turned upside down when he is provoked to make a miserable attempt at robbery. Malek Chibane, born in 1964 in France of Kabyle parents, made two features,

Hexagone (*Hexagon*, 1993), looking at the life of five young friends in a Parisian suburb as events serve to drive them apart, and *Douce France* (*Sweet France*, 1995). Here two young friends witness a robbery and are able to get their hands on the loot, with which they hope to realize their dreams. But life does not work out that way. Karim Dridi (b. 1961), the sole feature filmmaker of Tunisian origin active in France, made three films, only one of which related directly to immigrant problems. In *Pigalle* (1994), Véra, a stripper, and Fifi, a pickpocket, are thrown together when their respective partners are murdered in the violent atmosphere of Pigalle. *Bye-Bye* (1995) traces the adventures of two young brothers from Belleville preparing, in a racist, drug-ridden Marseilles, for the departure of the younger of them for Algeria. In *Hors jeu* (*Out of Play*, 1998), by contrast, the focus is on two young actors who find themselves by chance in the middle of a dinner party for film stars and decide to take them hostage.

Ahmed Bouchaâla, born in 1956 in Algeria and with Algerian nationality but living in France since the age of 6, made his debut with *Krim* (1995), in which a prisoner released after sixteen years in prison sets off to find his daughter, Yasmine. Lost and desperate in a world he does not recognize, he is saved by meeting a 17-year-old drug addict, Nora. Two new women directors also made features. Rachida Krim (b. 1955), after a number of shorts, made the low-budget feature *Sous les pieds des femmes* (*Under Women's Feet*, 1996), which traced a woman's progress to political awareness (and the great love of her life) within the context of the FLN's liberation struggle in France. By contrast, Zaîda Ghorab-Volta (b. 1966), with *Laisse un peu d'amour* (*Leave a Little Love*, 1998), moved away from Maghrebian concerns to offer a study of generational conflict and eventual understanding among three women (a mother and two daughters) who have to live under the same roof. Karim Traïdia (b. 1949), the only Algerian-born filmmaker resident in the Netherlands (where he has lived for twenty years), also began with a feature, *La financée polonaise* (*The Polish Bride*, 1998), which owes more to his life in Europe than to his Maghrebian origins. The film tells of a Polish illegal immigrant who is forced into prostitution but escapes and finds a new life with a Dutch farmer.

Among other works produced by this loose group of new filmmakers is the acclaimed documentary *In het Huis van mijn Vader* (*In My Father's House*, 1997), made by Fatima Jebli Ouazzani, who was born in Morocco in 1959 but has lived in the Netherlands since 1970, which looks at the issue of virginity before marriage in Morocco, mixing memories and personal experiences. The film won top prize at the 1998 Moroccan National Film Festival in Casablanca, though the director was unknown in Morocco and had had no contacts with the film industry there. Equally remarkable is *Vivre au paradis* (*Living in Paradise*, 1998), a fictional study in the shanty town of Nanterre in 1961–1962, where families are split in their struggle for existence, a husband turning to deceit while his wife chooses militancy. But within the community, there is a true solidarity. This first feature, shot in Tunisia by a Paris-born director of Algerian descent, Bourlem Guerdjou (b. 1965), beat all the Maghrebian opposition to win the first prize, the tanit d'or, at the Carthage Film Festival in 1998.

Of the seventy filmmakers responsible for the 101 features made in the Maghreb in the 1990s, almost half (thirty-four) were newcomers. But it is difficult to generalize about developments in the decade which saw the total collapse of the once-dominant Algerian film industry and the emergence of enlightened funding policies in Morocco.

In Algeria just over half the active directors were newcomers (fourteen out of twenty-six). Apart from one director born in the 1930s (Hilmi, a television veteran making a first film for cinema release) and one born in the 1960s (Mohamed Lakhdar Hamina's son Malek), all the newcomers were born in the 1940s or 1950s (five in each decade)—a remarkable rejuvenation for the national cinema. The increase in production of the early years of the decade was followed by a virtual cessation under the twin blows of organizational collapse and social unrest. At the end of the decade hardly any films were being shot in Algeria.

In Morocco, where a record number of forty-two features were produced, just eleven out of twenty-four active directors were newcomers, though four of these were able to complete more than one film. In terms of date of birth, there was the characteristic wide Moroccan spread (from 1936 to 1969). In the early part of the decade the CCM seemed to favor age over youth, allowing the directing debut of producer Mohamed Lotfi at 58 and funding the return, for a second feature, of Benani at 55, Zerouali at 56, Abbazi at 59, and Bennani at 65—even giving completion money to the 87-year-old French director Jean Delannoy, shooting his last film, *Marie de Nazareth,* in Morocco in 1995. But later in the decade the CCM switched its focus to younger filmmakers. From the start its funding schemes had covered short films as well as features, and it became accepted that the successful completion of, say, three short films qualified a young director for feature funding. This new approach helped the emergence of Ayouch and Aoulad Syad in the late 1990s.

In Tunisia seven of the nine newcomers of the 1990s were born in the 1950s. The only completely new representatives from the 1940s generation are, significantly, the two new women directors, Tlatli and Bornaz, both IDHEC graduates, whose male contemporaries had been given their first directing opportunities up to twenty years earlier.

As far as the backgrounds of the new Maghreb filmmakers are concerned, we find the familiar spread and a more or less equal divide between those with formal training and those without. On the one hand, the usual film schools were involved: Debboub had studied at Algeria's short-lived film school INC in 1967; Hadjadj at INSAS; Bakhti, Benallal, Tlatli, Bornaz, Lotfi, Gounajjar at IDHEC; Aoulad Syad at Fondation Européenne des Métiers de l'Image et du Son (FEMIS); and Benjelloun, Ben Mokhtar, and Zran at other Paris courses. Lagtaâ studied at Lodz, Bouberras and Meddour at the VGIK in Moscow, and Abidi in Rumania; Ktiri Idrissa studied in the United States. On the other hand, Dhouib came from the Tunisian amateur film movement (FTCA) and Chouika and Saâd Chraïbi from its Moroccan equivalent (the FNCCM), Fazaï Mellitti and Hilmi were actors, and Ben Smaïl and Ayouch studied drama in Paris and Malik

Lakhdar Hamina did the same in the United States. Others came from television (Hellal, Rahim, Ismaîl) and a few from quite different professions: Belhiba was a teacher, Chrigui a painter, Ould Khelifa a journalist, and Zinaï-Koudil a novelist.

The 1990s began with a comparatively high output in all three countries of the Maghreb, with no hint of the catastrophic reorganization which would bring Algerian cinema to its knees. And, with certain very clear exceptions, a sense of continuity with the 1980s is the most striking feature of the new decade. There is still very little attempt to look outside the Maghreb—Laskri's Algerian-Vietnamese co-production *Lotus Flower,* Behi's *Swallows Don't Die in Jerusalem,* and Benbarka's international co-productions are this decade's sole films with a wider perspective. Even in Algeria in the early 1990s we have a sense of this continuity: another study of children from Tsaki, another satire from Zemmouri, a further idiosyncratic feature from Lledo, another study of mixed, cross-racial loyalties from Touita. In Morocco, the increased levels of production allowed leading directors like Derkaoui, Noury, and Ferhati to expand their output, pursuing the same themes that had concerned them in the previous decade, but without making a significant breakthrough to international audiences. Gounajjar and Chrigui tried to revive Morocco's experimental film strand, but their 16mm black-and-white features provoked little response. In Tunisia too we find the same phenomenon: Bouzid completes his loose trilogy of films on male identity, Babaï completes a new realist adaptation, and Khemir offers a further look at the Andalusian heritage. Those filmmakers who had previously sought a more international audience by using foreign players and languages (Egyptian for Smihi, French for Behi and Ferchiou) continue to do so, but with the same lack of real commercial success. In several cases, the 1990s films are superior to work produced earlier, but the shock of the new, the unexpected, is absent in the work of most established directors.

The exceptions, of course, are among the key works of the decade. Tazi's *Looking For My Wife's Husband* was one of the first Moroccan films to compete successfully with imported US blockbusters at home, in addition to achieving (comparatively) wide foreign distribution. It is this new popularity of Moroccan-made films which leads Pierre Vermeren, in his study of *Le Maroc en Transition,* to argue that, of all art forms, it is Moroccan cinema which "shows itself to be most in touch with the social reality of modern Morocco," so that "the seventh art has certainly played an important role in the evolution and maturing of society."[8] In Algeria established filmmakers and experienced directors from television (Chouikh, Allouache, Hadjadj, Bouguermouh, and Meddour) made great efforts to overcome both declining production support and very real physical threats of fundamentalist violence. Together they made a series of masterly films about the current situation, both probing studies of the present and the sources of current misery (*Youssef* and *Bab el-Oued City*) and eloquent fables and allegories about honor, violence, and identity, questioning those traditions which seem to have offered little defense against chaos (*Machaho, The Forgotten Hillside, Baya's Mountain,* and *The Desert Ark*).

Some thirty-four filmmakers, more than half of them born in the 1950s or 1960s, made their feature debuts in the Maghreb in the 1990s and early 2000s. In terms of personnel, therefore, there is a real renewal of what was becoming an aging trio of national cinemas. But remarkably few of these newcomers brought a fresh, authentic voice to the film making of the period. In Algeria, Malik Lakhdar Hamina (with *Autumn—October in Algiers*) and the sole Algerian woman to complete a fictional feature, Zinaï-Koudil (with *The Female Demon*), produced distinctive first features which, unfortunately, have not been followed up. In Morocco, Lagtaâ achieved a great commercial success with his exposure of youthful sexuality (in *A Love Affair in Casablanca*) and Ayouch's second feature, *Ali Zaoua*, looked unsparingly at the lives of children living on the streets of Casablanca. The Moroccan government's funding policies mean that both can be expected to build up a real creative output in the coming years. In Tunisia, Ferid Boughedir (who really counts as a newcomer, though he did co-direct a French-language feature as early as 1970) achieved Tunisia's greatest national box office success, and an international critical success, with *Halfaouine*, and Tlatli directed the finest of all Maghreb fictional films by a woman director (and a film of truly world class), *Silences of the Palace*. It is with filmmakers such as these that the future of North African film making rests.

In Europe, where thirteen filmmakers of Maghrebian descent were responsible for twenty-one features in the 1990s, a much higher proportion were newcomers (ten out of thirteen) and all but one of these were born in the 1950s and 1960s. Given that these new directors almost all come from work within the French film and television industries and no longer feel the need to treat exclusively Maghrebian subjects, it is no longer possible to see the two strands of filmmaking—in the Maghreb and in Europe—as being closely related parallel streams. Paradoxically, this separation in terms of backgrounds, subjects, and styles comes at a time when an increasing number of Algerian filmmakers have been active in exile in Europe (Allouache, Benhadj, and Zemmouri among them), blurring national boundaries. It seems too that the very detachment from the Maghreb and its particular production structures and censorship (even self-censorship) codes has given the filmmakers born or brought up in Europe a new lucidity about North African issues, and the result is such insightful, prize-winning works as Guerdjou's *Living in Paradise* and the documentary *In My Father's House* (Jebli Ouazzani).

5   Into the Present

The beginning of the new century saw very different prospects for filmmakers from the various countries of the Maghreb. In the period up to the end of 2002, only five features were completed in Algeria, of which two were made by filmmakers from the immigrant community abroad and one by an Algerian filmmaker in exile in Europe. By contrast, sixteen features were made by directors with links to the Maghreb but working and living in Europe. Thanks to more generous government funding some twenty-two new features from Morocco were shown and many further projects given government funding. Even Tunisia saw its output rise, with a dozen features (and six new directors) in just three years. Remarkably, in 2000–2002, seven of the overall total of fifty features were directed by women, while an eighth woman co-wrote and co-directed a film with her husband.

Algeria

Algerian cinema continues to be virtually non-existent, with no sign of production and distribution structures being restored. But at least Ghaouti Bendeddouche's *La voisine* (*The Neighbor*, 2002), one of the films left incomplete when the production organizations were shut down in 1998, did finally get shown at the JCC in Tunis. The film, which shows the dramatic impact of the arrival of a beautiful newcomer on the cloistered, regulated life of a group of women in the Casbah, is described by its director as a human comedy and a voyage into the emotional and social malaise of Algeria. The best-known feature made in Algeria since the late 1990s is Merzak Allouache's *L'autre monde* (*The Other World*, 2001) and this is the story of a painful return. A young woman, Yasmine, born in France and speaking no Arabic, goes to Algeria to hunt for her Algerian lover, Rachid, who was reported lost in an ambush but who may, it is thought, have escaped. The plot, meandering and seemingly improvised, ends somewhat inevitably in a mindless slaying. The shooting of *The Other World* is an important event, but the film itself generates little emotion or suspense. More impressive was the first feature of the editor Yamina Bachir-Chouikh (b. 1954), *Rachida* (2002), the story of a young female teacher whose attempts to create a positive life for herself are constantly thwarted by the threat and reality of violence. In Europe, Mohamed Rachid Benhadj made *Mirka* (2000), an international co-production with French-Italian-Spanish backing, international stars (Vanessa Redgrave and Gérard Depardieu), and a world-renowned cinematographer (Vittorio Storaro). All this diverse talent is somewhat incongruously

Fig. 12. *Rachida* (2002), Yamina Bachir-Chouikh, Algeria

brought to bear on what is essentially a simple peasant drama about a boy who is persecuted because he is the product of a Balkan ethnic rape.

Morocco

The Moroccan government continued its ambitious program of funding film making from the late 1990s into the early 2000s, backing on average seven features a year (and a similar number of shorts). In 2002 funding reached the record level of eleven features and six shorts. This is a level of production almost three times that achieved in the 1970s and 1980s. Fifteen of these new films were shown at the National Film Festival in Marrakesh in 2001. More importantly, all but one of them had received a commercial distribution in Morocco by 2002. Moreover, Moroccan films are beginning to find consistently large audiences and in each year from 1998 to 2001 at least one achieved audiences of over two hundred thousand. This is in addition to Nabil Ayouch's *Ali Zaoua*—easily the best of recent Moroccan features—which was seen by over three hundred fifty thousand spectators.

The weakness of the Moroccan system is that the state funding continues to be the only way of setting up a feature or short fiction film, while films funded in Europe, like Fatima Jebli Ouazzani's *In My Father's House*, which won the top prize at the 1998 National Film Festival, simply do not get commercial distri-

bution in Morocco. The system's strength is its nicely eclectic selection proce-
dure. Obviously those filmmakers who came up with the biggest box office
hits of the past four years—Ayouch, Derkaoui, Noury, and Saâd Chraïbi—have
received further funding. But money has also been made available to well-
respected directors, whose work is better received at foreign festivals than at the
Moroccan box office. Thus the modest results obtained by Jillali Ferhati (a past
winner of the grand prix at the Paris Biennale of Arab Cinemas) with *Braids*
and the young Daoud Aoulad Syad with *Bye-Bye Souirty* have not prevented
them from receiving fresh funding in the 2000s. Even more promising for the
future is the fact that in each year from 1998 funding has been given to at least
one newcomer born in the 1960s: Omar Chraïbi (brother of Saâd) in 1998,
Myriam Bakir in 1999, Ismaïl Ferroukhi and the actor Faouzi Bensaïdi in 2000,
Mohamed Uland Mohand in 2001, and Yasmine Kassari and Hassan Legzouli in
2002. All these seven have followed the favored path of making (usually state-
funded) fictional shorts before getting feature film backing, and their work is
much anticipated.

This burst of state-funded production meant that by 2002, for the first time,
both the number of Moroccan directors and the number of feature films they
have produced exceeded figures for Algeria. Among the long-established directors, Souheil Benbarka, head of the CCM, showed his new feature, *Les amants
de Mogador* (*The Lovers of Mogador,* 2002). Jillali Ferhati directed a new realist
study of Moroccan society, *Tresses* (*Braids,* 2000), which once more depicts a
modest family—in Tangier this time—disrupted when a woman is raped by
a young man whose family is too powerful to be directly challenged. Hakim
Noury produced a highly successful new satirical comedy, *Elle est diabétique et
hypertendue et elle refuse de crever* (*She Is Diabetic and Hypertensive and She
Refuses to Die,* 2000), which depicts a man torn between wife and mistress,
but whose real problem is his dominating mother-in-law. Noury, one of the
most prolific of Maghrebian filmmakers, quickly followed this with *Une histoire
d'amour* (*A Love Story,* 2001). The appropriately titled *Les années de l'exil* (*The
Years of Exile,* 2002) marked the return of Nabyl Lahlou after ten years of silence. The film chronicles the misadventures of two policemen sent to a mountain village to arrest a so-called subversive.

Alongside these veterans, the martial arts specialist Saïd Souda (who trained
in the Far East) made his second action feature, *Du paradis à l'enfer* (*From
Heaven to Hell,* 2000), in which he again played the lead, this time as a hit man
on the run from a vengeful widow. Some of the key 1990s filmmakers also made
new features. Saâd Chraïbi's *Soif* (*Thirst,* 2000) was set in South Morocco and
brought together a number of stories of need and desire. Hassan Benjelloun, the
only man to have two features in the 2001 National Film Festival, offered three
films in quick succession: *Jugement d'une femme* (*A Woman's Judgment,* 2000),
about a female civil rights activist's search for justice; *Les lèvres du silence* (*The
Lips of Silence,* 2001), which looks at the issues faced by a couple confronted by
the problem of sterility; and *Le pote* (*The Pal,* 2002). Also shown for the first
time in 2001 were *Amour sans visa* (*Love without a Visa,* 2001), a drama about

AIDS by Najib Sefrioui, and *Les amours de Hadj Mokhtar Soldi* (*The Loves of Hadj Mokhtar Soldi*, 2001), a comedy starring the highly popular Bachir Skiredj and directed by Mostafa Derkaoui, which received top box office ranking in 2001.

Three of the younger filmmakers who had achieved their first breakthroughs in the late 1990s also continued their careers. Mohamed Ismaîl followed *Aouchtam* with a new feature, *Et après...* (*And Afterward...*, 2002), yet another study of the lure of Europe for Moroccans living in the north of the country. For his second feature, *Le cheval de vent* (*The Wind Horse*, 2001), Aoulad Syad again worked with Ahmed Bouanani as scriptwriter. The story tells of two ill-assorted men who meet by chance, one going to visit his wife's grave and the other going to the deathbed of his mother, who he had been told had died long ago. They set off on their journey on an old motorbike and sidecar (the "wind horse" of the title). Nabil Ayouch chose as the subject for his third—after the acclaimed *Ali Zaoua*—a mixture of thriller and love story, *Une minute de soleil en moins* (*A Minute of Sunshine Less*, 2002).

Seven newcomers made their debuts in 2000–2001, among them Ahmed Boulane (b. 1956) with *Ali, Rabia et les autres* (*Ali, Rabia and the Others*, 2000), about the difficulties of a man who is released from prison but finds that his world has changed totally. Jamal Belmejdoub (b. 1956) made *Yacout* (2000), a retelling of the classic tale of an ugly but eloquent man who misunderstands the feelings of the beautiful young woman he hopelessly loves. Omar Chraïbi (b. 1961 and the younger brother of Saâd) offered a story about the attempted rehabilitation of a poet, *L'homme qui brodait des secrets* (*The Man Who Embroidered Secrets*, 2000). Abdelhaï Laraki (b. 1949) made *Mona Saber* (2001), in which Mona, a young French woman, learns that her real father was a Moroccan. Armed with just a name, a black-and-white photo and a love letter to her mother, she sets out for Morocco to track him down and discovers some of the new political realities of the country. The oldest member of this group of newcomers, the veteran documentary filmmaker Abdelmajid Rchich (b. 1942), whose first short was made back in 1968, presented a feature about marital problems, co-scripted with fellow directors Farida Benlyazid and Omar Chraïbi, *L'histoire d'une rose* (*The Story of a Rose*, 2000). In 2002 Kamal Kamal (b. 1961) showed his first feature, *Taif Nizar*, and Imane Mesbahi (b. 1964 and daughter of the pioneer director Abdellah Mesbahi) finally completed *Paradis des pauvres* (*The Paradise of the Poor*), which she had begun in 1994.

Tunisia

Despite some truly striking films in the 1990s, Tunisia remains the "poor relation" among Maghrebian cinemas with fewer films and fewer directors in every decade since the 1960s. Now, in 2002, the problem is the lack of cinemas. *SeptièmArt*, Tunisia's uniquely long-lived bilingual film magazine (it was founded in 1964) notes in its ninety-eighth issue that a crisis has arrived, in that the number of film theatres has declined from 156 at the time of independence to just 36 at the beginning of the new millennium.[1] Clearly this is not a basis on which any independent national cinema can be built and inevitably filmmakers have to look abroad for both financial support and box office receipts. Ironically, thanks partly to renewed and more generous state production support, more features have been completed in 2000–2002 than at any time in Tunisian film history.

In 2000 Moufida Tlatli followed her highly successful debut feature, *Silences of the Palace,* with *La saison des hommes* (*The Men's Season,* 2000). This has the same basic subject matter—the sufferings of women over two generations—but is markedly more uneven, perhaps because of its sheer scope. It is set largely on the island of Djerba, where men traditionally left home to find work in Tunis, returning only once a year to their wives (hence the title). There are beautifully realized scenes of women's unity in adversity and striking juxtapositions in the editing, but the overall tone is unremittingly bleak. Also making a second film, but this time after a twenty-five-year gap, was Naceur Ktari, who returned with *Sois mon amie* (*Be My Friend,* 2000). Despite a clearly articulated plot line and moments of real drama, this did not quite match up to the power of his earlier work, *The Ambassadors.* The hero's trajectory toward death (backstage on the opening night of his new production) may be melodramatic, but there is a nice ambiguity in the relationship between his wife and girlfriend. In 2001 another established director, Mahmoud Ben Mahmoud, who had made a number of video documentaries from the 1980s onward, directed a feature-length "musical voyage through the lands and music of Islam," *Les mille et une voix* (*A Thousand and One Voices*). The same year Fadhel Jaziri made his feature-length documentary video study of a Sufi festival, *Hadhra,* also co-produced by Canal Horizons.

2002 saw the release of several new films by established Tunisian directors. Abdellatif Ben Ammar's first feature in twenty-two years, *Le chant de la noria* (*The Noria's Song*), lacks the stylistic originality of Ben Ammar's early work, being yet another tale of self-discovery by middle-aged urban dwellers, thanks to an exemplary trip to the underdeveloped South (the noria of the title is the traditional Arab water pump). Ridha Behi's latest film, *La boîte magique* (*The Magic Box*), is in a more personal vein than his recent work and tells of a disillusioned filmmaker, now in his forties. As he fulfills a commission from a European television channel, Raouf looks back at his own relationship with the cinema as a child. For his fifth feature, *Poupées d'argile* (*Clay Dolls*), Nouri Bouzid chose a subject familiar from the work of his Moroccan contemporaries, Hakim Noury (*Enfance volée*) and Jillali Ferhati (*Poupées de roseau*): the exploitation of young village children who are hired as maids by middle-class families living in the capital. The plotline traces the attempts by the middleman Omrane, accompanied by a new 9-year-old recruit, Fedhah (who makes the clay dolls of the title), to fulfill his obligations to the parents when one of his young charges absconds.

Six debuts by young Tunisian filmmakers also occurred in 2000–2002. Nidhal Chatta (b. 1959) made *No Man's Love* (2000). Very much a young man's film (though the director had just turned 40), this offers the distinctly strange combination of deep-sea diving and road movie (the customary therapeutic journey to the South). Khaled Ghorbal (b. 1950) made *Fatma* (2001), which premiered at Cannes and dealt with the problems faced by women in Muslim society. It is the story (from childhood, through study in Tunis, to marriage) of Fatma, whose life is blighted by the rape she suffered at the age of 17. *Khorma, la bêtise* (*Khorma: Stupidity,* 2002), directed by Jilani Saadi (b. 1962), tells the story of a young man, nicknamed Khorma (which means stupidity), who takes over from his aged benefactor the role of dealing with the dead in their little town, with unexpected results. Nawfel Saheb-Ettaba (b. 1959), who had studied in Canada, made *El-Kotbia* (*The Bookstore,* 2002), another study of a return from abroad, this time by a young man who finds little comfort there. Two women also offered first features. Nadia El Fani (b. 1960), who had worked extensively in production activities, made *Bedwin Hacker* (2002), the somewhat confused tale of a young Tunisian woman who, from a base in the South Tunisian desert, begins to hack into European satellite broadcasts with Arab slogans. Also in 2002, Raja Amari, who had studied at FEMIS in Paris, made her debut with *Satin Rouge* (*Red Satin*). Born in 1971, Amari is the youngest Maghrebian filmmaker. Her film deals with a concerned mother who visits a cabaret—the Satin Rouge of the title—because she is worried about her daughter's relationship with a musician, and discovers there a world which challenges her life's assumptions. Though generally well received abroad, the film's portrayal of a sexually active widow outraged many Tunisian critics.

Immigrant Cinema

The number of films made by directors of Maghrebian descent has increased strongly in the early 2000s. Eight features released in 2000–2002 deal directly with immigrant problems. Karim Traïdia's second feature, *Les diseurs de vérité* (*The Truth Tellers,* 2000), is a wordy, claustrophobic tale that moves between Europe and Algeria, though the contrast is muted since the Algerian scenes were shot in Portugal. The truth tellers of the title are the independent journalists so hated by the fundamentalists, and the focus is on an editor who rejects exile and returns to meet his death. Nadir Moknèche (b. 1965), born in Algiers but resident in France since the age of 18, made his debut with *Le harem de Mme Osmane* (*Madam Osmane's Harem,* 2000), a tragicomic farce in the manner of Pedro Almodóvar, set in 1993 Algiers but shot in Tangier. In this story of an apartment block of women dominated by the tyrannical Mme Osmane, Moknèche sets out to upturn all the clichéd images of the submissive Arab woman. Mostéfa Djadjam (b. 1952), who played the lead in Allouache's *The Adventures of a Hero,* directed *Frontières* (*Frontiers,* 2000), a powerful study of a group of six would-be emigrants from various parts of Africa and the difficulties they experience even before reaching the borders of Europe. Another filmmaker making his debut is the actor Abdellatif Kechiche with *La faute à Voltaire* (*Voltaire's Fault,* 2000), a rambling two-hour story chronicling the adventures and relationships of Jallel from his arrival as an illegal immigrant to his abrupt

Fig. 13. *The Truth Tellers* (2000), Karim Traïda, resident in the Netherlands

capture and repatriation by the French police. *Lettres d'Algérie* (*Letters from Algeria*, 2002), directed by Azize Kabouche (b. 1960), deals with a theatre group which bases a play on the "Letters from Algeria" column in the newspaper *Le Monde*. Two self-taught young filmmakers also offered their views on immigrant life in the communities within which they grew up. Mourad Boucif (b. 1967), working with a childhood friend, the Turkish immigrant Taylan Barman, offered a look at young love in the immigrant community in Belgium, *Au delà de Gibraltar* (*Beyond Gibraltar*, 2001), while Rabah Ameur-Zaïmèche (b. 1968) took as his chosen subject his own family's life in poor suburbs of Paris, *Wesh Wesh, qu'est-ce qui se passe?* (*Wesh Wesh—What's Happening?*, 2002). Another feature by a new director, also set among the immigrant community, is *17 rue Bleue* (2001), directed by Chad Chenouga (b. 1962). This is the (apparently autobiographical) study of a close mother-and-son relationship which culminates in the mother's slow and painful death. Like the works of Rachida Krim and Bourlem Guerdjou in the late 1990s and Yamina Benguigui in 2001, this is a look back by a filmmaker at the issues relating to his or her parents' generation.

Of the eight other 2000–2002 features, three involved women filmmakers. Yamina Benguigui followed her two three-part video documentary series, *Femmes d'Islam* (*Women of Islam*, 1994) and *Mémoires d'immigrés* (*Immigrants' Memories*, 1997), with her first fictional feature, *Inch'Allah dimanche* (*Inch'Allah Sunday*, 2001), the story of an Algerian woman, Zouina, who has to overcome enormous problems of adjustment when, with her children, she joins her husband in 1970s France. Zaîda Ghorab-Volta again looked outside the immigrant community in her tale of two young adolescent girls' exploratory journey across France, *Jeunesse dorée* (*Gilded Youth*, 2001). Zakia Bouchaâla (b. 1963), who had worked as actress and co-writer on her husband Ahmed's first feature, *Krim*, co-directed his second, *Origine contrôlée* (*Control of Origin*, 2001), an exuberant comedy which has a French character in the leading role. It is, however, typical of *beur* cinema in depicting a group of marginalized characters (one a transvestite) who are mostly of Maghrebian origin and who come together and achieve real friendship and mutual help.

Another newcomer, Naguel Belouad, shot for eight weeks in Algeria, but curiously the outcome was a study of the sufferings of women within polygamy in 1920s Algeria, *L'attente des femmes* (*Women's Expectations*, 2000). *La maîtresse en maillot de bain* (*The Mistress in a Swimming Costume*, 2001), written and directed by actor Lyèce Boukhitine (b. 1965), looks at the life in a small French town of three friends who have known each other since childhood. The two veteran directors of the 1980s, Mehdi Charef and Rachid Bouchareb, chose non-immigrant protagonists for their first films of the new millennium. Bouchareb, in *Little Sénégal* (*Little Senegal*, 2001), begins with the study of a Senegalese (played in masterly fashion by Sotigui Kouyate), who goes to the United States in search of what happened to his ancestors who were taken away as slaves, and ends with a dispassionate picture of the rivalries between Africans and Afro-Americans in the poorer quarters of New York. Charef's *Marie-Line* (2001) is the sensitive portrait of a French woman, Marie-Line, who is the wife of a National Front member but who gradually achieves solidarity with the illegal immigrant members of the all-night department store cleaning team of which she is the leader. This is a carefully constructed piece, full of precise observation. Charef followed it with a much more uneven work, *La fille de Keltoum* (*Keltoum's Daughter*, 2002), which, like Allouache's *The Other World*, is the tale of a young woman who quits the security of Europe, in this case to seek out the mother in Algeria who she thinks selfishly abandoned her.

Except in Algeria, the new millennium has seen a real upsurge of production, but as yet it is impossible to discern any new trends. Familiar themes recur: the purging, life-enhancing trip to the South (*The Noria's Song, No Man's Love, Thirst*), the so-called "return" to an unknown Maghreb (*The Other World, Mona Saber, Keltoum's Daughter, El-Kotbia*), the problems—past and present—of immigrant life in France or Belgium (*Inch'Allah Sunday, 17 rue Bleue, Control of Origin, Marie-Line, Voltaire's Fault, Beyond Gibraltar, Wesh Wesh, Letters from Algeria*), or the lure of life there (*Frontiers, And Afterward . . .*). Marginalized characters and/or victims, mostly women, provide the customary protagonists (as in *Rachida, Fatma, Women's Expectations, Braids, Bedwin Hacker*). Women directors have made an increasingly strong impact, and the work of young Maghrebian women in Europe making short documentaries and fictions promises further developments in the near future. The backgrounds of the twenty-five new directors of 2000–2002 (out of a total of fifty active filmmakers) have a similar mix to those in the 1990s. Ten have studied film making (though Rchich was at IDHEC back in 1963) and ten come from drama studies or acting. Of the rest, one was a film editor, two had worked within the film industry and just two (Boucif and Ameur-Zaïmèche) are self-taught. Eighteen of the twenty-five had previously made at least one short film. The age profile continues slowly to decline: of the twenty newcomers whose dates of birth are known, two were born in the 1940s, seven in the 1950s, ten in the 1960s, and one in the 1970s.

A number of critics have used the beginning of the new millennium as an opportunity to sum up thirty-five years of North African film making, and all emphasize that continuity, rather than radical change, has been characteristic of the overall development. Tahar Chikhaoui is happy to attribute to each cinematography a thirty-five-year focus: "If Algerian cinema has been above all a political cinema, and if Moroccan cinema in turn has been a cultural cinema, Tunisian cinema is for the most part a social cinema."[2] For Chikhaoui, all three cinematographies are characterized by "a will to move consciences and to play a role in the development of mentalities."[3] Michel Serceau agrees that Maghrebian filmmakers have, as a whole, been concerned less with entertainment than with personal expression and engagement, but argues that, faced with the need "to confront social, political and economic problems and the tensions and contradictions that afflict their societies,"[4] they have generally chosen an approach in which realism predominates. Their weakness—exemplified by their failure to relate to wider cultural developments (such as those in literature)—stems from the fact that that they belong "to a socio-cultural category which has hardly come more to grips with the (Arab-Berber) popular culture of their countries than with classical Arab-Muslim culture."[5]

The diversity of stance within the broad overall approach—whereby "it would not be exaggerated to discern as many currents as there are filmmakers"[6] and where individual filmmakers often change their individual style totally from one film to another—is, for Chikhaoui, "the expression of a need for research, a manifestation of a cinematography in search of its identity.'"[7] Raphaël Millet too sees Maghrebian cinemas as marked by striving: "Characters in search of authors. And authors in search of meaning."[8] In cinematographies shaped by low levels of production and marked by the constant lure of international (particularly Parisian) success, works of outstanding quality have been rare in the 1990s and early 2000s. Indeed for Millet—looking at Maghrebian cinemas within a Mediterranean context—the image which constantly recurs is that of the void. In Algerian cinema (Mohamed Chouikh or Benhadj) there is the desert, "the place of paradox" where "the experience of the void clogs that of life itself."[9] Moroccan filmmakers continue shooting, "even if at times they are shooting in a void,"[10] and if Tunisian cinema is melancholy, "it is simply that it is secretly in mourning for itself. As if it no longer believed totally in what it does, what it lives, what it sees."[11] More positively, Michel Amarger sees a new narrative focus: "The new fictions directly address the to-and-fro across national boundaries, the desire for exile and the emotions of return through the gaze of creators attentive to the evolutions of the Arab soul."[12]

Three of these critics see the new importance of women directors in Maghrebian cinema as crucial. Looking at Arab cinema as a whole, Millet notes that women behind the camera were rare: "They still are. And yet the movement has been under way for a dozen years or so and especially during the last three or four."[13] Behind those who have already completed a feature, he sees "'a crowd of new talents, showing that this 'New Wave' has depth and is almost a ground swell."[14] Chikhaoui, for whom the presence of women is one of the most important characteristics of Tunisian cinema in the past decade, points out that the proportion of women directors in Tunisia in the 1990s is relatively high in an Arab context and that their films "are far from being the worst of the decade."[15] Serceau—looking at the work of male directors as well as women—even goes so far as to claim that Maghrebian cinema "has effectively become in certain respects a feminist cinema."[16] Whatever the difficulties Maghrebian cinemas will have to face in the coming years, they will be able to draw strength from this growing importance of women as well as the increasing number of younger people among the ranks of their filmmakers.

Part Two   *Themes and Styles*

Authorial or expressive cinema is in a majority in the Maghreb, because the state prefers to subsidize an expressive cinema which can represent the country worthily abroad. Within this subsidized cinema there is space for works of high artistic quality as well as for propaganda films.

Linked to the state, the films of the Maghreb countries therefore often see their themes, their style and their degree of freedom linked to the political past or the film economy relevant to each country.

—Ferid Boughedir[1]

6 An Indigenous Film Culture: *El Chergui* (1975)

Though the issue of the impact of colonialism on North African societies is a highly complex one, we can agree with Albert Memmi when he asserts, in *The Colonizer and the Colonized,* that

> We have no idea what the colonized world would have been without colonization, but we certainly see what has happened as a result of it. To subdue and exploit, the colonizer pushed the colonized out of the historical and social, cultural and technical current. What is real and verifiable is that the colonized's culture, society and technology are seriously damaged.[2]

Post-independence film making forms part of the attempt to re-establish a valid cultural identity in many parts of the formerly colonized world. As Nouri Bouzid put it, expressing his discontent with the structures of traditional Arab (that is to say, Egyptian) melodrama: "We must show that the cinema is capable of saying everything and must break down the old forms to invent the new Arab cinema."[3] In an interview with Guy Hennebelle recorded after the completion of his first feature, the Moroccan filmmaker Moumen Smihi set out the possible outlines of a new program for North African filmmakers:

> There's a general problem here. Cinema is the product of western bourgeois society. It is therefore the production of this society's imagery of that society, that is to say, it is integrated into a novelistic, theatrical, dramatic tradition. From the moment when the same means of expression, the cinema, is manipulated in another cultural atmosphere, it is necessary, even if only to escape servile imitation, to interrogate the forms and cultural traditions of this different atmosphere.[4]

This interrogation, aimed at establishing a new form of cinema, has a number of implications. First of all, the role of the protagonist had to be re-examined. The result, for most North African filmmakers, is the emergence of a new protagonist who is unable to change the world by an imposition of will or even to develop his or her own individual potentialities to the full as the Western hero does. Instead, the new protagonist is essentially a character who submits. In Moumen Smihi's case, both his short film, *If Moh, No Hope/Si Moh pas de chance* (1971) and his first feature, *El Chergui* (1975), represent what he describes as a "Descent into Hell."[5]

This new protagonist is linked to a different notion of film structure: "It is true that it is hard to destroy narrative in cinema. . . . However, you can think of forms which would function precisely to translate another way of living and thinking, another culture, other social options than those put forward up to now by the West."[6] This new plot structure, in turn, will have roots in the national culture, insofar as this can be recovered. In the case of Morocco, in Smihi's view, "the particular character of Moroccan colonization, under the Protectorate structure, allowed the country to preserve its social core in a deeply authentic form, despite the viciousness of the aggression from outside."[7] The filmmaker's own approach

> consisted of proceeding by successive departures or entries derived from the film's main theme (the story of a Moroccan woman) but also in opposition to a linear narrative, which by this fact became disarticulated, or articulated in other ways.[8]

The purpose was to find an answer to those exclusions to which Edward Said has drawn attention: "After the colonial parenthesis, it is our task now to research what might constitute the African being, the Arab being, their imaginary, their culture."[9]

Experiments in Narrative

Moroccan cinema first established its international reputation in the 1970s with Souheil Benbarka's early political films and with a number of highly original experiments in film narrative made by filmmakers trained during the 1960s in European film schools, among which Moumen Smihi's El Chergui finds its place. The first of these experimental films was Wechma (1970), directed by Hamid Benani, who had studied at the IDHEC in Paris. The film is in two parts, the first dealing in masterful fashion with the protagonist's neglected, alienated childhood after he has been adopted from an orphanage by a harsh, self-torturing man who cannot give him the love he needs. The second part shows his subsequent disjointed, drifting progress through a series of petty crimes and meaningless encounters, until he is killed in a motorcycle accident. The film, which is shot through with symbolic imagery and enigmatic events, brought together some of the major future directing talents of Moroccan cinema (the cinematography is by Mohamed Abderrahman Tazi and the editing by Ahmed Bouanani). Benani, in turn, was involved in the production of El Chergui. As Fouad Souiba and Fatima Zahra el Alaoui write,

> Wechma was a true revolution in Maghrebian cinema. For the first time, a film maker had thought deeply about the filmic language which he was going to use, shot by shot, had sought and found an original form of expression which distinguished itself totally from the clichés of Western art or commercial cinema and went directly back to the sources of the Moroccan collective imaginary.[10]

Traces was followed four years later by another independent film, About Some Meaningless Events (1974), the debut feature of Mostapha Derkaoui, who had studied at the Polish film school in Lodz. This tale of a filmmaker who is drawn into a crime which he witnesses by chance was apparently never shown, but it began a series of films in which, over the next ten years, the director would explore the nature of film making and the role of the director. The best known of these is *The Beautiful Days of Sheherazade* (1982). As Ahmed Araib notes, "An elite cinema par excellence, Derkaoui's work constitutes a genre which has not received much support from the public but which always provokes reflection."[11] These early 1970s films, like *El Chergui* which followed them, were low-budget independently financed works. When the state resumed its interest in film production, one film which received full backing was *Mirage* (1979), made by another IDHEC graduate, Ahmed Bouanani. This uses the basic motif of a simple peasant who finds a bag of money and sets off for the city to create a mythical, labyrinthine world of stories and performers, of caricatures and filmic allusions (to Chaplin, Fellini, and others), shot through with hints of off-screen violence (shots and sirens). *Mirage* is, to quote Souiba and el Alaoui once more, "a great moment in the evolution of the national film language."[12]

There have been other examples of ambitious experimental approaches elsewhere in the Maghreb. Though the structure of the Algerian film industry did nothing to encourage an experimental approach, a number of isolated works do display truly distinctive Algerian approaches to film narrative: Mohamed Zinet's use of his narrator in *Tahia ya Didou* (1971), Merzak Allouache's direct-to-camera style in *Omar Gatlato* (1976), Farouk Beloufa's play with complex narrative in *Nahla* (1979), and Brahim Tsaki's use of space and silence in *Story of a Meeting* (1983). Perhaps the most resolutely consistent use of experiments to break narrative flow and create unexpected formal juxtapositions is to be found in the work of Mohamed Bouamari over the ten years, through four features, from *The Charcoal Burner* (1972) to *The Denial* (1982). Even the first of these, which was seen as a realistic peasant drama when first released in Europe, turns out on re-viewing to be full of play with narrative, beginning with a Charlie Chaplin-style chase, using sound, music, and silence in unexpectedly inventive ways and expressing duration through highly formalized sets of repeated compositions and gestures.

The two poles of the experimental approach to film narrative in Tunisia could hardly be more different. At one extreme are the theatrically trained collaborators from the Théâtre Nouveau de Tunis—Fadhel Jaïbi, Fadhel Jaziri, and their colleagues, Mohamed Driss, Jalili Baccar, and Habib Masrouki—who developed a quite distinctive style, much influenced by twentieth-century European drama, in their two complex theatrical adaptations, *The Wedding* (1978) and *Arab* (1988). By contrast, another Tunisian filmmaker not trained professionally in a European film school, Nacer Khemir, creates in his two features, *The Searchers of the Desert* (1984) and *The Dove's Lost Necklace* (1990), a dream image of Andalusia, using methods and approaches drawn from the Arab oral tradition (Khemir is a performing storyteller and sculptor as well as a filmmaker). In both films, which are shot in carefully framed images and formally enacted scenes, emphasis is placed on signs and objects that can take on a symbolic meaning. Apparently solid worlds are established and initially coherent stories are begun, but they cannot be held in place and exist only to be erased or obliterated, as the action moves on and a new narrative takes shape. Just as the wind can transform a desert landscape and a spoken text can evoke or elide a whole world, so shifts occur from reality to dream (and vice versa) and become the norm in a poetically shaped environment redolent of the Islamic past.

El Chergui

Moumen Smihi's *El Chergui* illustrates the precarious situation of Moroccan cinema in the late 1970s in the absence of any state funding:

> The technicians were badly paid or not paid at all. The camera crew worked on barely half the normal wage. Leïla Shenna (who played Aïcha) was nice enough to accept a ridiculously low fee. I got absolutely nothing at all. Everyone worked on the basis of sharing the eventual receipts.[13]

It was by intention "a Moroccan film, made for Moroccans before anyone else,"[14] but because of the lack of interest in local films shown by Moroccan distributors, it received very little public showing.[15] Smihi, who, alongside his film training at IDHEC, had also followed the seminars of Roland Barthes at the Ecole Pratique des Hautes Etudes, where he wrote a thesis on the sociology of spectacle in Morocco, brings an intellectual approach to his film making. He was able, for example, to draw inspiration from Arab literature:

> The classical Arab authors succeed very well at bringing together in the same text, approaches as different as narration, secondary exegeses, and so on, in fact several "genres" mixed together in a structure that can seem disorganised, but which has its own rationality.[16]

As he said, in *El Chergui* "it's not a question, precisely speaking, of a narrative or a plot, but of a texture in which the discourses overlap."[17] What interested him in the film was "to develop a multiple communication, a discourse which would go a little bit in every direction, perhaps in the likeness of our modern consciousness."[18] This he achieved, but though the film is indeed "based on the tangling together of small narratives,"[19] it does have three clearly identifiable principal narrative concerns. The first is the story of the woman, Aïcha, whose life is turned upside down when her husband decides to take a second wife, a story which, as Smihi observes, "evokes the condition of Arab women in general."[20] But this narrative is precisely located in place and time. The place is the city of Tangier, "whose international reputation is considerable, and exaggerated for the most part. A city whose body is wounded by the foreign presence. At least ten different imperialisms used to fight each other over Tangier."[21] The source of the title, as Moulay Driss Jaïdi explains, lies in the fact that "the Chergui and the Gharbi are the two winds which rule over Tangier, which, in addition, is the meeting place of the Atlantic and the Mediterranean."[22] It is also "a city shattered by injustice, exploitation and oppression."[23] The time is also a very specific period, Morocco on the eve of independence (1952–1954), which for Smihi is a key historical moment: "'Many things were decided then about the official decolonization of the country. Some things came to an end, others began to see the light of day.'"[24]

grand prix du Festival de Toulon 1975
prix international de la critique Toulon 75
prix art & essai Toulon 75

الشِّرْكَي
EL CHERGUI
ou le silence violent
un film de moumen Smihi

Fig. 14. *El Chergui* (1975), Moumen Smihi, Morocco

El Chergui is full of formal patterning. The film's opening credits are interspersed with shots of Tangier streets and buildings, accompanied by a significant sound track. Initially there is a woman's singing, which is answered by a male voice, while at the ending there will be shots of pupils in the French school and voice-over of the words they have been learning: feu, flamme, fou (fire, flame, madman). Throughout the film there is a play with effects in a very carefully constructed sound track which is designed to represent the "mosaic" quality of Moroccan society and the complexity of its linguistic makeup. Smihi explains that "the female voice reproduces the singing of the Rif, in the north, and the male voice the songs of the Atlas mountains,"[25] the slave singing on the beach is "a Gnawan, from the black population of Morocco, with its origins in Guinea,"[26] and in addition there are snatches of French, Spanish, and Egyptian radio (with their conflicting messages) and a brief passage of recitation from the Koran. Sound is often laid forward or allowed to continue after a shift in space (the sound of the Spanish policemen's horses, for example, which are heard in the city street before the young man enters the brothel and before the young woman begins her story about them).

In visual terms, Smihi adopts similar procedures, consistently fragmenting the space. In the credits virtually all the images we see allude to a colonial presence: the profusion of shots of huge white colonial buildings, street names in French as well as Arabic, glimpses of flags from many countries. Later there will be scenes featuring the indigenous population in the markets, the streets, and the docks and on the beach, but nothing coheres to establish the geography of Tangier. The same is true of the film's interiors, where the concentration on precisely framed compositions of individual characters leaves us with little sense of the way the spaces connect and often an uncertainty about whether characters are looking at each other or gazing blankly at a wall. Smihi's interest seems to be more in the transitions between spaces—or the blockages preventing transition—rather than the spaces themselves. At the very beginning, we have doors opening without any human agency to reveal, firstly the world of work (the baker with his loaves and oven) and the boy's dream (when Brahim sees himself running on the very beach along which his mother will pass to her death). At the end of the film the gates outside the lycée close similarly—seemingly of their own accord—to bring the narrative to an end. In an interview, Smihi lists seven such gates—the above three, plus gates representing, for him, concepts of story, power, madness, and hell[27]—but railings and barriers abound and other examples could be quoted (such as the barred windows by which the prison is introduced and the gates to the prison outside which women wait with food for their menfolk).

Aïcha's Story

The central element in the film's narrative is the situation of Aïcha and her story forms the core of the film. But at both the beginning and the end the film features other narratives, those of male work and the life of her son, Brahim. Among the initial work scenes is a shot of the grocer's shop, showing her husband in conversation with the grocer, but we are not aware, at this stage, of his identity or of the significance of the conversation. The scenes of Aïcha's domestic life are preceded and initially punctuated by the sounds and images of goats being driven by in the street outside. At first seen weeping, she is invited into the action by her mother-in-law, "Come and eat, Aïcha, don't cry. God

Fig. 15. *El Chergui* (1975), Moumen Smihi, Morocco

is merciful." But she remains immobile, indifferent to the actions around her (her son getting up, her husband's ablutions and prayers, the meal itself). The mother-in-law's words to her son explain the situation, as she rebukes him for wanting to take another wife, telling him that Aïcha and his son Brahim will both suffer and (in what is presumably the Moroccan equivalent of old dogs not being able to learn new tricks) tells him that "An old cat cannot learn to dance." He pays no attention, and throughout the scene no look or word is exchanged between husband and wife. Aïcha makes no protest; indeed she seems indifferent to family life. She is isolated and without speech ("The Violent Silence" of the full title), but she does have an unexpected ally in her mother-in-law.

While hanging out the washing on the terrace, Aïcha is greeted by her neighbor and their handshake, shown in close-up, is the warmest piece of human contact as yet in the film, just as her words to the neighbor are the only ones she speaks in the film. The neighbor suggests three ritual actions to prevent her husband from taking a new wife: a massage, an offering to the "Men of the Sea," and later a ritual bathe at the festival to celebrate Sidi Kacem. These actions form much of the remainder of Aïcha's story. The neighbor's sister Assia performs the massage while the mother-in-law prays, and Aïcha then sets out to make her offering. Though Brahim is dressed throughout in Western clothes, Aïcha and her husband always wear traditional Moroccan dress, and now she wears a white veil and an all-enveloping black cloak as she goes to perform the ceremony at the edge of the sea. Returning, she pauses once, at the prison. At this point other digressions occur (those involving the young prostitute's story and the boys' games) and when we next see her, Aïcha is savagely beating her son for going to the beach and to the cinema. The ferocity of her assault (which the mother-in-law tries to halt) is enhanced by the fact that Aïcha never gets far enough out of her own concerns to offer love or tenderness toward the boy; this beating is their only physical interaction in the film.

The mother-in-law comes up with another possible solution to Aïcha's problem and together the two women visit a "marabout" or traditional healer. He offers help: a potion which Aïcha drinks, an amulet to put under her husband's pillow, and support for the sacrifice of a black cock and a sevenfold bathe in the grotto at the Sidi Kacem festival. Back home, Aïcha follows his advice about the amulet and prepares to leave for the market. As she does so, she and her husband exchange looks—for the first and only time in the film—but not a single word passes between. It is left for the mother-in-law to wish Aïcha well: "God will be with you." A long sequence at the market, where she buys the cock, is followed by two pauses, when, unveiled, she first watches a laughing madman playing with a little girl swinging on a noisy gate and then observes a party of rich English people. Then she disappears into the background, while the film explores other themes, especially those related to her husband, reappearing at the beginning of the Sidi Kacem celebrations, when she listens to the musicians and the men chanting and sacrifices the cock. Again the film moves away from her story, returning only at the end of the day. While the others sleep, she is alone, weeping inconsolably, as if anticipating her fate. Making their way across the beach next morning, the group of Aïcha, her mother-in-law, the neighbor, and Brahim pass the lonely figure of a Gnawan singing and dancing. Aïcha, her face unveiled, proceeds into the grotto with the other women. While the mother-in-law prays, the neighbor anoints Aïcha with coins and holds on to her hand as she bathes, clad in white now, in the surging waves. But she loses hold and Aïcha drowns, seemingly accepting her fate (she does not struggle). The male voice from the opening credits enters, and Aïcha's story is at an end.

A Tangle of Narratives

In itself Aïcha's story is a simple linear narrative, moving slowly but seemingly inexorably to her death. But just as other themes are introduced before we see her, so too the film does not end with her death but in fact moves on to the male world of work in the harbor, to empty streets and to groups of men walking to work, accompanied by sirens and ships' hooters, and finally to the French school and the children's recitations. The school gate creaks shut, and the final titles unfold in silence. Smihi treats the women's magical rituals and superstitions with a cool detachment and, as the film progresses, greater emphasis is placed on the husband's actions. We see him emerge from the house where the prostitute lives, in discussion with the grocer, collecting his rents, celebrating at a picnic with his friends, and meeting his new bride and her family, and this too is a linear, if disrupted, narrative. But the other stories which make up Smihi's tangle of narratives are far more fragmentary, often incomplete and inconclusive. The sense of a colonial power is there, but only in enigmatic detail: a man arrested in a cafe, a line of shackled prisoners, sounds offscreen of shots and military bands, a group of rich English people partying, the omnipresent towering white buildings and foreign flags. Brahim is the only character whose dreams we see on-screen, but the images of him are without logical progression: How or why does he pass from Koranic school to French lycée? Who is the Gnawan on the beach? Often Aïcha stops in her wanderings to observe a scene (the prisoners, the madman, the English), but she offers no comment, and her expression does not indicate the slightest emotion. Occasionally too the camera seems to want to leave Aïcha and her story, as when it lingers on a group of boys she passes playing in the street or when it concentrates on the workmen at the end of the film.

Even on repeated viewing parts of the film remain quite enigmatic. Why do toads emerge from the couscous at the men's picnic? They are "the materialisation of the magical practices the wife has been engaging in," according to Smihi.[28] Why do we see the image of Mohamed V projected on the moon, followed by newsreel footage of riots calling for his return from exile? An expression of popular belief, according to Smihi: "The nationalist movement, launching mass protests, seems to have been the original force disseminating this strange watchword."[29] But despite, or because of, these enigmas *El Chergui*—like *Wechma* and *Mirage*—continues to be held in high regard as a major innovative force in Moroccan film making. On the eve of the film's release in Paris, Noureddine Ghali wrote that in the context of Moroccan cinema it is "a landmark film": "Its author shows here a stylistic mastery and the temperament of an authentic *cinéaste.*"[30] Its reputation has not diminished in the present era, as three 1990s evaluations show. *El Chergui* is, for Jaïdi, one of the 1970s films which "have as their project the affirmation of that freedom of expression ceaselessly demanded by Moroccan producer-directors."[31] For Souiba and el Alaoui the power of the work's thematic "lies in its constant oscillation between Moroccan reality and mythology."[32] For Araib, "Moumen Smihi ratchets up the level of Moroccan cinema" and his film belongs to "an experimental cinema inseparable from its social and philosophic environment."[33]

7 History as Myth: *Chronicle of the Years of Embers* (1975)

There was every reason for Algerians to celebrate the origins and success of their struggle for liberation in works of fiction, particularly since, as Philip Dine has noted, the colonizers' view of it was "essentially reflexive and ultimately selfish":

> For the French literature and cinema of this final and most bitterly opposed stage of the decolonisation of the Maghreb must, inevitably, be a literature and a cinema of *European* crisis. The relevant narratives are, it must be stressed, exclusively European phenomena, which have virtually nothing worthwhile to tell us about the history, people, and culture of Algeria: they are reflections of the European mind alone.[1]

But if both space and inclination for a depiction of the recent struggle existed for Algerian filmmakers, the immediate context in which they had to work could hardly have been less promising. The immediate censorship context is well known: in Algeria, as Monique Gadant notes, "the FLN did not arrive at independence with a really precise political program":

> This is even more the case where culture was concerned. In this area they stayed at the level of the slogan, thinking that the subordination of culture to politics went without saying.[2]

In terms of film, this meant that "productions are strictly designed for the defense and illustration of the official version of events."[3] It was bad enough that each form of expression had its (FLN-controlled) monopoly: ONCIC for the cinema, Société Nationale d'Edition et de Diffusion (SNED) for writers, and so on. Worse was the fact that the situation among the various forces struggling for power was unstable.[4]

What has been less remarked is that the year 1965, which saw the appearance of the first Algerian feature film, also saw the coup d'état by the military led by Houari Boumediene, who thereby turned against the man he had helped to power, Algeria's first post-independence president, Ahmed Ben Bella. The coincidence is remarkable and, indeed, some passersby who witnessed the tanks stationed at strategic positions during the coup apparently thought they were watching the shooting of Gillo Pontecorvo's *The Battle of Algiers,* which was currently in production.[5] Boumediene, former head of the "frontier army" stationed in Tunisia during the liberation struggle, had every reason to distrust the proclamation of the whole truth about Algeria's struggle, as Benjamin Stora notes:

> For the Algerian military who seize power in 1965, there is a need to rewrite Algerian history, negating the role of the resistance inside the country. There is

also a need to negate, through this fictional history where the military plays the central role, certain moments of the partisan history of Algerian nationalism.[6]

The emphasis was therefore on the encouragement of certain stories from which certain key figures were eliminated and others "projecting the mythical image of a Manichean universe, where roles are clearly defined between the heroes and the traitors, the liberators and the oppressors."[7] As Mouny Berrah has noted, films with an emphasis on the war depict "an ideal nationalism," whereas films about the land were able to "emphasize the contradiction of Algerian society in the same period."[8] Stora sums up the situation: "In the period 1965–1980, paradoxically, the 'Algerian revolution' had never been so celebrated, so commemorated. But what sort of history was it?"[9] The man whose work allows us the answer this question is Mohamed Lakhdar Hamina.

By 1975, Lakhdar Hamina had already established himself as a leading figure in Algerian cinema with three completed features, each of which tackled the liberation struggle from a different angle. *The Wind from the Aurès* (1966) was a powerfully dramatic story, using linear narrative and a basically Western style of dramatic structure. By contrast, *Hassan Terro* (1968) was a comic tale, adapted from one of his own plays by the actor Rouiched, who is a little man, an anti-hero, who gets caught up in events and is hailed as a hero. The third film, *December* (1972), returned to the serious tone of Lakhdar Hamina's first film to offer a study of torture, but seen, remarkably, from the viewpoint of a French officer who is responsible for the violence. Lakhdar Hamina, who had successfully turned the newsreel bureau (OAA) into the production base for his own initial feature film making career, is clearly a man able to operate within the constraints of the Algerian production context (he was to become head of ONCIC in 1981–1985). His films can be seen, as Berrah notes, "as the perfect expression of the code of good conduct governing the subject."[10]

The Film

Chronicle of the Years of Embers was very much an official work, produced by ONCIC to mark the twentieth anniversary of the beginning of the Algerian war on 1 November 1954, and shown to heads of state who visited Algeria for the celebrations. As a result Lakhdar Hamina was able to obtain an unprecedented level of financing for the shooting (in 70mm and Panavision) and the employment of foreign technicians and collaborators (most controversially the French composer Philippe Arthuys, whose lush Western melodies shape the audience response to the images throughout). Sabry Hafez argues that the film "nearly consumed the budget of the entire Algerian cinema (ONCIC and OAA) for three years, drying out its resources and depriving other film makers of the opportunity to produce their projects."[11] Inevitably it provoked hostility from Algerian critics and resentment on the part of Lakhdar Hamina's colleagues. Yet the director claims the film as a purely personal work:

Fig. 16. *Chronicle of the Years of Embers* (1975), Mohamed Lakhdar Hamina, Algeria

I've said and I repeat that I didn't make a historical work. My film gives only a personal vision, even if it is based on precise facts. I never had the pretension of furnishing an overall vision of the whole of Algeria at that historic period, all the more so, since I was brought up in a little village.[12]

And again:

This sort of historico-political film could never be made with all the required rigor and objectivity, since you can only make this sort of film with the greatest passionate subjectivity.[13]

Certainly it is personal in a way more common in art cinema than in epic film making: it is from an idea by Lakhdar Hamina, who co-scripted it (with the novelist Rachid Boudjedra), has the sole credit for production and direction, and appeared in a leading role, together with his three children. Perhaps the contradiction between official film and personal vision is only apparent, since Lakhdar Hamina's stance allows the film's various historical lacunae to be glossed over. Certainly Lakhdar Hamina achieved his own and the state's greatest wish by winning the Palme d'or at the Cannes Film Festival in 1976 (outstripping, in this respect, even the Egyptian film industry).

Chronicle of the Years of Embers has a running time of 177 minutes in the version viewed (other sources cite various lengths, up to three hours 50 minutes in the case of Wassyla Tamzali).[14] It adopts a loosely shaped, unevenly balanced seven-part episodic structure to trace the events in Algeria leading up to the outbreak of the war of liberation in 1954. The early episodes contain a mass of subject matter beyond that immediately indicated by their titles, but the later episodes are shorter and more focused. Insofar as the pre-credit sequence of a film customarily sets out to shape our response to the subsequent narrative, the scenes depicting despair at the drought and of the decision to leave the land for a life elsewhere seem to herald a film showing man's (and woman's) struggle against nature, which Lakhdar Hamina was in fact to treat in his next feature, *Sand Storm* (1982). The credit sequence itself sets the lyrical tone of the film, alternating Philippe Arthuys's lush string harmonies with the harsher, more elemental music of pipe and drum accompanying a peasant crowd setting off to a shrine to pray for rain, with the images blurred and only half decipherable through a heat haze.

"The Years of Cinders/Les années de cendre"

The film's first episode takes the protagonist, Ahmed, from his life as a peasant in the drought-ridden desert to life in town, where he encounters French rule and French exploitation of resources in a quarry and in the fields. The opening rural sequences have won praise from the sociologist Mostefa Lacheraf for their ethnographic value,[15] and Berrah has written of the film that "on the sociological level, it remains an irrefutable document which, regardless of the conception of history it mobilizes, has the merit of organizing and synthesizing . . . a determining era in the modern history of Algeria."[16] Yet this long opening sequence is in effect timeless, a characteristic shown by the critics' varied attempts to date the film's action (from the 1940s till 1954 for Berrah, 1939–1954 for Tamzali, 1941–1954 for Lacheraf, 1945–1954 for Lotfi Maherzi). The peasants' joy, when the rain actually comes, is joy at nature's bounty, and their despair, when the crop fails yet again, is a response to the harsh burning sun which dominates their lives. Insofar as there are disputes over water, these are between rival groups of peasants on different sides of the riverbed: there are no social hierarchies here and no trace of French exploitation. This is in fact a world outside history. Hafez's assertion that the film "reduces the element of self-awareness to the level of the peasants"[17] is certainly true of the opening sequence. Nevertheless this sequence is handled with the editing control of pace and rhythm, the visual flair and the exuberant acting (as when the peasants first encounter water) which will be characteristic of the film as a whole.

History (and, I would argue, self-awareness) enters the film in the person of the madman, Miloud (played with enormous relish by Lakhdar Hamina himself). He is the first to greet Ahmed and his family on their arrival in the town, which he describes as "an illusion." He shows them the buildings which represent colonial power—beginning of course with the jail—before leading them to the "paradise" of the poor. Ahmed gets a job working in a quarry, but when, defending himself from a French supervisor's whip, Ahmed knocks him unconscious, he is taken to the commissariat and beaten till he can hardly move. In the town square the French declare a general mobilization, to which Miloud responds by returning to the cemetery to summon up the dead. Ahmed is not involved (it seems that the French do not know of his existence) and he gets a new job, working in the fields. He is able to attend a clandestine meeting, where the men gather to listen to a broadcast by Hitler (speaking, oddly enough, in perfect Arabic!). All rejoice at France's downfall and most support Hitler, though warned by one of their number that for him "Arabs are less than toads." A Vichy rally, at which the French sing "Maréchal nous voilà," brings this sequence to a close. At this stage in the film Ahmed has made his first acquaintance with the city, colonial rule, and some concept of a wider world, but he remains a passive figure. His revolt is a purely personal response to unexpected aggression, and he is marginalized within the town where Miloud the madman is at home.

"The Years of the Cart/Les années de la charette"

When typhoid strikes the town, the French leave, but the Arab population suffers grievously when all the exits are sealed off. When the disease has disappeared, Ahmed departs for his home village with the sole survivor of his family, his young son. Back home he joins the peasants working for a French farmer. Another dispute over water arises, but this time Ahmed redirects the anger against the colonizers who have stolen their land. A group blows up a dam, but they are caught and deported to serve in the French army during the war in Europe. A montage sequence of warfare follows, but on 8 May 1945, when the Europeans are rejoicing the end of the war, there is a massacre in Algeria after some peasants rise up against the French. This second water dispute is a genuine political action, as Ahmed brings the rival groups together and, united, they vent their anger on the French. But this is merely an isolated, improvised act, not part of any organized mass movement, and it is swiftly swallowed up in world events. The film's handling of the 1945 massacre has caused some controversy among Algerian critics. When, on 8 May, Algerian demonstrators who had come under police fire turned their fury on the French settlers, killing over a hundred of them, the French response was devastating. In the following week, thousands of Algerians were slaughtered (fifteen thousand according to the French, forty-five thousand according to Algerian sources), and these killings were crucial, "definitively creating a gulf between the two communities and convincing a number of Algerian nationalists that only armed action would obtain concessions from the French."[18] As Lacheraf notes, we see "only rare almost allusive indications"[19] of these bloody events which were "the prelude to a true national realization of other means of struggle."[20]

"The Years of Embers/Les années de la braise"

Disillusioned when he returns from the war and alone after the death of all his companions, Ahmed is mocked by Miloud as he throws away his medal. He gets a job as a blacksmith and becomes a real part of the urban community. He and the others are suspicious when a political exile, Larbi, arrives in the town, but Larbi soon becomes their leader, advocating armed revolt. For speaking out in the mosque, he is beaten in scenes that echo Ahmed's own ill-treatment at the hands of the French. Among those drawn to the liberation struggle, much attention is a given to the rival claims of armed struggle and electoral participation, but followers of both camps are slaughtered together in the great massacre that follows.

"The Year of the Assault/L'année de la charge"

The elections called by the French, who have their own collaborator as a candidate, split the peasants, some urging participation, others (like Ahmed) advocating armed struggle. When both groups try to attend a political rally, they are mown down by the cavalry in a battle in which Larbi is killed and Ahmed is transformed into an expert rider and swordsman. Several critics have evoked Soviet cinema in their discussions of the film's epic qualities—Berrah, for example, talks of the film as being "in the great tradition of Soviet film making"[21]—but these scenes of battle recall far more the Hollywood tradition. Hassan Bouabdallah, who talks of *Chronicle* as being "arbitrarily cemented together by the growth to political awareness of its peasant hero, who suddenly becomes a superman in the style of American cinema,"[22] goes on specifically to evoke the basic rules of the most banal Hollywood western: "the peaceful farmer is suddenly called upon to transform himself into an avenger. He is shown, at the beginning, learning to shoot; in the middle he fights an equal duel;

then it is one against two, before, finally, he has to kill off a dozen or more bandits."[23] It is difficult to refute such claims, though this action sequence is handled with real vigor and assurance by Lakhdar Hamina and forms the action climax of the film. Yet for all its cinematic power, it is not shown as contributing significantly to the struggle, as the Algerian opposition is implacably crushed and its leaders are led away to prison.

"The Years of Fire/Les années du feu"

The action in the remaining three sections of the film is much more muted. In "The Years of Fire," Ahmed and his men take to the mountains when they return after two years in prison. Miloud again addresses the dead ("Your numbers are growing . . . ") and curses the living who remain passive: "May God curse those of you who miss this rendezvous with destiny." His words annoy the Caïd and he is punished viciously (dragged along in the sand behind a horse). As fresh French troops arrive, he takes Ahmed's young son to the mountains to warn Ahmed.

"1 November 1954/Le 1 novembre 1954"

One inevitable omission from Lakhdar Hamina's version of events in the film is the naming of the sole Algerian nationalist organization of the 1940s and early 1950s, the Parti du Peuple Algérien (PPA), and its charismatic leader, Messali Hadj, persona non grata for the post-1965 leadership. Because of this, the film is unable to show 1 November 1954 as a moment when these veteran nationalists, many of them imprisoned or exiled by the French, were replaced by the younger militants of the newly formed FLN, who came to lead the eight-year armed struggle.[24] One or two critics, lamenting that the film is not a more severe indictment of French colonialism, have questioned its concentration on conflicts between Algerians, with Hafez, for example, arguing that "it exaggerates internal conflicts."[25] But in fact the late 1950s saw bitter and bloody conflicts between the FLN and Messali's renamed organization, the Mouvement National Algérien (MNA), both in Algeria and in France. But Lakhdar Hamina, of course, working on behalf of a government whose slogan was national unity, could show none of this. Instead, the film offers us a strangely downbeat ending. At the very moment that the armed struggle gets under way, Ahmed is betrayed and surprised by the French. Trying to ensure his colleagues' escape to safety, he is shot and killed, to be mourned only by his son and the ever-present Miloud. The French in the town, meanwhile, hold elaborate ceremonies for those who have died supporting their cause.

"11 November 1954/Le 11 novembre 1954"

The somber mood of the film's ending is enhanced by the final episode, a kind of epilogue, set ten days into the struggle. Here Miloud too dies alone,

Fig. 17. *Chronicle of the Years of Embers* (1975), Mohamed Lakhdar Hamina, Algeria

though in his case blessing both the madness which gave him his insight and the years of struggle we have witnessed in the course of the film. A title tells us that a million Algerians died in order to achieve independence on 5 July 1962.

For a hymn to the necessity of armed struggle, *Chronicle* is strangely weighted in narrative terms. The first two episodes, which occupy over half the film's running time, are devoted largely to natural disasters (famine and typhoid) and at this stage no argument is advanced that these disasters are in any way a product of French colonial policies toward agriculture or urban life. Indeed the direct effects of French colonial rule are barely touched upon. There is no space in the film even for a purely symbolic depiction of the effects of such rule on the colonized; almost invariably the violence is inflicted not by the French in person but by their Algerian supporters, such as the *Caïd,* depicted as hostile and arrogant and as despising the peasants. Even in the central massacre scene, when French-led colonial forces are employed, Lakhdar Hamina is eager to show that the slaughter is watched and fully accepted by both the French and their collaborators, shown mounted side by side. There is never a conflict of any kind between the French and their collaborators—no argument over tactics or levels of violence, for example—although the Algerian freedom fighters are shown debating at length the rival merits of direct action and electoral reform. This leads Maherzi to argue that the colonizer "is represented as an element which is in practice exterior to the conflict, to the extent that an uninformed spectator might see the principal contradiction of the period as that between the people and a class of Algerians complicit with the colonial authority."[26] Given this view, the enthusiasm which the film provoked in France is very comprehensible.[27] Equally the ending of the film is very muted, in that both protagonists die in November 1954, just as the armed struggle gets fully under way. This is an elegiac and mournful conclusion to two intertwined personal histories, not a clear-sighted look to the coming battle.

Perhaps the most intriguing aspect of the film is Lakhdar Hamina's choice of his two principal protagonists, Ahmed and Miloud, activist and madman, who are seen as similarly forming part of the same struggle. Miloud cares for Ahmed's son when he becomes an activist, thereby himself becoming the second father figure for the next generation of Algerians who will take up the struggle. The combination of a chronological linear narrative and a protagonist who is an idealized man of action is not without its dangers, since much of the film is shaped by the level of his personal consciousness. It is clear that for Lakhdar Hamina socioeconomic awareness (the decision to leave the land) is a necessary precursor for political awareness, but because Ahmed makes his way to the city before achieving any sort of personal political insight, the two stages are not linked as clearly to the colonial situation as the director may have intended. Equally the move to become a skilled urban craftsman (a blacksmith) and participation in political debates led by an outsider (Larbi, the urban activist exiled to the town, who becomes the focus for the growing sense of a need to oppose violence with violence) is posited as a necessary precursor for the move toward direct action. But when Ahmed leaps (literally) into action during the massacre, he needs to be seen not as the naturalistically depicted peasant of the opening scenes, not as an individual at all, but as a symbolic figure representing the ideal development over time of the Algerian peasantry.

While Ahmed is the idealized man of action, Miloud, who constantly appears at key moments in the narrative—seen most often in the setting of the cemetery where he constantly harangues the dead—is the man of words. As the traditional wise fool, he first appears to introduce Ahmed (and us) to the reality and nature of the town, later warning constantly of the need for action and finally dying proclaiming the importance of the armed struggle which is under way by the time he dies. He gives us insights that Ahmed could never articulate, including an awareness of the forces that shape social life. But he can never (except perhaps in relation to Ahmed's son) be more than a man of words: when an army is needed, he turns to the dead in the cemetery, not to live recruits. The two figures—Ahmed and Miloud—complement each other, but neither directly influences the other's actions (they are from different worlds) and neither possesses the political awareness provided in the film only by the activist outsider, Larbi. As a result, the film can offer a mythologized pageant of the armed struggle but not a historical analysis of the motivation and interplay of its component forces.

8   A Fragile Masculinity:
Omar Gatlato (1976)

Omar Gatlato is the debut feature film of Merzak Allouache, who has since gone on to establish himself as one of Algeria's leading directors with a further six features made in Algeria or France. On its initial release, the film drew large audiences, running for months in two Algiers cinemas and smashing box office records.[1] In all it was seen by some 300,000 spectators in 315 cinemas. It has enjoyed a generally high reputation with critics in Algeria and abroad, and when the film was first shown in France in 1977, it received the kind of reviews which Allouache, who had studied film history in Paris in 1968, can hardly have anticipated in his wildest dreams. Its lasting interest is twofold: its use of voice-over narration as a stylistic device to probe the mind and emotions of the central character and its depiction of the difficulties of sexuality in a culture where young men and women are segregated. Abdou B., a distinguished film critic and the editor of the leading Algerian film review *Les Deux Ecrans,* described *Omar Gatlato* in 1987 as "the degree zero of depicted or spoken sex."[2]

The Concern with Virility

In the very first shot of the film, which runs for almost a minute of screen time, Omar talks directly to the camera, introducing himself and his problems to us: "My name is Omar. My friends nicknamed me Gatlato, 'it kills me.' That is: I'm obsessed with the idea of virility and macho . . . it kills me. They're right: virility is the only thing that matters." The whole film is a demonstration of the limitations of this code, which are explored principally through the contradictions within Omar as he attempts, in the second half of the film, to meet up with the woman, Selma, to whom he is attracted. In his opening words, Omar sets out his position: "A man has to defend his dignity every day," adding—as if in justification—"There are an awful lot of men in the world and they're all equal." But this bold statement is undercut by the initial visual presentation of the protagonist: the opening shot begins with a close-up of his feet, revealing clearly the holes in his socks, and only then pans up to reveal his face and allow him to address us.

Though Omar places himself unequivocally within the community of men (the *umma*), he reveals early on a real weakness: his susceptibility both to Algerian popular music (*chaâbi*) and to the songs of the Hindi film melodramas whose song tracks he records. His thirty cassettes of these, he tells us, are his "treasure." Significantly he applies to *chaâbi* the same terminology as that he uses for virility: "*chaâbi* is my passion: it kills me," but his comments on Hindi music reveal the extent to which he sees this love of music as a feminine weakness (and hence one he will never be able to confront fully within himself): "If I were a woman, I could cry listening to it." The central problematic of the film for Allouache is the emotional poverty of the male position in a Muslim society: How is it possible for a young man to mature in a segregated society which denies him all contact with women other than those of his own family? Even if they feel attraction, how can young Muslim men translate this into meaningful action? As Allouache has stated, he was "particularly interested in their relationships with women—how there were two distinct societies, one male, one female, being created through various forms of segregation."[3]

A useful aid in defining Omar's role as a comic hero is the distinction Jerry Palmer makes between plausibility and implausibility in comic characters and actions.[4] Omar is certainly a plausible product of a society founded on social segregation: he defines himself in masculine terms and constructs his life in terms of male friendships. But he becomes increasingly implausible as he attempts to act out this role. We see from the opening scene that he is both unaware and uneasy in his relationships with his sisters—the only females of his own generation with whom he has contact. He prides himself on his virility as "the only thing that matters," but when a girl's hand inadvertently touches his, as they stand side by side at the bus window, he recoils as if from an electric shock: Omar's notion of virility does not encompass encounters with real women. His values may be defined as those of the *umma*, the universe of male believers, and these are commendable values, but, from the very first shot in the film, Omar takes them too literally. He admits to being obsessed by macho values, but at the same time reveals a weakness for music; his "treasure" is his stock of cassettes of romantic music at which, if he were a woman, he admits he would cry. As the narrative develops, the gap between his supposed virility and his actual timidity widens.

A Narrated Film

The first and most obvious aspect of *Omar Gatlato* is its use of a protagonist who talks directly to us. Direct address to camera is a conventional method in documentary, particularly in its more recent television forms, and it has also been used in a wide variety of fictional films, both in Hollywood and elsewhere. But generally the speaker briefly introduces a story and, as this begins to take shape, the film switches to the conventional third person filmic narration in which the narrator has no privileged position within the enacted scenes. Here in *Omar Gatlato*, on the other hand, Omar's role as narrator is far in excess of what is common in fiction: he talks almost incessantly through the opening scenes. But he is generally not concerned to tell us stories. Far from being a simple "talking to camera" approach, Allouache's chosen style utilizes three methods of narration (direct address, voice-over, inner monologue) with three basic

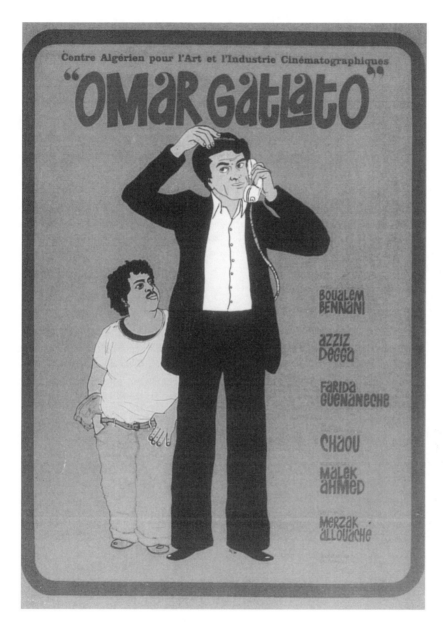

Fig. 18. *Omar Gatlato* (1976), Merzak Allouache, Algeria

functions (naming, describing, predicting). There is a general assumption that the use of a narrator within the text creates detachment or distance, but this effect is not borne out by Sarah Kozloff in her investigations of Hollywood films that use first person narrators. Her conclusion is that "this type of narration can greatly affect the viewer's experience of the text by 'naturalising' the source of the narrative, by increasing identification with the characters, by prompting nostalgia, and stressing the individuality and subjectivity of perception and storytelling."[5]

The direct-to-camera style gives Omar an initial authority—as source of the truth of the narration—akin to that conventionally claimed by the narrator of a documentary. But this is very different from the position he occupies either socially or in relation to women. In the first half of the film Omar is the apparently omniscient protagonist-narrator, master of what is a virtually unchanging daily world. Thus he is able to predict accurately what the women on the balcony will talk about as they hang out their washing or how the butcher Qasim will treat his apprentice. But his self-proclaimed mastery comes to an end in day two, when he is humiliated and robbed of his wallet and cassette recorder by muggers as he walks through the Casbah with his friend Ali. He does not have time to rebuild his confident mastery because the very next day—the mid-point of the film in terms of its duration—he receives, with a replacement cassette recorder, a partially recorded tape which will plunge his life into chaos. The voice of Selma, which by chance is recorded on the tape, becomes the new verbal power which makes itself increasingly felt. This is an event which Omar has not been able to foresee, and it is with this entry of the unnameable, indescribable, and unexpected that the true drama of the film begins to gain weight and solidity. Now, as Omar loses his command of the events of his life, his confident speech—his naming, describing, and predicting—is replaced by obsessive listening and by self-reflective monologues. Like so many Arab film narratives *Omar Gatlato* is a story of defeat. It is Allouache's inventive strategy of using the sound track as the battleground which gives the film its stylistic freshness and continuing power to hold our attention.

In Search of Music

For Wassyla Tamzali, *Omar Gatlato* is important because it is "the first Algerian film to draw a portrait of the popular culture of a significant part of the populations of the big cities."[6] The key scenes in this respect are the two outings Omar makes in search of the music he loves so passionately: to the Olympia cinema, where he can listen to Hindi film music, and to the variety show, where he can hear a performance of his beloved Algerian *chaâbi* music. The attraction of the Hindi film music for Omar is easily explained by the role of filmic song-and-dance routines in Indian society:

> In a rigidly structured conventional society that seeks to control all romance, action and excitement in life, their accessibility offers young and old a much needed

escape—a privileged moment or two alone with one's fantasies when the real, the mundane, is thrown to the winds.[7]

For the working-class urban Indian, the experience of such a film is "perhaps the only true communal experience there is,"[8] and this describes Omar's situation remarkably closely, though he has his beloved *chaâbi* too. He does not understand Hindi, of course, but then many in the vast Indian audiences will have no knowledge of the language of the songs, so the music has been structured to arouse emotion directly through its rhythms and melodies. Clearly the fact that these Hindi films which Omar loves are tales of thwarted passion and unconsummated love is also significant, since this again ties in with his passion for *chaâbi* music, whose themes are similar.

Omar's reasons for attending the variety show with a number of his friends and work colleagues are very clear from the voice-over which accompanies the very first shot in the scene: "We don't get much entertainment, but tonight there's a show. It's a variety evening. Some numbers are good, some are bad. What brings us is the music. We have to sit here through the first part, but we'll put up with it for the songs." Before they hear the *chaâbi* singer, Cheik Chaou, they have to endure a stagy drama in classical Arabic[9] and a modern mime. The drama, concerning the troubles of a sad, lovesick prince and the grand vizier's beautiful daughter Safouan, fails to engage the largely male audience. One spectator shouts: "Kill the prince," but the play continues to murmurs, which change to whistles on the arrival of Safouan. The prince's offer—as a pledge of love—of ten black slaves, four handmaidens, and a flock of sheep, provokes the cry "Long Live the Agrarian Revolution!" With the audience making its own entertainment chanting, clapping, and dancing in the aisles, the play comes to an embarrassed halt. The mime, Fouad, fares no better and is soon hustled off the stage. The lights go down, Omar gets out his recorder, and the performance of Cheik Chaou begins. The male audience, of which Omar and his friends form an indissoluble part, is shown to reject both the official version of traditional culture and the modern imported Western culture. Throughout the film, Omar himself shows little interest in stories: there are no books in his room, we never see him reading, and at best he talks of intending to borrow a newspaper. It is music alone which affects him.

One of the Boys

Omar has no real relationship or close communication with any of the members of his family and lives completely segregated from women. His relationships with his male friends are therefore of the greatest importance to him—a part, as Allouache says, of his concept of virility. Over half the film is made up of Omar's interaction with his male friends, his three colleagues at the office and the boys from his neighborhood with whom he sits, talking quietly and listening to guitar music, high above the city. With a mixture of friends from both groups he goes at the cinema, to the variety show, and to the club.

Together they attend a wedding, go swimming at the harbor, and cheer on their team at the football match. In addition, when the more dominant Moh replaces Ali as his closest friend, they are together constantly.

Tamzali sees this male group as "a closed world which will develop its own language, its code of honor, its morality, outside of the rules of society."[10] Allouache, in his interview with Tamzali, is at pains to point out that these young men are not delinquents, "they are not marginalized. They have jobs and families."[11] Allouache also denies that the culture of Omar and his friends can be defined as homosexual: "The word homosexuality isn't the right one because it covers different notions from what happens here," but he does go on to admit it involves "very strong and exclusive male friendships" and may lead to "real scenes of jealousy."[12] But to Western eyes at least, the dancing of the male guests at the wedding seems to indicate more than a simple "buddy" friendship, and Omar's relationship with Ali is at best ambiguous. When Omar walks Ali home "to keep him company" through the Casbah, in the scene which forms the first turning point of the film, the framing of the images gives a sense that Omar is protective toward the slim, frail-looking Ali. Up to this point in the film (on the bus, for example) Omar has made a point of keeping out of trouble. Now, as if stimulated by Ali's presence, he finds the need to stand up for himself, despite the fact that he and Ali are outnumbered. For the first time in the film, Omar behaves like a real film hero, smashing his adversary in the mouth and disarming him of his knife. But ironically this leads to his downfall, since Ali has meanwhile been captured by the two other muggers, who hold an axe to his throat. Omar, distraught, has to yield not just his wallet but also his treasured cassette recorder.

Omar and Selma

Selma enters Omar's life purely by chance, simply because she did not erase the tape on which she recorded a few sentences when trying out the cassette recorder Moh had loaned her. The sentences themselves are banal: "One. Two. Three. What can I say? It's silly talking to yourself. I can hear the bus outside. The children won't go to sleep. The walls of my room are painted with flowers. It's Ramadan—the days are so long. Another bus stops. The last one tonight. Tell me, why are the flowers red? Can't you hear me? So what if you can't. I'm talking to myself. What's wrong with that? I don't know if . . . " Yet when Omar listens to them, late at night in his room while his sister and the children are asleep (in a shot which lasts three minutes and is the longest in the film), his life is changed totally. The infatuation which grows from this moment is, of course, absurd, and a key factor in making Omar a comic character. But it is not difficult to see why Selma's voice has such an impact. The moment is propitious. Late at night is the only time that Omar has any space to himself in the crowded flat, when, with the children asleep, he can at least pretend that he is alone. He is excited: after the anguish of having his cassette recorder stolen in the Casbah, he now has a replacement machine. The tapes which are so crucial to him are now accessible again. Then there is the total surprise at hearing a woman's voice, seemingly talking to him, here, in his own room.

There are a number of things which serve to make Selma (though he does not yet know her name) real to him. She too is alone at night (the last bus has gone) and she too is plagued by children who will not go to sleep. Like Omar, she names and describes the things around her. But at the same time she is absent. We have already seen Omar's inability to deal with real flesh-and-blood women, but Selma is imaginary. Everyone in his life up to this moment has a name, a nickname, a few key attributes he can put into words: this is the source of his power as narrator of the film. But this voice belongs to someone who has no name, and about whom he knows nothing except what he can deduce from the tape. The voice reaches him by the very means through which he is emotionally most vulnerable and by which his sensibility is daily fuelled. A woman's voice comes to him out of the blue, when he is alone late at night. It is as if the tales of romance have taken on a personal voice, one which is half introspective, "I'm talking to myself. What's wrong with that?" and half addressed seemingly directly to him: "Can't you hear me?" As we have seen, Omar lives in an exclusively male world, and the film adopts his perspective (we never see the bride, her bridesmaids, or any of the female guests when Omar and his friends attend a wedding, for example). Yet here a woman's personal thoughts and private feelings (however banal) are suddenly available to him. For Omar this is a unique and unimagined moment: the voice of a woman in her own solitude, a seemingly close intimacy with someone who is present on the tape, through the sound of her voice, but absent physically. This combination of circumstances is bound to be lethal for him. The impact can be measured by the fact that the following day is the only one on which he does not address us directly, either by speaking to the camera or by voice-over; he is, in this sense, quite literally speechless.

He now starts to cultivate Moh, so as to find out more about the girl whose voice now obsesses him. But the description Moh gives undercuts Omar's fantasies: "She's a typist. One day I got fired and she fought for me. She's in the union." A job, trade union activity—how can such activities be the attributes of Omar's dream woman? She is a girl he could certainly take home to his mother: "She has dark hair. Not much makeup. She's not at all stuck up." Moh is curious as to why he has such an interest in a girl he has never seen. His demand that Moh should do more angers his friend: "Show me a bit of respect. I'm not a marriage bureau." Omar bridles at this, "Who said anything about marriage?" But the remark does raise the question of why Omar is to meet her, what is he offering her? He says he wants to hear her voice, to talk to her. But in a society which denies the possibility of casual relationships between members of the opposite sex, what can she expect of a meeting with an unknown outsider? The absurdity of Omar's situation is very clear, but Moh relents and gives him Selma's phone number.

The call next day to Selma, shot in close-up in a single two-and-a-half-minute take, involves a rush of emotion, in which he introduces himself, talks about her impact on him ("I hear your voice every night. It lulls me to sleep"), and uses all the little facts he knows (the red flowers on the walls, the child who cries) to demonstrate his power: "You see, you can't keep any secrets from me, I know everything." Then, after lying about his plans to join a union, he arranges to meet her at midday the following day. This phone call, for which Omar is given a musical accompaniment worthy of the hero of a spaghetti western, marks a significant stage forward. Omar has spoken to Selma and she has replied: the communication is no longer simply one way. But still their contact is solely aural: it is just that they are now linked by telephone as well as by the tape. The next step, a face-to-face meeting, is still a huge one.

Omar goes out with Moh to celebrate his phone call, but their drinking, accompanied by Arab music on an old gramophone, soon makes them both melancholy. Omar recites a poem of unhappy love: "My creator is my master. He alone knows my secret. He has destined me, forced on me her beauty. He showed me her wonder, her charm. What came over me on Thursday? I met Fatma of the long eyelashes and her love destroyed me." When Moh gets up to go to the toilet, Omar draws on his cigarette and stubs it out on the palm of his hand. This new low point for Omar is marked on the sound track by the same drum roll heard when he was mugged. This moment is a perfect illustration of the fears which, according to Fatima Mernissi, female sexuality arouses in Muslim males:

> The Muslim woman is endowed with a fatal attraction which erodes the male's will to resist her and reduces him to a passive acquiescent role. He has no choice; he can only give in to her attraction, whence her identification with *fitna*, chaos, and with the anti-divine and anti-social forces of the universe.[13]

It is fascinating that the word *fitna* means both chaos or disorder and also "a beautiful woman—the connotation of a *femme fatale* who makes men lose their self-control."[14] At home Omar falls onto his bed and falls asleep listening to Selma's voice, "One. Two. Three . . . " As Maryse Léon notes, "what kills him, in everyday reality, is his nervousness and indeed it's a case of a 'feminine' characteristic which men have used up till now to emphasize the constitutional inferiority of women!"[15]

On the morning of the meeting he looks smart in his dark suit. But as soon as Selma appears, he hesitates and turns away. His imagined vision of their meeting, shot with distorted colors and accompanied by the ominous drum roll, is one of the bleakest images in the film. A handheld camera circles the couple as they shake hands, but both—in Omar's mind—are tense and uncommunicative: the very image of a non-meeting. The moment is lost. Next morning the film comes a full circle. The opening shot of the last scene is identical to shot one, and the subsequent shots in the scene pick out some of the stages of Omar's normal route to work. But this time there is no direct address, we merely hear Omar's words in voice-over. He tells us that today he is going to phone Selma, but everything that has happened in the film leads us to doubt that. He moves off through the crowded streets and is soon swallowed up in the traffic.

Fig. 19. *Omar Gatlato* (1976), Merzak Allouache, Algeria

Omar Gatlato is not simply a comedy, it is also a profound social analysis of the impact of social segregation in a society in which—to quote Mernissi once more—"the Muslim system does not favour men; the self-fulfillment of men is just as impaired and limited as that of women."[16] Many of the difficulties that may hinder fruitful relationships between men and women—such as arranged marriages—are ignored in the film, while such very real social issues as shortage of accommodation and insecure employment are merely touched upon. But the central issue of the effects on men of a system of social segregation is handled with wit and precision. The principal stylistic devices which Allouache uses to give us this insight into the social reality of 1976 Algiers—comedy and a system of direct narration—serve simultaneously both to distance and to involve us. Omar's active pursuit of the dream woman who inadvertently enters his life and his resilience (even on day nine he convinces himself that all is not lost and that he will phone Selma) allow us the kind of empathy which a protagonist needs, while the comic excesses of his responses and their constant frustration help distance us and allow us to see the social problems of Algerian society with a new clarity. There are few gags as such, but there are well-observed little moments of comic incongruity to accompany Omar's comically inept attempts to cope with his emotions. We are carried along, but at the end of the film it is clear that our narrator-guide has lost his ability to convince us.

9 Memory Is a Woman's Voice: *La Nouba* (1978)

The status—even existence—of autobiography within Arabic literature is controversial. The predominant view in the West has till recently been that most clearly expressed by Georges Gusdorf: "It would seem that autobiography is not to be found outside our cultural area; one would say that it expresses a concern peculiar to Western man,"[1] whereas Dwight Reynolds argues in *Interpreting the Self* that "there are clearly far more premodern Arabic autobiographies in existence than have previously been assumed."[2] While admitting that "the elements that we as twenty-first-century individuals most associate with the realm of 'private' life were never the central focus of premodern Arabic autobiographical texts,"[3] he argues that for Arabic writers autobiography constitutes "rather a frame or summation for revealing a certain portrait of the whole, a context within which one's work would then be placed and evaluated."[4] Reynolds also posits that "a degree of continuity"[5] can be discerned in twentieth-century autobiographies, but other critics—particularly women critics—perceive the elements of "private" life as vital, and therefore see a clear rupture. Hilary Kilpatrick, for example, argues that

> It is only with the cultural contacts between Europe and the Arab world, which started in the seventeenth century and increased markedly in the nineteenth, that Arab intellectuals acquired the impetus to reformulate the foundation on which their literature should be constructed.[6]

Similarly, Fadwa Malti-Douglas argues that "it is only in the last few decades that modern Arabic literature, and with it modern Arabic women's literature, has achieved a level of relative frankness on questions of corporality and sexuality."[7]

Certainly women's autobiography has always been problematic in Arab society: "Self-representation of women in public was not desired. Therefore the genre of autobiography, the most extreme form of literary self-representation, was not acknowledged at all for women."[8] Indeed, to quote Malti-Douglas again, "While certain carefully defined poetic subgenres were assigned to women, the world of prose was effectively closed to them."[9] Yet autobiographical writings by women do exist and indeed serve as a critique of male-dominated concepts of autobiography. As Dinah Manisty observes:

> Women's writing shows that the very coherence of such conventional autobiography is a sign of its falseness and alienation; it challenges the concept of a coherent self. A woman cannot experience herself as an entirely unique entity because she is

always aware of how she is being defined by the dominant male culture. In the process of forming an identity she is always looking at herself through the eyes of others.[10]

Arab cinema has traditionally been similarly reticent about matters of a personal, autobiographical nature, but between 1978 and 1989 Youssef Chahine, the veteran Egyptian filmmaker whose first feature dates from 1950, released three films—*Alexandria . . . Why?*, *An Egyptian Story*, and *Alexandria Again and Again*—which, though probably not intended to form a coherent series, together constitute a remarkable autobiographical trilogy. As Ibrahim Fawal perceptively notes, "What is startling about this trilogy, from an Arab perspective, is that it exists at all. It is unprecedented in the annals of Arab cinema for an artist to bare his soul for the whole world to see."[11] Faced with the opposition in Egypt to the first of the three films, Chahine reacted angrily: "Listen! I've been talking about Egyptian and Arab society all my life, so why don't they let me talk about myself for once."[12] Khémais Khayati has no doubt about the real reason why the film was (temporarily) banned: "In reality, it's the fact that Chahine talks in the first person about himself, his family, his dreams and his disappointments as well as his society. In short, Chahine stripped naked in front of his audience. What a shock!"[13] Chahine's audacity opened the way for a whole new generation of filmmakers in the Arab world in the mid-1980s and early 1990s, among them the Tunisians, Nouri Bouzid and Ferid Boughedir, whose work is considered here. Bouzid has noted that, in the case of his own (1940s) generation, "with the development of the individualistic and personal, there was a development of the autobiographical: The directors embarked on a process of self-questioning, seeing this as a step that must be taken before they may begin to question others."[14] But the Algerian novelist-turned-filmmaker Assia Djebar followed a rather different route toward personal self-expression.

Assia Djebar

In her book of collected observations about her life as a French-language novelist of Maghrebian origin, *Ces voix qui m'assiègent*, Assia Djebar offers two images of herself as a child: "a little girl going out into the street with a lady (my mother), a city dweller enveloped in her white silk veil . . . who went, every Thursday, to the *hammam*"[15] and "a little Arab girl going to school for the first time, one autumn morning, hand-in-hand with her father."[16] The school, where her father taught, was a French-language school and, when she went on to further school studies in Algiers and Paris, followed by enrollment in the Ecole Normale Supérieure de Sèvres, the language of the colonizer became, for Djebar, the language of personal liberation. Initially she wrote her novels (the first was published when she was just 21) as a product of this education, in an untroubled "pure joy of inventing."[17] The first three novels, each written in a matter of months, were trouble-free, but the writing of the fourth, the beginning of which coincided with Algerian independence, took her three years to complete, and it was not published until 1967. Looking back later on this experience, she realized that her situation as a publishing author was paradoxical: "I was writing while still remaining veiled. I would even say that that was deliberate: writing as a veil."[18] The problem was that she experienced a fifty-page section in her fourth novel, though narrated in the first person by a male character, to be autobiographical, hence as an "unveiling."[19] The result was ten years of silence as a writer.

On her return to Algeria in 1974 to take up a university post, she hoped to be able to write in Arabic, but found that this "had become the language of political discourse . . . and, at the same time, more and more a masculine language."[20] Then she hit upon the idea of writing for the cinema. Djebar was excited by the potential that the camera offered for a distinctive reversal of the female gaze, as she writes in *So Vast the Prison:*

> This strange slit that the tourists photograph because they think it is picturesque to have a little black triangle where the eye should be, this miniature gaze will henceforth be my camera. All of us from the world of the shadow women, reversing the process: We are the ones finally who are looking, who are beginning.[21]

Djebar's experience of the film medium at this time was that of an enthusiastic viewer of Hollywood films during three years in Morocco and as a spectator in the early post-1962 years in Algeria. When she approached the Algerian television authorities, they suggested the adaptation of one or more of her novels. But she insisted on following through with her own project, which required a minimal budget, a jeep, a technical crew and, above all, a sound recordist.[22] So it was that, in 1975, she began work, researching in the mountains from which her mother's family came. She discovered that filming was not just a new form of looking but also a way of "capturing words in space."[23] Her chosen task of "writing for the cinema" involved setting out "from recorded sound, from sound listened to, and listened to again."[24] Finding cinema was rediscovering literature, but moving from written literature to oral literature,[25] and, as Mildred Mortimer notes, "in the oral tradition of women she found the authentic expression of Algerian culture."[26] In response to the question as to why she turned to an audiovisual medium, Djebar's reply was, "for the sound and the speech, for women's speech which I wanted to seek out, if possible, at its source."[27] It was in this way that *La nouba des femmes du mont Chenoua (La Nouba,* 1978) was born.

Subsequently, the RTA, which had funded *La Nouba,* also backed a second film, *La zerda ou les chants de l'oubli (La Zerda,* 1980), but Djebar's relationship with the state organization was never happy, and she has complained that six further projects were blocked in one way or another, because she "was a woman" and because she "practiced a cinema of research, not a cinema of consumption."[28] One of these projects, devised in 1979 with her future husband, the poet Malek Alloula, has been published under the title *La zerda ou Maghreb, années 30 (La Zerda or The Maghreb in the Thirties).*[29] A decade later, Djebar collaborated with Merzak Allouache on the fifty-minute video *Femmes en mouvement*

Fig. 20. *La Nouba* (1978), Assia Djebar, Algeria

(*Women on the Move*, 1989) and then, in the early 1990s, with the young Kamal Dehane on two 16mm documentary films. The experience of making *La Nouba* and the impact of the women's testimonies were crucial to Djebar in recovering her own voice as a novelist, and there are specific references in many of the novels she has published since the 1980s: some of the interviews appear in *L'amour, la fantasia* (1985), extracts from her diary of the shooting are incorporated into *Vaste est la prison* (1995), and the novel *La femme sans sépulture* (2002) is devoted entirely to the story of the rebel heroine, Zoulikha.

La Nouba

A *Nouba*, Djebar tells us, is a six-part ancient Andalusian urban dance form, which is not rigidly structured (there are regional variants), and where each part has its own distinctive rhythm—slow or fast or dreamlike, for instance. In a *Nouba*, musicians take turns to come to the forefront to perform.[30] In *La Nouba* the film's credits are interspersed with isolated images (which will recur later in the narrative) and accompanied by a collage of sounds: water flowing, the noise of battle, snatches of Arab music. There is a double dedication: to Bela Bartók, who researched Algerian music in and around Biskra in 1913, and to Zoulikha, killed in the *maquis* in 1959, whose story is told and retold by the women of the mountains. This indicates both the importance of the sound track (music and voice) and the pattern of opposites brought together in the film: the sounds of the *Nouba* and the Western music of Bartók, the Arabic oral storytelling and the French-language commentary, the documentary shooting and the dramatic re-enactment.

In this two-hour film, the six-part structure of the *Nouba* itself is preceded by an overture (Touschia), which, though composed of a single narrative line with a total chronological coherence, has two stylistically different halves. The first interior scene contrasts the free movements of Lila and the clumsy ones of her husband, Ali, temporarily confined to a wheelchair. They exchange glances —but no words—for this is a relationship in crisis. Lila's principal relationship is a formal one with the camera, his is that typical of an Arab male: attempting to control her through his gaze. She struggles to escape this: "I speak, I speak, I speak. I don't want anyone to see me . . . as I really am" and to come to terms with the images of the war years that obsess her. Lila talks of her loss: "I was fifteen, with a hundred years of suffering." The second scene is less formalized, shot in a more documentary style with synchronous dialogue. Again the characters, here Lila and the doctor visiting Ali, are constantly on the move, crossing and recrossing each other's paths. At the close, the group of young musicians present in the background throughout the scene come to the foreground, and a girl sings of love, absence, and the mountains.

The *Nouba* itself opens with a prelude (Istikhbar) in which Lila makes her first explorations, her voice-over making clear her motivation: "I'm not looking for anything. But I'm listening. Oh, how I love to listen." First she visits Djamila, who sings her a fragment of a song from the South of the country, and then Djamila's mother, who tells the story of Chenoua's saint, Abdel Rahman el Shamr, whose seventh wife opened the food jars feeding the village, releasing the doves they contained. The enactment of this story is accompanied by the music of Bartók, and here the choice is particularly apposite, since Bartók's own sole opera is *Bluebeard's Castle,* another tale of an over-inquisitive wife (in this case Duke Bluebeard's fourth). Later, Lila retells the story to her daughter Aïcha at bedtime, their loving interaction contrasting strongly with the coldness of her relationship with Ali. The sequence ends with the images of war, which haunt Lila, even in her sleep.

In the second sequence, adagio (Meceder), Lila continues her meetings with older women who can tell her about the past, and the recurring image is of her driving through a sparsely populated landscape in her jeep, accompanied on the sound track by Arab music. Her method, recorded in the voice-over, is simple: "Open the door, say hello, don't say anything, just listen. Is it the past or the present that's whispering?" There are successive meetings with elderly women who tell about their experiences of the war against the French, and gradually a picture of the women's contribution emerges: "I am beginning to hear you, women of Mount Chenoua . . . You were the strength of the struggle." We get only fragments of the women's testimonies, since by Djebar's own account, twenty hours of recorded conversations resulted in just five three-minute extracts in the film.[31] We hear the sound of these women's voices clearly, but often they are speaking offscreen or with their faces turned away. At times the meditative, narrating voice in French intrudes, denying us direct contact with the women, in order to give us the narrator's thoughts. The sequence ends with a visit to the former colonial town of Cherchell (where Djebar herself was born).

In the slower and more reflective third sequence, the allegro (Btaïhi), we get the now familiar range of domestic scenes—here Lila bathing her daughter Aïcha—and scenes of travel. This three-part sequence also fills in a great deal of information about the characters, confirming aspects of Lila's life and family left ambiguous in earlier parts of the film. In the first part, a collage of voices tell us about Zoulikha who, after the death of her husband, abandoned her young children and took to the mountains, only to be captured by a French patrol. She remained defiant to the end, but her dead body was later thrown into the town square. The images which accompany this form a kind of homage to Cherchell and its monuments. The second part, a visit to the tomb which Juba II built for his wife, confirms the distance between husband and wife, and Lila is identified as the woman behind prison bars seen earlier. The third part also confirms the couple's professions: she is an architect, he a vet. She reveals that she has always wanted to build houses of glass, transparent houses, claiming that the many deaths were caused by the fact that "there are walls between people, between hearts." She addresses her first (and only) words in the film to Ali: "I'm going to the mountains, where I grew up with my brother. I'll leave Aïcha with you." The last we see of him in the film is as he watches her silently from the doorway.

The fourth sequence (Derj), set in the mountains, moves to the heart of the film's concerns. It begins with the testimony of three women, each of whom is, the narrator tells us, "the shadow of a living truth, submerged in the past." After a brief re-enactment of a 13-year-old girl finding her dead brother, we move to Lila as a child, sitting in an ornate cagelike bed with her grandmother, who tells her stories of her "tribe." Within this framework are set enactments of the 1871 revolt led by Sidi Malek and scenes of the women who had to await the outcome of the battles, hidden within the mountain caves at Dahra. To the music of Bartók, the grandmother's story is widened out to embrace a whole generation of older women: "So it was, in a silent Algeria, old women whispering by night and their stories becoming wonders in the dreams of children. And history revisited by the fireside, in broken words and voices seeking one another."

In the fifth sequence, moderato (Nesraf), the tone changes again and the mood becomes more lyrical. Lila is now back by the sea, but alone. She takes a boat trip around the coast, lying in the boat, looking up at the cliffs, sleeping. Her meetings with the women of Mount Chenoua are now the substance of her dreams: "All these women wandering in the past become my mother. I am the little girl who once drank from their hands." The music shifts from a Bartók piano piece to flute music and on to Arab drum music, as the women clap and dance the *Nouba* in the caves beneath the rocks.

The finale (Khlass) opens with an image of the sea from which Lila emerges as she climbs up the cliff, passing a group of seated women as she enters the cemetery. The final song (with words by Djebar) is accompanied by a collage of

Fig. 21. *La Nouba* (1978), Assia Djebar, Algeria

shots or outtakes (mostly images of women) from scenes in earlier parts of the film. Her song, the singer tells us, always speaks of freedom. Women shall never return to the shadows, since now the sun of freedom has risen. Celebrating Zoulikha who "still lives in the mountains," the poem ends on a note of total optimism: "All that was difficult will become easy . . . We'll live in a dream of bounty and ease. We'll reign in freedom and joy."

Fiction and Autobiography

On the surface *La Nouba* is a formally structured fictional story about a woman, Lila, whose marriage is in crisis and who goes back to the scenes of her childhood, now scarred by war. By doing this she frees herself from the inhibiting male gaze (that of her husband), which attempts to pin her down. But on a deeper level this is a highly personal and indeed autobiographical work. Production stills taken during the shooting of the film show the close physical similarities between Assia Djebar and her chosen actress, Sawan Noweir. Djebar was born in Cherchell and the mountains explored in the second half of the film are those where her mother's family still lives. In researching the film she anticipated Lila's journeying, and—as a Westernized woman and an outsider—she was accepted by the community and given the access she needed, not because of her fame as a French-language novelist but because she was part of her mother's extended family and welcomed as such. As she has written, "Filming places in this way—preserving within me the litany of words murmured in my maternal language—was as much a 'diary' of myself and my family which I was beginning, as a return to the places spared from the destruction caused by so terrible a war."[32] Certainly in her retelling of women's stories and the probing of her own personal responses, she is fulfilling one of the demands of autobiography defined by Robin Ostle, namely that it "becomes an instrument of strategy through which a position of relative powerlessness or marginality is transformed into something which is able to challenge or occupy the centre."[33]

A key to *La Nouba,* as to all of Djebar's work, is the question of language. It is clear from all her writings that she is deeply aware of the contradictions involved in being, as she has put it, "a woman with a French education" but with "an Algerian or Arabo-Berber, or even Muslim sensibility."[34] Making *La Nouba* was not just rediscovering the scenes of her childhood nor just meeting remote members of her extended family. Essentially it was a linguistic experience: rediscovering the Arabic spoken by her mother, from which she had distanced herself by her French-language education. Whereas a documentary filmmaker, an outsider, might have used the twenty hours of recorded interviews to give us direct access to these women who had survived war and grievous losses—using, say, long-held close-ups of gnarled faces and long passages filled with the hesitant cadences of people not accustomed to public speech—Djebar's concerns are very different. Throughout the film we get only brief glimpses of the women's faces and mere fragments of their testimony. The key to Djebar's approach—what the film uniquely offers us—is the translation of this raw material through her own sensibility and through the French language (in which the commentary is spoken). It is this verbal text—supported by the densely edited sound track—which is the core element of the film, and it was her success in this act of translation of feeling—from women's spoken Arabic to literary French—that unblocked her creative inspiration as a novelist.

La Nouba is a complex work that begins as a formalized interior drama and ends as a celebratory song. In tackling its subject matter, it adopts a variety of stylistic approaches: formal fictional drama, conventional documentary shooting and interviewing, enacted reconstructions, and voice-overs. Throughout there is a play with sound. This occurs within the sound track itself, which uses silence to powerful effect and also sets, one against the other, natural sound and distorted newsreel sound, direct-to-camera speech and a questioning voice-over commentary, Arab song and dance and Western musical forms. In addition—and equally importantly—there is a constant interplay between this sound track and the image track, and here juxtaposition rather than synchronization is the rule. The audiovisual texture is thus dense and complex and, as Mireille Calle-Gruber has noted, shows the same concern with a musical structure as that apparent all Djebar's novels.[35]

Though the basic narrative structure—a personal journey to explore the past—is straightforward, the film juggles four separate time levels: the present of the filmed exploration, the immediate past as remembered by female witnesses, the distant past evoked by the grandmother, and the retrospective meditation on the images by the narrator. The story told emerges only gradually, through delicate touches, added details, repetitions, and embroidered variants, which together give the film its slow rhythm and its lyrical quality. Always—most notably in the portrait of the marriage—we are left with only part of the story: the film draws us in to fill its gaps and omissions. Indeed the film moves steadily away from the tight dramatic narrative of the opening, so that it—like Lila herself—is free to roam in search of a past accessible only in fragmentary form from the film's elderly female participants. *La Nouba* is an outstanding formal feminist experiment in film narrative which is far removed from the prevailing male-oriented and male-dominated realistic conformities of 1970s and 1980s Algerian cinema.

10 Imag(in)ing Europe:
Miss Mona (1987)

One current concern within film studies is with representations of self and Other, specifically with displaced minorities, with exile and diaspora, with the search for transnational identities, with the exploration of emigration—in a word, with cultural hybridity. The facts about emigration—as far as the Maghreb is concerned—are well known. The number of emigrants—mostly to France, but also to the Netherlands, Belgium, and Germany—has risen steadily from around six thousand in 1912, to one hundred thirty-two thousand during World War I, to over three hundred thousand after World War II, and on to reach to reach an estimated one million eight hundred thousand in France alone today. Over this period, the nature of the migrants has continually shifted. If the initial migrants were single men employed in heavy industry and mining around Marseilles, Paris, and in the North, the number of emigrant families— mostly lodged in shanty towns (bidonvilles) like those around Nanterre—came to predominate in the postwar period. More recently there has been an increasing number of educated young people seeking abroad the opportunities denied them at home in the Maghreb (80 percent of those moving to Canada, for example, have higher education qualifications).[1]

In addition to those with valid visas, there are, of course, innumerable illegal migrants. As Winifred Woodhall has pointed out, when considering the issues raised by emigration, there is "the need to differentiate among various groups of cultural others living in exile"; that is, to distinguish between, on the one hand, émigré intellectuals, writers, and filmmakers and, on the other, the peasants and industrial workers driven by purely economic circumstances to undergo a forced emigration.[2] Both groups may have to cope with both the pressures of integration and assimilation and with a loss of identity (childhood, family, landscape), but this does not make them a single entity. The Other is a social, as well as national, religious, or racial product. When we look at the representation of this phenomenon in cinema, we need to distinguish between the depictions of the dreams, aspirations, and illusions of the emigrant and those of the lived experience of the immigrant.

Europe as Other

If we consider the image of Europe that emerges from the films of Maghreb-based filmmakers, the first feature of note is the paucity of direct representations of emigrant life. The dazzling exception is the Tunisian Naceur

Ktari's masterly *The Ambassadors* (1975), which takes on board the problems and challenges of solidarity against racism and is a forceful and committed study of the lives of emigrant workers in France. The ironic title derives from the words of the politician who addresses the workers as they leave for Europe and in no way reflects their actual status there. The film's strong narrative line traces the group's shift from individual concerns to real friendship and, after two racist killings, the move to political action. But here too Ktari refuses rhetorical notions, avoiding clichés such as the unity of the workers of the world. Apart from this award-winning feature, North African filmmakers have offered little direct insight into the lives of North African workers in France. There is the amiable but slight comedy by another Tunisian, Lotfi Essid, *What Are We Doing This Sunday?* (1983), which traces the adventures of a Tunisian and an Algerian who spend the weekend looking—with little success—for female company. Much more significant is the Algerian Ahmed Rachedi's *Ali in Wonderland* (1979), in which the protagonist shares a tiny apartment with two friends and very strict rules: no women, no animals, no visits, no heating, no kitchen smells, and no Arab music. His job is as a crane operator, and from his lofty perch he works out his own philosophy: "Open your eyes and look at them, but don't go so far as to judge them. Your view is superficial. They've looked at us too, without trying to understand us. And that's how the gulf between us has come about. Look, but don't rush to judge them." When Ali does attempt to intervene—to try to save a man he has seen suffer a heart attack—he is assumed to be the killer by the man's white neighbors.

Otherwise, Europe is depicted as an unattainable Other. The Moroccan Ahmed El Maânouni's first feature, *The Days, The Days* (1978), was based on three months' research and shot with a crew from INSAS, the Belgian film school where he had studied. At the center of the film is the young peasant who wishes to achieve his independence and sees only one way of doing this: emigration to Europe. The director uses the real words and gestures of the peasants to animate his script. Drawing on the real problems and conflicts of rural life which he discovered, the film emerges as a close, perceptive, and realistic look at everyday life in a Moroccan village, depicted without any trace of folklore or exoticism but within which Europe is ultimately no more than a dream. *The Big Trip* (1981), the first film of another Moroccan director, Mohamed Abderrahman Tazi, also offers precise insights into contemporary Moroccan society. It utilizes the classic motif of the journey; in this case the trip is that undertaken by a lorry driver who drives from the South to Casablanca. Everywhere along the way he is cheated and robbed. He decides to emigrate, but realizes too late—when already at sea—that he is about to be cheated again and will not see land again. Most poignantly of all protagonists in Moroccan film narratives, the two main characters in Jillali Ferhati's *Make-Believe Horses* (1995) die attempting the narrow crossing from Tangier in a seaside pedal boat. The film focuses on an ill-matched group of individuals who meet up in Tangier, all nursing hopeless dreams of going to Europe: Mohamed to see a horse race, Ali to have an operation to restore his sight, Fatima to rejoin her mother. Mohamed enters a fantasy world, pretending to his wife that he is already in Paris and stealing to pay for his visa. Ferhati creates a suffocating world, reminiscent in some ways of French 1930s poetic realism: the enigmatic blind man, rain-swept, darkened streets, characters whose dreams are blocked, escape which is in sight but always just beyond reach. The ending, inevitably, is death.

Two Tunisian films offer perceptive insights into the notion of emigration. Perhaps the most pessimistic view of exile is to be found in Taïeb Louhichi's *The Shadow of the Earth* (1982), the tale of an isolated rural family community —patriarchal father with his sons and nephews and their families—whose life is slowly torn apart by natural forces and the impact of the modern world. As natural disasters increase pressure on the group, the young men leave, but life continues, with incongruous intrusions from the modern world—identity cards, conscription, a battery-operated television set—as well as the regular exploitative visits of the carpet merchant. The film is an elegy for the passing of a traditional way of life, but the emigration of the young is seen to offer no solution: the film ends with the frozen image of the coffin in which the body of the young man who has chosen emigration is returned to his family. The most sophisticated and universally relevant parable about emigration, exile, borders, rules, and bureaucracy is Mahmoud Ben Mahmoud's *Crossing Over* (1982), where two passengers are trapped on a cross-channel ferry: The film is set on 31 December 1980 and plots the parallel fates of two refugees, a working-class Polish dissident and a middle-class Arab intellectual, trapped on the same ferry. They both lack the necessary passport documents—because a new year begins at midnight—and neither the British nor the Belgian authorities will allow them ashore. Separated by language, class, and culture, they are unable to take a common stand and each goes his separate way, the Pole toward the suicidal killing of a policeman, the Arab toward an inner world, strengthened by a casual sexual encounter. A settled life in Europe is never a possibility in this Kafkaesque tale.

The View from Europe

On the other hand, there is the work of those filmmakers, of North African origin or born in Europe of Maghrebian parents, who operate broadly within the cultural and production context of the immigrant in Europe. Virtually all the 1970s works—such as those of Ali Akika and Ali Ghalem—were firsthand accounts of the problems and pressures of life as an immigrant, and they were generally considered by critics in relation to the work of contemporary socially committed French filmmakers, such as Michel Drach and Yves Boisset, whose films contained—from an outside perspective—images of Maghrebian immigrants living in France. Since the mid-1980s the perspective has changed, however, with new directors—such as Abdelkrim Bahloul, Rachid Bouchareb, and Mehdi Charef—coming from within the immigrant community. Their first features—*Mint Tea* (1984), *Bâton Rouge* (1985) and *Tea at Ar-*

chimedes' Harem (1985), respectively—are key works of a new kind of immigrant cinema. But these filmmakers have a range of interests that go beyond those of their own personal backgrounds, and the subsequent works they have produced, far from being mere social documentaries, are works of considerable interest in their own right as film narratives, bringing new voices to Francophone cinema.

All these films serve as examples of the extremely fruitful cultural interaction of France and the Maghreb, and the work of the whole group offers real insight into the issues raised by lives shaped or distorted by immigration. Such films reflect the position outlined in an interview by the Algerian-born, French-language novelist Leïla Sebbar:

> My writings are marked by Algeria—Algeria and the Maghreb in exile in France—and by France, through the contact between the Maghreb and Europe, East and West. I would not have recreated a world of interaction, of love and violence, in my novels had I stayed in Algeria—that Algeria of monolithic thought, of the single and controlled body. Algeria without the Other would not have inspired me.[3]

The position of these writers and filmmakers is unique. As Alec Hargreaves notes,

> Writers of Maghrebi immigrant origin are undoubtedly postcolonial in the sense that they have their origins in former French colonies and are still grappling in many ways with the unfinished business of decolonisation.[4]

Brought up in Europe, "they are also profoundly hybrid in their cultural references" and though in a sense cultural outsiders, "to the extent that they live and write in the country where they were born and raised, they cannot in any literal sense be described as exiles, migrants or nomads."[5] They are in this way very different from the many Algerian filmmakers—such as Merzak Allouache or Mohamed Rachid Benhadj—who have been forced to live in Europe by the current situation in Algeria.

Mehdi Charef

Mehdi Charef was born in 1952 at Maghnia in Algeria and retains his Algerian citizenship. Hargreaves gives a vivid picture of his upbringing. He arrived in France in 1962 at the age of 10 and has admitted that the rupture was tearful.[6] Reflecting on the tensions caused by his sudden removal to France, he has remarked: "If I had stayed in Algeria, I would have perhaps been all right, I wouldn't perhaps have felt the need to express myself."[7] He was raised initially "in one of the many bidonvilles [shantytowns] that sprawled across Nanterre, in the western suburbs of Paris."[8] Later, he spent ten years in a "cité de transit," one of the temporary accommodation centers set up by the French authorities to offer a better accommodation for immigrants. The situation was difficult: "At home, all the time it's: 'Take care, don't do this, because you're an Arab. . . . Don't do that. . . . Don't forget you're a Muslim!' In the street the kid finds himself

Fig. 22. *Miss Mona* (1987), Mehdi Charef, resident in France

smack in the middle of another world, which his parents know nothing about,"[9] and Charef has spoken eloquently about what it meant to be brought up in this way:

> Always torn between two societies which, at the same time, forget us—but what has Algeria done for us, the young people?—and want to enroll us, hardly tempted by a return to Algeria, pushed, on the contrary, I would even say condemned to live in France, flayed alive, the young immigrant people think that now the best way to assert themselves is to live as they are, to set themselves up as sons of immigrants living in France, valuing what can be saved from their culture of origin, but insisting also that they already belong more and more to French society.[10]

From the age of 17 Charef worked for over ten years as a mechanic in a tool factory, writing film scripts in his spare time. The fairy-tale success story of how one of these scripts, turned into a novel as *Le thé au harem d'Archi Ahmed*, was published in February 1983 (when he was just 30) by a leading French publishing house and how this novel was read by the internationally renowned director Costa-Gavras, who first commissioned a script from Charef and then engaged him to direct the film, is told by Hargreaves.[11] Since the film was released in 1985, two other French-language novels have followed, and Charef has gone on to direct four further films, as well as a number of telefilms for La Sept Arte.

Miss Mona

Mehdi Charef's second feature, *Miss Mona,* is one of the first indications of the way in which the *beur* filmmakers of the 1980s have turned away from merely chronicling immigrant communities to look, in particular, at other examples of urban alienation and deprivation. As Christian Bosséno notes, "the central characters of *beur* films are not 'Arabs' on one side and 'the rest' on the other, since the dividing line is never regarded as essential by second-generation film makers."[12] Indeed, as René Prédal observes, "if the cinema is to be believed, then the process of integration has its best chance of starting off from the bottom—setting wretchedness against wretchedness."[13] In *Miss Mona,* the central character is a young Maghrebian, Samir (played by the Tunisian actor and future film director Mohamed Ben Smaïl), but the most vivid portrait is that of Miss Mona, the aging French transvestite played by Jean Carmet, who befriends him. In the course of some two hours, the film recounts in delicate, deeply felt detail the growth of this friendship which—largely because it is so sincerely felt on both sides—leads to Samir's downfall.

The film opens with an unresolved shot (behind the credits), filmed through the driver's window of a Paris metro train, which recurs enigmatically from time to time throughout the film—with or without the back of the driver's head—and is resolved only at the very end. This pattern of repetition and delayed revelation is one of the formal structuring elements of the film. From this opening, the film comes above ground to chronicle Samir's miserable life as an illegal immigrant: work in a rag trade sweatshop, fear of being picked up by the police in one of the raids that occur again and again in the film, and living in a shared tenement room with five or six other immigrants. When one of their number dies, they offer him prayers and take a collection for his family, but they have to bury him themselves at night, so as to avoid betraying their own existence. Samir's life enters crisis when, out of the blue, he is fired by his boss, who refuses to take him back despite his subsequent pleas.

One night, in order to avoid being picked up by the police, Samir, now reduced to stealing his food, allows himself to be taken home by the aging transvestite, Miss Mona, who also works as a fortune-teller and has a caravan by a canal. It is Mona who teaches Samir how to sell the only commodity he has, his body, showing him how to pick out a client at a public urinal and urging him to follow the man downstairs in a nearby café. Samir takes the money offered and submits, but the experience makes him throw up and threaten Mona. We subsequently return from time to time to the sad and friendless life of this first client (putting out a pair of pajamas on the empty second bed in his room, feeding his goldfish with spaghetti, attending a male strip show, visiting a gay dating agency), but these scenes are not integrated into the main plot. Just as Samir needs money to buy forged identity papers, so Mona needs it for the sex-change operation he had never been able to afford. The money was once raised, but Mona's partner stole it, went off to Switzerland for the operation and returned, as a woman, to run a nearby café, where Mona regularly watches "her" from afar. Continuing his life of prostitution, Samir visits a rich old gay who wants not his body, but just someone to talk to, and also participates in a naked session with a young boy, watched through a glass panel in the floor by the client below who masturbates and shouts abuse. Samir now finds that he can no longer enter the mosque and splits up from Mona for a while, giving blood, living in a ruined building with a group of French drunks, sampling life at a hostel for the homeless. But when Mona is beaten up by a client, Samir takes him back to the caravan and nurses him.

Meanwhile Mona's life continues. From the early scene of him emerging from the caravan after their first night together, dressed as a man but brushing imaginary dust from Samir's jacket with nervous feminine gestures, the complexities of Mona's life are illustrated. He works (fairly unsuccessfully it seems) as a prostitute, but daily he tends to his senile father (also a transvestite) who lives with him. Every Thursday he visits his blind mother, who has the appearance (but presumably not the sexuality) of a six-foot transvestite. Sometimes Mona is half-man, half-woman, as when he sits by the canal side, wearing a dress but no wig, plucking a chicken. This method of building a character through little observational touches and details, rather than through big scenes of dramatic interaction, is typical of Charef's approach, in which the art lies, as Abbas Fahdel notes, in making the images say what the words do not.[14] Even when they behave foolishly or break the law, there is always a total respect for the characters, and to talk, as Carrie Tarr does, of "the film's fundamental homophobia"[15] or to see Mona as an example of "the perverse feminised French"[16] who are responsible for Samir's downfall is to misread the film totally.

The basic tone of a Charef film is observational and realistic, but he allows his characters moments when they can express their (often transgressive) dreams and desires to the full. Here we see Mona in a dream sequence in which he expresses his desire for Samir in the guise of a Marcel Marceau-type mime. Mona also poses in black lace underwear in front of a mirror to the singing of Marlene Dietrich and later he puts on a flowing white dress and imitates Marilyn Monroe standing over the air vent in *The Seven Year Itch*. Such open attempts to express his female side lead inevitably to disaster (Samir smashes the record, a customer beats him up), but Charef's sympathy is always with the dreamer, who is never caricatured or ridiculed. Fahdel is not exaggerating when he observes that "there is something of Dostoevsky in Charef's great compassion for the humble."[17] Equally sympathetic is the manner in which Charef recounts Samir's similarly disastrous attempt to become a "real" homosexual, by bringing home the boy prostitute—a dancer in a male strip show—who has saved him from the police. Seemingly inevitably, the boy steals Mona's life savings next morning. When Samir pursues him to get the money back, the boy hangs himself on stage, an act which chillingly provokes not concern but jeers and catcalls from the audience. To counterbalance these extreme moments are little incidents of banal, if incongruous, domesticity. There is an air of ordinary family life sought and achieved, for example, when Mona baths his sulky, child-

Fig. 23. *Miss Mona* (1987), Mehdi Charef, resident in France

ish old father, when Samir playfully helps the old man with his lipstick, or when the three of them go picnicking in the woods.

But overall the mood darkens, as Samir and Mona increasingly prey on those as badly off as themselves, hiring a van and pretending to be removal men to steal a young couple's furniture, kidnapping a male prostitute and stealing his earnings, and robbing one of Mona's fortune-telling clients at knife point. Finally, to recoup Mona's lost savings, they decide to rob his ex-partner, the café owner. Just as they seem to have succeeded, the woman returns and recognizes Mona, who is terrified. While Mona takes off with the money, Samir returns to kill the woman. The film's ending brings all its various repeated threads together. In the caravan Mona waits with Samir's newly forged papers and a bottle of champagne for his return. But Samir is stopped by police in a seemingly chance encounter in the metro. He almost makes his escape, being caught only when the train driver opens the train doors rather than driving off. In the penultimate shot we see the driver's face for the first time: it is Samir's lonely first customer, whose forward view through the train window we share for the closing titles.

The customary form in France for this immigrant cinema (and its contemporary literary equivalent) is *beur*. Bosséno has pointed out one of the abiding qualities of the *beur* cinema, of which *Miss Mona,* and indeed all Mehdi Charef's work, forms a key part:

> It would be no exaggeration to argue that *beur* films have revived a tradition of French populist cinema which has often been lost sight of. One of their greatest merits is that they succeed in doing what very few French movies do . . . they set their stories in a real country, and one that is in crisis.[18]

Prédal, who is in broad agreement with this stance, observes that the lives of *beur* protagonists are hardly ever successful:

> Cinema certainly doesn't show them as winners or as pampered by life, and though they are always shown with warmth and without "miserabilism," there is no way they could provoke envy in the audience or feed the spectator's dreams.[19]

This in turn requires filmmakers to define a new kind of film structure:

> So constructing a film around a *beur* character leads the film maker to modify his practice as well as his aesthetic, since the new "hero" breaks the narrative rules just as much as the psychological conventions.[20]

Mehdi Charef is in the forefront of this redefinition. Though he has continued to remain true to the approaches and attitudes displayed in *Miss Mona,* not all his work echoes its slow descent toward disaster and not all has predominantly Maghrebian subject matter. His 2000 film *Marie-Line,* for example, takes as its protagonist a French woman, the wife of a National Front activist, whose work as leader of a night cleaning team in an urban hypermarket gradually leads her to achieve solidarity with the dispossessed women in her charge. In Charef's work, the fascist supporter, like the transvestite or the illegal immigrant, requires our sympathetic understanding, not our instant dismissal.

11 Defeat as Destiny:
Golden Horseshoes (1989)

The Arab Protagonist

The state-controlled Algerian cinema was unique in the Maghreb in demanding a positive male hero: the freedom fighter active in the liberation struggle or the urban intellectual politicizing the peasants, for example. The result is the paradox of a would-be revolutionary cinema following the plot patterns and final resolutions of Hollywood cinema, opening up a gap between the film rhetoric and the actual experience of the audience. This is what made the hesitant, defeated hero of Merzak Allouache's *Omar Gatlato* such a key figure in 1976. But since the collapse of the state funding structure, the new protagonist of the films of Mohamed Chouikh, Belkacem Hadjadj, and Abderrahmane Bouguermouh in the 1990s is a hero who struggles but faces ultimate defeat. Elsewhere too the defeated hero is the norm. For Moulay Driss Jaïdi, the trajectories of Moroccan film protagonists are "journeys toward failure,"[1] whether the setting is the city or the countryside. The pattern begins with the early 1970s experimental narratives, such as Hamid Benani's *Wechma* and Ahmed Bouanani's *Mirage,* and continues through to the 1980s and 1990s films, which re-edit and accentuate this "image of failure."[2] From Jaïdi's 1995 perspective, most Moroccan films "reflect a pessimist vision. Almost all the protagonists experience a defeat,"[3] and the same is true of more recent films, such as Jillali Ferhati's *Make-Believe Horses* and the work of the best of the younger directors, exemplified by Daoud Aoulad Syad's *Bye-Bye Souirty.* Even Hadj Ben Moussa, hero of Mohamed Abderrahman Tazi's light comedy, *Looking for My Wife's Husband,* ends in a hopeless position, trying to reach Europe as an illegal immigrant.

In Tunisia, death is the fate of all the heroes in Omar Khlifi's pioneering depictions of the liberation struggle, and this sets a pattern for Tunisian cinema's portrayal of the male protagonist. Tahar struggles in vain against the forces of "modernization" in Ridha Behi's *Hyenas' Sun,* just as the aging patriarch fails to preserve his traditional lifestyle in Taïeb Louhichi's *The Shadow of the Earth,* and the overwhelming love felt by Qaïs drives him to madness in the same director's *Leïla My Reason.* The two male protagonists in Mahmoud Ben Mahmoud's *Crossing Over* (1982) are irrevocably trapped abroad the cross-channel ferry, and the same theme is picked up by newcomer Mohamed Ben Smaïl in *Tomorrow I Burn* (1998), where the protagonist is doomed from the very first sequence and goes slowly and inexorably toward his death. But perhaps the key examples of stories of defeat in Tunisian cinema are Nouri Bouzid's three initial studies of male protagonists—*Man of Ashes* (1986), *Golden Horseshoes* (1989), and *Bezness* (1992)—where the one constant is the notion of "defeat as destiny."[4] In his essay "New Realism in Arab Cinema: The Defeat-Conscious Cinema," Bouzid gives his definition of the Arab protagonist as seen by the younger generation of Arab filmmakers of which he forms a part:

> The male is not strong as he is traditionally portrayed. On the contrary, he is lost and confused and is plagued with a set of dilemmas that shake him to the core. . . . The projected image of a constantly victorious and honourable Arab hero has been abandoned. Admitting defeat, the new realism proceeds to expose it and make the awareness of its causes and roots a point of departure.[5]

Nouri Bouzid

With four features of his own and work on five scripts for other directors in just over a decade from the mid-1980s, Bouzid is a dominant force in Maghrebian cinema. All three of his first three feature films opened up new areas of subject matter for Arab cinema, particularly those relating to male identity: the rape of young boys in *Man of Ashes*, the fate of a released political prisoner in *Golden Horseshoes*, male prostitution in *Bezness*. In each case the tone is highly personal, and the pain endured by the characters is shared by Bouzid himself: "In all my films, and most of the scripts I've done, I've worked through pain."[6] His aim is to communicate his image of pain to his audiences:

> I speak directly to audiences. . . . Cinema helps them understand themselves and the reasons for this burden of sorrow we carry around within us. Humiliation, defeat, so many shattered dreams have made us a people scarred by grief. I try to help them discover its causes through the emotions, not by moralising.[7]

In all of his films, as Martin Stollery notes, a tension between past and present is crucial, as "characters suffer intense physical or emotional pain":

> This pain bursts into the present through involuntary subjective flashbacks which threaten to overwhelm those experiencing them. Suppressed, uncontrollable visual memories challenge the precarious integrity of these characters' present existences.[8]

Golden Horseshoes anticipates the confusion and self-doubt of Western-educated artists and intellectuals throughout the Arab world when they were confronted by Islamic fundamentalism in the mid- and late 1990s. Bouzid admits that *Golden Horseshoes* is his favorite film—"It's the film closest to my heart, my existence and my life"[9]—but insists that the film is not autobiographical: "There's a little of me in all the characters but it's not my life. . . . Maybe it's even a film against myself."[10] But the film was scripted in the first person,[11] and though he has sought various distancing devices—a protagonist physically very different from himself, a voice-over in which the protagonist talks of himself in the third person—the sense of direct, lived pain is one of the film's strongest qualities. In any case it would be difficult not to see this study of a man released from torture and prison who fails in his attempts to reintegrate himself into life as being at least partially an autobiographical confession, when one knows that Bouzid himself, after a brief spell working in the Tunisian national television service Radio-Télévision Tunisienne (RTT), was arrested in 1973 for participation in the activities of a left-wing group, Perspectives Tunisiennes, the Tunisian socialist study and action group. In all, he spent almost six years in prison and was not able to resume his career, initially as an assistant director, until 1979.[12] But whatever the autobiographical content of the film, Bouzid views his protagonist with pitiless lucidity and allows no room for any attempt at self-justification. Even the torture scenes, though filmed with their full brutality, are not presented in such a way as to arouse pity or sympathy for Youssef, As Denise Brahimi has noted, Youssef "though sometimes overwhelming, is not totally sympathetic and does nothing to be so. We may judge his fate to be tragic, but for all that we do not feel totally at ease with him."[13] But, at the same time, "the ex-revolutionary intellectual, with all his failures and weaknesses, is a character much less negative or prone to negativity than he seemed to be at first sight."[14] It is this double portrait which sets the whole tone of the film.

Golden Horseshoes

Bouzid has an acute sense of film structure (this is his major contribution to the scripts of his colleagues, such as Moufida Tlatli and Ferid Boughedir), and here in Golden Horseshoes the setting in time and place is precisely chosen. The place is Tunis, but not the Tunisian capital as we customarily imagine it: "It is Tunis in winter, a city where people are shivering and everything is wet and cold. Symbolically the protagonist, Youssef Soltane, wears a big black coat and (white) scarf, clothing which isolates him from the city to which he returns after six years in prison, but which does not manage to give him the slightest inner warmth."[15] The generally dilapidated settings match the weather: the film is set in half-lit, evidently cold and inhospitable rooms or the wet and shadowy streets and squares of the medina. Nothing could be less like the tourist image of colorful Tunisia than the nighttime shots of Sidi Bou Saïd, where Youssef's son, Adel, lives. Only the scenes depicting the early stages of Youssef's relationship with Zeineb and some scenes of his early family life are bathed in light: the scenes with Zeineb after his release from prison match the gloom of the rest of the film. The chosen time is the festival of Ashura—the Night of the Martyrs—which serves to give a temporal unity to the action. As Bouzid himself points out, Ashura has a double face: "Ashura is the night of tolerance, of forgiveness. It celebrates the salvation of the prophets . . . Soltane, who saw himself as a prophet, will not be saved," but "Ashura is also the night on which Hussein, the Prophet's grandson, was murdered. That's why there's a lot of blood in the film."[16] Since this is a festival when children dress up, sing, and dance, Youssef inevitably recalls his own three children, the product of a traditional marriage, his two daughters, Meriem and Raja, and his son, Adel, who are now grown up

Fig. 24. *Golden Horseshoes* (1989), Nouri Bouzid, Tunisia

and leading their own lives. He also remembers himself as a child in the sprawling family house.

The key to the power of the film is the way in which the protagonist is conceived and presented. As Bouzid told a seminar of young scriptwriters, for him, "it's the character that determines everything":[17] "The character is going to be the source of everything. He is going to impose his own evolution, he is going to claim complete freedom, and he is going to impose his own needs, provided he is a character with roots."[18]

Defeat as Destiny: Golden Horseshoes 135

Youssef Soltane totally fulfills Bouzid's theoretical definition. Everything in the film is seen through his eyes; "the audience sees only what he sees, what he hears from his past or present or what he imagines."[19] Youssef certainly has roots. He is weighed down by his past: two years in hiding, six in prison, and, since then, two years trying to rediscover his identity. Everything we see and hear relates directly to him, but significantly there are no images—even dreamed or imagined ones—of a possible future. Youssef is caught between a past that no longer makes sense to him (he has no answer to those who treat his ideas as outdated and mock his former ambition, as an intellectual, to shape the rule of his country) and a present with which he does not have any way of connecting.

His plight is not simply that of a solitary human being but is a comment on the way of life of a whole generation in postcolonial North Africa. Youssef has chosen a path which sets him apart as an individual in an Arab culture: a French-language education (which his son now seeks to emulate), imported left-wing political views (such as those of Antonio Gramsci), divorce, drinking. Even before he was imprisoned, he had wondered aloud why he had had a family, so it is hardly surprising that he finds himself unable to reconnect with his children when he re-emerges from prison. Cut off from them, distant too from his mother, and facing his brother's hostility, Youssef finds his closest human contact with the old weaver and drunkard Sghaier, a father figure who was part of his childhood and who is, like him, a wounded man (he still has a bullet in his side from the time when he was conscripted to fight for the French forces in Indochina). But in the course of their nocturnal wandering, Youssef abandons even Sghaier. Youssef the intellectual had tried to fight his political battle with words and now these are all he has left. He finds even they no longer help or comfort him, and so he burns the manuscript he has come to recover. In a sense, Youssef has aspired to live out the role of the Western fictional protagonist, to conquer the city, metaphorically crying "A nous deux, maintenant!" like Rastignac confronting Paris at the end of Balzac's novel *Le Père Goriot,* and has attempted to succeed through acting positively after making his own decisions, just like a Hollywood protagonist. But he has failed. Nowhere in the film is there a sense that this failure is personally motivated, the result of flaws in Youssef's character. The failure is depicted as the total inability of a whole generation to live out this alien, individualist dream in the reality of 1970s Tunisia or to recover from it in the 1980s.

A Life in Fragments

There is, in *Golden Horseshoes,* a total unity of protagonist, plot, and style. Structurally the film reflects Youssef's efforts. As he tries successively, but in no perceptible order, to pick up the broken pieces of his life, so too the film sets off, seems about to make a significant breakthrough, and then falls away, only to start again on a different track. The actions do not fit together to form a coherent whole: over and over again the film gets itself under way, only to shudder to a sickening halt. The actions never reach the kind of completeness

Fig. 25. *Golden Horseshoes* (1989), Nouri Bouzid, Tunisia

which would allow them to form conventional scenes and sequences, and there is no play with patterns of suspense and no possibility for the successful resolution of the action. As Bouzid himself puts it, Youssef

> is searching to put back together the pieces of his life. As he searches for those who were important in the past, he discovers the pieces have fragmented. The harder he tries to reconstruct them, the more he encounters things that shock and scatter the fragments even further. In putting himself together he destroys. The film had to be structured in the same way: it gathers and then destroys with shocking images.[20]

The editing of individual shots reflects the overall structure of the film, being full of unexpected transitions, jumps in time and space, which take us, in an initially confusing manner, through several decades of Youssef's life: his childhood, his marriage, his three children, his love affair with the beautiful Zeineb, his time in prison and his emergence from it. These shots, often single images triggered off by some detail of his immediate surroundings, come without warning and in what seems, on initial viewing, a random order.

To give two tiny examples: when he first arrives at the old family house to meet his mother at the opening of the film, he finds a group of children outside, singing around a bonfire. He imagines one of them to be his youngest daughter, Raja. The child turns and it *is* Raja as a child dressed in red, and she comes toward him, arms outstretched. But the person he actually embraces (in a false cut on the movement) is Raja as she is now, dressed in black and an adolescent. Later in the film, he revisits Zeineb's flat and imagines her, in a red dress, in the mirror. The mirror moves and we are back in time with Zeineb, now dressed in black, smiling at Youssef before his arrest. As the film progresses, these disjointed fragments can be sorted chronologically, but, like Youssef's life, they do not make a coherent pattern: constantly there are gaps and unexplained details. While Youssef's ultimate fate may be foreseen, the unfolding of the final events of his life remains inscrutable, and the film offers no hint of an answer to the problems which his life poses.

The film is shaped as a succession of encounters, almost all of which are broken up by memories or imaginings of past events and circumstances. The first visit is to his mother, who feels abandoned by her two sons, living in a deserted house ("like a funeral") and preoccupied with her own impending death. There he meets his youngest daughter, Raja, but she cannot forgive him for not being there when she was growing up, for divorcing her mother and not attending her mother's funeral. Within the family home, he has to confront the futility of his past life as a militant: "After twenty-five years you realize you haven't accomplished anything. You're not even allowed to dream. You liked those magic words—Socialism, Nasserism, Marxism—but they slipped through your hands like grains of sand." He also recalls his failure to recreate his relationship with Zeineb, who now resents his self-pity and his attempts to control her. Bored with his politics, she too confronts him with his failure: "Who do you think you are? The conscience of the world? A prophet from God?"

Leaving with the manuscript of his writings which he has collected from the house, he sets off alone, but is lured by music downstairs into the basement, where his old friend and mentor Sghaier now lives. Here in the basement nothing has changed, but outside everything is different. Youssef finds Sghaier's continued faith in him as troubling as Zeineb's rejection, and, alone while Sghaier fetches wine, he recalls the beginning of his relationship with Zeineb. When he and Sghaier set out to find more wine, they encounter the dark and labyrinthine world of the old medina, now largely in ruins and inhabited by whores and threatening male figures. New memories come to his consciousness and the discovery of a dead horse triggers memories of the torture endured in prison. These scenes are handled with brutal realism, as Bouzid shows how Youssef's spirit is broken by the pain and humiliation inflicted on his naked body in the torture sessions, the images of his suffering intercut with the slaughter of the stallion from the title sequence. Further memories flood through his mind as he drives drunkenly through the night with Sghaier and the pair stop off for a quiet smoke. Looking for Adel, he instead has a passionate chance encounter with Nana (the girlfriend of his old friend Raouf, now in exile). But even this cannot hold him and he rushes off into the night to find Sghaier.

Bouzid's audacious handling of this nude love scene, like his treatment of the torture sequence and the shots of animal slaughter, shows the extent to which his approach to the body is a key to the intense physicality of his cinema: "The body in all its aspects should be available to drama. . . . The body is the key to one's identity. I'm all for a cinema of the body."[21] The scenes in *Golden Horseshoes* have a brutal force: human torture and animal slaughter are shown without reticence and the scene of lovemaking has an explicit directness rare—if not unique—in the Arab cinema of the 1980s. In the United Kingdom, the Channel Four screening of the film was preceded by a warning for viewers of a sensitive disposition, and inevitably there were censorship problems in Tunisia, as Bouzid notes:

> The censors in Tunisia were shocked by the torture scenes in *Golden Horseshoes*, also by the love scene; by the body in both guises: broken by torture and transported by joy. They refused a certificate for the distribution of the film in Tunisia in its original version. They wanted to cut it by 14 minutes. . . . In the end, and after more haggling, we got that down to 35 seconds: 20 from a torture scene; 15 from the lovemaking. And only for screening in Tunisia; the negative remains intact.[22]

Finally meeting Adel, he drives off with him to see his elder daughter, Meriem, who shocks him by living openly with her boyfriend. As dawn breaks, he drives alone for his final confrontation, with his brother, Abdallah, an Islamic fundamentalist who works in a slaughterhouse. Of this crucial scene between the two brothers Bouzid has said that it is "one of the strongest moments in the film," that he would have made the whole film "for that moment alone."[23] The clash is bitter, as a whole lifetime of rivalry comes to the fore, against a background of slaughtered animals and hanging carcasses. When Youssef expresses his hatred of fundamentalism—"Politics don't allow doubts. I need to doubt"—his brother openly scorns him as a loser and a man who cannot even take care of his family. His view is unambiguous: Youssef is doomed. Running off, sickened by the blood as well as by his brother's words, Youssef pauses to destroy his precious manuscript and then prepares for his own death. His ritual washing prior to suicide is intercut with the stallion brought for slaughter. Then there is a final abrupt transition of space, time, and reality to the white stallion running free along the seashore, the image frozen for the final titles.

One of the strongest unifying features in the dramatic narrative of *Golden Horseshoes,* lifting it out of a purely realistic mode, is the recurrent paralleling of the life of the tormented hero, Youssef Soltane, and that of the crippled white stallion that serves as a symbol of endangered freedom and gives the film its title. The film opens with a close-up of the horse's eye (cut across, in *Un chien andalou* style, by the producer's credit in red lettering), just as it will include a close-up of Youssef's eye toward the end of the film, as he washes himself in preparation for suicide. Already in the opening credit sequence the linkage is direct: the horse is under threat—being fattened up for slaughter—while Youssef's opening voice-over words as he watches the scene announce his own fate, "Youssef Soltane, you are banished for ever." The figure of the horse recurs regularly in the narrative, sometimes as a dream image (wandering in the moonlight through the courtyard of Youssef's home, or standing by the shore, outlined against sky and sea), sometimes as a nightmare reality (the dead horse in the medina and on the seashore which Youssef stumbles across during his night-time wanderings with Sghaier through the medina). On occasion Youssef and the horse are brought together with brutal directness, as when the film intercuts between Youssef being dragged back to his cell after torture and the dead and bleeding horse being pulled across the slaughterhouse floor. The horse arrives at its place of death just as Youssef himself prepares to die.

Yet the mythic overtones which the animal also possesses within the narrative are hinted at earlier in the film. When, in a rare moment of peace, the dissidents are together before their capture, we hear the song (specially composed by Bouzid): "Run, run over the waves, you lovely horse." There is a second reference when the song is heard again when old Sghaier is introduced to us, and this is re-echoed in drunken revelry later in the film, during Sghaier's journey through the night with Youssef. At the end, the symbolic role of the white horse is unambiguous in the film's epilogue, when we see shots of the horse galloping free and hear the Arab song with its simple musical accompaniment:

> I heard you coming from afar
> Down the path.
> The pavement fell in love
> With the sound of your shoes.
> You throw away the saddle and run,
> You leave the square without a statue
> Have you forgotten the secret?
> Would you be surprised to know
> That your shoes were made of gold?
> Run, run over the waves, you lovely horse.

12 Sexuality and Gendered Space: *Halfaouine* (1990)

We are accustomed in the West to a division between public and private space and, as Judith Mayne has pointed out, our conventional novels and films deal with the implications of this, but not as "a simple mode of expression which reflects, in a one-dimensional and direct way, the social concerns of class society":

> Narrative is a mode of understanding, a structure within which questions are raised and answers tested, a fiction of possibilities and hypotheses. In narrative, then, the relationship between the two spheres of public and private life is examined, articulated and thought through.[1]

At first sight, the result of this is that "men would appear to move freely between the realms of private and public space, whereas women's involvement in the public sphere is bound by the private sphere, the family."[2] But Mayne, drawing on research by Carroll Smith-Rosenberg, argues that "the separation of male and female realms of activity does not correspond, in simplistic one-to-one fashion, to the separation of public and private spheres."[3]

This is not the case in the Muslim world, which redefines this distinction, since public and private spaces, firstly, are not only differentiated but also rigidly gendered and, secondly, the distinction is not open for discussion or debate. Fatima Mernissi offers a useful initial schema for examining this division of space. On the one hand, there is the public world of the *umma*, the world of the believers, of religion and power, a male world where women's position is ambiguous: "Allah does not talk to them directly."[4] On the other hand, there is the private world of domesticity, essentially the world of women and children. One can argue that a man's presence here is ambiguous, that he does not belong here. But it is a world over which he has total authority, and his presence turns this domestic world into the very opposite of the public world of the believers.

Fatima Mernissi sets out the distinction thus:

The *umma*	The family
Equality	Inequality
Reciprocity	Lack of Reciprocity
Aggregation	Segregation
Unity, Communion	Separation, Division
Brotherhood, Love	Subordination to Authority
Trust	Mistrust[5]

The exclusion of women from public space, their seclusion from the world of men (symbolized by the veil), means that domestic space—as far as adults is concerned—is one occupied exclusively by sexual beings. In Mernissi's words: "Men and women are supposed to collaborate in only one of the tasks required for the survival of society: procreation."[6]

Mernissi is not alone in such a linking of sexuality and space in the Muslim world. Abdessamad Dialmy, for whom "space and sexuality are two privileged expressions which society uses to express its profound identity,"[7] sees the two concepts as closely related in terms of both structure and history. Sexuality and space obey "the same binary, manichean logic":[8] "It is a manichean logic which seems to rule the traditional patriarchal universe in its totality, a logic whose starting point is the human body itself."[9]

Dialmy tabulates this as follows:[10]

Binary Schemes	Sexuality	Space
pure—impure	+	+
clean—dirty	+	+
dry—wet	+	+
light—dark	+	+
central—peripheral	+	+
high—low	+	+
vertical—horizontal	+	+
manifest—concealed	+	+
exterior—interior	+	+
square—circular	+	+
straight—curved	+	+
masculine—feminine	+	+

Dialmy explores four modes of relationship between sexuality and space: the functional (the physical location of sexual intercourse), the territorial (the division of space into masculine or feminine), the lexical (the existence of words which designate both spatial and sexual objects), and the symbolic (the ordering of spatial objects according to the masculine/feminine dichotomy). Here we are concerned principally with the territorial. Looking at the Arab city which forms the setting of *Halfaouine*, we find numerous complexities which offer a rich dramatic potential. Historically, as Dialmy observes, there is the link between the tribal origins of the Arabs and their practice of endogamy (marriage within the tribe) and the architecture of the medinas which they established when they first became urbanized: an introverted space, houses closed to the outside (no windows or balconies), unobtrusive (no external signs of the distinction of rich and poor or virtually no external indication of the sacredness of a building such as a mosque), and a zigzag approach protecting an inner domestic space housing the women of the household (a source of intense concern for males, whose "honor" is at the mercy of the sexual activity of their women and whose wealth can be depleted thanks to Islamic laws on female inheritance).

Nor should this form of architecture be seen as merely a historical relic. An examination of an Arab bidonville (slum) in Nanterre in the mid-1960s showed that it retained, to a totally unexpected extent, the traditional North African typology:

> The main street through the slum was punctuated by a series of parallel passage-ways all leading to a courtyard and house by way of a zigzagging passageway in which the lavatory was located. Entering the house, the sequence of rooms was always the same, leading from the kitchen through the living room to the mother's bedroom, which thus took pride of place, being protected by the other rooms.[11]

In symbolic terms there is an intense sexual ambiguity about the medina. Ostensibly phallic and male, with its high ramparts and towering minaret (allowing man untrammeled access to Allah), the geographic shape of the medina nevertheless offers other symbolic readings. Are we, as Dialmy suggests, to view its rounded shapes, containing at their center "a place with a secret, hidden, protected interior," as "a form of uterus"?[12] Should we conceive of the labyrinthine passageways of the medina as a passive form of defense against outsiders?[13] Or should we see mastery of the labyrinth as a long and painful initiation rite, allowing a "horizontal ascension to Allah," a woman's pathway to parallel that enjoyed by men in the mosque?[14] Whatever our approach, the ambiguity is evident: "Torn between its phallic signs and its feminine forms, between the vertical and the round, the Arab-Islamic city (the medina) offers proof of a bisexual origin, in the image of the body of which it is the architectural and urban transposition."[15]

Halfaouine

This may seem a somewhat heavy introduction for Ferid Boughedir's first solo fictional feature, *Halfaouine* (1990), which is, after all, a comedy. But, as I have argued at length elsewhere,[16] an understanding of African film making demands that we lose our Hollywood-fostered expectation that film is simply the art of manipulating time (in which the underlying principle is the combination of logic and surprise and a key element is the creation of suspense). We must turn our attention as well to questions of spatial division, spatial organization, and spatial conflict. If we look for suspense, *Halfaouine* is bound to disappoint: it follows a totally predictable pattern, moving gently from the initial arousal of sexual interest to the gratification of desire with the body of a beautiful, submissive young girl. A spatial approach is more fruitful, and here we shall be looking at just one element of this: space as it concerns the protagonist.[17] Boughedir himself has defined *Halfaouine* as a world "seen through the eyes of a child trying to find his way in an adult world, within a conservative society where strict separation of the sexes rules."[18] The child protagonist Noura's status as half-child, half-adult male is crucial to the organization of the dramatic action, since he thereby inhabits two spaces. He is young enough (or at least small enough) to be still treated by his mother as a child and hence inhabits both the

Fig. 26. *Halfaouine* (1990), Ferid Boughedir, Tunisia

female domestic space at home and—despite the growing suspicions of the bathhouse keepers—the sole female semi-public space, the *hammam*. But at the same time he is free to inhabit the public (male) space of streets and roof-tops to meet his older friends, Moncef and Mounir, and his mentor, Salih. This freedom is denied to the women of the household, who leave the domestic interior only in groups—to go to the *hammam* or "for an injection."

For Michel Serceau, *Halfaouine* is "perhaps at one and the same time the most mature and intelligent of Maghrebian films,"[19] as well as "one of the Maghrebian films, if not *the* film, which deals most not only with women's bodies, but also with the vision and fantasies of the body, in both sexes."[20] Serceau argues that the rare comedies made in the Maghreb advance the cause of women (as well as *Halfaouine,* he cites *Omar Gatlato, Looking for My Wife's Husband,* and Farida Benlyazid's *Women's Wiles*), noting that "Maghrebian cinema has perhaps never spoken about women as well as in these comedies which deal with men's immaturity."[21] The central paradox of Noura's life, as Denise Brahimi has observed, lies in the fact that "on the one hand everything and everyone around him reflects to him this obsession, because he lives in a world where sexuality is omnipresent and exhibited, while on the other hand this sexuality is held out of reach by a system of complex and perverse taboos."[22] *Halfaouine's* particular concern with nudity has to be seen in the context of Arab culture and the history of Arab film making. As is evidenced by the institution of the veil, the look has a particular force in Arab society; indeed the theologian Al-Ghazali has stated: "To look at anyone else's wife is a sinful act. . . . The look is fornication of the eye."[23] Afsanej Najmabadi links the gaze with the movement from the women's world of childhood to the male, adult world:

> The experience of expulsion from the world of women is above all an experience of a lost sight, lost vision. Having entered the world of men, the boy's gaze becomes subjected to *ahkam-i nigah,* rules of looking. . . . Sighting itself is thought of as magically powerful and hazardous.[24]

Hence Boughedir's notion of centering his film on expulsion from the *hammam* could not be more apt.

Within the context of the Arab cinema in which Boughedir was working, nudity had been virtually non-existent before the 1990s, aside from rare exceptions by European-trained directors, such as the Palestinian Michel Khleifi's *Wedding in Galilee* (1987) and Bouzid's *Golden Horseshoes* (1989). Indeed, writing in 1987, the former editor of the Algerian film review *Les Deux Ecrans,* Abdou B., was scathing about the self-censorship customarily practiced by Arab filmmakers whose works, he claimed, showed an "exemplary chastity."[25] *Halfaouine* was passed by the Tunisian censors but provoked, according to Boughedir,[26] a five-day debate in the Tunisian National Assembly led by deputies who wished to ban the film. This action no doubt helped make the film the greatest box office hit in Tunisian film history, with five hundred thousand admissions in a country of just eight and a half million people.

Ejection from the *Hammam*

The women's *hammam* experienced during their childhood figures largely in the imagination of many Arab men.[27] When, in the pre-credit sequence of *Halfaouine,* we see the protagonist, Noura, in the *hammam* with the women of his family, he seems a child like any other. Later, as he listens to his mother's tales of ogres eating little boys, we can again see he is still very much a child. But when we meet him with his older friends, Moncef and Mounir, we can see that he is also already beginning to share their obsession: what do the girls who pass veiled on the street look like naked? As the film's protagonist, Noura will act to resolve the ultimate mystery—what a woman's body is like—and this forms the shaping action of the film. The importance of this action, as the film's co-scriptwriter Nouri Bouzid notes, is that in Arab culture "a boy becomes a man when he has discovered the female body."[28]

There are two further visits by Noura to the women's *hammam*, placed respectively one-third and two-thirds of the way through the film. During the first visit, he looks with new eyes at the half-naked girls, whose breasts he subsequently describes—in terms of melons and pears—to Moncef and Mounir. During the second, on the day before the party to celebrate the circumcision ceremony for his baby brother, he shows far too much active interest in how women are below the waist and is caught spying. His expulsion from his childhood paradise is a scandal for the family.

The film, which seems to be set during the rule of Tunisia's first post-independence ruler, Habib Bourguiba (that is, before 1987), paints a vivid picture of life in the Halfaouine district of Tunis. The full title of the film is *Halfaouine—L'enfant des terrasses* and, as Martin Stollery notes, "The sparrow-like rooftop-hopping of *Hafaouine*'s adolescent protagonist and his role as errand boy for various people within the community enable him and the film's spectator to observe gaps in the gendered spatial divisions ostensibly regulating the neighbourhood he inhabits."[29]

There is rising tension between the population and the police, with increased bursts of violence (there is even a brief reference to "Youssef Soltane," the political activist hero of co-scriptwriter Bouzid's *Golden Horseshoes*). Noura's idol is the shoemaker-cum-poet Salih, a drinker and womanizer, who foresees the film's ending when he tells Noura that "women know what they want and decide where and when." At home too, where Noura's father Si Azzouz rules severely, the tensions rise with the arrival of his mother's cousin, the newly divorced Latifa, who both provokes and challenges the men (including Noura's father) with her liberated dress and behavior. Noura steals her bra for Mounir (who complains it has been washed) and her chewed gum for Salih. Leïla, a young orphan a little older than Noura, is taken into the family as a servant. This is supposed to be an act of charity, but she is harshly treated by Noura's mother and denied access to the *hammam*.

Restaging the *Hammam*

Noura has a sad time at the circumcision ceremony and hides from the family. Leïla is sent to look for him but does not betray his whereabouts when she finds him. Meanwhile, despite his absence, the party goes well, though Moncef and Mounir are ejected because of their behavior toward the young girls present. Everyone is dressed in their best clothes—often traditional robes—and when Salih sings a sad love song and is applauded by the men, Latifa responds from the women's side of the curtain, mocking him. As Lieve Spaas observes,

"A powerful sexual atmosphere pervades the strongly segregated male and female societies. In both, songs and jokes are imbued with eroticism and sexual innuendo."[30] Later Noura goes out on his own to Salih's shop, where he witnesses the seduction of Latifa, who protests verbally but shows by her actions that she intends to stay.

This seduction provides the model for Noura's behavior toward Leïla. On his return home, when he finds Leïla sleeping on the patio with his aunt Salouha, he tries to unbutton her nightdress, but she turns away in her sleep. Next morning Noura finds Salih and Latifa together again, joking about Salih's pretended inability to make wedding slippers, and then revisits the women's *hammam*, where he remembers his times there and also his mother's tales of ogres. On his return at night he finds Leïla's necklace under his pillow and visits her in her room. He strokes her bare breast as she sleeps but has to leave quickly when his father comes down the corridor. Salih, who had previously protested publicly at the closure of the shop of his friend Ali, who has been arrested, gets drunk and draws an anti-government slogan on the wall. Next morning he is arrested, jokingly asking Noura to tell Latifa that the wedding will have to be postponed. Unwilling to take Noura to the *hammam*, his mother tells Leïla to wash his hair, which she does in a position—squatting behind him on the floor—that echoes the mother's position in the *hammam* during the pre-credit sequence. Noura uses the situation, and his knowledge of the *hammam*, to persuade Leïla to take off her wet clothes, promising to show her how the women behave together in the *hammam*. He gets her to strip to the waist, but his attempts to undress her completely are thwarted by the return of the women from the baths. Leïla, in disgrace, is told she must leave in the morning. But that night, when he goes back to his room, Noura finds Leïla naked in his bed, waiting for him. Next morning, when Leïla leaves, the pair exchange smiles. Then Noura leaps off across the free spaces of the terraces and rooftops, defying his father, but at the same time leaving behind forever the childish pampered comfort of the women's world of shared intimacy.

Halfaouine is fresh, funny, and inventive. Boughedir claims that the film is autobiographical, in the literal sense that it is "very largely inspired by events I personally experienced as a child in Halfaouine, the old popular district of Tunis."[31] But there is also another autobiographical thread. As the film's co-scriptwriter Bouzid has observed, Boughedir "celebrates the act of becoming a man in discovering the female body. It's interesting, you could almost say that about cinema. Cinema is the art of discovering and seeing; this can be an aim in itself, and it's Ferid's cinema."[32]

In *Halfaouine*, in the four successive scenes that have the space of the *hammam* (or its reconstruction) as their setting, we have a metaphor for the birth of a filmmaker: moving from a childishly indifferent gaze, to a more focused look, on to spying (looking—or trying to look—without being seen), and then finally to a restaging (with suitable props) of the paradisical space of the *hammam* from which Noura has been expelled. The film shows us at the end a young

Fig. 27. *Halfaouine* (1990), Ferid Boughedir, Tunisia

man freed from the tyranny of his father and the oppression of the family. Noura has triumphed over the barriers which have constrained him as a child. As Houria Zourgane puts it, Boughedir "gives painless birth to our collective unconsciousness" and offers a portrait of "the Arab man, with his wounds, his frustrations and his desires."[33]

Why then is this ending not wholly satisfying? The reason, I think, is that the film, having depicted its world of gendered spaces so well, ultimately avoids the full implications of growing up in a society where the sexes are segregated. As Tahar Chikhaoui puts it, "For a film about the awakening of desire, *Halfaouine* lacks weight, lacks what is destructive and regenerative in desire, death, life, what is at work in this society."[34] In such a reading, *Halfaouine* is not a tale of young love, the story of the youthful discovery of bodies and the mutual plea- sure they can give. Rather it is a tale of seduction. Noura's hero outside the family is the shoemaker Salih, an old drunkard and womanizer, who lives alone with a caged bird. He eventually sees the old man's political views lead to the wrath of the authorities, but not before he has listened to Salih's songs and fol- lowed at firsthand his elaborate games of seduction with Latifa. Just as the influ- ence of his older friends, Moncef and Mounir, prompted Noura to look at the young women in the bathhouse in a new way, so too Salih's lessons in seduction become the model for his own sexual initiation. The strategy of seduction is, as Mernissi notes, a direct and inevitable consequence of the social systems of sexual separation and seclusion.[35] Boughedir, who has depicted the social situation of segregation so vividly throughout the film, shows himself, at the end, to be complicit with the power imbalance that underlies it and with the distortions of sexual relationships it brings about. Noura embarks on his plan of seduction, using his childish knowledge of the *hammam*, from which Leïla, as a servant, is excluded, as his way of making his intentions clear. But seduction, as Mernissi notes, is "a way of seeming to give yourself and of procuring great pleasure without actually giving anything."[36] Noura takes, but gives nothing in return. To quote Mernissi for one last time: "It is very rare that an individual who has invested years in learning the art of seduction as a mode of interchange can suddenly open up and lavish all his (or her) 'emotional treasures' on the person he has finally chosen to love."[37]

Noura's liberation at the end of the film, when he defies the authority of his father and leaps over the rooftops, constitutes a dubious freedom, having been achieved at the expense of someone for whose fate he shows no concern. One questions the maturity Boughedir implies he has achieved and queries what will become of him—after this beginning—as a male in a divided society. The original (unpublished) script is more realistic. After he is denied the ability to re-create the *hammam* at home, Noura's older friends, Moncef and Mounir, take him to a brothel, where he gets his answer. A whore (who, the script tells us, could be Leïla, but older) loosens her robe and opens her legs. Unable to cope with what he sees, Noura runs away. . . . The film as it stands lacks this edge. It is, in the end, a lyrical piece of wish fulfillment which consciously and skillfully avoids any depiction of the pain of adolescence, either for Noura or for the young servant girl he eventually sleeps with. It remains caught within the power structure underlying the separation of male and female space in Arab culture. This is a tale of power, not love, of exploitation, not initiation.

13 A Timeless World: *Looking for My Wife's Husband* (1993)

In *The Wretched of the Earth* Frantz Fanon draws a vivid picture of two contrasting urban spaces in the colonized world, between which, in his view, "no conciliation is possible":

> The settler's town is a strongly-built town, all made of stone and steel. It is a brightly-lit town; the streets are covered with asphalt, and the garbage-cans swallow all the leavings, unseen, unknown and hardly thought about. . . . The town belonging to the colonized people, or at least the native town, the Negro village, the medina, the reservation, is a place of ill fame, peopled by men of ill repute. They are born there, it matters little where or how; they die there, it matters little where or how.[1]

But at least since independence, the medinas of the principal cities of Tunisia and Morocco (such as Tunis, Marrakesh, or Fez) have shown a considerable resilience and durability, even if they are now threatened by deterioration and decay. In Maghrebian films they tend to be depicted as spaces complementary—not inferior—to the modern urban quarters of the town. But their lack of all markings of modernity (except for satellite dishes on the roofs)—the absence of cars, street furniture, public buildings, modern department stores, and so forth—means that they constitute a very distinctive space in film narrative: the site of memory and myth, tradition and nostalgia, essentially a timeless world.

The medina figures strongly in Tunisian cinema, appearing, as Kamel Ben Ouanès notes, "as an inescapable 'ritual' passage and a hermeneutic instrument, leading to an exploration, sometimes of the nostalgic past, sometimes of the disenchanted present."[2] In treating this subject, the cinema "transforms memory into a mirror and the vague impression of a relationship of emotion or identity into an iconographic expression, submitted to the curiosity—or perhaps the examination—of the spectator."[3] The medina forms, for example, the perfect labyrinth for Youssef's nocturnal quest for identity with Sghaier in Bouzid's *Golden Horseshoes.* It is also one of the contrasting but contiguous worlds (of tourist sites and domestic interiors) which, in the same director's *Bezness,* combine to provide a perfect symbol for the inner conflict of the film's protagonist, Raouf, who sells himself to the tourists (both men and women) in the public spaces of hotels and bars, while maintaining a rigidly macho stance vis-à-vis his sister and fiancée in the domestic space of the medina. The opening shots of the film say it all: during the credits the European photographer Fred is lost in the narrow, labyrinthine streets of the medina, but as he emerges, the film cuts directly to a young woman stripping to her bikini on the beach, and a few shots later Fred captures the classic Maghrebian image of a topless tourist and a Tunisian woman totally clad from head to foot (like an early Victorian bather) emerging side by side from the waves.

In contrast, films set wholly in the medina, such as Ferid Boughedir's *Halfaouine* and Moncef Dhouib's first feature, *The Sultan of the Medina* (1993), tend to be timeless works which cannot be dated with any confidence (as Tahar Chikhaoui asked in his review of *Halfaouine*: "At what precise moment is this film set?"[4]). Dhouib's film centers on an old crumbling home in the medina, haunted by genies and totally dominated by men, though the abode of women, and hence of charms, superstitions, and poems. The action brings together the innocent virgin Ramla and Fraj, the "holy fool," who is able to move through the male world but also enter the women's world. But he can do this latter only naked like a small child, to be used by women seeking cures and spells. The medina here is a world of cruelty (toward the weak) and violence (toward women). Fraj tries to help Ramla to fulfill her dream of escape but draws back at the sight of the modern world outside. Ramla, alone and unprotected, is raped and destroyed by a gang of criminals. In this tale of isolation and imprisonment, the only touch of modernity is the old man who lives in the cellar and makes his living by painting out the nipples on posters for imported films.

Perhaps this sense of tradition and modernity existing side by side, or of time standing still, has prompted Tunisian filmmakers to play seemingly illogical games with time and duration in some of their film narratives. Boughedir's second feature, *One Summer at La Goulette,* is explicitly set in the summer of 1966, but contains several scenes featuring the return to her native Tunis of Claudia Cardinale, a 58 year old when the film was shot in 1995, who would have been in her late twenties and in her prime as a world star in 1966. Similarly, Moufida Tlatli's second feature, *The Men's Season,* covers a twenty-year time span within a family and, while employing different actors to play the young people as children and as adolescents, uses the same players to portray the couple both on their wedding day and in the film's present, twenty years later. Equally disconcerting, in this sense, is Mohamed Abderrahman Tazi's Moroccan feature *Looking for My Wife's Husband,* which combines, without an apparent sense of incongruity, meticulously reconstructed interiors and medina scenes set in Fez in the 1950s with shots elsewhere reflecting how the city outside the medina looks at the time of shooting (in 1993).

Looking for My Wife's Husband

Tazi approaches time in a way that he recognizes is not Western: "Here, in an Arab-Muslim society, we have a different approach to time, we don't calculate it in the same way."[5] The double framework which he uses in *Looking for My Wife's Husband* is in part autobiographical in origin: "When I go into the Fez medina I'm taken out of the present, out of the period in which I normally live."[6] This is clear too when he explains why he has situated the film in "a time-

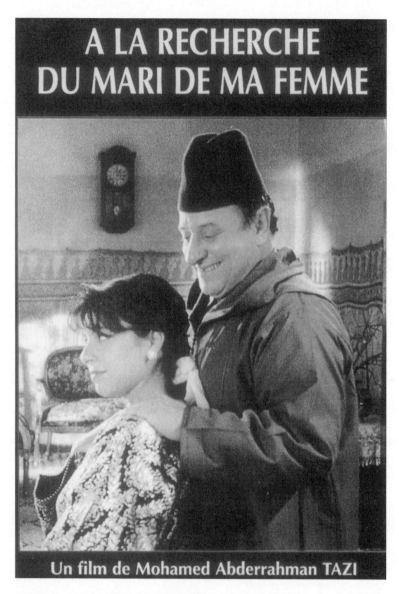

Fig. 28. *Looking for My Wife's Husband* (1993), Mohamed Abderrahman Tazi, Morocco

less space-time": "When you are inside the walls, in the medina, you can imagine we are in the 1950s. . . . But when you pass to the other side of the walls, you are squarely in 1993."[7]

For Tazi, it is important "to highlight the fact that Morocco lives at two different speeds. There are those who, like the weavers, the tanners, and so on, live at the speed of traditional Morocco; then there are those who live the rhythm of modern life."[8] For him his "atemporality" has a critical function:

> "Atemporality" means taking something that is happening today and situating it in a rather timeless period, allowing you to be critical but not in too obvious a way. In fact, that's one of the best ways to be socially critical—to adopt some historical distance with regard to the present.[9]

Tazi claims that as well as distancing the present, this technique also throws the past into a new perspective: "In the film, when we are within the city walls, we are in another time, a kind of indeterminate era. That's what I am evoking, the sort of internal beauty of Fez."[10] For the director, the difference between the beginning and end of the film is crucial:

> We created atemporality at the outset with the photo of Mohamed V but at the end of the film, when we raise the problem of clandestine immigration, we're right in the present. Public awareness of this problem really had to be sharpened.[11]

The reason why Tazi's atemporality causes few problems for the spectator (except perhaps with regard to the film's ending) is his belief in narrative simplicity:

> As far as narration is concerned, I don't think it's appropriate for Moroccan films to narrate in the style of Bergman or Antonioni. I think simplicity is primary—we don't need to create a complicated scheme in order to construct a narrative. We need a linearity in narration, in telling the story.[12]

And again:

> I think "plot" is something of a Western notion. . . . My main concern is to capture and carry the spectator along; the plot or suspense is secondary, as is the element of the unexpected—I think the unexpected is minimal in my stories.[13]

In addition to its treatment of time, *Looking for My Wife's Husband* is also notable for being a comedy. Comedies are rare in Maghrebian cinema, but it is remarkable that three of the greatest box office hits with local audiences and the most successful exports in the history of Maghrebian cinema have been comedies: *Omar Gatlato* in Algeria, *Halfaouine* in Tunisia, and *Looking for My Wife's Husband* in Morocco. All three also are concerned with aspects of male sexual identity, dealing with immature, adolescent, and inadequate males, respectively. Of the three, Tazi's film was by far the most successful commercially in Maghrebian terms and, with something like one million tickets sold in Morocco alone (twice as many as its nearest competitor), it can claim to be the most popular film ever in the Maghreb. Tazi's previous two features, *The Big Trip* and *Badis,* had both been serious dramas ending in disaster for their protagonists, yet the choice of comedy here was, Tazi tells us, far from deliberate:

> I didn't say to myself, "I'm going to make a comic film. I'm going to get people to laugh." No. I said, "I'm going to tell a story that really touches me." . . . This gave me the pretext I wanted, to show my native soil, my native city of Fez, in a way different from the way it has been shown in foreign productions.[14]

Polygamy in an Idyllic World

Considering Tazi's film from an outsider's perspective, one would never think that, in Morocco in the mid-1990s, polygamy and repudiation were the subject of concern for both a national council for the participation of women in political life and a national council for the reform of the law concerning personal rights (*moudawana*) and resulted in "tumultuous debates between fundamentalists and modernists."[15] Tazi's view of the institution of polygamy in *Looking for My Wife's Husband* is basically lyrical. The portrait of a polygamous household reflects his personal experience, in that his grandfather was polygamous and his father had two wives.[16] Like so many Maghrebian men of his generation (Boughedir, for example), he has a real nostalgia for the experience of growing up in an extended family where "the children grew up with the women and the female servants, in this communication which exists between them and the mothers, the concubines."[17] But though the real issues of polygamy are barely touched upon in the film, the choice of this issue as the film's subject is as appropriate as the medina setting, as Abderrahmane Koudjil's account of polygamy in the Maghreb makes clear:

> The problematic of polygamy in the Maghrebian context is very complex. This act is marked, on the one hand, by ancestral traditions and customs and, on the other, by the superimposing of two laws: Muslim law and the positive law inherited from the French juridical system. This recurring dialectic between tradition and modernity, the particular and the universal, links with another dialectic, that between human rights and cultural diversity.[18]

The house in which much of the action of *Looking for My Wife's Husband* occurs, with its traditional layout of separate apartments leading off a central courtyard and its exquisite mosaic tiling, has been lovingly furnished by Tazi to capture a sense of the 1950s (the time of his own childhood). The household of the protagonist, Hadj Ben Moussa (played with enormous comic gusto by Bachir Skiredj), is initially depicted as an idyllic world. The three wives each have their own specific roles—Lalla Hobby as the mother figure, Lalla Rabea as the child rearer, and Houda as the young (childless) mistress figure—and there is no jealousy between them. Lalla Hobby's position as head of the household is fully accepted by the others, and there is real love between Houda and Lalla Rabea's children, whom she willingly looks after. When Lalla Hobby emerges unscathed when a wardrobe falls on top of her, the wives and servants celebrate with an informal party and agree on the preparations for the circumcision celebration for Lalla Rabea's youngest son, with Lalla Hobby providing the robe she had acquired long ago for the son she never had.

Though Lalla Hobby's daughter Miriam is a doctor, married to a busy businessman, residing and leading an active life outside the medina, there is no tension between the generations and no hint of criticism or even disapproval of the father's way of life—a situation very different to that depicted in Ousmane

Sembene's study of polygamy, *Xala*. The young wife Houda has a remarkably realistic approach to her situation. We learn that she first met the Hadj when she went with her mother so sell the latter's bracelet, and she openly treats the marriage as a financial arrangement, urging the Hadj to give her more valuable jewelry, to match that of her co-wives. Demanding a gold bracelet, she asks openly, "Otherwise, what's the use of being married to a jeweller?" For the Hadj, serious jewelry has to wait until she has had a child, but she has already shown herself aware of the problems this implies, namely that "the children of an old man will soon be orphans." She keeps strictly to the rules of a polygamous household. Though very aware of how much the Hadj is attracted to her, she sends him off when he visits her on one of Lalla Rabea's nights. At the same time, she is attracted by the idea of romantic love. We first see her (in the pre-credit sequence) hanging out washing on the balcony and mildly flirting with a man. She and her widowed friend Khadija eye the passing men from a balcony window, assessing their physical qualities. She dreams of being visited by a prince who recites traditional love poetry (from *Layla majnun*) and envies Khadija's freedom. But it is clear that she has little awareness of life outside the family (her own home or the Hadj's).

The idyll is shattered when Houda innocently opens the door (the servants are busy upstairs) and is greeted by the man delivering the sheep which the Hadj has purchased for the *Aïd* ceremony. Hadj returns to find her framed in the doorway, wearing her indoor clothes, and is outraged. He accuses her of being naked, which seems comically odd to a Western viewer, though Fatima Mernissi tells us that "the Moroccan term for a woman who is not veiled is *aryana* ('nude')."[19] Totally beside himself, he calls her every name he can think of—shameless, provocative, and a bitch—and is totally hurt (and no doubt astonished) when she reacts by deriding him as an old moaner. His response is to divorce her on the spot, as is his right under Moroccan law. As Mernissi notes, in the Muslim institution of verbal repudiation, the characteristic is

> the unconditional right of the male to break the marriage bond without any justification, and without having his decision reviewed by a court or a judge. In reenacting the seventh-century institution, the Moroccan Code limits the judge's role simply to registering the husband's decision.[20]

The Third Renunciation

The opening third of the film, which was scripted by Tazi's fellow filmmaker Farida Benlyazid (who had earlier scripted his second feature, *Badis*), with dialogue by Ahmed Taïeb El Alj (who plays Hadj's mocking neighbor in the *souk*), is well scripted, setting out the context clearly and building up neatly well to its comic climax, the confrontation of the Hadj and Houda. The contrasting characters are well drawn and the strength of the women, in a situation which might be seen simply as male domination, is nicely conveyed. The middle portion of the film is equally effective, intercutting short scenes of the Hadj in his medina world realizing the implications of what he has done and of Houda sampling the supposed joys of freedom in modern Moroccan society.

Houda's departure from the Hadj's house is carefree (after all, this is the third time he has repudiated her) and she even does a little comic impersonation of the Hadj in anger. After the co-wives and children have all promised to visit her, she sets off with her cart full of belongings back to her mother's house, where she has already booked her room. Declaring that she has no intention of moping between four walls, she immediately sets off to visit her friend Khadija. As she and Khadija go shopping for clothes and she has her hair cut short in Western style, her mother becomes more and more upset by her behavior, particularly when she appears in a miniskirt. Assuring her worried mother that she is not pregnant by the Hadj, she shows her lack of resentment of him, describing him as generous and as having a good heart.

Meanwhile the Hadj finds his house bleak and empty without Houda's laughter and singing. The children sulk and the co-wives are silent. The Hadj reacts badly, complaining about the food and dragging his elder son off to the Koranic school as a punishment (one which Tazi himself experienced).[21] Now he comes to experience one of the characteristics of polygamy noted by a Western psychologist, namely that "polygamy has a general 'lowering effect' on the emotional importance of the husband-wife bond and that this applies to the wife as well as to the husband. She also invests less in her husband and invests more in other relationships."[22] At this point in the film the bond between the co-wives becomes very clear. Neither wants him in her bed, so he has to drink and sleep alone in Houda's old room. Both threaten to leave him and cause a scandal if he takes a new wife, so there is only one path open to him: to take back Houda. If we ask why he has to go to whatever extremes are required to remarry Houda (rather than just take her back and continue his relationship with her as before), we have to understand that in Muslim society repudiation is a social, familial act:

> Repudiation is not only a trap for the man and the woman, it also morally binds all members of the family, who feel uncomfortable when they have witnessed a verbal repudiation. If the man does not perform the legal remarriage, they feel they are living with fornicators who are committing *zina*.[23]

Elsewhere Mernissi defines *zina* as "illicit copulation."[24]

The Awful Truth

Urged by his mocking neighbor in the *souk,* the Hadj visits a lawyer to find out what is necessary if he is to remarry Houda after repudiating her three times. The answer is that under Islamic law, Houda must have remarried and been divorced. The marriage need only have lasted one night, but it must have been consummated. Kevin Dwyer notes that this process "is commonly seen as a way to punish a man who has lost self-control and behaved whimsically in a matter as serious as marriage and divorce. Of both these offences the Hadj is certainly guilty."[25] From this point onward the humiliation of the Hadj grows ever greater, as he becomes increasingly a figure of fun in the medina. His wives choose someone they think will be suitable, the local "idiot," who seems to like the idea but whose upper-class mother refuses on the grounds that such an action would ruin the family's reputation. The mother, incidentally, is played by Fatima Mernissi, the noted Moroccan sociologist whose book *Beyond the Veil: Male-Female Dynamics in a Muslim Society* (1985) offers many insights into the issues of polygamy and repudiation treated in the film and which has been regularly cited here. Miriam also tries without success, and the local butcher and baker each take the opportunity to poke fun at the Hadj. Finally the local tailor finds him a suitable husband, a migrant worker who has come briefly for a family visit before returning to Belgium.

Meanwhile Houda has found the limits to a woman's freedom in modern Morocco. Out with Khadija at a café recommended by Miriam, she encourages the attentions of two young men. When they agree to go with the men for a ride in their car, they discover that the men expect sex as well as conversation. Abandoned when they refuse, they have to walk back home, provoking other men to stop and talk to them, assuming they are whores. Perhaps for this reason, Houda agrees to go along with the Hadj's scheme, and we next see her sitting on the wedding bed, waiting for a new husband she has never met (the normal situation, of course, for a traditional Moroccan bride). The film's focus, however, is not on her wedding night but on the Hadj's experience of it: he sits on Houda's old bed, shouting and crying, to be comforted by Lalla Hobby and mocked by Lalla Rabea. His all-night agony is increased when he goes next morning to reclaim Houda and finds that no one will answer the door. Then, days later, he discovers the truth: the husband, Mustapha, has had to flee back to Belgium, because the police have found that the Mercedes he sold on his return was stolen. He has promised to return, but when?

Up to this point *Looking for My Wife's Husband* has been unequivocally a comedy. The opening scenes skillfully built up our sense of a pompous and self-important figure ripe for a fall. Though some of the film's humor may grate for a Western audience (the scenes making fun of the local "idiot" and Houda's incontinent, bedridden father, for instance), the central figure of Hadj Ben Moussa is a richly comic figure, whose increasing discomfiture can only provoke laughter. Similarly the double timescale has been lightly handled, with no real clash of generations or between life inside and outside the medina. There has been no real attack on the patriarchal system or on the practice of polygamy. But the film's conclusion plunges us totally into the harsh immediacy of 1993. Seeking a visa for Belgium, the Hadj has the (for him) humiliating experience of standing for hours in a queue. When, finally, he is confronted by an official and asked his reasons for wanting to visit Belgium, he can only mumble "I'm going to look for my wife's husband. The wretch." Just as Houda showed herself unequipped to deal with life as a modern liberated woman, so too the Hadj is clearly ill prepared to be a migrant.

Fig. 29. *Looking for My Wife's Husband* (1993), Mohamed Abderrahman Tazi, Morocco

In a closing scene which was not in Benlyazid's script and was not disclosed to the cast before shooting, we get our last glimpse of the Hadj, boarding one of the frail little open motor boats which constantly take out would-be migrants. When one knows the statistics for the possible survival of such illegal migrants, laughter is no longer an option. The change of tone is a deliberate move by Tazi, whose three other films all confront serious social issues. In 1993 what concerned him most was illegal immigration, an issue ignored by the government-controlled media in Morocco. From what might be regarded as a loving, even self-indulgent recreation of a dream world of childhood, Tazi has shifted in a tiny scene (just nine shots and a fade to black before the end credits) to a virtually improvised documentary image of contemporary reality. As he himself has noted, "Some of the extras I used had actually tried to emigrate once or even several times, and they all assured me that the next time they had opportunity, they would try to do so again."[26] Though disconcerting for the spectator, this sudden change of mood fits totally with Tazi's view of Moroccan society, not as something with its own clear specificity but as a mosaic of many cultures and peoples and of differing but co-existing levels of time.[27]

14 A New Future Begins:
Silences of the Palace (1994)

Though Tunisia is the smallest of the three Maghrebian cinemas (fewest films, directors, and film theatres), it has the largest number of women directors. The reasons for this undoubtedly lie in the 1956 post-independence law (strengthened further in 1993) giving women social status unprecedented in the Arabo-Muslim world: establishing the equality in law between men and women, abolishing polygamy and religious divorce (based on simple repudiation), setting a minimum age of 17 for marriage, and establishing a mother's custody of her children in the case of the husband's death. Six Tunisian women directors, all but one educated at film schools in Europe, have produced eight feature films in the course of twenty-four years. Four of these—Selma Baccar, Nejia Ben Mabrouk, Moufida Tlatli, and Kalthoum Bornaz—belong to the generation born in the 1940s, which dominates Maghrebian cinema, while Nadia El Fani was born in 1960. Raja Amari (born in 1971) is the youngest of the new generation of filmmakers which has made its presence felt since the very end of the 1990s. In addition there are two female "outsiders"—Najwa Tlili, the Tunisian-born director of *Rupture* (1998), who lives and works in Canada, and the Swiss-based Nadia Fares, who shot *Miel et cendres* (*Honey and Ashes*) in Tunisia in 1996. Abdelkrim Gabous, who lists thirty female technicians,[1] notes that the paucity of production means that "no Tunisian woman director is able to live from directing. If she is not an editor or producer, she has a job outside the cinema or lives on her husband's income."[2]

What is remarkable about all these films is that, while recognizing the difficulties women face in the Arab world, they refuse to turn their protagonists into passive, helpless victims. The pattern is set by Baccar's *Fatma 75* (1978), which mixes documentary and fiction to evoke the history of Tunisian women from Carthage to the present, in order to "help open a dialogue between women and give women subjects for discussion."[3] Ten years later Ben Mabrouk was able to show *The Trace* (1982–1988), which shows a young working-class girl's successful struggle to obtain a university education. In the 1990s Tlatli made *Silences of the Palace* (1994); Baccar completed a second feature, *The Fire Dance* (1995), on the life of the singer Habiba M'sika, who shocked 1920s male audiences; and Bornaz completed *Keswa* (1997), a humorous look at contemporary Tunis centered on a wedding ceremony as seen through the eyes of woman returning from Europe. The 2000s have seen Tlatli's second feature, *The Men's Season* (2000), El Fani's *Bedwin Hacker* (2002), and Amari's debut film, *Red Satin* (2002). In two key ways these films confront the customary pattern of Maghrebian cinema.

Here the trajectories of the protagonists are not the customary therapeutic journeys to the South but a visit to Europe (*The Fire Dance*) or an intrusion into European media (*Bedwin Hacker*), a questioning return to the family (*Keswa*) or a positive movement towards Tunis in pursuit of education (*The Trace*) or career (*The Men's Season*). There is also a concern with positive women characters who refuse to be beaten, such as Sabra in *The Trace*, Aïcha in *The Men's Season*, Kalt in *Bedwin Hacker*, or, in comic mode, Nozha in *Keswa*. This is reinforced by the interest in women who brave the male world by appearing as performers: Habiba M'sika and also Khedija and Alia in *Silences of the Palace* and Lilia in *Red Satin*. As Tlatli notes, "A woman artist has difficulty in finding her place in our society."[4] The concern to address and involve the female spectator is never allowed to obscure an appeal to a wider audience.

Moufida Tlatli

Moufida Tlatli is very much in the mainstream of Maghrebian film making in that she studied at IDHEC in Paris, where she subsequently worked for four years in production roles for the Office de Radiodiffusion et deTélévision Française (ORTF). What is unique about her—and contributes so much to the quality of her films—is her experience as a film editor on some eighteen feature films made between 1974 and 1992, during which time she established her reputation as one of the Arab world's leading film editors. The Tunisian directors with whom she worked include many major figures, such Abdellatif Ben Ammar (*Sejnane* and *Aziza*), Taïeb Louhichi (*The Shadow of the Earth* and *Leïla My Reason*), Mahmoud Ben Mahmoud (*Crossing Over*), Ferid Boughedir (*Halfaouine*), Nacer Khemir (*The Searchers of the Desert*), and two female colleagues, Baccar (*Fatma 75*) and Ben Mabrouk (*The Trace*). In addition she has worked with other leading Arab filmmakers: the Algerians Merzak Allouache (*Omar Gatlato*) and Farouk Beloufa (*Nahla*), the Palestinian Michel Khleifi (*La mémoire fertile/Fertile Memory*) and the Moroccan woman director Farida Benlyazid (*Gateway to Heaven*).

Both Tlatli's films have a broad scope, following the problems, and also the reticences, of women through from one generation to the next. As she said of *Silences of the Palace*, "To understand the silences which surround us in our everyday life, I wanted to go back in time and find the distant causes, the origin."[5] She does not see herself as being in any way a militant feminist, but both her features fit her description of her first feature as "a testimony, a cry, a woman's work for women, whether they are Tunisian or not. . . . We must change and shake up mentalities. From my position as film maker, I try to do that."[6]

The Film: *Silences of the Palace*

Silences of the Palace has a personal motivation. It was, Tlatli tells us, "born out of absolute necessity," when a sudden and serious illness of her mother made her realize that she knew very little about her: "Like many people

Fig. 30. *Silences of the Palace* (1994), Moufida Tlatli, Tunisia

of her generation, she didn't talk about herself, her past, her ordeals and the constraints linked with her being a woman."[7] It was also made in relation to her own daughter, who "lives in a modern Tunisia but where the burdens of tradition continue to play very important political, social, family and religious roles."[8] Like many of the key films of Tunisian cinema of the late 1980s and 1990s, works such as Nouri Bouzid's *Man of Ashes* (1984) or Boughedir's *Halfaouine* (1990), *Silences of the Palace* is a deeply felt look at the past while not being directly autobiographical.

There are two keys to an understanding of how *Silences of the Palace* works. The first is the concept of melodrama. Tlatli has spoken of recent Tunisian cinema as being characterized by a return to the melodrama, "but in a more nuanced manner," admitting a debt to the Egyptian cinema of the 1950s—no doubt thinking of the work at this period of Youssef Chahine and Salah Abou Seif—which she describes as "a cinema of excess."[9] Certainly *Silences of the Palace* has many characteristic features of the genre: the importance of music throughout the film, the sudden and unexpected appearance of Khedija as an oriental dancer, the sudden shifts of mood (Khedija is dreamily happy with Sid Ali and brutally raped by his brother on the very same day), the explicit threat from upstairs to Alia's virginity as a constant source of anxiety for the audience, the coincidence of Alia's revolt and her mother Khedija's death from a failed abortion attempt which forms the film's climax.

Melodrama is about playing with temporality and audience expectation. A second key is the spatial organization of the dramatic action. Ostensibly the film is about past and present: the Tunisia of the beys and the modern Tunisia of today (or at least the 1960s). But the spatial differentiations are equally important for an understanding of the film. As Dinah Manisty notes,

> The notion of space is taken far beyond that of transcending the private world of women to the public and sacred domain of men. Increasingly we observe that space enters a metaphorical domain in which the journey and the struggle involve creating increasingly complex narrative strategies to express the need for psychological space.[10]

The boundaries dividing space express, moreover, in Fatima Mernissi's phrase, "the recognition of power in one part at the expense of the other."[11] This is certainly true of *Silences of the Palace*. Sid Ali descends to the kitchen only to demand services, "Bring us some refreshment upstairs," and his wife, Jneina, comes only to give orders: "This soup is too salty for Sid Ali. . . . Don't just sit there, go and lay the table upstairs." In *Silences of the Palace*—as so often in African (including Maghrebian) cinema—we can talk meaningfully of a "spatialization of narrative."

Spaces of the Palace

The climax of *Silences of the Palace* is so powerful because it brings together in a vividly edited sequence the parallel and contrasting fates of the film's two protagonists. Their lives, together with the film's double time scheme as Alia visits the scene of her childhood ten years after, set up the binary contrasts that help to shape the film's narrative. But equally important is the binary organization of space: the climax is also the film's most brutal depiction of the violent contrasts between its various spaces. Throughout the film there is the obvious upstairs/downstairs, rich/poor contrast. The Tunisian princes, the beys, now compromised by their too willing collaboration with the French Protectorate, live out their idle lives. There is opulence and a veneer of culture. Sid Ali plays his lute but also takes the chance to flaunt his mistress's charms before his guests (and his long-suffering wife). Si Bechir looks scholarly as he strolls the garden, book in hand, but on finding the unconscious Alia he lifts her skirt to stroke her thigh and, aroused, rapes her mother before her eyes. The assumption of power is absolute: the servant women mount the stairs only to offer the services demanded of them, which include sexual services. The disregard of any female identity is clear from the way Si Bechir rapes his brother's mistress and openly contemplates using the daughter. But nothing is said, no complaint raised. As the old housekeeper Khalti Hadda tells Alia at the end of the film, "We were taught one rule in the palace: silence."

Space is also divided between inside and out. The gardens belong very much to the beys, and virtually the only time we see the servants there is when they stand by to watch the family portrait being taken. It is a sign of Alia's ambiguous position—daughter of a servant but close friend of Si Bechir's daughter, Sarra—that she is able to wander here. Against this open, attractive, and often empty space is set the drab and enclosed world of the kitchen, which Tlatli has described as the "living heart of the film."[12] While the film's first flashback is the curiously choreographed simultaneous birth of Sarra, Si Bechir's legitimate daughter, and Alia, Khedija's illegitimate child, the second is a thirty-second shot of the women in the kitchen celebrating Alia's birth. The central action first gets properly underway in the subsequent flashback sequence, which again begins in the kitchen and shows Alia spying on her mother as the latter is summoned to serve upstairs.

The way in which the kitchen scenes are shaped sets the pattern for the film's treatment of the women's work. Tlatli has said that she "was interested in the bodies of women who move, and work, with all the time in the world" and "had to show them in their own rhythm, in their own way of living and breathing."[13] To show the slowness of their lives through her camera, she begins the third flashback scene with a close-up (here Alia's face as she joins the group's singing) and slowly draws back to show the whole semi-circle of women, holding the shot for almost a minute and a half before going on to capture other aspects of the action. Together with duration, Tlatli is concerned with detail: "A camera is somewhat sly and hidden. It's there and it can capture small details about something one is trying to say, so in a sense it can be an instrument for poetry."[14] We return to the kitchen a dozen times at intervals in the film, almost always in the same way, beginning with a close-up and with the camera then pulling back for a long-held wide shot: beginning, for example, with a close-up of cotton being treaded, hands and a watermelon, food preparation, the radio, washing, and so forth.

Even within the palace, for the women the act of crossing the boundaries and going upstairs is to make themselves sexually available to the beys. After Si Bechir has asked for Alia to bring him his tea, Khedija admonishes her daughter: "You'll never leave this room again. You mustn't go upstairs. Is that understood?" But in order to protect her daughter, she herself has to take up Si Bechir's medicine and, in effect, offer herself to a man who has raped her. For the women, the kitchen forms the core of their existence, their place of work, and also their refuge, where they sing and exchange confidences. But, in addition, the palace is a prison. This sense of enclosure is most graphically conveyed in the shot which immediately follows the rape of Khedija. Alia, in long shot, runs desperately forward toward the open gateway, which slowly and inexorably closes to imprison her within the palace grounds, the force of the image being enhanced by the fact that though she is screaming in agony, we hear no sound at all.

Twin Destinies

The spaces of the palace form the context in which the parallel and contrasting fates of the two women unfold. Khedija, sold to the beys as a child of 10 and having, as a consequence, no proper family to turn to outside the palace, can be seen an example of "the female child" as defined by Nawal El Saadawi in *The Hidden Face of Eve*:

> The education that a female child receives in Arab society is a series of continuous warnings about things that are supposed to be harmful, forbidden, shameful or outlawed by religion. The child therefore is trained to suppress her own desires, to empty herself of authentic, original wants and wishes linked to her own self, and to fill the vacuum that results with the desires of others. . . . A girl who has lost her personality, her capacity to think independently and to use her own mind, will do what others have told her and will become a toy in their hands and a victim of their decisions.[15]

Significantly Khedija has become a dancer, exhibited by her master at his parties, fulfilling quite literally El Saadawi's prediction that such a female child is reduced to an outside shell, "the body, a lifeless mould of muscle and bone that moves like a wound-up rubber doll."[16]

As an adult, she has no other perspective to pass on to Alia: "Be careful. Don't let anyone come near you. If a man touches you, run away. If anything happens to you you're lost." Khedija shares moments of mutual tenderness with Sid Ali, but does not complain to him when she is raped by his brother. She is desperate in her efforts to protect her child but refuses to talk about her to Sid Ali after Alia has made what she knows has been a perilous public appearance as performer upstairs, drawing to her male attention which is bound to take a sexual form. She knows that Alia's father will never acknowledge his role, fond though he is of his daughter: the social gulf is too vast. Khedija fully fits Tlatli's description of the character: "the type that in our countries is sometimes said to be 'colonised by the colonised,' a woman inferior by birth, a woman born to serve man." [17]

Alia herself is initially driven by curiosity, endlessly spying on her mother and asking questions about who her father is. She starts as a child, with her innocence typified in the scene of the family photograph when, arriving with Sarra, she assumes she should line up with the immaculately clad family. After she has been brushed aside and realigned with the servants, the cause of her misunderstanding becomes clear, when Sid Ali poses for a second photograph, standing between her and Sarra. A key stage of Alia's growing up is the moment when she cuts her own image off this photograph. Her mother's gift of the lute and her own discovery of her singing voice both liberate her and make her more vulnerable: as soon as she is noticed, she becomes the focus of male sexual interest, with both Si Bechir and the new inhabitant of the palace, the teacher, Lotfi, who is in hiding from the authorities, paying attention to her.

Alia's singing indeed leads her directly into the relationship with Lotfi which will in turn lead to her revolt and her departure from the palace. But in becoming a performer she takes on the same equivocal social status as her mother, though the status of singer has, it seems, traditionally been more highly regarded than that of the dancer. As Karin van Nieuwkerk observes in her study of honor and shame in relation to Egyptian entertainers, women are "generally perceived as more enticing than men":

> The fact that excitement is most strongly aroused by the eye rather than by the ear also affects the various categories of female performers. Female performers are mainly listened to; female singers are both listened to and, at least at present, observed; while female dancers are solely eye-catchers. Female dancing is accordingly considered the most shameful form of entertainment. [18]

The sense of Alia following in her mother's footsteps is wonderfully expressed in the scene depicting the two of them by the mirror. We first see Khedija sitting at the mirror in her bedroom, putting on her makeup. Alia appears standing behind her and is framed in the upper right-hand corner of the mirror. After a two-shot of the pair by the wardrobe, the film returns to the first composition, but this time it is Alia who sits at the mirror, putting on her makeup, while Khedija's anguished face appears in the upper right-hand corner.

Political Film?

The early part of the narrative of *Silences of the Palace*—up to the midpoint constituted by the rape of Khedija—is devoted largely to the lives of the servant women and the personal relationship of mother and daughter. There is a little political discussion among guests at the party, where the beys are advised by the French to stick with their colonizers, although it is not denied that "common subjects are thrown into jail, others are killed for no reason." Later Hussein brings news of the disturbances that accompany the call for independence: "The

Fig. 31. *Silences of the Palace* (1994), Moufida Tlatli, Tunisia

street is on fire, the French have surrounded the city. They've shot demonstrators and it's not over yet. Too much blood."

But the beginning of serious political discussion comes only after the rape, when the comments of the servants listening to the radio in the kitchen ("if the bey leaves, the country is lost") are paralleled by comment on the bey's precarious situation and the condemnation of the nationalist song, "Green Tunisia," upstairs. Political information increases, spread by the radio: "Upheavals and riots are spreading throughout Tunisia. The French government has refused to receive the nationalist delegation. There have been demonstrations for independence in several cities. A nationwide strike has been declared." Hussein is able to back this up with his personal experience: "There's a strike. The police are everywhere. There are barricades at every post. I was arrested at Bab Saadoun. They kept me for two hours. I was lucky." On the eve of Sarra's engagement party, the political crisis reaches its climax: "An important communiqué. The French government, in agreement with the bey and in view of the serious situation, has declared a state of emergency and a curfew from 9 P.M."

It is clear that Tlatli attaches importance to the political events which coincide with the personal stories she is depicting. But she approaches politics only obliquely, through the lives of women who never leave the palace and the beys who are politically inactive. This is in keeping with her feelings about the camera, apparent in her comparison of cinema and poetry in terms of a "culture of the indirect":

Poetry is made up of a superimposition of images on words. Perhaps this culture of the indirect has advantages over a culture valuing simple and direct expression. Here everything is a little bit devious, a bit unformulated—the unsaid, and so on. This is why the camera is so amazing. It's in complete harmony with this rather repressed language.[19]

The arrival of Hussein's friend Lotfi brings a potentially new political dimension, since he is hiding from the police. But in fact we learn nothing of his supposed political activity outside the palace and, within it, his sole role is to politicize Alia's singing. When she begins to sing alone, outside, in performance upstairs and even at the beginning of Sarra's engagement party, she sings conventional material (in fact, Arab friends tell me, Oum Kalsoum songs dating from slightly later than the presumed action of the film). It is a surprise to us, as it is to the audience at the party, when she begins to sing "Green Tunisia." Presumably she is responding to Lotfi, perhaps to his extremely naive equation of her future and that of the independence struggle: "You're as indecisive as our country. One word thrills you, the next scares you. Things are going to change. A new future awaits us. You will be a great singer. Your voice will enchant everyone."

Whatever the case, Alia makes her stand and leaves the palace forever with the man she loves, failing even to attend her mother's funeral. The reality, as we see from the framing shots ten years later, is very different from her expectations. Much of the reason for this lies in Lotfi, who has refused to marry her (she is illegitimate and a singer) or to start a family: "I thought that Lotfi would save me. I have not been saved." Tlatli shows clearly in her films that women are ready for the choice of modernity. But are men? Lotfi is clearly not. In *The Eloquence of Silence*, writing specifically of the Algerian experience, Marnia Lazreg offers general insights very applicable to the figure of Lotfi:

A colonized man is just a man whose basic right to food, shelter, clothing and happiness are not recognised. Fighting for those rights does not make him a perfect human being. For him to understand the meaning of modes of suffering and inequality other than those inflicted on him by colonial might requires attaining a form of consciousness that is willing to rise above its victimisation and implicate itself in that of others. The history of revolutions in other parts of the world has not provided concrete examples of how such consciousness might be reached.[20]

As a result:

Consciousness of difference between women and men as an instance of *social* inequality, instead of the expression of biological difference ordained by a divine force, is not the automatic outcome of militancy in a decolonisation movement.[21]

The powerful climax of *Silences of the Palace* brings together the passing of the beys and the death of Khedija, the freeing of Alia, and the independence of Tunisia. At the end of the film, Alia explicitly compares her life to Khedija's: "Like you I've suffered, I've sweated. Like you I've lived in sin. My life has been a series of abortions. I could never express myself. My songs were stillborn." Can we also see Alia as a symbol of Tunisia? In Tlatli's view cinema "has to make use of metaphors and symbols, in keeping with this lack of directness that so characterises Islamic society."[22] To me, at least, *Silences of the Palace* demands to be read as another instance of the "national disenchantment" of which Hélé Béji wrote so eloquently in 1982.[23] But Tlatli does not end without hope. Rediscovery of the past together with the recovery of her mother's story make Alia determined to keep the child Lotfi wishes her to abort: "This child, I feel it has taken root in me. I feel it bringing me back to life, bringing me back to you. I hope it will be a girl, I'll call it Khedija." A new future, however painful, begins.

15 A New Realism? *Ali Zaoua* (1999)

Nouri Bouzid's concept of a "New Realism," which proved so useful for an analysis of the new Arab protagonist to be found in *Golden Horseshoes,* also offers clear insights into the work of the whole dominant generation of film-makers in post-independence Maghrebian cinema—those born in the 1940s. These Arab filmmakers—with their contemporaries in Syria, Lebanon, and Palestine—saw themselves as the filmmakers who would take forward the work of an earlier generation of Egyptian filmmakers, such as Tewfik Saleh and Youssef Chahine, who had made remarkable advances, but within the context of the Egyptian film industry. The newcomers were working outside any sort of comparable industrial production structure and the new realism

> projected the particular ideas and personal attitudes of the *auteur* director, making each film different from the other, developing the individualistic stance and, eventually, imbuing the work with a hitherto almost unknown authenticity.[1]

And, as Bouzid notes,

> all this gave the new films a distinctly and intimately personal flavour, thereby destroying the old, ossified moulds and making the *auteur* director the pivotal element in the film.[2]

The new realism these directors were seeking "is not a form, but a specific content that has a form; it is concerned with reality—a new reality."[3]

This approach had an impact on several key aspects of the structure of film narrative. As we have seen, the new realism set out "to demolish the myths which classical literature and classical cinema had perpetuated":[4]

> New character types came into being, all of them departing from the old stereo-types and, thereby, appearing authentic. They interacted with the medium and with the dramatic action. None of them were flat characters; they all had histories and roots, weaknesses and strengths, in addition to all sorts of minute individualis-ing details. All these elements were then wrapped up, as it were, in the director's feelings about, and love for, these characters.[5]

Intimately connected with the search for new characters was the search for a new identity. In addition, there was an impact on the films' structure and mode of narration which "began to possess an internal dynamic which, in turn, was based on a certain visual concept, instead of being merely a series of sentences and scenes strung together."[6] Nor was the aesthetic aspect neglected, as the new realism was also "an attempt to say something new, and to say it beautifully."[7] Writing in the later 1980s, Bouzid saw two main threats to this new realism: firstly, the influence of state funding and the kind of "official" film making this brought with it (as in Algeria during the existence of ONCIC) and, secondly, the emigration to Europe of Arab filmmakers seeking a new context of production. It is interesting today to reconsider Bouzid's approach in the light of one of the most important developments in Maghrebian cinema at the end of the 1990s and the beginning of the new millennium: the significant new state funding in Morocco, which is lifting film output to hitherto unattained levels and enticing back the Maghrebian filmmakers who have trained and begun their careers from a base in Europe.

Nabil Ayouch

Nabil Ayouch, author of the searing study of Casablancan slum children, *Ali Zaoua* (1999), is undoubtedly the leading young Moroccan filmmaker of today. But he was born in 1969 in Paris, where he grew up, with dual nationality thanks to his French mother and Moroccan father. He studied at the Ecole Supérieure du Commerce Extérieur and took drama courses in Paris. There too he began his professional film making career, working initially as assistant in various production roles and directing about fifty publicity shorts and advertisements. He still lives in Paris and has his own production company based there. Yet in establishing himself as a feature filmmaker in Morocco, he has followed the preferred pattern of the CCM, which administers the state funding scheme there. He made three short 35mm fictional films in the early 1990s, the first of them, *Les pierres bleues du désert* (*The Blue Stones of the Desert*, 1992), thanks in part to a state advance ("aide sur dossier"). Then, in 1995, he received funding for his first feature, *Mektoub*, which appeared two years later and achieved a considerable commercial success in Morocco. This was the key breakthrough for the younger generation of Moroccan filmmakers—those born in the 1950s and 1960s—and Ayouch himself built on this success with the internationally acclaimed *Ali Zaoua*, which was again highly successful at the Moroccan box office—the most popular film since Mohamed Abderrahman Tazi's *Looking for My Wife's Husband* in 1993.

While *Mektoub* did well with audiences within Morocco, its adoption of a pseudo-Hollywood thriller format was only partially successful. But with *Ali Zaoua*, Ayouch put himself fully within the mainstream of Moroccan film making. Though the latter has a multi-faceted identity, from very early on a realist approach to social problems has been an important feature of its output and one which has received consistent state funding. The approach has its tentative beginnings with Latif Lahlou's CCM-produced *Spring Sunshine* as early as 1969, but it reaches its full flowering with the socially committed studies of urban poverty and oppression—also state funded—made in the 1980s and 1990s by directors such as Jillali Ferhati, Hakim Noury, and Mohamed Abderrahman Tazi. There are also parallel strands of politically committed film making which also uses a realist style, exemplified by the early work of Souheil Benbarka—especially *A Thousand and One Hands* (1972) and *The Oil War Will Not Happen*

(1974)—and also the more documentary approach of Ahmed El Maânouni, exemplified by his first feature *The Days, The Days* (1978).

Tazi's protagonists may be victims, but they are always adults—the constantly abused and put-upon lorry driver of *The Big Trip* (1981) and the two women whose friendship cannot save them from the prejudice and hostility of the local community in *Badis* (1988), for example. In contrast, both Ferhati and Noury have made studies of children and young women whose lives are blighted. Though separated by a decade, Ferhati's *Reed Dolls* (1981) and *The Beach of Lost Children* (1991) both look at fragile young girls' lives destroyed in an indifferent society. Neither for Aicha—married as a child, made pregnant as soon as she begins menstruation, and then rejected by her husband's family when he dies—nor for Mina—left pregnant after the death of her lover and tormented by a hostile stepmother—is there any prospect of a meaningful life outside the bounds of marriage. Equally poignant is the double pattern of Rkia's life story in Noury's *Stolen Childhood* (1993): sold off into household work at the age of 10 and then seduced and abandoned as a teenager, she can end only as a prostitute. Both filmmakers demonstrate deep concern, but neither can offer an answer. Ferhati disclaims any pretension of offering solutions in *Reed Dolls:* "I wanted to show as much as possible a reality I live myself, even if this is a film about a woman . . . to say that the woman's problem is not exceptional, and that it is a struggle that involves us all."[8] This approach is very much in line with that of Noury, of whose film making the Moroccan critic Ahmed Araib writes that it is "a *cinéma vérité* where the filmmaker's effort comprises a faithful reflection of this reality whose principal witness is the spectator. . . . His films disconcert at times because of the bitterness which emanates from this reality based on injustice and inequality which Noury denounces courageously."[9]

Ali Zaoua

Ali Zaoua opens in a slightly disconcerting manner with Ali—off camera —talking about his private dream about an island with two suns, explaining his ambition of becoming a sailor, and lying about his life as "Ali Steel Teeth," who pulls cars with his teeth and who left home because he overheard his mother planning to sell his eyes. Eventually we become aware that this is a television news item being filmed by a woman reporter, and we see the 15-year-old Ali, surrounded by the many street children whose life he shares. The sequence ends with a close-up of Ali looking straight at us. This opening echoes Ayouch's own first experience during the months of researching the film, which began when he took a video camera to the waste ground where the boys congregated: "The kids immediately directed themselves, saying whatever came into their heads. . . . They know exactly how to give what society expects of them in terms of 'miserabilism.' The film intended to take another direction."[10]

The children in the film are all played by genuine orphans and abandoned children whom Ayouch met through Dr. Najat M'Djid, who had founded the

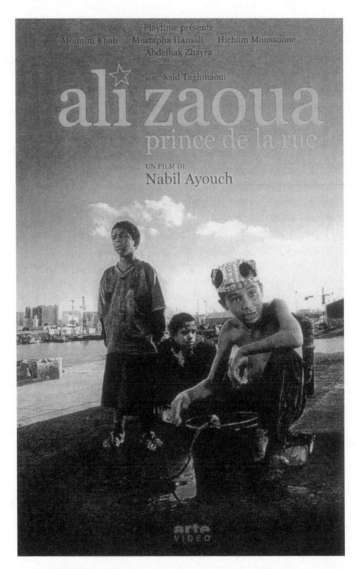

Fig. 32. *Ali Zaoua* (1999), Nabil Ayouch, Morocco

Bayti Association six years earlier to care for Casablanca's street children. In
Dr. M'Djid's view the association took risks in participating in the project, "since
it was vital that they [the children] did not see it as a way out, but as a transition stage whose consequences could only be measured in two years' time."[11]
Though the children certainly contributed enormously to the film through their
performances, and certain scenes of the film were improvised during the shoot-

ing, the overall structure was pre-scripted by Ayouch and Nathalie Saugeon, with the assistance of another French writer, Philippe Lamblin, and with Arab adaptation and dialogue by the Moroccan dramatist Youssef Fadel (who had worked in the same capacity on *Mektoub*). This was a very conscious strategy for Ayouch: "I knew that I had to work with this destructured universe by building a fiction. That meant bringing these children into a structure."[12]

An interplay between dream and reality is the characteristic feature of this overall structure. When Ali talks afterward to his closest friend, Kwita, his dream of his island is mixed up with the real-life opportunity of working on a boat, offered him by a friendly fisherman. His most prized possession, a compass, has a similar dual role: it shows him where north and west are but will also take him "straight to his island." All these dreams and ambitions are brutally destroyed in reality, as Ali and his little group of three younger companions (Kwita, Omar, and Boubker) are attacked by the gang from which they have separated themselves. This gang, whose chant is "What is life? Life is shit," is led by the evil, if slow-witted, Dib (played by one of the film's few professional actors, Saïd Taghmaouï, who had played one of the leading roles in Mathieu Kassowitz's celebrated study of the Parisian *banlieue, La haine*). In the melee, a stray rock hits Ali and he falls dead. His three young companions cannot believe what has happened—"a rock doesn't kill you—like a dog"—and they sleep with his body, expecting him to wake up. But next morning they have to face the truth. They wash the body and hide it when they are disturbed by the police. Kwita declares that they must bury Ali properly, "like a prince," and the film's central section is devoted to the trio's efforts to do this. Thus, though Ali dies very early in the film, he continues to dominate the narrative, through this concern with his burial. By the end he has become a mythical figure for the three boys. Equally important, but more controversial, are Ali's dreams—particularly his story about the island with two suns—which are illustrated at intervals throughout the film by animated sequences of childlike drawings. For some critics these sequences constitute a sentimentalization of what should be a harsh realistic narrative. But, for the children, the stories are very real: since Ali was a prince, his stories must be true. If these animations—and the parallel series illustrating Kwita's longings—are understood as representations of how the children themselves imagine these stories, they make perfect dramatic sense as part of the film's double perspective.

The core of the film is the central section, which traces the trio's efforts to give Ali a proper burial, in which the disorder of their lives—dominated by glue sniffing—becomes particularly apparent. Though they are all similarly victims of society, their characters are very different. Kwita is thoughtful and serious. He is the driving force behind the project to bury Ali with dignity, and he follows in Ali's footsteps by imagining a better life and struggling to begin to reintegrate himself into society, though like the others he turns to glue sniffing in moments of tension. Omar shows little such awareness and is constantly involved in violence: beaten up by Dib's gang, he accuses Kwita of letting him down and threatens him with a broken bottle. It is he who is seemingly the worst affected by drug abuse. Boubker, the youngest, is always trailing behind the other two, desperate when they fight but given to wild bursts of enthusiasm when anything even slightly positive occurs. At one point, feeling neglected, he proclaims his desire to die so that they will care about him, as they do about Ali. The performances Ayouch has extracted from the three young non-professionals are never less than totally compelling.

The trio try to raise money in all kinds of ways—stealing, selling cigarettes, and hawking shell necklaces they've made themselves—but then they immediately spend it all on glue. When Omar visits Ali's mother, he cannot prevent himself from stealing the coins he sees in an ashtray. When they encounter someone weaker than themselves—the little cigarette seller Nouredinne, who wants to be known as Winston (after the cigarette brand)—they aggress him. They have moments of warmth, humor, and laughter, but their mutual alliances are constantly shifting, and there is one moment of vicious violence (when Omar comes close to cutting Kwita's throat). At times too they drift into private worlds, especially Kwita, who has developed Ali's taste for dreaming, both of the loving family he sees depicted in a photograph contained in a schoolgirl's wallet he has stolen and of the escape symbolized by the compass he has inherited from Ali. All three are touchingly in need of love and affection, constantly inventing non-existent families (an uncle, a fiancée . . .). In a beautifully shaped scene, Boubker—oblivious to the danger of which we are aware—is delighted when a doll appears at the window of the abandoned truck he is playing in, only to find it is attached to Dib's stick. The film gives only hints of what happens after Dib enters the truck. Kwita twice throws a friendly dog down a flight of steps, but falls peacefully asleep when it wraps itself around his neck. Omar, who has briefly become a kind of substitute son for Ali's mother, opens up in response to her emotion on hearing of Ali's death, but is rejected when he tries to hug her.

The trio's efforts with regard to the burial get nowhere and, as Kwita discovers, Ali's body is beginning to stink in the hole in which they have hidden it. At this point Hamid, the fisherman whom we have seen looking for Ali and whom Kwita has met at the harbor, takes over. He organizes them to cover the body with ice and next day begins work on the boat which is to be Ali's coffin. The boys want to help but are drawn back into their glue sniffing and toward Dib's gang. Kwita, now wearing Ali's T-shirt and becoming more and more like his hero, successfully confronts Dib, recovers Ali's watch, and leads the other two away through the massed ranks of the gang. Back on the quay side, they descend their hole, using matches to look again at the pictures of his island with two suns which Ali has drawn on the walls. It is only later that they realize that Ali's body is no longer there. Hamid has taken care of that too and allows them to spend the night on his boat where, looking at the stars, they tell each other stories about Ali the Prince. Next day they visit the flat belonging to Ali's mother and hear the source of Ali's story of his island: the tape of a fairy tale his mother had used to help him get to sleep. Eventually they find her and she takes them in a taxi to the harbor, where the film's final confrontations take place. Dib and his gang are disconcerted—they cannot even manage their chant—as the boys set sail with Ali's mother to bury Ali at sea, like a real sailor, if not like a prince.

The children in *Ali Zaoua* are treated with affection within the narrative, but no attempt is made to disguise the total waste that these lives represent. There are moments of harsh precision in the children's interaction with the real world, as when Boubker goes to a shop looking for nails and the shopkeeper immediately calls him over and casually thumps a tin of glue in front of him. Otherwise the adults are far less convincing. Ali's mother (played by the director's sister, the actress Amal Ayouch) is a very beautiful and very romanticized whore, seemingly untouched by the sordid reality of her life, with the result that her dreams and sense of loss do not fully engage us. Hamid is a totally idealized figure, a deus ex machina who resolves the problem of the burial and allows the film to end on a note of optimism (perhaps Kwita will himself escape). Quite why he acts as he does is never clear—perhaps because he feels some responsibility for dislocating Ali's life and hence provoking the confrontation which led to his death? The ending undoubtedly softens the film's impact, but it shows how carefully the film has been constructed. All the major plot points have been resolved: we have seen Kwita assert himself against Dib and discovered the source of Ali's island. As the narrative comes to its climax, the music swells and a repeated overhead track along the quay, which had three times been enigmatically cut off abruptly, now finds resolution as it is completed to show the boat now out at sea. Then the animation is resolved with a shot of Ali and his beautiful girlfriend on his island, frozen into the drawing he had made on the cellar wall, dissolving to black as the camera leaves the cellar and goes on to a very composed shot of Casablanca harbor with two apparent suns, accompanied by a voice-over echo of the opening interview, in which Ali talks of his ambition to become a sailor.

It is a measure of the film's quality that, when one seeks parallels for *Ali Zaoua,* an obvious choice is Luis Buñuel's Mexican masterpiece, *Los olvidados* (1950), which also looked at the fate of slum children and used a mixture of professional and non-professional actors. Ayouch could certainly have employed Buñuel's opening caption to that film, with Casablanca replacing Mexico City as one of those huge modern cities which

> hide behind their imposing buildings places of wretchedness, sheltering children, without hygiene and without school, breeding grounds for future delinquents. Society tries to cure this social wound, but the results of its efforts are very limited. . . . That is why this film is based on real events. It is not optimistic and leaves the solution of the problem to the progressive forces of society.[13]

An equally significant link is the use of dream sequences. As Ado Kyrou noted, "with *L'âge d'or* Buñuel discovered everyday reality in the surreal," while *Los olvidados* began a series of films where "surreality appears beneath the real." [14] *Los olvidados* contains a memorable dream sequence in which the young Pedro imagines a loving mother offering him a side of meat, which is snatched

Fig. 33. *Ali Zaoua* (1999), Nabil Ayouch, Morocco

away by the villainous Jaïbo. There is also the dying vision of Jaïbo himself. The connection with *Ali Zaoua* would have been even closer if Buñuel had been allowed by his producer to fulfill his ambition

> to insert a few bizarre images which would flash onto the screen just for an instant, just long enough for the audience to wonder if it had really seen them or not. For example, when the boys pursue the blind man across the empty lot, they pass a huge building under construction. I wanted to put a hundred-piece orchestra on the scaffolding, playing soundlessly.[15]

For Ayouch too, "oneirism is also part of reality," particularly in the case of *Ali Zaoua,* where the children "have dreams of belonging which connect them to material reality: having a car, a home, a house, a boat. They dream of the real, of the promise of the real." When they have sniffed glue, "they look at the television aerials and tell each other film stories. You have to admit that violence is not the only thing in their lives."[16] This is particularly true of Kwita, who, when he steals from the middle-class schoolgirl, finds a photograph of her and her parents—all smiling. This becomes his dream—a normal family life—about which he makes up stories, and toward the end of the film there is a hint that perhaps he, alone among the three, may be able to reintegrate himself.

As far as Bouzid's concept of a new realism is concerned, it is clear that Ayouch, twenty-four years his junior and representing a new generation of Maghrebian filmmakers, does bring a fresh voice. The look at Casablanca from a Paris production base and with the use of Moroccan state funding has not prevented the film from offering a very powerful and lucid personal view of the poverty, deprivation, and other social problems to be found in Casablanca. Indeed it is the combination of thorough research and use of non-professionals with careful script writing and a very conscious shaping of the plot which gives *Ali Zaoua* its particular power. This is no detached documentary about poverty as seen from afar, but a fictional *auteur* film which succeeds in achieving authenticity through its closeness to its subject. For Ayouch, the key demand during the shooting was: "Never lie to yourself, never lie to them."[17] In this he succeeded: while certain aspects may have been softened and the violence is at times muted, the film is totally honest in depicting lives for which there is very little hope. But despite this, the characters are not simply helpless victims. They have their histories, friendships, failings, and dreams, and they can therefore engage us emotionally as spectators, despite the fact that they have—in Bouzid's phrase—defeat as their destiny.

Conclusion

Since the 1960s, we have been living in a rapidly globalizing world and media environment. Indeed globalization is the norm against which people are now determining their individual and national identities. Access to multiple channels of communication and types of local and transnational media and the displacement of an unprecedented number of people have challenged our received notions of national culture and identity, national cinema and genre, authorial vision and style, and film reception and ethnography.

—Hamid Naficy[1]

The National Cinemas of the 1960s

To a quite surprising degree the film structures set up by the newly independent states of the Maghreb echoed the colonial past. The CCM, set up in 1944 to serve the needs of the French Protectorate, continues as the focus of Moroccan national cinema to this day. Indeed, for the first decade or so after independence, the bulk of the short films it produced were barely distinguishable from those of the colonial era, apart from the gradual replacement of French directors by Moroccan nationals. The reliance on foreign directing expertise is also to be found at the beginnings of fictional feature film production in the Maghreb. In each of the three countries, indigenous feature film making was preceded by the production of a fictional film directed by a foreigner: *Such a Young Peace* (1965) by the Frenchman Jacques Charby in Algeria, *H'mida* (1966) by Jean Michaud-Mailland in Tunisia, and a film known as both *La route du Kif* (*The Kif Road*) and *Alerte à la drogue* (*Drug Alert,* 1966) by the Spaniard N. Zanchin (and for which Mohamed B. A. Tazi is variously credited as co-director or screenwriter) in Morocco. The most surprising continuity is that in Algeria, where film is generally seen as having been born, literally, in the struggle for liberation in which hundreds of thousands died. Here the post-independence structure of the nationalized film industry exactly matched the divisions and focuses of French colonial structures. As Lotfi Maherzi points out in his study, *Le cinéma algérien,* the would-be revolutionary rural "ciné-bus" distribution network (the CDC) mirrors precisely the colonial propaganda network (the SDC),[2] and the new structure set up for feature production (the CNCA) took its inspiration from the French Centre National de la Cinématographie (CNC).[3]

Each national cinema developed its own special style and characteristics, wittily captured by Ferid Boughedir in 1981:

—Algerian cinema or the dignity of the humiliated: "We were a great people. Have confidence in us and we will build mountains. In my film I repeat what my government says," insists every Algerian film maker, "because I intend to push it, if possible, to be even more progressive."
—Moroccan cinema or the silent complaint: "I'm suffocating, I'm suffocating, it's the Middle Ages," protests the Moroccan film maker. "How can I push back these walls? Air, air! If only I could speak. But meanwhile unravel what I have to tell you."
—Tunisian cinema or the demands of truth: "It's not true, it's not true. Here's the truth, the truth about emigration, about tourism, about the rural exodus, about the national struggle, about the situation of women. I demystify," says the Tunisian film maker, "I make counter-cinema. I have a little freedom of expression and I speak. If only I could say more! If only I had the means! I'd also talk about myself. But who am I? An orphan looking for his own face. Which one? There are too many faces. Wait, I'm looking . . . "[4]

The state defined the filmmakers' precise orientation on entering the film industry. If they were Algerians, they had to seek employment as state functionaries —with the particular constraints that this implies. In Morocco and Tunisia their only path was some version of low-budget independent "art" cinema. In Algeria the authorities' control was obviously total, but in Morocco and Tunisia too filmmakers have faced strong censorship pressure. In Tunisia, Nouri Bouzid was faced with a censor's demand to cut fourteen minutes from his second film, *Golden Horseshoes*, but after a year of negotiating, he finally had this reduced to just thirty-five seconds. As he wryly observed, "While we can look at a foreign couple, we don't have the right to look at Arab bodies making love."[5] The Moroccan Abdelkader Lagtaâ's *The Closed Door*, already delayed because of the bankruptcy of its French co-producer, faced a similar long battle with the censor, who demanded cuts to four scenes. As the director has reported, "After a year of fruitless struggle, I had to resign myself, death in the soul, to release it in a mutilated form in April 2000, and even then several cinemas refused to program it, so as not to shock their family audiences."[6]

The political situation and the censorship context have meant that there was no possibility of creating a political counter-cinema, and only a couple of filmmakers, Souheil Benbarka in Morocco and Mohamed Lakhdar Hamina in Algeria, have managed to obtain really big budgets for international-style production (and both, interestingly, were at one time heads of their respective national film corporations). The limits and aspirations of Third World art cinema, as set out in relation to the Indian situation by Wimal Dissanayake, apply fully to the Maghrebian context. The filmmaker, "while not totally abandoning commercial imperatives, seeks to explore through willed art facets of indigenous experiences and thought worlds that are amenable to aesthetic treatment," while art cinema itself "endeavours very often to be critical of the nation-state and its diverse social, political, cultural institutions and discourses."[7]

The state has played a huge role in shaping Maghrebian film production. In each of the three countries a state monopoly within the ministry of information and culture was established after independence: ONCIC in Algeria, CCM in Morocco, and SATPEC in Tunisia. These organizations controlled the import, distribution, and exhibition of films, as well as production. They were the censorship bodies, controlled access to the profession, and, when and where state funding for production was available, they distributed this too. Their gross limitations in dealing with their multiple responsibilities are clearly revealed in the expensive European co-production deals they all indulged in during the 1970s and after. All these efforts were complete financial disasters, though it is only fair to note that ONCIC did co-fund three major Youssef Chahine films in the later 1970s and also the Tunisian Ben Ammar's *Aziza* in 1980, while the CCM in the 1990s made interesting co-productions with filmmakers from Mali, the Ivory Coast, and Tunisia.

Some of the difficulties in structuring suitable schemes of state funding are shown by the experience of Morocco. The first three Moroccan features were produced by the state organization (CCM) in the 1960s, but then the state drew back and was not involved in the burst of early 1970s innovative cinema (the first films of Souheil Benbarka, Moumen Smihi, and Hamid Benani), which gave Moroccan cinema its first international reputation. The CCM returned toward the end of the decade, funding or co-funding seven features of very variable quality in 1977–1979. In 1980 it introduced a funding scheme—the "fonds de soutien"—for filmmakers (supported by a tax on cinema admissions—mostly to see foreign films). But since the sole criterion was simply being "Moroccan," the outcome was the production of films lacking in both quality and audience appeal. After the scheme was changed in 1987—to become the "fonds d'aide" and take on board issues of quality—the results have been far more successful, and at least a few Moroccan films each year can hold their own against the competition of US imports. The system of aid has also managed to raise the planned output of Moroccan films to around eight a year in the 2000s, but the real drawback is that it remains the only real source of production finance. As Lagtaâ has noted, "A film project which does not manage to get this state funding is in practice buried, given there are no other support structures which could allow it to see the light of day."[8]

The most extreme example of a national state cinema is that developed in Algeria during the monopoly of ONCIC between 1968 and 1984. The Algerian government believed in the total subjugation of culture to politics. As a result, ONCIC controlled all aspects of cinema, and though there was some freedom of maneuver for filmmakers—as is shown by the experience of Merzak Allouache when making *Omar Gatlato* (1976)[9]—the government imposed its chosen subject matter on the national cinema. Algerian cinema took on all the narrow and uncritical aspects of a national cinema as defined by Dissanayake, privileging "ideas of coherence and unity and stable cultural meanings associated with the uniqueness of a given nation," while at the same time being "imbricated with national myth-making and ideological production."[10] It is illuminating to compare the Algerian situation with that confronting filmmakers in

Turkey. There—as Kevin Roberts and Asu Aksoy demonstrate—cinema was similarly expected to fulfill two irreconcilable roles: "to play its part in project-ing the ideal image of the nation,"[11] while at the same time satisfying "the need to give visibility and sense to the actual social realities of modern Turkey."[12] Looking at the crisis in Algeria the historian Benjamin Stora has argued that it is "fed in part by the myths forged in the independence struggle": "This excess of falsified memory appears as an obstacle to a true reappropriation of the past, the construction of a nationalism based on the republican spirit and a tolerant Islam."[13] If we follow this view, then the cinema can be seen as complicit in the falsification of the Algerian struggle by the FLN which led eventually to the tragic breakdown of democratic structures in 1992.

Since the 1980s and early 1990s the situation of world (and Maghrebian) cinema has changed enormously, but, as Philip Schlesinger observes, "the new wave of concern with global interconnectedness should not make us now envis-age the world as definitively 'postnational.' The continuing strong links between modes of social communication and national political spaces remain funda-mental for conceptions of collective identity."[14]

Maghrebian Cinemas and Transnational Cinema

In all three states of the Maghreb the number of cinemas has been de-clining since the early 1990s. In Morocco, where there is still considerable state aid, the number of film theatres (155 at independence) rose to a 1955 peak of 247 before falling to fewer than 170 today.[15] In Tunisia there has been a steady decline from 156 at independence to less than a quarter of that number (just 36) today. In Algeria the situation is catastrophic, with a reduction from over 300 at independence to barely a dozen today. This diminution of film theatres has been accompanied by a huge development of alternative distribution struc-tures using video and cable, backed up by satellite television transmission from Europe. This now reaches hundreds of thousands of homes, and VHS cassettes are beginning to be on sale, with increasing video-club viewing. The current novelty is the showing of the latest local and foreign films (often before their cinema release) in cafés signed up to international satellite channels. Nowhere is cinema economically viable, and Kevin Dwyer has calculated that even the most successful Maghrebian film of all time—*Looking for My Wife's Husband,* with a million entries in Morocco alone—"earned just over 60% of its budget."[16]

In this context, local film production is inevitably under threat. The disband-ing of the state production structures and aid systems in Algeria has led to pro-duction of just four features—all largely foreign funded—in the past five years. In contrast, Moroccan cinema is protected by the state funding system (for filmmakers as well as for film exhibition) and Morocco has become the leading film-producing country in the Maghreb. But for filmmakers in Tunisia, where state aid is less generous and the local market is tiny, the setting up of a feature film is a complex financial operation. Moufida Tlatli has listed the network of local sources that she has to approach:

To make my films I obtained a subvention from the production funding commission of the ministry of culture, which meets three times a year. This funding corresponds to about 15 percent of the film's budget and you can also benefit from funding, or rather services, from the ministry of tourism, from Tunisian television, from an advance by the distributor and funding from Canal+ Horizons. In all this funding covers about half the cost of a normal film.[17]

The credits of Boughedir's film *Halfaouine* offer a telling example, listing five co-producing companies: Cinétélefilms and Radio-Télévision Tunisienne (from Tunis), together with Scarabée Films, France Média, and La SEPT (all based in Paris). In addition the credits acknowledge the participation of ten other funding sources from five different countries: the Centre Nationale de la Cinématographie in Paris, the Tunisian ministry of culture and information, Tunis Air, the Tunisian National Office of Tourism, the Hubert Bals Foundation in Rotterdam, Channel Four in London, Westdeutscher Rundfunk in Cologne, Nederlandse Omroepstichting (NOS) and Nationale Commissie Voorlichting Bewustworging Ontwikkelingssamenwerking (NCO) in Holland, and the Fonds d'Action Sociale (FAS) in France.

Films made with this kind of mixed funding cannot help but reflect the (perhaps unspoken) priorities of the two areas where a Tunisian film can make its reputation before local release: international film festivals and Paris art cinemas. But, as Olivier Barlet has noted, these demands are contradictory: on the one hand, "a demand for exoticism: to confine oneself to a territory which is both geographical (the location must be Africa . . .) and ideological (magical, immemorial, legendary, mythical etc. Africa)" and, on the other, "a demand for reality: to document present-day Africa through its problems, generally seen as those of the urban environment."[18] In this context, it is difficult to talk of a Moroccan or Tunisian cinema as if there were any kind of straightforward definition. In Mohamed Abderrahman Tazi's view, "there are Moroccan films but no Moroccan cinema,"[19] while Bouzid, asked for his personal self-definition, replied, "I exist as a tiny part of Tunisian cinema (even if that term is meaningless)."[20]

For Tunisian filmmakers the key source of external funding is France, and their chances here are much enhanced by the policies of the French state. Analyzing what he terms "filmic deterritorialisation," Raphaël Millet points to the role of the French government (particularly in the years 1984–1996) in fostering film production in all areas of French interest and influence (sub-Saharan Africa, the Maghreb, Vietnam, etc). This is partly through government agencies: the ministry of cooperation, the ministry of foreign affairs, the Fonds Sud (administered by the CNC), and the Agence de la Francophonie (ex-Agence de Coopération Culturelle et Technique [ACCT]), and partly through laws supporting the rise of co-productions (formal agreements with almost forty countries, giving automatic right to aid) and the decree of 6 July 1992 (favoring film production in developing countries).[21] Though this aid structure is not centralized, it does have specific criteria which shape the kinds of work produced. The Fonds Sud, for example, to which Maghrebian filmmakers have access, specifies works "with a strong cultural identity" shot by a director resident in the country concerned and not involving any shooting in France or Europe.[22] Of course the impact of this aid is increased by the French film school training many filmmakers have received and the encouragement (sometimes requirement) to use French technicians and resources (especially for editing). The result, in Millet's view, is "the inauguration, perhaps only partially and involuntarily, of a Westernized international film order where independence is a value not only sought but is also, and above all, very relative."[23] Looking at the wider aspects of French international policy, he also argues that "it is less the case of a French aid policy serving the cinemas of the South than of the latter being used to help French cultural policy."[24] In similar vein, Isabel Schäfer questions the whole concept of "a Mediterranean community," which underlies much European Community support for Maghrebian film making, and concludes: "In the end we can place the *mediterraneanist* discourse of the Europeans in a whole tradition of *orientalist* analysis."[25]

We certainly have a particular type of transnational cinema in the Maghreb which is dependent on the initiatives of a foreign state. In this respect it is instructive to compare the Tunisian situation with that in China. The issues to be confronted in an attempt to evaluate any so-called national cinema within such an international context are admirably listed by Sheldon Hsiao-peng Lu at the beginning of his study of *Transnational Chinese Cinemas*. In addition to a necessary examination of the nature of a "national cinema" itself, issues such as "the advent of 'transnational cinema,' the relation of film to the modern nation state, the nexus between visual technology and gender formation, and film culture in the age of global capitalism after the end of the Cold War"[26] need to be considered. These issues are obviously relevant to a consideration of Maghrebian cinemas in the 1990s, and Lu's central question—"How does one recreate the Third World *national* allegory, through the cinematic apparatus, in the new *transnational* setting?"[27] is fundamental.

The key difference in context between the Tunisian Boughedir and Lu's chosen Chinese exemplar Zhang Yimou is that while the latter's production possibilities are shaped by private capitalist companies and investors in Hong Kong and Taiwan, Boughedir's situation results almost wholly from decisions taken by a foreign government, namely France. Despite this, responses to the films of Zhang Yimou and Boughedir are remarkably similar. As Lu admits, Zhang has been taken as "an exemplary instance of the wilful surrender of Third World cinema to the Orientalist gaze, as a classic case of the subjugation of Third World culture to Western hegemony."[28] Similarly Boughedir's second feature, *One Summer at La Goulette,* was attacked by Mustapha Nagbou, the editor of the long-established Tunisian film journal *SeptièmArt,* who wrote: "We say straightaway to international public opinion that this film has nothing Tunisian about it, it doesn't even belong to La Goulette. . . . Tunisia of today is quite different from this idiocy."[29] Clearly Boughedir's frank depiction of sexuality, so different from that in mainstream Arab cinema and to which Nagbou takes such exception, is only possible because of the film's international financing (which is not to say that this depiction was shaped solely to make the film commercially viable in the West). As Lu observes, "under the conditions of global capitalism, Zhang has been able to pursue and sustain a critical project that has become impossible in his home country."[30] Boughedir is in many ways the epitome of the transnational filmmaker, proclaiming that his work "belongs at one and the same time to a national cinema (Tunisian) and a regional one (Maghreb and the Arab world), to a continental cinema (Africa), and, of course, to a universal one (humanity)."[31] Yet his film art has the same potential as that possessed by Zhang's, namely "to become an oppositional practice on the domestic front and as an alternative discourse in the international arena."[32]

Toward Cultural Hybridity?

Hybridity, *The Shorter Oxford English Dictionary* tells us, is the condition of being hybrid, and the latter word is a term initially applied to the "offspring of a tame sow and a wild boar" (an apt analogy, perhaps, for the relation between Third World cinemas and Hollywood). Here I am using the word in its figurative sense of "anything derived from heterogeneous sources," the sources being, in this case, Europe and North Africa. Today hybridity is a universal phenomenon and it is possible to posit "the exemplary status of the immigrant as the 'central figure' of a modernity that deprives everyone of familiar landmarks, forcing everyone to adopt new codes."[33] Maghrebian cinema offers many revealing insights into the cultural aspects of this phenomenon.

From the mid-1970s to the early 1990s there was a constant and fruitful coming and going of filmmakers between Algeria and France. But since 1997 there has been virtually no feature film production in Algeria, and film directors and technicians—together with writers and journalists—have been driven into exile. Few filmmakers have been able to continue their careers. Of those who have, Allouache and Mahmoud Zemmouri have both made studies of the immigrant community, but Mohamed Rachid Benhadj's work has taken him further and further away from Maghreb concerns. His 1999 feature *Mirka*, for example, is an international co-production, with French, Italian, and Spanish producers; an Italian cinematographer; French and English stars; and a Balkans setting. Many critics were astonished when it was shown in competition as an "Algerian" film at the Journées Cinématographiques de Carthage in 2000. This dispute echoes the problems faced by Adolfo Aristarain's Argentinian-Uraguayan co-production *A Place in the World/Un lugar en el mundo,* which was disqualified from the 1993 Academy Awards "after a debate surrounding the film's identity," the quarrel underlining the clash pointed out by Ann Marie Stock, between "the way in which cinema participates in the construction and negation of national identity on the one hand, and the critical insistence on cultural purity on the other."[34]

Throughout the world questions of national identity are continually raised about cinema. In a 1997 article significantly entitled "Will There Be Latin American Cinema in the Year 2000? Visual Culture in a Postnational Era," Néstor

García Canclini puts the questions from a Mexican perspective: "What remains of national identities in a time of globalization and interculturalism, of multinational co-production and the Chain of the Americas, of free trade agreements and regional integration? What remains when information, artists and capital constantly cross borders?"[35]

Certainly it is increasingly difficult to ascribe a clear national identity to films shown, and even winning prizes, at Arab and African festivals, and their authors are often not listed in national filmographies. To take two "Tunisian" examples: *Honey and Ashes/Miel et cendres* (1996) is set in Tunisia, but its director, Nadia Fares, is of Egyptian-Swiss origin and divides her time between Switzerland and New York,[36] and Tunisian-born Najwa Tlili's *Rupture* (1998) looks at the Tunisian community in Canada, where the director lives and works. Similarly, Mohamed Soudani was born at El Asman in Algeria in 1949, but is of Malian descent and, since graduating from IDHEC in Paris, he has lived and worked in Switzerland. His best-known fictional work, *Waalo fendo* (1997) is Swiss produced and set among the Senegalese community of illegal immigrants in Milan (though since this was written, Soudani has returned to Algeria after thirty years to document memories of the war in the feature-length *Guerre sans images* (*War without Images*, 2002).

The problem promises to become even greater in the future. In 1998, 2000, and 2002, all the ostensibly Maghrebian fictional short films which were shown in competition at the Paris Biennale of Arab Cinemas—the works of tomorrow's likely feature filmmakers—were European produced. Though the films were mostly shot in North Africa, the filmmakers were almost all trained in European film schools, currently live in Europe, and have their production base there. One of these young filmmakers is Hassan Legzouli (b. 1963), who was born in Morocco but has lived abroad since 1980. He studied and made short films in Lille and Brussels before shooting a first short in Morocco in 1999. When questioned about his views on Moroccan cinema, he replied that while the label "Moroccan cinema" was justified in the 1970s, "today I prefer to talk of films made by Moroccans. What I mean by that is that there has not been any real reflection on what it means to make films in Morocco."[37] The notion of a simple North African identity seems to have vanished.

The most striking example of cultural hybridity is the work of the fictional feature filmmakers—mostly, but not exclusively, Algerian—who either left the Maghreb as children or were born, as second-generation immigrants, in France; that is, the film equivalent of those sometimes termed *beur* writers. When the first of these filmmakers—Abdelkrim Bahloul, Rachid Bouchareb, and Mehdi Charef—arrived on the scene in the mid-1980s, they were broadly comparable to their Maghrebian colleagues: a little younger perhaps, but with the same range of backgrounds (student at IDHEC, trainee in the French film industry, factory-worker-turned-novelist, respectively). Their initial films reflected the lives and concerns of the French immigrant communities in which they had grown up.

But the careers of this initial trio, and the two dozen or so newcomers who have joined them since the beginning of the 1990s, have since developed in para-doxical ways. They have given us some of the keenest insights into Maghrebian beliefs and aspirations through studies of the community couched in terms in-conceivable within a state-controlled industry. But because Algeria is currently inaccessible as a location for shooting, it has become a kind of phantom in the works of certain of these filmmakers. The Dutch-based Karim Traïdia, in *The Truth Tellers* (2000), chose to shoot his "Algiers" in Portugal, thereby blurring the film's ostensible contrast between Europe and North Africa. But the most remarkable film in this respect is *Madam Osmane's Harem* (2000) by the Paris-based Nadir Moknèche, which is a film structured around absence, as Stora notes in his study of Algeria in the 1990s. Everything is there in this film about a block of flats inhabited by an array of women in 1993 Algiers, but at the same time nothing is there: "the absence of the men who have left for the war, for work in the oil fields or in France, the absence of the real Algiers (the film was shot in Morocco), the absence of ideological engagements, the absence of the blood shed in the war."[38] Inevitably the protagonist is played by a Spanish actress (Carmen Maura).

Most of the immigrant or second-generation immigrant filmmakers have felt a need to treat other subjects. Even Charef, whose work remains close to his origins, has recalled his frustrations when working in television: "I had to free myself from the weight of my parents' culture, but at the same time come to terms with it, since it does form part of me," and "I wanted to go somewhere else, not to deal with immigration any more. It seemed to me that my education prevented me from working with freedom."[39] Even where the films do con-tinue to deal with the lives of immigrant communities, the protagonist is of-ten French (as in Charef's *Marie-Line* and the Ahmed and Zakia Bouchaâlas's *Control of Origin*). Other filmmakers have taken a further step away from di-rectly Maghrebian concerns. Bouchareb, for example, has made films about the mixed race (Vietnamese/American) children left behind after the fall of Saigon (*Life Dust*) and about the tensions between Senegalese immigrants and Afro-Americans in contemporary New York (*Little Senegal*).

At first sight the existence of this diasporic Maghrebian cinema seems a natural part of the contemporary world. But when we look at the wider situa-tion of "the films that post-colonial, Third World filmmakers have made in their Western sojourn since the 1960s," dealt with by Hamid Naficy in his book *An Accented Cinema: Exilic and Diasporic Filmmaking*, it is clear that the films by directors of North African origin do not fit in with the overall world pic-ture.[40] Naficy's own exhaustive categorization of the exilic and diasporic film making, which he terms "accented cinema," comprises marginalized modes of production, epistolary forms, constant concern with the homeland, and themes of memory, claustrophobia, and journeying. Neither the works made by exiles from the troubles in Algeria nor those by first- or second-generation Maghreb immigrants in France fit comfortably within this definition. Naficy sees clearly that the situation in France is different, admitting that "*beur* cinema is generally a realist, narrative, commercial and popular cinema in France."[41] But he still tries to include the films by claiming that *beur* cinema "embodies the accented style more in its themes, characters and structures of feeling than in its style of visualisation or narration."[42]

But what Naficy's work in fact makes clear is the extent and ease with which North African filmmakers in exile or from the diaspora have been drawn into the (admittedly loose) structures of French commercial film making, where international co-production and a range of "participating institutions" are common. Once more the explanation must be sought in the policies of the state. As Susan Hayward has noted, "Ever since World War II, France's cinema, more than that of any other country, has been at the receiving end of state aid and legislation intended to facilitate its growth."[43] The French government's concern with the "cultural exception" and its clear intention of fostering the creation of a broad-ranging French "author's cinema," alongside the Francophone one discussed earlier, have provided a uniquely welcoming and extremely creative base for filmmakers of Maghrebian origin. Indeed, looking for a forerunner for the *beur* filmmakers, Christian Bosséno suggests a French director of the 1960s and early 1970s, arguing that "*beur* cinema taps a realistic, tender source of inspiration that distinguished, for example, the highly innovative film making of a director like Jean Eustache."[44]

In the opening to a recent article René Prédal begins—as he admits a little provocatively—by asking, "Do the North Africans become French in the cinema?"[45] His central focus is on the filmic depiction of mixed-race couples in the 1990s, and here he finds virtually no distinction between the work of filmmakers of Maghrebian descent and that of their purely French colleagues. From the mid-1980s, *beur* filmmakers "are concerned with an author's cinema (*cinéma d'auteur*) aimed at a wide audience: fiction, professional actors and community problems capable of interesting both communities."[46] Simultaneously there exists a French author's cinema (*cinéma d'auteur*)—and Prédal cites specifically Christian Vincent's *Save Me/Sauve-moi* (2000) and Philippe Faucon's *Samia* (2000)—whose "metaphysical gloom and sociological greyness" is ideally suited to the depiction of Maghrebian second-generation immigrants' lives and loves.[47] This leads Prédal to conclude by reposing his opening question: "Do the North Africans become French? Perhaps, but they are principally engaged in changing the meaning of the two terms, in a much needed way."[48] In his 2002 book-length study of *Le jeune cinéma français*, Prédal is even more explicit, observing that "the *beur* current is now twenty years old and no longer constitutes a entity apart from the rest of cinema."[49] With regard to *beur* cinema, then, it is better to talk not of an accented cinema but rather of a cinema of integration or assimilation, one which is now so French in style and tone that its hybrid origins are increasingly obscured.

Appendix A
Dictionary of Feature Filmmakers

Abbazi, Mohamed (Moroccan filmmaker). Born in 1938 in Khémisset, he studied film direction at UCLA and cinema studies at Harvard in the United States. He has worked extensively as assistant on foreign films shot in Morocco and for foreign television companies and made a number of shorts in the 1960s and 1970s. Feature films: *From the Other Side of the River/De l'autre côté du fleuve/Mel wad lhih* (1982), *The Treasures of the Atlas/Les trésors de l'Atlas/Kounouz latlas* (1997).

Abdelwahab, Ali (Tunisian filmmaker). Born in 1938 in Tozeur, he worked for many years in the theatre. He worked as assistant to Jacques Baratier and Omar Khlifi. Feature film: *Om abbes/Um 'Abbâs* (1970).

Abidi, Ali (also known as **Ali Labidi**) (Tunisian filmmaker). Born in 1950 in Redeyef, he studied film and theatre in Romania. He made three shorts before beginning his feature film career. Feature films: *Barg Ellil/Eclair nocturne/Barg al-leil* (1990), *Redeyef 54/Rdeyef 54* (1997).

Aboulouakar, Mohamed (Moroccan filmmaker). Born in 1946 in Marrakesh, he studied at VGIK, the Moscow film school. He is a painter and has made a number of short films, both documentary and fiction. Feature film: *Hadda* (1984).

Achouba, Abdou (Moroccan filmmaker). Born in 1950 in Rabat, he studied at IDHEC in Paris. He lives in France, working as teacher and critic. He made a number of shorts in the late 1970s. Feature film: *Taghounja/Tarounja* (1980).

Akdi, Ahmed Kacem (Moroccan filmmaker). Born in 1942 in Chefchaouen, he worked as a trainee in Gibraltan television and made a number of short films. Feature films: *The Drama of the 40,000/Le drame des 40,000* (1982), *What the Winds Have Carried Away/Ce que les vents ont emportés* (1984).

Akika, Ali (French-based filmmaker of Algerian descent). Born in 1945 in Gigel in Algeria, he has lived in France since 1965. He studied political economy at university and became a schoolteacher and film critic. He participated in the eighty-five-minute collective film *The Olive Tree/L'olivier* (1976) and made several shorts. He has subsequently made a number of video documentaries. Feature films: *Journey to the Capital/Voyage en capital* (with Anne-Marie Autissier, 1977), *Tears of Blood/Larmes de sang* (with Anne-Marie Autissier, 1980).

Allouache, Merzak (Algerian filmmaker). Born in 1944 in Algiers, he studied at INC in Algiers and IDHEC in Paris. He worked for the OAA and CNC before joining ONCIC as a director in 1975. He worked as assistant director to Mohamed Slim Riad and made two mid-1970s documentaries. Feature films: *Omar Gatlato/Umar gatlatu* (1976), *The Adventures of a Hero/Les aventures d'un héros/Mughamarat batal* (1978), *The Man Who Looked at Windows/L'homme qui regardait les fenêtres/Rajul wa nawâfidh* (1982), *A Parisian Love Story/Un amour à Paris/Hubbub fi Bâris* (in France, 1986), *Bab el-oued City/Bab al-wad al-humah* (1994), *Hello Cousin!/Salut cousin!* (in France, 1996), *Algiers-Beirut: In Remembrance/Alger-Beyrouth, pour mémoire* (in France, 1998), *The Other World/L'autre monde* (2001).

Amari, Raja (Tunisian filmmaker). Born in 1971 in Tunis, she completed a degree in French literature at the University of Tunis before studying at FEMIS in Paris (1994–1998). She made three shorts from 1995. Feature film: *Red Satin/Satin rouge* (2002).

Ameur-Zaïmèche, Rabah (French-based filmmaker of Algerian descent). Born in 1968 in France, he studied social sciences in Paris. His first feature was shot on video and transferred to 35mm for cinema release. Feature film: *Wesh Wesh—What's Happening?/Wesh Wesh, Qu'est-ce qui se passe?* (2002).

Aoulad Syad, Daoud (Moroccan filmmaker). Born in 1953 in Marrakesh, he completed a doctorate in physical sciences at Nancy in France and teaches at the Faculty of Science in Rabat. He attended courses at FEMIS and worked as a photographer, publishing three books, *Marocains*, in 1989; *Boujaâd, Espace et mémoire*, in 1996; and *Territoires de l'instant*, with Ahmed Bouanani in 2000. His film making career began in 1989 and he made five shorts and a first feature in the 1990s. Feature films: *Bye-Bye Souirty/Adieu forain* (1998), *The Wind Horse/Le cheval de vent* (2001).

Ayouch, Nabil (Moroccan filmmaker). Born in 1969 in Paris, he studied drama and directing there, graduating in 1990. Producer and director of a number of shorts and advertisements, he made his first fictional shorts in the early 1990s. Features: *Mektoub* (1997), *Ali Zaoua/Ali Zaoua, prince de la rue* (1999), *A Minute of Sunshine Less/Une minute de soleil en moins* (2002).

Azizi, Mohamed Nadir (Algerian filmmaker). Born in 1941 in Miliana, he made one short film. He was part of the collective that made the documentary feature *So That Algeria May Live/Pour que vive l'Algérie* (with Ahmed Kerzabi, 1972). Feature film: *The Olive Tree of Boul'Hilet/L'olivier de Boul'Hilet* (1978).

Babaï, Brahim (Tunisian filmmaker). Born in 1936 in Béja, he studied at IDHEC in Paris. He worked as trainee at ORTF and as assistant on a number of Italian and French features. In Tunisia he worked for television and made a number of shorts and documentaries. Subsequently he made a feature-length documentary, *A People's Victory/Victoire d'un peuple/Intissâr chaâb* (1975). Fictional features: *And Tomorrow?/Et demain?/Wa ghadan?* (1972), *The Night of the Decade/La nuit de la décennie/Laylat al-sanawât al-'achr* (1991).

Baccar, Selma (Tunisian filmmaker). She was born in 1945 in Tunis and is a product of the FTCA (the Tunisian amateur film movement), in the context of which she made her first two shorts. She studied at IFC in Paris and worked in television and as assistant director on feature films. She has also made a number of documentaries. Features: *Fatma 75* (1978), *The Fire Dance/La danse du feu/Habbiba Messika* (1995).

Bachir-Chouikh, Yamina (Algerian filmmaker). Born in 1954 in Algiers, sister of Mohamed Chouikh. She joined ONCIC in 1974 and worked as script girl and then as editor on numerous documentaries and features, including Chouikh's *The Citadel* and *The Desert Ark.* Feature film: *Rachida* (2002).

Badie, Mustapha (Algerian filmmaker). Born in 1928 in Algiers, he has worked mainly for television, completing a number of television films and series. His debut feature was one of the first (and most important) of the films on the war of liberation. Features: *The Night Is Afraid of the Sun/La nuit a peur du soleil/Al-lailu yahkaf ash-shams* (1965), *Hassan Terro's Escape/L'évasion de Hassan Terro/Hurub Hasan Tiru* (1974).

Bahloul, Abdelkrim (French-based filmmaker of Algerian descent). Born in 1950 at Rebahia in Algeria, Bahloul came to France in 1970 at the age of 20. He has Algerian nationality. He studied first modern languages and then film at IDHEC in Paris from 1972 to 1975. After working in television and making two shorts he turned to feature film making. He has also made occasional film appearances, as in Allouache's *The Other World.* Feature films: *Mint Tea/Le thé à la menthe* (1984), *A Vampire in Paradise/Un vampire au paradis* (1991), *The Hamlet Sisters/Les soeurs Hamlet* (1996), *The Night of Destiny/La nuit du destin* (1997).

Bakhti, Benamar (Algerian filmmaker). Born in 1941 in Tlemcen, he studied at IDHEC and worked as assistant in French television and on various French feature films. On his return to Algeria he worked for RTA, directing a number of noted television features. Feature films: *The Epic of Cheikh Bouamama/L'épopée de Cheikh Bouamama* (1983), *Moonlighting/Le clandestin* (1991).

Behi, Ridha (Tunisian filmmaker). Born in 1947 in Kairouan, he studied literature and sociology in Tunis and Paris. A product of the Tunisian amateur film movement (FTCA), he made a number of shorts. Feature films: *Hyenas' Sun/Le soleil des hyènes/Chams al-dhibâ* (1977), *The Angels/Les anges/Al-malâika* (1984), *Bitter Champagne/Champagne amer/Wachmun 'ala-l daâkira* (1988), *Swallows Don't Die in Jerusalem/Les hirondelles ne meurent pas à Jérusalem/Al-khuttâf lâ iyamût fi al-quds* (1994), *The Magic Box/La boîte magique* (2002).

Belhiba, Fitouri (Tunisian filmmaker). Born in 1950 in Zarzis, he trained as a teacher and worked in theatre. He has made a number of shorts in France and Tunisia. Feature film: *Wandering Heart/Coeur nomade/Ruqayya* (1990).

Belmejdoub, Jamal (Moroccan filmmaker). Born in 1956 in Sidi Kacem, he studied film making at INSAS in Belgium and worked as a film critic. He also worked in television and as assistant director. In the 1990s he made three short films and co-scripted Saâd Chraïbi's feature *Women . . . and Women/Femmes . . . et femmes* (1998), followed by work on the script of Abdelhaï Laraki's debut feature, *Mona Saber* (2001). Feature film: *Yacout* (2000).

Belouad, Naguel (French-based filmmaker of Algerian descent). He studied for a master's degree in communications at the American University in Washington, D.C., and shot a first short documentary in Maryland in 1991. He worked as assistant director on a number of CAAIC productions. Feature film: *Women's Expectations/L'attente des femmes* (2000).

Beloufa, Farouk (Algerian filmmaker). Born in 1947 at Oued Fodda, he studied briefly at the short-lived Algerian film school, INC, before graduating from IDHEC in Paris. He also studied in Paris under Roland Barthes. His first major work on his return to Algeria, the feature-length compilation film *Insurrectionary/Insurrectionelle* (1973), was banned and the material was re-edited and released unsigned. His sole feature film is one of the rare Algerian films to deal with matters outside Algeria (in this case, Lebanon on the eve of the 1975 civil war). Feature film: *Nahla* (1979).

Ben Aicha, Sadok (Tunisian filmmaker). Born in 1936 in Sidi Alouane, he studied in Tunis and then at IDHEC in Paris and the Centro sperimentale di cinematografia in Rome. He was a trainee at ORTF and later worked as editor on shorts and features in Tunisia. He also completed several shorts. Feature films: *Mokhtar/Mukhtar* (1968), *The Mannequin/Le mannequin/Aridhat al-aziâ* (1978).

Benallal, Rachid (Algerian filmmaker). Born in 1946 in Algiers, he studied at INC in Algiers and completed his studies at IDHEC in Paris. On his return to Algeria, he worked as assistant director in Algerian television and directed two short films. From the early 1970s he edited around a dozen Algerian features films, some of them among the most significant of the period. Feature film: *Ya ouled* (1993).

Ben Ammar, Abdellatif (Tunisian filmmaker). Born in 1943 in Tunis, he studied at IDHEC in Paris. On his return he worked for the Tunisian newsreel company and worked as assistant on a number of foreign productions. He also worked as cameraman and made a few short films. More recently he has worked as producer through his company, Latif Productions. Feature films: *Such a Simple Story/Une si simple histoire/Hikâya basîta kahâdhihi* (1970), *Sejnane/Sajnân* (1974), *Aziza/'Aziza* (1980), *The Noria's Song/Le chant de la noria* (2002).

Benani, Hamid (Moroccan filmmaker). Born in 1940 in Meknes, he studied at IDHEC in Paris. He made a few shorts, worked on the film journal, *Cinéma 3*, and formed part of the short-lived film collective Sigma 3. A pioneer of Moroccan cinema in 1970, his second feature was not made until twenty-five years later. Features: *Traces/Wechma/Washma* (1970), *A Prayer for the Absent/La prière de l'absent/Sirr al-majarra* (1995).

Benayat, Mohamed (French-based filmmaker of Algerian descent). Born in 1944 in Algeria, Benayat arrived in France at the age of 4 and retains Algerian nationality. After a first short film, he went on to make five feature films in the 1970s and 1980s. Feature films: *The Mask of an Enlightened Woman/Le masque d'une éclaircie* (1974), *Savage Barricades/Barricades sauvages* (1975), *The New Romantics/Les nouveaux romantiques* (1979), *Child of the Stars/L'enfant des étoiles* (1985), *Arizona Stallion* (1988).

Benbarka, Souheil (Moroccan filmmaker). Born in 1942 in Timbuktu in Mali, son of a Southern Moroccan family, he studied sociology in Rome before switching to film at the Centro sperimentale di cinematografia. He worked as assistant on Italian features, including two by Pier Paolo Pasolini, and made three short films. He became head of the CCM in 1986 and also developed his own production and distribution complex, Dawliz. Feature films: *A Thousand and One Hands/Mille et une mains/Alf yad wa yad* (1972), *The Oil War Will Not Happen/La guerre du pétrole n'aura pas lieu/Harb al-bitrui* *ian yaqa'* (1974), *Blood Wedding/Noce de sang/Urs al-dam* (1977), *Amok* (1982), *Horsemen of Glory/Les cavaliers de la gloire* (1993), *The Shadow of the Pharaoh/L'ombre du pharaon/Delo pheraoun* (1996), *The Lovers of Mogador/Les amants de Mogador* (2002).

Ben Brahim, Rachid (Algerian filmmaker). Born in 1951 in La Lambèse, he began his career with two fictional shorts and three documentaries. In the 1980s he worked in television, making both features and documentaries, and in 1998 contributed an episode to the collectively made *The Other Algeria: Views from Within/L'autre Algérie: regards intérieurs*. Feature film: *The Third Act/Le troisième acte* (1991).

Benchrif, Hamid (Moroccan filmmaker—1940–1986). Born in Fez, he worked in radio and television and as editor on a number of Moroccan features. Feature film: *Steps in the Mist/Des pas dans le brouillard/Khutawât fî dabâb* (1982).

Bendeddouche, Ghaouti (Algerian filmmaker). Born in 1936 in Tlemcen, he studied at IDHEC in Paris. Back in Algeria he worked as assistant on feature films and, for ten years, as documentary filmmaker. He contributed one episode to the collective film *Hell for a 10 Year Old/L'enfer à dix ans* (1968). Feature films: *The Fishermen/Les pêcheurs/Al-shabaka* (1976), *Dead the Long Night/Morte la longue nuit* (compilation film, with Mohamed Slim Riad, 1979), *Harvests of Steel/Moissons d'acier* (1982), *Hassan niya/Hasan niya* (1989), *The Neighbor/La voisine/Al jara* (2002).

Benguigui, Yamina (French-based filmmaker of Algerian descent). Born in Paris, she began her career in television, producing works on women's issues, including two series each comprising three fifty-two-minute videos: *Women of Islam/Femmes d'Islam* (1994) and *Immigrants' Memories: The Maghreb Inheritance/Mémoires d'immigrés: L'héritage maghrébin* (1997). She has also made *Kate's House, A Place of Hope/La maison de Kate, un lieu d'espoir* (1995) and the fifty-two-minute video *The Perfumed Garden/Le jardin parfumé* (2000). Feature film: *Inch'Allah Sunday/Inch'Allah dimanche* (2001).

Benhadj, Mohamed Rachid (Algerian filmmaker). Born in 1949 in Algiers, he studied architecture at the École Supérieure d'Arts Décoratifs in Paris before studying film at the Université de Paris. He continues to work as a painter. From 1979 he made a series of television features and several documentaries. Currently he lives in Italy, where he has made a forty-five-minute documentary, *The Last Supper/L'ultima cena* (1995), and his latest features. Feature films: *Desert Rose/Rose des sables/Louss* (1989), *Touchia/Tushia* (1993), *The Tree of Suspended Fates/L'albero dei destini sospesi* (in Italy, 1997), *Mirka* (in Italy, 2000).

Ben Halima, Hamouda (Tunisian filmmaker). Born in 1935 in Moknine, he studied at IDHEC. He worked as editor for the Tunisian newsreel company and as producer for RTT. After two documentaries he made a pioneering feature and contributed an episode to *In the Land of the Tararani/Au pays de Tararani/Fî bilâd al-Tararany* (1972). Feature: *Khlifa Ringworm/Khlifa le teigneux/Khalifa al-aqra'* (1969).

Benjelloun, Hassan (Moroccan filmmaker). Born in 1950 in Settat, he studied first pharmacy and then film, at the CLCF, in Paris. Graduating in 1983, he made a couple of short films before embarking on his feature film career. Features: *Other People's Celebrations/La* *fête des autres /Ayad al-akhain* (1990), *Yarit* (1993), *Yesterday's Friends/Les amis d'hier* (1997), *A Woman's Judgement/Jugement d'une femme* (2000), *The Lips of Silence/Les lèvres du silence* (2001), *The Pal/Le pote* (2002).

Benlyazid, Farida (Moroccan filmmaker). Born in 1948 in Tangier, she studied film at ESEC in Paris. A journalist, she has worked as screenwriter with Jilali Ferhati (*A Hole in the Wall/Une brèche dans le mur*, 1978, and *Reed Dolls/Poupées de roseau*, 1981), Mohamed Abderrahman Tazi (*Badis*, 1990, and *Looking for My Wife's Husband/A la recherche du mari de ma femme*, 1993), and Abdelmajid Rchich (*The Story of a Rose/L'histoire d'une rose*, 2000). She contributed one episode to the collective feature *Five Films for a Hundred Years/Cinq films pour cent ans* (1995). Feature films: *A Gateway to Heaven/Une porte sur le ciel/Bâb al-sama'maftûh* (1987), *Women's Wiles/Ruses de femmes/Keid Ensa* (1999).

Ben Mabrouk, Nejia (Tunisian filmmaker). Born in 1949 in El-Oudiane, she studied literature in Tunis and film at INSAS in Brussels. She worked as trainee in Belgian television before completing a feature and contributing an episode to *After the Gulf?/La guerre du Golfe . . . et après?/Harbu al-khalîj wa ba'du?* (1992). Feature film: *The Trace/La trace/ Al-sâma* (1988).

Ben Mahmoud, Mahmoud (Tunisian filmmaker). Born in 1947 in Tunis, he studied film at INSAS and aspects of art and communication at the Free University of Brussels in Belgium. He worked in the 1970s as both scriptwriter and sound recordist. He has made various documentaries—some in video—since the 1980s. Feature films: *Crossing Over/ Traversées/'Ubur* (1982), *The Dust of Diamonds/Poussière de diamants/Chichkhân* (co-directed with Fadhel Jaïbi, 1992), *The Pomegranate Siesta/Les siestes grenadine/Kouaïl er-roummen* (1999), *A Thousand and One Voices/Les mille et une voix* (documentary, 2001).

Ben Mokhtar, Rabie (Algerian filmmaker). Born in 1944 in Amalou, he studied film making in France, specializing in cinematography. In Algeria he made a number of documentaries and worked as director of photography. Feature film: *Marathon Tam* (1992).

Bennani, Larbi (Moroccan filmmaker). Born in 1930 in Fez, he graduated from the French film school, IDHEC, in 1954. He joined the CCM in 1959 and made a dozen short films before co-directing the second Moroccan feature film in 1968. He had to wait twenty-seven years to complete his own second feature. Feature films: *When the Dates Ripen/ Quand murissent les dattes/Hinama yandhuju al-tamr* (with Abdelaziz Ramdani, 1968), *The Unknown Resistance Fighter/Le résistant inconnu* (1995).

Bensaïd, Hamid (Moroccan filmmaker). Born in 1948 in Meknes, he worked as assistant curator at the Cinémathèque Française in Paris and studied film at Lodz in Poland. He has made several shorts and documentaries. Feature film: *The Bird of Paradise/L'oiseau du paradis* (1981).

Ben Salah, Mohamed (Belgian-based filmmaker of Algerian descent). Born in 1945 in Algeria, he made his sole 16mm feature-length film as his diploma film at INSAS, where he studied. Feature film: *Some People and Others/Les uns, les autres* (1972).

Ben Smaïl, Mohamed (Tunisian filmmaker). Born in 1953 at La Goulette, he studied first biology and then dramatic arts, the latter at the University of Paris VIII and in

Los Angeles. He began work as an actor in the 1980s, appearing in both French and Tunisian features, including Mehdi Charef's *Miss Mona* (1987). He made two documentaries in the 1990s. Feature film: *Tomorrow I Burn/Demain je brûle/Ghoudwa nahrek* (1998).

Bornaz, Kalthoum (Tunisian filmmaker). Born in 1945 in Tunis, she studied at IDHEC in Paris, graduating in 1968. She worked as assistant on a number of foreign and local films made in Tunisia and edited over a dozen shorts as well as several features. She scripted and directed her own short films from the late 1980s. Feature film: *Keswa—The Lost Thread/Keswa—le fil perdu/Kiswâ al-khayt al-dhâi'* (1997).

Bouamari, Mohamed (Algerian filmmaker). Born in 1941 in Setif, he had no formal film training. From the mid-1960s he worked as assistant director and short filmmaker. Feature films: *The Charcoal Burner/Le charbonnier/Al-fahâm* (1972), *The Inheritance/ L'héritage/Al-irth* (1974), *First Step/Premier pas/Al-khutwat al-ula* (1979), *The Denial/Le refus/Al-raft* (1982).

Bouanani, Ahmed (Moroccan filmmaker). Born in 1938 in Casablanca, he studied at IDHEC in Paris and was involved in the short-lived Sigma 3 collective. From 1970 he has worked as editor and scriptwriter on a number of Moroccan short and feature films. He has published several volumes of poems and wrote the scripts for Daoud Aoulad Syad's first two features. The pair also collaborated on a book of photographs and poems, *Territoires de l'instant* (2000). At the same time he has directed several short films. Feature film: *Mirage/Al-sarab* (1979).

Bouassida, Abdelhafidh (Tunisian filmmaker). Born in 1947 in Sfax, he is a product of the FTCA, the Tunisian amateur film movement. He studied at FAMU, the Prague film school, and on his return worked as journalist, short filmmaker, and assistant on a number of features. Feature film: *The Ballad of Mamelouk/La ballade de Mamelouk/Sarâb* (1981).

Bouberras, Rabah (Algerian filmmaker). Born in 1950 in Algeria, he was a trainee at RTA before studying at VGIK, the Moscow film school. From 1982 he has made a series of 16mm features for RTA. Feature film: *Sahara Blues* (1991).

Bouchaâla, Ahmed (French-based filmmaker of Algerian descent). Born in Algeria in 1956, he has lived in France since 1962 and has Algerian nationality. He has worked as assistant director and made a first short in 1984. His wife, **Zakia Bouchaâla**, born in 1963 in Lille and née Tahiri, is an actress. She co-wrote his first feature and co-directed the second. Together they also collaborated on the script of the Moroccan newcomer Abdelhaï Laraki's first feature, *Mona Saber* (2001). Feature films: *Krim* (1995), *Control of Origin/ Origine contrôlée* (2001).

Bouchareb, Rachid (French-based filmmaker of Algerian descent). Born in France in 1953 and of French nationality, Bouchareb began his career in French television, working as an assistant and making a number of shorts. Feature films: *Bâton Rouge* (1985), *Cheb* (1990), *Segou* (1992), *Shattered Years/Des années déchirées* (1992), *Life Dust/Poussière de vie* (1994), *My Family's Honor/L'honneur de ma famille* (1997), *Little Senegal/Little Sénégal* (2001).

Boucif, Mourad (Belgian-based filmmaker of Moroccan descent). Born in 1967 in Algeria of Moroccan parents, he arrived in Belgium at the age of 5. He received no film school training. All his films—two shorts and his sole feature—have been made in collaboration with his childhood friend, a fellow Belgian immigrant from Istanbul, Taylan Barman. Feature film: *Beyond Gibraltar/Au delà de Gibraltar* (with Taylan Barman, 2001).

Boughedir, Ferid (Tunisian filmmaker). Born in 1944 in Hammam-Lif, he is a product of the FTCA, the Tunisian amateur film movement. Film critic and historian, he has combined an academic career with his work as a filmmaker. Active from the late 1960s, he made short films, acted as assistant director on foreign features, contributed one episode to the collective feature *In the Land of the Tararani/Au pays de Tararani/Fi bilâd al-Tararany* (1972), and co-directed a first fictional feature. In the 1980s he made two key documentaries, *African Camera/Caméra d'Afrique/Kâmira Ifrqiya* (1983) and *Arab Camera/Caméra arabe/Kâmira 'arabiya* (1987). His solo feature career began in 1990. Feature films: *Murky Death/La mort trouble/Al-mawt al-akhîr* (with Claude d'Anna, 1970), *Halfaouine/Halfaouine—l'enfant des terrasses/Halfawîn—'Usfûr stah* (1990), *One Summer at La Goulette/Un été à la Goulette/Saîf halqu-al wâdiy* (1995).

Bouguermouh, Abderrahmane (Algerian filmmaker). Born in 1936 in Akbou, he studied at IDHEC in Paris. From the late 1960s he made a number of shorts and contributed one episode to the collective feature *Hell for a 10 Year Old/L'enfer à dix ans* (1968). Subsequently he made two 16mm television features for RTA, *Summer Birds/Les oiseaux de l'été* (1978) and *Black and White/Noir et blanc/Kahla wa beida* (1980). Feature films: *Cry of Stone/Cri de pierre/Ourâkh al-hajar* (1986), *The Forgotten Hillside/La colline oubliée* (1996).

Boukhitine, Lyèce (French-based filmmaker of Algerian descent). Born in 1965 in Digoin, France, he studied drama in Lyon and Paris and appeared in a number of films. He made three short fictional films before completing his first feature. Feature film: *The Mistress in a Swimming Costume/La maîtresse en maillot de bain* (2001)

Boulane, Ahmed (Moroccan filmmaker). Born in 1956 in Salé, he studied drama at the National Conservatoire for Dramatic Art and Music in Rabat and then worked in theatre. He began (but did not complete) formal studies of film in Italy. On his return he worked as an actor and as assistant on foreign productions. In the 1990s he made a number of documentaries and two fictional shorts. Feature film: *Ali, Rabia and the Others/Ali, Rabia et les autres* (2000).

Bourquia, Farida (Moroccan filmmaker). Born in 1948 in Casablanca, she studied drama at the State Theatre Institute in Moscow, graduating in 1973. On her return, she worked in Moroccan television, directing numerous dramas and series throughout the 1980s and 1990s. Feature film: *The Embers/La braise/Al-jamr* (1982).

Bouzid, Nouri (Tunisian filmmaker). Born in 1945 in Sfax, he studied at INSAS in Belgium. On his return, he worked in Tunisian television before being arrested for political activities and imprisoned for five years. On his release he worked as assistant director on a large number of Tunisian and foreign features. He made his directing debut in 1986 and has subsequently worked as a scriptwriter on five features (for Boughedir,

Tlatli, Babaï, and Dhouib) and contributed an episode to the collective feature *After the Gulf?/La guerre du Golfe . . . et après?/Harbu al-khalîj wa ba'du?* (1992). Feature films: *Man of Ashes/L'homme de cendres/Rih al-sid* (1986), *Golden Horseshoes/Les sabots en or/ Safâ'ih min dhahab* (1989), *Bezness/Baznâs* (1992), *Girls from a Good Family/Tunisiennes/ Bent familia* (1997), *Clay Dolls/Poupées d'argile* (2002).

Charef, Mehdi (French-based filmmaker of Algerian descent). Born in 1952 at Maghnia in Algeria, he arrived in France at the age of 10. He retains Algerian nationality. Trained as a mechanic, he worked in a factory from 1970 until 1983. That year he published the first of three French-language novels, *Le thé au harem d'Archi Ahmed* (translated into English as *Tea in the Harem*), followed by *Le harki de Meriem* (1989) and *La maison d'Alexina* (1999). He also made several téléfilms for La Sept Arte in the 1990s, including *Pigeon volé* (1995) and a version of *La maison d'Alexina* (1998). Features: *Tea in Archimedes' Harem/Le thé au harem d'Archimède* (1985), *Miss Mona* (1987), *Camomile/ Camoumille* (1988), *In the Land of the Juliets/Au pays des Juliets* (1992), *Marie-Line* (2001), *Keltoum's Daughter/La fille de Keltoum/Bint Keltoum* (2002).

Chatta, Nidhal (Tunisian filmmaker). Born in 1959 in Tunis, he studied ecology and oceanography in the UK. He made a number of short underwater films and also worked in production roles for the BBC. Feature film: *No Man's Love* (2000).

Chenouga, Chad (French-based filmmaker of Algerian descent). Born in 1962 in Paris, he studied first economics and then drama at the Cours Florent in Paris, where he later became a teacher. He has appeared in a number of French films and television dramas. He made four shorts in the 1990s. Feature film: *17 rue Bleue* (2001).

Chibane, Malek (French-based filmmaker of Algerian descent). Born in 1964 in France of Kabyle parents, he began his feature film making career in the early 1990s. Feature films: *Hexagon/Hexagone* (1993), *Sweet France/Douce France* (1995).

Chouika, Driss (Moroccan filmmaker). Born in 1953 in Kalaa Sraona, he studied economics, became part of the Moroccan amateur film movement (FNCCM), and worked as a trainee in film production. For television he made *The Silence of the Night/Le silence de la nuit* (1996) and *Sower of Wind/Semeur de vent* (1997), as well as a series about cinema, *Zawaya* (from 1994). Feature film: *Mabrouk* (1999).

Chouikh, Mohamed (Algerian filmmaker). Born in 1943 in Mostaganem, he worked as an actor in the theatre and appeared in leading roles in a number of films by Algerian and French directors. In the 1970s he directed two 16mm features for RTA, *The River Mouth/L'embouchure* (1972–1974) and *The Wrecks/Les paumés* (1974). Feature films: *Breakdown/La rupture/Al-inqita'* (1982), *The Citadel/La citadelle/Al-qal'a* (1988), *Youssef: The Legend of the Seventh Sleeper/Youcef: la légende du septième dormant/Youcef kesat dekra sabera* (1993), *The Desert Ark/L'arche du désert* (1997).

Chraïbi, Omar (Moroccan filmmaker). Born in 1961 in Casablanca, he studied photography at Liège in Belgium and communication studies at the University of Grenoble and completed a DEA in film at the Sorbonne in Paris. He worked as assistant director on a number of features, directed a few short films, and contributed an episode to the collective feature *Five Films for a Hundred Years/Cinq films pour cent ans* (1995). Feature film: *The Man Who Embroidered Secrets/L'homme qui brodait des secrets* (2000).

Chraïbi, Saâd (Moroccan filmmaker). Born in 1952 in Fez, he studied medicine and began his career in the context of the FNCCM, the Moroccan film club movement, founding the Al-azaim film club in Casablanca. He formed part of the collective which made *Cinders of the Vineyard/Les cendres du clos/Ramâd al-zariba* (1977) and also made a variety of short films. Feature films: *Chronicle of a Normal Life/Chronique d'une vie normale/Waqâi'a min hatât âdia* (1991), *Women . . . and Women/Femmes . . . et femmes* (1998), *Thirst/Soif* (2000).

Chrigui, Tijani (Moroccan filmmaker). Born in 1949 in Azemmour, he worked initially as a painter. He co-scripted Mohamed Aboulouakar's *Hadda* (1984) before making his own first 16mm feature. Feature film: *Ymer or The Flowering Thistles/Ymer ou les chardons florifères* (1991).

Damak, Mohamed (Tunisian filmmaker). Born in 1952 in Sfax, he is a product of the FTCA, the Tunisian amateur film movement. He studied in France at the CICF and the Ecole Pratique des Hautes Etudes, worked on a number of foreign features, and made short films. Feature film: *The Cup/La coupe/Al-ka's* (1986).

Damardjji, Djafar (Algerian filmmaker). Born in 1934 in Algiers, he studied theatre at the Berlin Humboldt University in the GDR. He taught at INC, the short-lived film school in Algiers, and worked in various government film-related posts. He has made shorts in Algeria and in the Arab Emirates, where he founded an audiovisual center. Feature films: *The Good Families/Les bonnes familles/Al-usar al-tayyibah* (1972), *Wanderings/Errances* (1993).

Debboub, Yahia (Algerian filmmaker). Born in 1940, he studied at the Algerian film school (INC) in the 1960s and worked in administrative roles in film and television. His first feature waited six years for release. Features: *The Old Lady and the Child/La vielle dame et l'enfant* (1991–1997), *The Resistance Fighters/Les résistants* (1997).

Derkaoui, Mohamed Abdelkrim (Moroccan filmmaker). Born in 1945 in Oujda, brother of Mostafa Derkaoui. He studied film at Lodz in Poland and on his return became one of Morocco's leading cinematographers. In 1979 he formed part of the collective responsible for *Cinders of the Vineyard/Les cendres du clos/Ramâd al-zariba* and later co-directed a first feature. His first solo feature appeared in 1998. Feature films: *The Travelling Showman's Day/Le jour du forain/Yawm al-id* (with Driss Kettani, 1984), *Cairo Street/Rue le Caire* (1998).

Derkaoui, Mostafa (Mococcan filmmaker). Born in 1944 in Oujda, brother of the filmmaker and director of photography Mohamed Abdelkrim Derkaoui. He studied theatre and literature in Tunisia and film making at Lodz in Poland, graduating in 1972. He directed various shorts during his studies and subsequently made a range of short films and television dramas. He participated in the collective responsible for *Cinders of the Vineyard/Les cendres du clos/Ramâd al-zariba* in 1979 and contributed one episode to the collective Arab film *After the Gulf?/La guerre du Golfe . . . et après?/Harbu al-khalîj wa ba'du?* (1992). He is one of the Maghreb's most prolific feature filmmakers. Feature films: *About Some Meaningless Events/De quelques événements sans signification/Anba'dh al-ahdâth biduni ma'nIa* (1974), *The Beautiful Days of Sheherazade/Les beaux jours de Charazade/Ayyâm chahrazad al-hilwâ* (1982), *Provisional Title/Titre provisoire/'Unwânun mu'aqqat* (1984), *First Fiction/Fiction première/Riwâya 'ûlâ* (1992), *(Ga)me in the Past/ Je(u) au passé* (1994), *The Seven Gates of the Night/Les sept portes de la nuit* (1994), *The Great Allegory/La grande allégorie* (1995), *The Loves of Hadj Mokhtar Soldi/Les amours de Hadj Mokhtar Soldi* (2001).

Dhouib, Moncef (Tunisian filmmaker). Born in 1952 in Sfax, he studied in Paris and worked in puppetry and street theatre. He also participated in FTCA, the Tunisian amateur film movement, worked as assistant, and, from the early 1980s, he has made a series of remarkable short films. Feature film: *The Sultan of the Medina/Soltane el Medina!/Ya sultan al madina* (1993).

Djadjam, Mostéfa (French-based filmmaker of Algerian descent). Born in 1952 in Oran, he has retained his Algerian nationality. Originally an actor, he played the lead in Allouache's *The Adventures of a Hero* (1978). In addition to his appearances as an actor on screen and stage, he has worked as assistant director (for Werner Schroeter and Mahmoud Zemmouri) and as scriptwriter. He began making short films and documentaries in 1982. Feature film: *Frontiers/Frontières* (2000).

Djebar, Assia (Algerian filmmaker). Born in 1936 in Cherchell, she studied at the Ecole Normale Supérieure in Sèvres. She is best known as a French-language novelist, author of over a dozen novels and collections of stories. In addition to her two features, made for RTA but given international distribution at film festivals, she also co-directed a fifty-minute documentary on *Women on the Move/Femmes en mouvement* (1990) with Merzak Allouache. Feature films: *The Nouba of the Women of Mount Chenoua/La nouba des femmes du Mont Chenoua/Noubat nissâ jabal chnouwwa* (1978), *The Zerda, or Songs of Forgetfulness/La zerda ou les chants de l'oubli/Zerda wa aghani al-nisyan* (1980).

Djemaï, Ahmed (Tunisian filmmaker). He learned film making in the film industry in France, where he lives, and where he made a few short films. He returned to Tunis for his first feature. Feature film: *Wind of Destinies/Le vent des destins/Rih al-aqdar* (1993).

Dridi, Karim (French-based filmmaker of Tunisian descent). Born in Tunis in 1961, but living in France, Dridi produced various industrial films and directed a number of short films before beginning his feature film career. Features: *Pigalle* (1994), *Bye-Bye* (1995), *Out of Play/Hors jeu* (1998).

El Fani, Nadia (Tunisian filmmaker). Born in 1960 in Paris of a French mother and Tunisian father. She spent her childhood in Tunis but has since lived in both France and Tunisia. She worked as assistant director on numerous foreign films, as well as Bouzid's *Man of Ashes,* before making four personal short films in the 1990s. Feature film: *Bedwin Hacker* (2002).

El Maânouni, Ahmed (Moroccan filmmaker). Born in 1944 in Casablanca, he studied drama in Paris at the Université du Théâtre des Nations and film making in Brussels at INSAS. He has worked as director of photography on several films, directed a number of shorts, and made a fifty-minute video documentary, *The Moroccan "Goumiers"/Les* *goumiers marocains.* His two feature-length films both mix documentary and fiction. Feature films: *The Days, The Days/O les jours/Al-ayyam al-ayyam* (1978), *Trances/Transes/Al-hal* (1981).

El Okbi, Mohamed Ali (Tunisian filmmaker). Born in 1948 in Tunis, he studied first in Paris—at IDHEC and the Sorbonne—and then in Los Angeles. In Tunisia he made a number of shorts and worked as assistant on a number of foreign-made feature films. His first feature is a semi-documentary featuring the 1978 Tunisian football team. Feature films: *A Ball and Some Dreams/Un ballon et des rêves/Kurra wa ahlâm* (1978), *The Teddy Boys/Les zazous de la vague/Al-zâzuwwât* (1992).

Essid, Lotfi (Tunisian filmmaker). Born in 1952 in Tunisia, he studied literature and cinema and worked as an actor before turning to film making. He made a couple of short films before completing his sole feature. Feature film: *What Are We Doing This Sunday?/Que fait-on ce dimanche?/Al-sabt fât?* (1983).

Fares, Tewfik (Algerian filmmaker). Born in 1937 in Bordj-Bou-Arreridj, he studied at the Sorbonne in Paris. On his return he worked at the Tunisian newsreel company and in television and collaborated on a number of early Algerian short films. He scripted two features directed by Mohamed Lakhdar Hamina. Feature film: *The Outlaws/Les hors-la-loi/Al kharijoun an-alkanoun* (1969).

Fazaî Mellitti, Ezzedine (Tunisian filmmaker). Born in 1957 in Tunis, he worked as an actor in Europe and the United States. Feature film, shown at the JCC but not otherwise distributed in Tunisia: *The Magic Box/Le magique/Al-sahir* (1994).

Ferchiou, Rachid (Tunisian filmmaker). Born in 1941 in Bardo, he studied film making in Berlin and worked as a trainee in both French and Italian television. Back home, he worked extensively in Tunisian television. Feature films: *Yusra/Yusrâ* (1972), *The Children of Boredom/Les enfants de l'ennui/Atfâl al-qujaq* (1975), *Autumn '86/Automne '86/Al-kharîf '86* (1991), *Check and Mate/Echec et mat/Kich mât* (1995).

Ferhati, Jillali (Moroccan filmmaker). Born in 1948 in Khemisset, he studied literature, sociology, and drama in Paris, where he lived for ten years. He made two short films before beginning his feature film career in 1978. He also contributed an episode to the collective feature *Five Films for a Hundred Years/Cinq films pour cent ans* (1995). Feature films: *A Hole in the Wall/Une brèche dans le mur/Charkhun fi-l hâ'it* (1978), *Reed Dolls/Poupées de roseau/Araïs min qasab* (1981), *The Beach of Lost Children/La plage des enfants perdus/Shâtiu al-atfâl al-mafoûdin* (1991), *Make-Believe Horses/Chevaux de fortune/Kuius al-has* (1995), *Braids/Tresses* (2000).

Fettar, Sid Ali (Algerian filmmaker). Born in 1943 in Algiers, he studied at INC, the short-lived Algerian film school, completing his studies at Lodz in Poland, where he worked as a trainee in television. Back home, he worked for RTA. Feature films: *Rai* (1988), *Forbidden Love/Amour interdit* (1993).

Ghalem, Ali (also known as **Ali Ghanem**) (Algerian filmmaker). Born in 1943 in Constantine, he received no formal education beyond that received at a Koranic school. In France he made two low-budget features and wrote the novel *A Wife for My Son/Une* *femme pour mon fils,* which forms the basis of his Algerian feature. Feature films: *Mektoub?* (in France, 1970), *The Other France/L'autre France* (in France, 1975), *A Wife for My Son/Une femme pour mon fils/Zawja li lbny* (1982).

Ghorab-Volta, Zaïda (French-based filmmaker of Algerian descent). Born in 1966, she began with work in the social sector before turning to cinema. She made three short fiction films before beginning her feature career. She also co-scripted Romain Goupil's feature, *Her Life/Sa vie à elle* (1995). Feature films: *Leave a Little Love/Laisse un peu d'amour* (1998), *Gilded Youth/Jeunesse dorée* (2001).

Ghorbal, Khaled (Tunisian filmmaker). Born in 1950, he had extensive training in drama both in Tunis (at the Centre d'Art Dramatique) and in Paris (at the Université Internationale du Théâtre de Paris, Université Paris VIII, and the Ecole Jacques Lecoq). He has worked as actor, writer, and director in theatre. He also coordinates a project on "School and Cinema" and has been director of a number of art cinemas. He made a first short in 1996. Feature film: *Fatma* (2001).

Gounajjar, Nour Eddine (Moroccan filmmaker). Born in 1946 in Berguent, he studied at IDHEC in Paris. He directed several shorts and formed part of the collective responsible for *Cinders of the Vineyard/Les cendres du clos/Ramâd al-zariba* in 1979. He has made a number of videos: a documentary on the Sahara, *Blue Memory/La mémoire bleue/Al-dakira al-zarka* (1991), and two fifty-minute fictions for RTM, *The Seven Approaches/Les sept accès* (1996) and *Anirar* (1998). Feature film (16mm): *The Waiting Room/La salle d'attente/Qâ at al-intidhar* (1991).

Guerdjou, Bourlem (French-based filmmaker of Algerian descent). Born in 1965 in Asnières (Paris) of Algerian descent. He directed a number of short films before completing his first feature. He also appeared as an actor in Mehdi Charef's *Tea at Archimedes' Harem* (1985). Feature film: *Living in Paradise/Vivre au paradis* (1998).

Haddad, Moussa (Algerian filmmaker). Born in 1937 in Algiers, he worked as assistant in French television and then for Casbah Films in Algiers. He was assistant to Gillo Pontecorvo and Luchino Visconti before co-directing a first feature (*Three Guns Against Caesar/Trois pistolets contre César,* with Enzo Peri, 1967). Most of his subsequent work comprised 16mm features for RTA. After a twelve-year absence he returned with a feature-length video, *Mad In* (1999). Feature films: *Beside the Poplar Tree/Auprès du peuplier/Min ourb al-saf saf* (1972), *Inspector Tahar's Holiday/Les vacances de l'Inspecteur Tahar/'Utla al'mafattish Tahar* (1973).

Hadjadj, Belkacem (Algerian filmmaker). Born in 1950 in Algiers, he studied film making at INSAS in Belgium and then worked in Belgian television. On his return he worked for RTA making the feature-length *The Cork/Le bouchon/Al-marja* (1980) and the prize-winning short *The Drop/La goutte* (1982). Three further RTA features followed: *Variations on an Absent Character/Variations sur un personnage absent/Buziân al-kal'l* (1983), *Djillali Gataa* (1984), and *The Five/Les cinq/El Khamsa* (1988), a collection of short films first produced in 1982. He has subsequently made three fifty-minute videos, *La sebeida* (1992), *The Shattered Rainbow/L'arc-en-ciel brisé* (1999), and *A Woman Taxi Driver in Sidi Bel Abbès/Une femme taxi à Sidi Bel Abbès* (2000). Feature film: *Once Upon a Time/Il était une fois/Machaho* (1995).

Hakkar, Amor (French-based filmmaker of Algerian descent). Born in 1958 in Khenchela in Algeria, Hakkar grew up as the child of immigrants in Besançon. Feature film: *Bad Weather for a Crook/Sale temps pour un voyou* (1992).

Hammami, Abderrazak (Tunisian filmmaker). Born in 1935 in Kairouan, he studied theatre in Strasbourg. He subsequently worked as an actor on stage and in television and film. After working as a trainee in ORTF he returned to Tunisia and became a director for RTT, working in a whole range of genres. Feature film: *Omi Traki/Ummy Trâky* (1973).

Hammami, Mohamed (Tunisian filmmaker). Born in 1951 in Tunis, he spent six years in Moscow, studying film at the Mosgow film school VGIK and journalism at the Patrice Lumumba University. Returning home to work for RTT, he directed shorts, documentaries, and two 16mm television features: *Land of Sacrifice/Terre des sacrifices* (1974) and *The Spark/L'étincelle* (1976). Feature film: *My Village/Mon village/Çirû* (1979).

Hellal, Abderrazak (Algerian filmmaker). Born in 1951, he joined ENTV in 1979 and has continued making television documentaries and features into the late 1990s. He has also written a number of novels. Feature film: *Question of Honor/Question d'honneur* (1997).

Hilmi, Mohamed (Algerian filmmaker). Born in 1931 in Azzefoun, he worked as an actor. He has also written extensively for radio and television and directed a series of 16mm RTA features. Feature film: *El ouelf essaib* (1990).

Ismaîl, Mohamed (Moroccan filmmaker). Born in 1951 in Tetuan, he studied law in Rabat. From 1974 he worked in Moroccan television, directing dramas, films, and variety shows. In the 1980s and 1990s he also worked as a film producer. Feature films: *Aouchtam* (1998), *And Afterwards . . . /Et après . . .* (2002).

Jaïbi, Fadhel (Tunisian filmmaker). Born in 1945 in Ariana, he studied theatre in Paris and, in the early 1970s, co-founded a number of theatrical groups, including the Nouveau Théâtre de Tunis. With Fadhel Jaziri he was actively involved in the company's stage productions and later co-directed several video versions. Feature films: *The Wedding/La noce/Al-'urs* (Collectif du Nouveau Théâtre de Tunis, 1978), *Arab/'Arab* (with Fadhel Jaziri, 1988), *The Dust of Diamonds/Poussière de diamants/Chichkhân* (with Mahmoud Ben Mahmoud, 1992).

Jaziri, Fadhel (Tunisian filmmaker). Born in 1948 in Tunis, he was involved, with Fadhel Jaïbi, in a number of theatrical collectives, including the Nouveau Théâtre de Tunis. Together they participated in the company's stage productions and later co-directed several video versions. He has also appeared as an actor in several films, most notably Mahmoud Ben Mahmoud's *Crossing Over* (1982), and made a ninety-minute video, *Hadhra* (2001). Feature films: *The Wedding/La noce/Al-'urs* (Collectif du Nouveau Théâtre de Tunis, 1978), *Arab/'Arab* (with Fadhel Jaïbi, 1988).

Jebli Ouazzani, Fatima (Dutch-based filmmaker of Moroccan descent). Born in 1959 in Meknès, she emigrated in 1970 with her parents to the Netherlands, where she has lived since. After studying psychology, she took a diploma course in directing and scriptwriting at NFTVA in Amsterdam. From 1983 she worked as a reporter in Dutch radio and television and made a number of short documentaries on social issues. Her first feature won the top prize at the Fifth Moroccan National Film Festival in Casablanca in 1998. Feature film: *In My Father's House/Dans la maison de mon père/In het Huis van mijn Vader* (1997).

Kabouche, Azize (French-based filmmaker of Algerian descent). Born in 1960 in Lyon, France, he studied drama in Paris and made numerous appearances on stage and in films. He made two shorter films before completing his first feature. Feature film: *Letters from Algeria/Lettres d'Algérie* (2002).

Kamal, Kamal (Moroccan filmmaker). Born in 1961 at Berkane, he did his university studies at the Mohamed 1st Faculty in Oujda. Later he studied scriptwriting at the Institut Libre du Cinéma in Paris. He produced a television series, *Idriss al Akbar,* and made numerous video shorts. Feature film: *Taif Nizar* (2002).

Kateb, Mustapha (Algerian filmmaker). An actor in the FLN company, he appeared in a number of Algerian features, including early films by Mustapha Badie, Mohamed Lakhdar Hamina, and Ahmed Rachedi. His sole feature film is an adaptation of play by the actor Rouiched. Feature film: *El ghoula/Al-ghûla* (1972).

Kechiche, Abdellatif (French-based filmmaker of Tunisian descent). Worked as an actor, in the theatre and on screen, taking leading roles in Abdelkrim Bahloul's *Mint Tea* (1984) and André Téchiné's *The Innocents/Les innocents.* Feature film: *Voltaire's Fault/La faute à Voltaire* (2000).

Kettani, Driss (Moroccan filmmaker—1947–1994). Born in Salé, he trained in the theatre in Paris, he also worked there as actor and assistant on films and in television (ORTF). He also worked as a trainee for the BBC. Feature film: *The Travelling Showman's Day/Le jour du forain/Yawm al-id* (with Mohamed Abdelkrim Derkaoui, 1984).

Khayat, Mustapha (Moroccan filmmaker). Born in 1944 in Casablanca, he studied cinematography at ORTF in Paris. On his return he worked in Moroccan television, first as cameraman, then as producer-director. Feature film: *Dead End/L'impasse/Al-wata* (1984).

Khechine, Ahmed (Tunisian filmmaker). Born in 1940 in Kairouan, he worked initially as a schoolteacher. He began his film work in the context of the Tunisian amateur film movement, making a number of short films in the 1960s. Feature film: *Under the Autumn Rain/Sous la pluie d'automne/Tahta matar al-Kharif* 1970.

Khemir, Nacer (Tunisian filmmaker). Born in 1948 in Korba, he has worked in a variety of media, active as sculptor, writer, and performing storyteller. He has also made a two-hour video, *In Search of the Thousand and One Nights/A la recherche des 1001 nuits* (1991). His feature film career began after four very varied shorts. Feature films: *The Searchers of the Desert/Les baliseurs du désert/Al-hâ'imoûn* (1984), *The Dove's Lost Necklace/Le collier perdu de la colombe/Tawq al-hamâma al-mafqûd* (1990).

Khlifi, Omar (Tunisian filmmaker). Born in 1934 in Soliman, he studied in Tunisia and France. He learned his film making in the context of the Tunisian amateur film movement, making a dozen short films in the early 1960s. His early features make him the great pioneer of independent Tunisian cinema. Feature films: *The Dawn/L'aube/Al-fajr* (1966), *The Rebel/Le rebelle/Al-mutamarrid* (1968), *The Fellagas/Les fellagas/Al-fallâga* (1970), *Screams/Hurlements/Çurrakh* (1972), *The Challenge/Le défi/Al-tahaddi* (1986).

Krim, Rachida (French-based filmmaker of Algerian descent). Born in 1955 at Alès, she studied painting at the schools of fine art in Montpellier and Nîmes. She has made a number of short films since 1992. Feature film: *Under Women's Feet/Sous les pieds des femmes* (1996).

Ktari, Naceur (Tunisian filmmaker). Born in 1943 in Sayada, he studied in Paris (at IDHEC, the CLCF, and the Sorbonne) and in Rome (at the Centro sperimentale di cinematografia). He subsequently worked as assistant for Tunisian and foreign filmmakers. Feature films: *The Ambassadors/Les ambassadeurs/Al-sufarâ* (1975), *Be My Friend/Sois mon amie/Hlou morr* (2000).

Ktiri Idrissi, Naguib (U.S.-based filmmaker of Moroccan descent). Born in Casablanca, he has lived with his family in the United States since 1977. There he studied at UCLA and now teaches film at Loyola Marymount College in San Francisco. For his first 16mm feature film, *Aziz and Itto: A Moroccan Wedding/Aziz et Itto: Un mariage marocain* (1991), he was producer, director, scriptwriter, editor, and sound recordist and shared the camera credit with Susan Pollack.

Labidi, Ali. *See* **Abidi, Ali**

Lagtaâ, Abdelkader (Moroccan filmmaker). Born in 1948 in Casablanca, he studied film making at the Lodz film school in Poland. He has made a number of short films for both film and television distribution and formed part of the collective which made *Cinders of the Vineyard/Les cendres du clos/Ramâd al-zariba* in 1979. Feature films: *A Love Affair in Casablanca/Un amour à Casablanca/Hubb fî al-dâr al-bayda* (1991), *The Closed Door/La porte close/Bâb al-nasdûd* (1995, released 2000), *The Casablancans/Les Casablancais/Bidawa* (1998).

Lahlou, Latif (Moroccan filmmaker). Born in 1939 in El Jadida, he studied in Paris, film making at IDHEC and sociology at the Sorbonne, graduating in 1959. He joined the CCM in 1960 and remained there for over a decade. He worked extensively in short film production as director, editor, and producer. He also had production roles on Moroccan features and French films shot in Morocco. Feature films: *Spring Sunshine/Soleil de printemps/Chams al-rabi'* (1969), *The Compromise/La compromission/Al-musâwama* (1986).

Lahlou, Nabyl (Moroccan filmmaker). Born in 1945 in Fez, he studied drama in Paris and established himself first as a playwright, writing in both French and Arabic. He made a medium-length film before turning to feature film making. Feature films: *Al Kanfoudi* (1978), *The Governor-General of Chakerbakerben Island/Le gouverneur-général de l'île de Chakerbakerben/Al-hakim al-'am* (1980), *Brahim Who?/Brahim qui?/Brahim yach?* (1982), *The Soul That Brays/L'âme qui braît/Nahiq al-ruh* (1984), *Komany* (1989),

The Night of the Crime/La nuit du crime/Laylat qatl (1992), *The Years of Exile/Les années de l'exil* (2002).

Lakhdar Hamina, Malik (Algerian filmmaker). Born in 1962, he is the son of Mohamed Lakhdar Hamina. As a child he had roles in various films—Costa-Gavras's *Z* and two of his father's features—and later studied drama in the United States. He played the leading role in his first feature. Feature film: *Autumn—October in Algiers/Automne—Octobre à Alger /Al-karif—October fi al-jaza'ir* (1991).

Lakhdar Hamina, Mohamed (Algerian filmmaker). Born in 1934 in M'sila, he worked for the GPRA, the provisional Algerian government in exile in Tunis, and went to Prague to study briefly at the film school there, FAMU, and to work in the Czech studios. The dominant figure in Algerian cinema, he was head of the OAA and later of ONCIC and won the Palme d'or at Cannes, with his superproduction *Chronicle of the Years of Embers.* Feature films: *The Wind from the Aurès/Le vent des Aurès/Rih al-awras* (1966), *Hassan Terro/Hasan Tiru* (1968), *December/Décembre/Dicember* (1972), *Chronicle of the Years of Embers/Chronique des années de braise/Waqâ sanwât al-jamr* (1975), *Sand Storm/Vent de sable/Rih al'rimâl* (1982), *The Last Image/La dernière image/Al-sûr al-akhîra* (1986).

Lallem, Ahmed (Algerian filmmaker). Born in 1940 in Sétif, he studied briefly at IDHEC in Paris. Committed to the FLN, he later worked in the studios of Belgrade and studied at the Lodz film school in Poland. He has continued to make short films from the 1960s through to the 1990s. Feature films: *Forbidden Zone/Zone interdite/Al-fâiza* (1974), *Barriers/Barrières/Al-hawâjiz* (1977).

Laradji, Rabah (Algerian filmmaker). Born in 1943 in Bordj-Benaim, he studied at INC. He made numerous shorts in the 1960s and 1970s, contributed an episode to the collective fictional feature *Stories of the Revolution/Histoires de la révolution* (1969), and was part of the collective team that made the feature-length documentary *So That Algeria May Live/Pour que vive l'Algérie* (1972). Feature film: *A Roof, a Family/Un toit, une famille/Saqat wa'aila* (1982).

Laraki, Abdelhaï (Moroccan filmmaker). Born in 1949 in Fez, he studied film making at the Ecole Supérieure Louis Lumière (Vaugirard) and film history at the Sorbonne in Paris. During and after his studies he made a number of short films. He has also worked in video, taught audiovisual production, made a number of programs for RTM, and directed numerous advertising shorts. He also produced a number of short films by young directors and also one feature film, Omar Chraïbi's *The Man Who Embroidered Secrets/ L'homme qui brodait des secrets.* Feature film: *Mona Saber* (2001).

Laskri, Amar (Algerian filmmaker). Born in 1942 in Aïn Berda, he studied film in Belgrade. After three short films, he contributed an episode to the collective fictional feature *Hell for a 10 Year Old/L'enfer à dix ans* (1968). He was head of CAAIC from 1996 until it was closed down in 1998. Feature films: *Patrol in the East/Patrouille à l'est/Dawriyyah nahwa al-sharq* (1972), *The Benevolent/El moufid/Al-mufid* (1978), *The Gates of Silence/ Les portes du silence/Abwâb al-çoumt* (1987), *Lotus Flower/Fleur de lotus* (1998).

Lledo, Jean-Pierre (Algerian filmmaker). Born in 1947 in Tlemcem, he studied at the Moscow film school, VGIK. On his return he made several short films before beginning his feature career. More recently he has made some short video documentaries. Feature films: *The Empire of Dreams/L'empire des rêves* (1982), *Lights/Lumières* (1992).

Lotfi, Mohamed (Moroccan filmmaker). Born in 1939 in Oujda, he studied at IDHEC in Paris. He worked as reporter and head of service for the Moroccan newsreel organization within the CCM and then at RTM. He also worked for many years as a documentary filmmaker, making *The Green March/La marche verte* in 1975. He worked increasingly in production before making his feature directing debut at the age of 58. Feature film: *Rhesus or Another Person's Blood/Rhésus ou le sang de l'autre* (1996).

Louhichi, Taïeb (Tunisian filmmaker). Born in 1948 in Mareth, he studied in Paris at the IFC and the Ecole Normale Louis Lumière, "Vaugirard." He made his first films in the context of the FTCA, the Tunisian amateur film movement. He has made over a dozen short and medium-length films. Feature films: *The Shadow of the Earth/L'ombre de la terre/Dhil al-ard* (1982), *Leïla My Reason/Layla ma raison/Majnûn Layla* (1989), *Moon Wedding/Noces de lune/'Urs al-qamar* (1998).

Mansour, Ali (Tunisian filmmaker). Born in 1944 in Mahdia, he studied for about ten years in Paris, first graphic design, then drama, and eventually film making at the CICF. On his return he worked on a great variety of productions for RTT. Feature film: *Two Thieves in Madness/Deux larrons en folie/Faraw'ilqut oukthâ* (1980).

Mazif, Sid Ali (Algerian filmmaker). Born in 1943 in Algiers, he studied at INC in Algiers and made a number of shorts. He contributed episodes to two collective features, *Hell for a 10 Year Old/L'enfer à dix ans* (1968) and *Stories of the Revolution/Histoires de la révolution* (1970). Feature films: *Black Sweat/Sueur noire/Al-'araq al-aswad* (1972), *The Nomads/Les nomades/Masirat al-ruhhal* (1975), *Leila and the Others/Leila et les autres/ Laîla wa akhawâtuha* (1978), *I Exist/J'existe* (documentary, 1982), *Houria/Hûria* (1986).

Meddour, Azzedine (Algerian filmmaker—1947–2000). Born in Sidi Aich, he studied for seven years at VGIK, the Moscow film school. On his return he joined RTA, where he made the compilation series *Colonialism Without Empire/Le colonialisme sans empire* (1978) and a dozen or so short films in the 1980s and 1990s. His final work was the episode *Silent Sorrow/Douleur muette*, which he contributed to the collectively made *The Other Algeria: Views from Within/L'autre Algérie: regards intérieurs*. Feature film: *Baya's Mountain/La montagne de Baya/Djebel Baya* (1997).

Mefti, Tayeb (Algerian filmmaker). Born in 1942 in Alger, he received no formal film training. After three short films he made his first feature for ONCIC. Feature film: *Moussa's Wedding/Le mariage de Moussa* (1982).

Merbah, Mohamed Lamine (Algerian filmmaker). Born in 1946 in Thigenif, he took a degree in sociology, worked as a trainee in Polish television, and studied at INC. From 1970 he combined work for the Algerian publishing house SNED and directing for RTA. He made short films and TV features for RTA, including *Al-mountasser* (1969), *The Mission/La mission* (1971), *Yadès* (1971), *The Medals/Les médailles* (1973), and *Châabia 73* (1974). In the 1990s he became head of ENPA. Feature films: *The Plunderers/Les spoliateurs/Al-mufsidûn* (1972), *The Uprooted/Les déracinés/Beni hindel* (1976), *Radhia* (1992).

Mesbahi, Abdellah (Moroccan filmmaker). Born in 1936 in El Jadida, he studied film making at the ESEC in Paris and was a trainee at the TNP. He occupied senior administrative posts in the ministry of information and the CCM. His last completed feature was shot in 1980 but not finished till nine years later, and he left two features unfinished in the early 1980s. Feature films: *Silence, No Entry/Silence, sens interdit/Sukut al-ittliah al-mamnu* (1973), *Tomorrow the Land Will Not Change/Demain la terre ne changera pas/Ghaganian tatabaddala al-ardh* (1975), *Green Fire/Feu vert/Al-dwaw'al-akhdar* (1976), *Where Are You Hiding the Sun?/Où cachez-vous le soleil?* (1979), *Land of Challenge/La terre du défi/Ardhu-l tahaddy* [also known by its original title, *I Shall Write Your Name in the Sand/J'écrirai ton nom sur le sable*] (1989).

Mesbahi, Imane (Moroccan filmmaker). Born in 1964 in Tetouan in Morocco. As a child, she appeared in the first two features directed by her father, Abdellah Mesbahi. In the 1980s she made several short films and also studied in Cairo: film making (for five years at the Higher Institute of Cinema) and psychology (at the Univerity of Aïn Chams). She began her first feature in 1994, but completed it only eight years later. Feature film: *The Paradise of the Poor/Paradis des pauvres* (2002).

Mesnaoui, Ahmed (Moroccan filmmaker). Born in Rabat in 1926, he died there in 1996. He followed a variety of courses and traineeships but was essentially a self-taught filmmaker. He joined CCM in 1962 and remained there until retirement in 1986, making about twenty short films over a period of thirty-five years. He co-directed the first Moroccan feature. Feature film: *Conquer to Live/Vaincre pour vivre/Inticar al-hayat* (with Mohamed B. A. Tazi, 1968).

Moknèche, Nadir (French-based filmmaker of Algerian descent). Born in 1965 in Paris, he grew up in Algiers from the age of one month. He left Algeria at the age of 18 to study law in Paris. After a stay in London and a traineeship at the Théâtre de Chaillot in Paris, he went to the United States to study film at the New School of Social Research in New York from 1993 to 1995. There he made two short films. Feature film: *Madam Osmane's Harem/Le harem de Mme Osmane* (2000).

Moufti, Hassan (Moroccan filmmaker). Born in 1935 in Tetouan, he studied scriptwriting at the Cinema Institute in Cairo and worked as assistant to several leading Egyptian directors, including Youssef Chahine, Salah Abou Seif, and Henri Barakat. He has worked extensively in Moroccan television and wrote the dialogue for Hakim Noury's first film, *The Postman* (1980). Feature film: *Tears of Regret/Les larmes du regret* (1982).

Mrini, Driss (Moroccan filmmaker). Born in 1950 in Salé, he studied mass communications in Hamburg and worked for two years as production assistant and assistant director in German television (NDR). He made a number of short films in the early 1980s and worked extensively in television. Feature film: *Bamou* (1983).

Mselmani, Habib (Tunisian filmmaker). As a director with RTT, he made numerous programs of all kinds. Feature film: *Sabra and the Monster from the Forest/Sabra et le monstre de la forêt/Sabra wa-l wahch* (1986).

Noury, Hakim (Moroccan filmmaker). Born in 1952 in Casablanca, he studied drama at the National Conservatoire of Dramatic Art from 1966 to 1970. Subsequently he worked as assistant to Souheil Benbarka, made his first short in 1977, directed three television dramas in the mid-1980s, and contributed one episode to *Five Films for a Hundred Years/Cinq films pour cent ans* (1995). In the 1990s he became one of the most prolific of Maghrebian filmmakers. Feature films: *The Postman/Le facteur/Sâi al-barîd* (1980), *The Hammer and the Anvil/Le marteau et l'enclume/Al-mitroqa wa alk-sindân* (1990), *Stolen Childhood/Enfance volée/Atoufoula al-mortasaba* (1993), *The Dream Thief/Le voleur de rêves* (1995), *A Simple News Item/Un simple fait divers* (1997), *A Woman's Fate/Destin de femme* (1998), *She Is Diabetic and Hypertensive and She Refuses to Die/Elle est diabétique et hypertendue et elle refuse de crever* (2000), *A Love Story/Une histoire d'amour* (2001).

Osfour, Mohamed (Moroccan filmmaker). Born in 1927 in Abda, he became enthusiastic about cinema at the age of 12 but received no formal film training. He made a number of short amateur films—which he showed to paying customers in his garage—from the 1940s through to the 1960s. The best known of these early films is the fifty-minute *The Accursed Son/Le fils maudit* (1958). He also worked on a large number of foreign films as actor or assistant. Feature film: *The Devil's Treasure/Le trésor infernal/Al-kinz al-jahannany* (1970).

Ould Khelifa, Saïd (Algerian filmmaker). Born in Tunisia, he worked as a critic before making his first feature. Feature film: *White Shadows/Ombres blanches/Al-dhilâl al-bidh* (1991).

Rachedi, Ahmed (Algerian filmmaker). Born in 1938 in Tebessa, he worked in the film section of the FLN in Tunis. On his return to Algiers he was one of the founding members of CAV and, subsequently, first director general of ONCIC. He made numerous short films and contributed to the collective documentary *So That Algeria May Live/Pour que vive l'Algérie* (1972). In 1981 he made a twelve-part series for RTA, *Barbed Wire/Barbelés/Silane*, followed eleven years later by *It Was the War/C'était la guerre* (with Maurice Fallevic, in France, 1992). Feature films: *Dawn of the Damned/L'aube des damnés/Fajr al-mu'adhhabin* (documentary, 1965), *Opium and the Stick/L'opium et le bâton/Al-afyun wal-'asa* (1969), *A Finger in the Works/Le doigt dans l'engrenage* (1974), *Ali in Wonderland/Ali au pays des mirages/Ali fi bilad al-sarab* (1979), *Monsieur Fabre's Mill/Le moulin de M Fabre/Tabûnat al-sayyid Fabre* (1984).

Rahim, Hadj (Algerian filmmaker). He received no formal film training but worked for RTA from the early 1970s. In the 1980s he made a series of television features for RTA. Feature film: *The Portrait/Le portrait* (1994).

Ramdani, Abdelaziz (Moroccan filmmaker). Born in 1937 in Saïdia in Morocco, he studied at the French film school IDHEC in Paris during the late 1950s. On his return in 1959 he joined the CCM. He also worked as assistant director or director of production on a number of foreign films shot in Morocco and made a number of short documentaries before he co-directed the second Moroccan feature. Feature film: *When the Dates Ripen/Quand murissent les dattes/Hinama yandhuju al-tamr* (with Larbi Bennani, 1968).

Rchich, Abdelmajid (Moroccan filmmaker). Born in 1942 in Kinetra, he studied film making at IDHEC in Paris, graduating in 1963. He joined CCM in 1964, taking time off to study anthropology and the history of art at the Université Libre de Belgique in Brussels. He made a number of documentary and short fictional films from 1968 onward. His first feature was co-scripted by Farida Benlyazid and Omar Chraïbi. Feature film: *The Story of a Rose/L'histoire d'une rose* (2000).

Reggab, Mohamed (Moroccan filmmaker—1942–1990). Born in Safi, he studied film at the Ecole Normale Louis Lumière, "Vaugirard," in Paris and then at VGIK, the Moscow film school. He also studied psychology at the Free University of Brussels and gained a diploma in audiovisual studies in Germany. He joined Moroccan television in 1967 and made a number of shorts. He taught in the audiovisual department of the Institute of Journalism in Rabat and was a member of the collective that made *Cinders of the Vineyard/Les cendres du clos/Ramâd al-zariba* (1979). Though his first feature won awards at several foreign festivals, Reggab was unable to pay the debts he had incurred in making it and was sentenced to some time in prison. He was preparing a second feature, *Memories of Exile/Mémoires d'exil,* when he died in Paris in 1990. Feature film: *The Barber of the Poor Quarter/Le coiffeur du quartier des pauvres/Hallaq darb al-fouqara* (1982).

Riad, Mohamed Slim (Algerian filmmaker). Born in 1932 in Cherchell, he received no formal film training. He worked for some years for French television and was imprisoned as an FLN supporter. He made shorts for CNC and one television feature, *Inspector Tahar/L'inspecteur Tahar* (1969), for RTA. Feature films: *The Way/La voie/Al-tariq* (1968), *Sana'oud/Sana'od* (1972), *Wind from the South/Vent du sud/Rih al-janub* (1975), *Autopsy of a Plot/Autopsie d'un complot/Tachrih mouâmara* (1978), *Dead the Long Night/Morte la longue nuit* (documentary, with Ghaouti Bendeddouche, 1979), *Hassan Taxi/Hasan taxi* (1982).

Saadi, Jilani (Tunisian filmmaker). Born in 1962 in Bizerte, he studied film making in Paris. From 1994 he made several short films. Feature film: *Khorma: Stupidity/Khorma, la bêtise* (2002).

Saddiki, Tayeb (Moroccan filmmaker). Born in 1937 in Essaouira, he has worked extensively as author, translator, and director in both theatre and television. He has also appeared in numerous plays, television dramas, and feature films, but made only one film as director. Feature film: *Zeft* (1984).

Saheb-Ettaba, Nawfel (Tunisian filmmaker). Born in 1959 in Tunis, he studied visual communication and film at the University of Quebec, graduating in 1991. In Canada he worked in various assistant roles on feature films. From 1993 he has made commercials and commissioned documentaries in Tunisia. There he also wrote various scripts and made a personal fifty-two-minute video documentary, *Stambali.* Feature film: *The Bookstore/La librairie/El-Kotbia* (2002).

Sefrioui, Najib (Moroccan filmmaker). Born in 1948 in Fez, he studied widely in Paris in the early 1970s: Arab literature at the Sorbonne (with a master's thesis on "Film Imperialism, the Case of Morocco"), with parallel studies at the Institute of Art and Architecture as well as film studies at the Ecole Normale Louis Lumière at the Université de Paris. He completed a second master's degree—on film history—under the direction of Jean Mitry. He worked as a film critic and completed a 16mm feature-length documentary, *The Children of Benbarka/Les enfants de Benbarka,* in 1981. Feature films: *Chams* (1985), *Love without a Visa/Amour sans visa* (2001).

Smihi, Moumen (Moroccan filmmaker). Born in 1945 in Tangier, he studied philosophy at the University of Rabat. He graduated from the French film school IDHEC in Paris in 1967 and attended Roland Barthes seminars at the Ecole Pratique des Hautes Etudes. He made two short films before beginning his feature career and made a fifty-minute video documentary, *With Matisse in Tangier/Avec Matisse à Tanger,* for France 3 in 1993. His 1999 feature is one of the few Moroccan films made without state support. Feature films: *El Chergui/El chergui ou le silence violent/Chaqiaw al-çoumt al-'anif'* (1975), *Forty-Four, or Tales of the Night/Quarante-quatre ou les récits de la nuit/4 aw usturat al-layl* (1981), *Caftan of Love/Caftan d'amour/Qaftân al-hubb* (1987), *The Lady from Cairo/La dame du Caire/Sayyidat al-qâhira* (1991), *Moroccan Chronicles/Chroniques marocaines/Waqa'i maghribia* (1999).

Souda, Saïd (Moroccan filmmaker). Born in 1957 in Meknes, he received no formal film training but went to Asia in 1972 to work in cinema there. He worked for some years for the Shaw Brothers in Hong Kong and for six years as producer-director in the Japanese film studios. He became a distributor of Hong Kong films in Europe in 1987. A martial arts specialist, he appeared in numerous films, including both of those he has directed. Feature films: *Shadow of the Guardian/L'ombre du gardien/Dhil al-hâris* (1985), *From Heaven to Hell/Du paradis à l'enfer* (2000).

Tazi, Mohamed Abderrahman (Moroccan filmmaker). Born in 1942 in Fez, he studied film at IDHEC in Paris and mass media communication at Syracuse University in New York. He worked as director of photography on two Moroccan features and as assistant on several foreign productions. He has also made several short films. Features: *The Big Trip/Le grand voyage/Abir sabil* (1981), *Badis* (1988), *Looking for My Wife's Husband/A la recherche du mari de ma femme/Abkhath ghari jawh imraaythi* (1993), *Lalla Hobby* (1997).

Tazi, Mohamed B. A. (Moroccan filmmaker). Born in 1936 in Fez, he graduated from the French film school IDHEC in 1960. After joining the CCM he made a number of documentaries in the 1960s and co-directed the first Moroccan feature. He worked extensively, as director and administrator, in television in the 1970s. Feature films: *Conquer to Live/Vaincre pour vivre/Inticar al-hayat* (with Ahmed Mesnaoui, 1968), *Amina* (1980), *Medicine Woman/Madame la guérisseuse/Lalla chafia* (1982), *Abbas or Jouha Is Not Dead/Abbas ou Jouha n'est pas mort* (1986).

Tlatli, Moufida (Tunisian filmmaker). Born in 1947 in Sidi Bou Said, she studied at IDHEC in Paris and then worked as a trainee and assistant at ORTF. From the mid-1970s she established herself as one of the leading film editors in the Arab world, working on numerous major features. Feature films: *Silences of the Palace/Les silences du palais/Samt al-çoumt* (1994), *The Men's Season/La saison des hommes* (2000).

Tolbi, Abdelaziz (Algerian filmmaker). Born in 1938 in Tamlouka, he fought in the ranks of the ALN and, when wounded, was sent to Tunis. He studied film in Cologne and worked in German television. He made a range of work for RTA in the late 1960s and early 1970s. Feature film: *Noua/Nua* (1972).

Touita, Okacha (Algerian filmmaker). Born in 1943 in Mostaganem, he studied film at IFC in Paris. He worked as a film actor and as assistant on various French and Tunisian features. After two shorts he began his feature career. His first feature was made in France and his second was not released. Feature films: *The Sacrificed/Les sacrifiés* (1982), *The Survivor/Le rescapé* (1986), *The Cry of Men/Le cri des hommes* (1990).

Traïdia, Karim (Dutch-based filmmaker of Algerian descent). Born in 1949 in Annaba, Algeria, he has lived in Holland since 1980. He studied sociology in Paris and film at NFTVA in Amsterdam, graduating in 1991. He has made a number of short films, beginning in 1991, and worked as an actor. In 1996 he published a collection of short stories written in Dutch. His first feature was shown at Cannes in 1998. Feature films: *The Polish Bride/La fiancée polonaise* (1998), *The Truth Tellers/Les diseurs de vérité* (2000).

Tsaki, Brahim (Algerian filmmaker). Born in 1946 in Sidi Bel Abbes, he studied at INSAS in Brussels. On his return he joined ONCIC. His first feature comprised three separate episodes. A concern with children and with the disabled has been a constant feature of his work. Feature films: *Children of the Wind/Les enfants du vent/Abna al-rih* (1981), *Story of a Meeting/Histoire d'une rencontre/Hikaya liqa* (1983), *The Neon Children/Les enfants des néons* (in France, 1990).

Yachfine, Ahmed (Moroccan filmmaker). Born in 1948 in Casablanca, he studied design in Rome, Islamic studies in Strasbourg (where he received his doctorate in 1979), and film at Indiana University–Bloomington. Feature films: *Nightmare/Cauchemar/Al-kabus* (1984), *Khafaya* (1995).

Yala, Mohamed Meziane (Algerian filmmaker). Born in 1946 in Akfadou, he studied film at Lodz in Poland and worked as a trainee for Radio-televisione italiana (RAI) in Rome. He made numerous shorts in the 1970s and 1980s. Feature film: *Autumn Song/Chant d'automne/Angham al-kharif* (1983).

Zemmouri, Mahmoud (Algerian filmmaker). Born in 1946 in Boufarik, he studied at IDHEC and began his career in France, making a short film and serving as assistant to Ali Ghanem. Feature films: *Take a Thousand Quid and Get Lost/Prends dix mille balles et casses-toi* (in France, 1981), *The Crazy Years of the Twist/Les folles années du twist/Sanawât al-twist al-majnouna* (1983), *From Hollywood to Tamanrasset/De Hollywood à Tamanrasset* (1990), *The Honor of the Tribe/L'honneur du tribu/Charaf al-gabilu* (1993), *100% Arabica* (in France, 1997).

Zerouali, Abdallah (Moroccan filmmaker). Born in 1939 in Taza, he studied at the French film school IDHEC in Paris. He began work as cameraman for the Moroccan newsreel service, became a documentary filmmaker, and also worked as cinematographer for Abdellah Mesbahi's *Silence, No Entry*. He directed five short films and worked as production manager on foreign and Moroccan features. His first feature, initially called *The Whirlpool/Le tourbillon,* was begun in 1980, but completed—with a new title—only in 1995. Feature films: *Pals for the Day/Les copains du jour/Rifâq al-nahâr* (1984), *I'm the Artist/Moi l'artiste* (1995).

Zinaï-Koudil, Hafsa (Algerian filmmaker). Born in 1951 in Ain Beïda. Before turning to film, she made a reputation as a novelist: she published four novels in Algeria and, more recently, she has published one in France, where she now lives in exile. She worked as assistant director before making her first 16mm feature for RTA. Feature film: *The Female Demon/Le démon au féminin/Ash-shaytan imra'* (1993).

Zinet, Mohamed (Algerian filmmaker—1932–1995). Born in Algiers, he worked as an actor and playwright, fought with the ALN, and, when wounded, was sent to Tunis. He studied drama in East Berlin and Munich and worked as an actor in Paris. He appeared as an actor in a variety of foreign and North African films and also worked as assistant director. Feature film: *Tahia ya Didou/Alger insolite/Tahia ya dîdû* (1971).

Zran, Mohamed (Tunisian filmmaker). Born in 1959 in Zarzis, he studied film making in Paris. He worked as assistant on two films in France and made three noted shorts. In 2002 he made a seventy-five-minute video, *Millennium Song/Chant du millénaire*. Feature film: *Essaïda/Al-sayida* (1996).

Appendix B
List of Films

1965

Algeria   Dawn of the Damned/*L'aube des damnés*/Fajr al-mu'adhhabin (Ahmed Rachedi)
              The Night Is Afraid of the Sun/La nuit a peur du soleil/Al-lailu yahkaf ash-shams (Mustapha Badie)

1966

Algeria   The Wind from the Aurès/*Le vent des Aurès*/Rih al-awras (Mohamed Lakhdar Hamina)

Tunisia   The Dawn/*L'aube*/Al-fajr (Omar Khlifi)

1968

Algeria   Hassan Terro/*Hasan Tiru* (Mohamed Lakhdar Hamina)
              Hell for a 10 Year Old/*L'enfer à dix ans* (collective)
              The Way/*La voie*/Al-tariq (Mohamed Slim Riad)

Morocco   Conquer to Live/*Vaincre pour vivre*/Inticar al-hayat (Mohamed B. A. Tazi and Ahmed Mesnaoui)
              When the Dates Ripen/*Quand murissent les dattes*/Hinama yandhuju al-tamr (Abdelaziz Ramdani and Larbi Bennani)

Tunisia   Mokhtar/*Mukhtar* (Sadok Ben Aicha)
              The Rebel/*Le rebelle*/Al-mutamarrid (Omar Khlifi)

1969

Algeria   Opium and the Stick/*L'opium et le bâton*/Al-afyun wal-'asa (Ahmed Rachedi)
              The Outlaws/*Les hors-la-loi*/Al-kharijoun an-alkanoun (Tewfik Fares)
              Stories of the Revolution/*Histoires de la révolution* (collective)

Morocco   Spring Sunshine/*Soleil de printemps*/Chams al-rabi' (Latif Lahlou)

Tunisia   Khlifa Ringworm/*Khlifa le teigneux*/Khalifa al-aqra' (Hamouda Ben Halima)

1970

Immigrant Cinema	*Mektoub?* (Ali Ghalem, in France)
Morocco	*The Devil's Treasure/Le trésor infernal/Al-kinz al-jahannany* (Mohamed Osfour)
	Traces/Wechma/Washma (Hamid Benani)
Tunisia	*The Fellagas/Les fellagas/Al-fallâga* (Omar Khlifi)
	Murky Death/La mort trouble/Al mawt al-akhîr (Claude d'Anna and Ferid Boughedir)
	Om abbes/Um 'Abbâs (Ali Abdelwahab)
	Such a Simple Story/Une si simple histoire/Hikâya basîta kahâdhihi (Abdellatif Ben Ammar)
	Under the Autumn Rain/Sous la pluie d'automne/Tahta matar al-Kharif (Ahmed Khechine)

1971

Algeria	*Tahia ya Didou/ Alger insolite/Tahia ya dîdû* (Mohamed Zinet)

1972

Algeria	*Beside the Poplar Tree/Auprès du peuplier/Min ourb al-saf saf* (Moussa Haddad)
	Black Sweat/Sueur noire/Al-'araq al-aswad (Sid Ali Mazif)
	The Charcoal Burner/Le charbonnier/Al-fahâm (Mohamed Bouamari)
	December/Décembre/Dicember (Mohamed Lakhdar Hamina)
	El ghoula/Al-ghûla (Mustapha Kateb)
	The Good Families/Les bonnes familles/Al-usar al-tayyibah (Djafar Damardjji)
	Noua/Nua (Abdelaziz Tolbi)
	Patrol in the East/Patrouille à l'est/Dawriyyah nahwa al-sharq (Amar Laskri)
	The Plunderers/Les spoliateurs/Al-mufsidûn (Mohamed Lamine Merbah)
	Sana'oud/Sana'od (Mohamed Slim Riad)
	So That Algeria May Live/Pour que vive l'Algérie (collective)
Immigrant Cinema	*Some People and Others/Les uns, les autres* (Mohamed Ben Salah)
Morocco	*A Thousand and One Hands/Mille et une mains/Alf yad wa yad* (Souheil Benbarka)
Tunisia	*And Tomorrow?/Et demain?/Wa ghadan* (Brahim Babaï)
	In the Land of the Tararani/Au pays de Tararani/Fi bilâd al-Tararany (collective)
	Screams/Hurlements/Çurrakh (Omar Khlifi)
	Yusra/Yusrâ (Rachid Ferchiou)

1973

Algeria   *Inspector Tahar's Holiday/Les vacances de l'Inspecteur Tahar/'Utla al'mafattish Tahar* (Moussa Haddad)
The War of Liberation/La guerre de libération (collective)

Morocco   *Silence, No Entry/Silence, sens interdit/Sukut al-ittliah al-mamnu* (Abdellah Mesbahi)

Tunisia   *Omi Traki/Ummy Trâky* (Abderrazak Hammami)

1974

Algeria   *A Finger in the Works/Le doigt dans l'engrenage* (Ahmed Rachedi)
Forbidden Zone/Zone interdite/Al-fâiza (Ahmed Lallem)
Hassan Terro's Escape/L'évasion de Hassan Terro/Hurub Hasan Tiru (Mustapha Badie)
The Inheritance/L'héritage/Al-irth (Mohamed Bouamari)

Immigrant Cinema   *The Mask of an Enlightened Woman/Le masque d'une éclaircie* (Mohamet Benayat, in France)

Morocco   *About Some Meaningless Events/De quelques événements sans signification/Anba'dh al-ahdâth biduni ma'nla* (Mostapha Derkaoui)
The Oil War Will Not Happen/La guerre du pétrole n'aura pas lieu/Harb al-bitrui ian yaqa' (Souheil Benbarka)

Tunisia   *Sejnane/Sajnân* (Abdellatif Ben Ammar)

1975

Algeria   *Chronicle of the Years of Embers/Chronique des années de braise/Waqâ sanwât al-jamr* (Mohamed Lakhdar Hamina)
The Nomads/Les nomades/Masirat al-ruhhal (Sid Ali Mazif)
Wind from the South/Vent du sud/Rih al-janub (Mohamed Slim Riad)

Immigrant Cinema   *The Other France/L'autre France* (Ali Ghalem, in France)

Savage Barricades/Barricades sauvages (Mohamed Benayat, in France)

Morocco   *El Chergui/El chergui ou le silence violent/Chaqiaw al-çoumt al-'anif'* (Moumen Smihi)
Tomorrow the Land Will Not Change/Demain la terre ne changera pas/Ghaganian tatabaddala al-ardh (Abdellah Mesbahi)

Tunisia   *The Ambassadors/Les ambassadeurs/Al-sufarâ* (Naceur Ktari)
The Children of Boredom/Les enfants de l'ennui/Atfâl al-qujaq (Rachid Ferchiou)

A People's Victory//Victoire d'un peuple/Intissâr chaâb
(Brahim Babaï, documentary)

1976

Algeria   *The Fishermen/Les pêcheurs/Al-shabaka* (Ghaouti Bended-douche)
         Omar Gatlato/Umar gatlatu (Merzak Allouache)
         The Uprooted/Les déracinés/Beni hindel (Mohamed Lamine Merbah)

Morocco   *Green Fire/Feu vert/Al-dwaw'al-akhdar* (Abdellah Mesbahi)

1977

Algeria   *Barriers/Barrières/Al-hawâjiz* (Ahmed Lallem)

Immigrant   *Journey to the Capital/Voyage en capital* (Ali Akika and
Cinema   Anne-Marie Autissier, in France)

Morocco   *Blood Wedding/Noces de sang/Urs al-dam* (Souheil Benbarka)

Tunisia   *Hyenas' Sun/Le soleil des hyènes/Chams al-dhibâ* (Ridha Behi)

1978

Algeria   *The Adventures of a Hero/Les aventures d'un héros/
         Mughamarat batal* (Merzak Allouache)
         Autopsy of a Plot/Autopsie d'un complot/Tachrih mouâmara
         (Mohamed Slim Riad)
         The Benevolent/El moufid/Al-mufid (Amar Laskri)
         Leïla and the Others/Leïla et les autres/Laîla wa akhawâtuha
         (Sid Ali Mazif)
         *The Nouba of the Women of Mount Chenoua/La nouba des
         femmes du Mont Chenoua/Noubat nissâ jabal chnouwwa*
         (Assia Djebar)
         The Olive Tree of Boul'Hilet/L'olivier de Boul'Hilet (Mohamed
         Nadir Azizi)

Morocco   *Al Kanfoudi* (Nabyl Lahlou)
         The Days, The Days/O les jours/Al-ayyam al-ayyam (Ahmed
         El Maânouni)
         A Hole in the Wall/Une brèche dans le mur/Charkun fi-l hâ'it
         (Jillali Ferhati)

Tunisia   *A Ball and Some Dreams/Un ballon et des rêves/Kurra wa
         ahlâm* (Mohamed Ali El Okbi)
         Fatma 75 (Selma Baccar)
         The Mannequin/Le mannequin/Aridhat al-aziâ (Sadok Ben
         Aicha)
         The Wedding/La noce/Al-'urs (collective)

1979

Algeria   *Ali in Wonderland/Ali au pays des mirages/Ali fi bilad al-sarab* (Ahmed Rachedi)
Dead the Long Night/Morte la longue nuit (Mohamed Slim Riad and Ghaouti Bendeddouche)
First Step/Premier pas/Al-khutwat al-ula (Mohamed Bouamari)
Nahla (Farouk Beloufa)

Immigrant Cinema   *The New Romantics/Les nouveaux romantiques* (Mohamed Benayat, in France)

Morocco   *Cinders of the Vineyard/Les cendres du clos/Ramâd al-zariba* (collective)
Mirage/Al-sarab (Ahmed Bouanani)
Where Are You Hiding the Sun?/Où cachez-vous le soleil? (Abdellah Mesbahi)

Tunisia   *My Village/Mon village/Çirû* (Mohamed Hammami)

1980

Algeria   *The Zerda, or Songs of Forgetfulness/La zerda ou les chants de l'oubli/Zerda wa aghani al-nisyan* (Assia Djebar)

Immigrant Cinema   *Tears of Blood/Larmes de sang* (Ali Akika and Anne-Marie Autissier, in France)

Morocco   *Amina* (Mohamed B. A. Tazi)
The Governor-General of Chakerbakerben Island/Le gouverneur-général de l'île de Chakerbakerben/Al-hakim al'-am (Nabyl Lahlou)
The Postman/Le facteur/Sâi al-barîd (Hakim Noury)
Taghounja/Tarounja (Abdou Achouba)

Tunisia   *Aziza/'Aziza* (Abdellatif Ben Ammar)
Two Thieves in Madness/Deux larrons en folie/Faraw'ilqut oukthâ (Ali Mansour)

1981

Algeria   *Children of the Wind/Les enfants du vent/Abna al-rih* (Brahim Tsaki)

Morocco   *The Big Trip/Le grand voyage/Abir sabil* (Mohamed Abderrahman Tazi)
The Bird of Paradise/L'oiseau du paradis (Hamid Bensaïd)
Forty-Four, or Tales of the Night/Quarante-quatre ou le récits de la nuit/4 aw usturat al-layl (Moumen Smihi)
Reed Dolls/Poupées de roseau/Araïs min qasab (Jilali Ferhati)
Trances/Transes/Al-hal (Ahmed El Maânouni)

| Tunisia | The Ballad of Mamelouk/La ballade de Mamelouk/Sarâb (Abdelhafidh Bouassida) |

1982

| Algeria | Breakdown/La Rupture/Al-inqita' (Mohamed Chouikh)
The Empire of Dreams/L'empire des rêves (Jean-Pierre Lledo)
Harvests of Steel/Moissons d'acier (Ghaouti Bendeddouche)
Hassan Taxi/Hasan taxi (Mohamed Slim Riad)
I Exist/J'existe (Sid Ali Mazif)
The Man Who Looked at Windows/L'homme qui regardait les fenêtres/Rajul wa nawâfidh (Merzak Allouache)
Moussa's Wedding/Le mariage de Moussa (Tayeb Mefti)
The Denial/Le refus/Al-raft (Mohamed Bouamari)
A Roof, a Family/Un toit, une famille/Saqat wa'aila (Rabah Laradji)
Sand Storm/Vent de sable/Rih al'rimâl (Mohamed Lakhdar Hamina)
A Wife for My Son/Une femme pour mon fils/Zawja li lbny (Ali Ghalem) |

| Morocco | Amok (Souheil Benbarka)
The Barber of the Poor Quarter/Le coiffeur du quartier des pauvres/Hallaq darb al-fouqara (Mohamed Reggab)
The Beautiful Days of Sheherazade/Les beaux jours de Charazade/Ayyâm chahrazad al-hilwâ (Mostapha Derkaoui)
Brahim Who?/Brahim qui?/Brahim yach? (Nabyl Lahlou)
The Drama of the 40,000/Le drame des 40,000 (Ahmed Kacem Akdi)
The Embers/La braise/Al-jamr (Farida Bourquia)
From the Other Side of the River/De l'autre côté du fleuve/Mel wad lhih (Mohamed Abbazi)
Medicine Woman/Madame la guiérisseuse/Lalla chafia (Mohamed B. A. Tazi)
Steps in the Mist/Des pas dans le brouillard/Khutawât fî dabâb (Hamid Benchrif)
Tears of Regret/Les larmes du regret (Hassan Moufti) |

| Tunisia | Crossing Over/Traversées/'Ubur (Mahmoud Ben Mahmoud)
Shadow of the Earth/L'ombre de la terre/Dhil al-ard (Taïeb Louhichi) |

1983

| Algeria | Autumn Song/Chant d'Automne/Angham al-kharif (Mohamed Meziane Yala)
The Crazy Years of the Twist/Les folles années du twist/Sanawât al-twist al-majnouna (Mahmoud Zemmouri) |

	The Epic of Cheikh Bouamama/L'épopée de Cheikh Bouamama (Benamar Bakhti)
	Story of a Meeting/Histoire d'une rencontre/Hikaya liqa (Brahim Tsaki)
Morocco	Bamou (Driss Mrini)
Tunisia	African Camera/Caméra d'Afrique/Kâmira Ifrqiya (Ferid Boughedir, documentary)
	What Are We Doing This Sunday?/Que fait-on ce dimanche?/Al-sabt fât? (Lotfi Essid)

1984

Algeria	Monsieur Fabre's Mill/Le moulin de M Fabre/Tabûnat al-sayyid Fabre (Ahmed Rachedi)
Immigrant Cinema	Mint Tea/Le thé à la menthe (Abdelkrim Bahloul)
Morocco	Dead End/L'impasse/Al-wata (Mustapha Khayat)
	Hadda (Mohamed Aboulouakar)
	Nightmare/Cauchemar/Al-kabus (Ahmed Yachfine)
	Pals for the Day/Les copains du jour/Rifâq al-nahâr (Abdallah Zerouali)
	Provisional Title/Titre provisoire/'Unwânun mu'aqqat (Mostapha Derkaoui)
	The Soul That Brays/L'âme qui brait/Nahiq al-ruh (Nabyl Lahlou)
	The Travelling Showman's Day/Le jour du forain/Yawn al-id (Abdelkrim Derkaoui and Driss Kettani)
	What the Winds Have Carried Away/Ce que les vents ont emportés (Ahmed Kacem Akdi)
	Zeft (Tayeb Saddiki)
Tunisia	The Angels/Les anges/Al-malâika (Ridha Behi)
	The Searchers of the Desert/Les baliseurs du désert/Al-hâ'imoûn (Nacer Khemir)

1985

Immigrant Cinema	Bâton Rouge (Rachid Bouchareb)
	Child of the Stars/L'enfant des étoiles (Mohamed Benayat)
	Tea in Archimedes' Harem/Le thé au harem d'Archimède (Mehdi Charef)
Morocco	Chams (Najib Sefrioui)
	Shadow of the Guardian/L'ombre du gardien/Dhil al-hâris (Saïd Souda)

1986

Algeria   *Cry of Stone/Cri de pierre/Ourâkh al-hajar* (Abderrahmane
Boughermouh)
Houria/Hûria (Sid Ali Mazif)
The Last Image/La dernière image/Al-sûr al-akhîra (Mohamed
Lakhdar Hamina)
A Parisian Love Story/Un amour à Paris/Hubbub fi Bâris
(Merzak Allouache, in France)

Morocco   *Abbas or Jouha Is Not Dead/Abbas ou Jouha n'est pas mort*
(Mohamed B. A. Tazi)
The Compromise/La compromission/Al-musâwama (Latif
Lahlou)

Tunisia   *The Challenge/Le défi/Al-tahaddi* (Omar Khlifi)
The Cup/La coupe/Al-ka's (Mohamed Damak)
Man of Ashes/L'homme de cendres/Rih al-sid (Nouri Bouzid)
*Sabra and the Monster from the Forest/Sabra et le monstre de
la forêt/Sabra wa-l wahch* (Habib Mselmani)

1987

Algeria   *The Gates of Silence/Les portes du silence/Abwâb al-çoumt*
(Amar Laskri)
We Shall Go onto the Mountain/Nous irons à la montagne
(collective)

Immigrant   *Miss Mona* (Mehdi Charef)
Cinema

Morocco   *Caftan of Love/Caftan d'amour/Qaftân al-hubb* (Moumen
Smihi)
*A Gateway to Heaven/Une porte sur le ciel/Bâb
al-sama'maftûh* (Farida Benlyazid)

Tunisia   *Arab Camera/Caméra arabe/Kâmira 'arabiya* (Ferid
Boughedir, documentary)

1988

Algeria   *The Citadel/La citadelle/Al-qal'a* (Mohamed Chouikh)
Rai (Sid Ali Fettar)

Immigrant   *Arizona Stallion* (Mohamed Benayat)
Cinema
                Camomile/Camoumille (Mehdi Charef)

Morocco   *Badis* (Mohamed Abderrahman Tazi)

Tunisia   *Arab/'Arab* (Fadhel Jaziri and Fadhel Jaïbi)

Bitter Champagne/Champagne amer/Wachmun 'ala-l daâkira
(Ridha Behi)
The Trace/La trace/Al-sâma (Nejia Ben Mabrouk)

1989

Algeria

Desert Rose/Rose des sables/Louss (Mohamed Rachid Benhadj)
Hassan niya/Hasan niya (Ghaouti Bendeddouche)

Morocco

Komany (Nabyl Lahlou)
Land of Challenge/La terre du défi/Ardhu-l tahaddy (aka *I
    Shall Write Your Name in the Sand/J'écrirai ton nom sur le
    sable)* (Abdellah Mesbahi)

Tunisia

Golden Horseshoes/Les sabots en or/Safâ'ih min dhahab
    (Nouri Bouzid)
Leïla My Reason/Layla ma raison/Majnûn Layla (Taïeb
    Louhichi)

1990

Algeria

The Cry of Men/Le cri des hommes (Okacha Touita)
El ouelf essaib (Mohamed Hilmi)
From Hollywood to Tamanrasset/De Hollywood à Tamanrasset
    (Mahmoud Zemmouri)
The Neon Children/Les enfants des néons (Brahim Tsaki, in
    France)

*Immigrant
Cinema*

Cheb (Rachid Bouchareb)

Morocco

*The Hammer and the Anvil/Le marteau et l'enclume/
    Al-mitroqa wa alk-sindân* (Hakim Noury)
Other People's Celebrations/La fête des autres/Ayad al-akhain
    (Hassan Benjelloun)

Tunisia

Barg Ellil/Eclair nocturne/Barg al-leil (Ali Abidi)
*The Dove's Lost Necklace/Le collier perdu de la colombe/Tawk
    al-hamâma al-mafqûd* (Nacer Khemir)
*Halfaouine/Halfaouine—l'enfant des terrasses/Halfawîn—
    'Usfûr stah* (Ferid Boughedir)
Wandering Heart/Coeur nomade/Ruqayya (Fitouri Belhiba)

1991

Algeria

*Autumn—October in Algiers/Automne—Octobre à Alger/
    Al-karif—October fi al-jaza'ir* (Malik Lakhdar Hamina)
Moonlighting/Le clandestin (Benamar Bakhti)
Sahara Blues (Rabah Bouberras)
The Third Act/Le troisième acte (Rachid Ben Brahim)

White Shadows/Ombres blanches/Al-dhilâl al-bidh (Saïd Ould Khelifa)

Immigrant Cinema

A Vampire in Paradise/Un vampire au paradis (Abdelkrim Bahloul)

Morocco

Aziz and Itto: A Moroccan Wedding/Aziz et Itto: Un mariage marocain (Naguib Ktiri Idrissa)

The Beach of Lost Children/La plage des enfants perdus/Shâtiu al-atfâl al mafoûdin (Jillali Ferhati)

Chronicle of a Normal Life/Chronique d'une vie normale/ Waqâi'a min hatât âdia (Sâad Chraïbi)

The Lady from Cairo/La dame du Caire/Sayyidat al-qâhira (Moumen Smihi)

A Love Affair in Casablanca/Un amour à Casablanca/Hubb fî al-dâr al-bayda (Abdelkader Lagtaâ)

The Waiting Room/La salle d'attente/Qâ at al-intidhar (Nour Eddine Gounajjar)

Ymer or The Flowering Thistles/Ymer ou les chardons florifères (Tijani Chrigui)

Tunisia

Autumn '86/Automne '86/Al-kharîf '86 (Rachid Ferchiou)

The Night of the Decade/La nuit de la décennie/Laylat al-sanawât al-'achr (Brahim Babaï)

1992

Algeria

Lights/Lumières (Jean-Pierre-Lledo)

Marathon Tam (Rabie Ben Mokhtar)

Radhia (Mohamed Lamine Merbah)

Immigrant Cinema

Bad Weather for a Crook/Sale temps pour un voyou (Amor Hakkar)

In the Land of the Juliets/Au pays des Juliets (Mehdi Charef)

Segou (Rachid Bouchareb)

Shattered Years/Des années déchirées (Rachid Bouchareb)

Morocco

First Fiction/Fiction première/Riwâya 'ûlâ (Mostapha Derkaoui)

The Night of the Crime/La nuit du crime/Laylat qatl (Nabyl Lahlou)

Tunisia

After the Gulf?/La guerre du Golfe . . . et après?/Harbu al-khalîj wa ba'du? (collective)

Bezness/Baznâs (Nouri Bouzid)

The Dust of Diamonds/Poussièrre de diamants/Chichkhâhn (Mahmoud Ben Mahmoud and Fadhel Jaïbi)

The Teddy Boys/Les zazous de la vague/Al-zâzuwwât (Mohamed Ali El Okbi)

1993

Algeria
The Female Demon/Le démon au féminin/Ash-shaytan imra'
(Hafsa Zinaï-Koudil)
Forbidden Love/Amour interdit (Sid Ali Fettar)
The Honor of the Tribe/L'honneur du tribu/Charaf al-gabilu
(Mahmoud Zemmouri)
Touchia/Tushia (Mohamed Rachid Benhadj)
Wanderings/Errances (aka Land of Ashes/Terre en cendres)
(Djafar Damardjji)
Ya ouled (Rachid Benallal)
Youssef: The Legend of the Seventh Sleeper/Youcef: la légende
du septième dormant/Youcef kesat dekra sabera (Mohamed
Chouikh)

Immigrant
Cinema
Hexagon/Hexagone (Malek Chibane)

Morocco
Horsemen of Glory/Les cavaliers de la gloire (a re-edited ver-
sion of Drums of Fire/Tambours de feu/Tubûl al-nâr, 1991)
(Souheil Benbarka)
Looking for My Wife's Husband/A la recherche du mari de
ma femme/Abkhath ghari jawh imraaythi (Mohamed
Abderrahman Tazi)
Stolen Childhood/Enfance volée/Atoufoula al-mortasaba
(Hakim Noury)
Yarit (Hassan Benjelloun)

Tunisia
The Sultan of the Medina/Soltane el Medina!/Ya sultan al
madina (Moncef Dhouib)
Wind of Destinies/Le vent des destins/Rih al-aqdar (Ahmed
Djemaï)

1994

Algeria
Bab el-oued City/Bab al-wad al-humah (Merzak Allouache)
The Portrait/Le portrait (Hadj Rahim)

Immigrant
Cinema
Life Dust/Poussière de vie (Rachid Bouchareb)

Morocco
(Ga)me in the Past/Je(u) au passé (Mostapha Derkaoui)
The Seven Gates of the Night/Les sept portes de la nuit
(Mostapha Derkaoui)

Tunisia
The Magic Box/Le magique/Al-sahir (Ezzedine Fazaî Mellitti)
Silences of the Palace/Les silences du palais/Samt al-çoumt
(Moufida Tlatli)
Swallows Don't Die in Jerusalem/Les hirondelles ne meurent
pas à Jérusalem/Al-khuttâf lâ iyamût fi al-quds (Ridha
Behi)

1995

Algeria   *Once Upon a Time/Il était une fois/Machaho* (Belkacem Hadjadj)

Immigrant Cinema   *Krim* (Ahmed Bouchaâla)

Morocco   *The Dream Thief/Le voleur de rêves* (Hakim Noury)
Five Films for a Hundred Years/Cinq films pour cent ans (collective)
I'm the Artist/Moi l'artiste (a completed version of *The Whirlpool/Le tourbillon*, 1980) (Abdallah Zerouali)
Khafaya (Ahmed Yachfine)
Make-Believe Horses/Chevaux de fortune/Kuius al-has (Jillali Ferhati)
A Prayer for the Absent/La prière de l'absent/Sirr al-majarra (aka *The Secret of the Milky Way/Le secret de la voie lactée*) (Hamid Benani)
The Unknown Resistance Fighter/Le résistant inconnu (Larbi Bennani)

Tunisia   *Check and Mate/Echec et mat/Kich mât* (Rachid Ferchiou)
The Fire Dance/La danse du feu/Habbiba Messika (Selma Baccar)
One Summer at La Goulette/Un été à la Goulette/Saîf halqu al-wâdiy (Ferid Boughedir)

1996

Algeria   *The Forgotten Hillside/La colline oubliée* (Abderrahmane Bouguermouh)
Hello Cousin!/Salut cousin! (Merzak Allouache, in France)

Immigrant Cinema   *The Hamlet Sisters/Les soeurs Hamlet* (Abdelkrim Bahloul)

Under Women's Feet/Sous les pieds des femmes (Rachida Krim)

Morocco   *Rhesus or Another Person's Blood/Rhésus ou le sang de l'autre* (Mohamed Lotfi)
The Shadow of the Pharaoh/L'ombre du pharaon/Delo pheraoun (Souheil Benbarka)

Tunisia   *Essaïda/Al-sayida* (Mohamed Zran)

1997

Algeria   *Baya's Mountain/La montagne de Baya/Djebel Baya* (Azzedine Meddour)
The Desert Ark/L'arche du désert (Mohamed Chouikh)
The Old Lady and the Child/La vielle dame et l'enfant (Yahia Debboub)

100% Arabica (Mahmoud Zemmouri, in France)
Question of Honor/Question d'honneur (Abderrazak
    Hellal)
The Resistance Fighters/Les résistants (Yahia Debboub)
The Tree of Suspended Fates/L'albero dei destini sospesi
    (Mohamed Rachid Benhadj, in Italy)

Immigrant Cinema	*In My Father's House/Dans la maison de mon père/In het Huis van mijn Vader* (Fatima Jebli Ouazzani, in the Netherlands) *My Family's Honor/L'honneur de ma famille* (Rachid Bouchareb) *The Night of Destiny/La nuit du destin* (Abdelkrim Bahloul)
Morocco	*Lalla Hobby* (Mohamed Abderrahman Tazi) *Mektoub* (Nabil Ayouch) *A Simple News Item/Un simple fait divers* (Hakim Noury) *The Treasures of the Atlas/Les trésors de l'Atlas/Kounouz latlas* (Mohamed Abbazi) *Yesterday's Friends/Les amis d'hier* (Hassan Benjelloun)
Tunisia	*Girls from a Good Family/Tunisiennes/Bent familia* (Nouri Bouzid) *Keswa—The Lost Thread/Keswa—Le fil perdu/Kiswâ al-khayt al-dhâi'* (Kalthoum Bornaz) *Redeyef 54/Rdeyef 54* (Ali Abidi)

1998

Algeria	*Algiers-Beirut: In Remembrance/Alger-Beyrouth, pour mémoire* (Merzak Allouache, in France) *Lotus Flower/Fleur de lotus* (Amar Laskri) *The Other Algeria: Views from Within/L'autre Algérie: regards intérieurs* (collective)
Immigrant Cinema	*Leave a Little Love/Laisse un peu d'amour* (Zaïda Ghorab-Volta) *Living in Paradise/Vivre au paradis* (Bourlem Guerdjou) *The Polish Bride/La fiancée polonaise* (Karim Traïdia)
Morocco	*Aouchtam* (Mohamed Ismaïl) *Bye-Bye Souirty/Adieu forain* (Daoud Aoulad Syad) *Cairo Street/Rue le Caire* (Mohamed Abdelkrim Derkaoui) *The Casablancans/Les Casablancais/Bidawa* (Abdelkader Lagtaâ) *A Woman's Fate/Destin de femme* (Hakim Noury) *Women . . . and Women/Femmes . . . et Femmes* (Saâd Chraïbi)
Tunisia	*Moon Wedding/Noce de lune/'Urs al-qamar* (Taïeb Louhichi) *Tomorrow I Burn/Demain je brûle/Ghoudwa nahrek* (Mohamed Ben Smaïl)

1999

Morocco   *Ali Zaoua/Ali Zaoua, prince de la rue* (Nabil Ayouch)
      Mabrouk (Drissa Chouika)
      Moroccan Chronicles/Chroniques marocaines/Waqa'i maghribia (Moumen Smihi)
      Women's Wiles/Ruses de femmes/Keid Ensa (Farida Benlyazid)

Tunisia   *The Pomegranate Siesta/Les siestes grenadine/Kouaïl erroummen* (Mahmoud Ben Mahmoud)

2000

Algeria   *Mirka* (Mohamed Rachid Benhadj, in Italy)

Immigrant Cinema   *Frontiers/Frontières* (Mostéfa Djadjam)

      Madame Osmane's Harem/Le harem de Mme Osmane (Nadir Moknèche)
      The Truth Tellers/Les diseurs de vérité (Karim Traïdia, in the Netherlands)
      Voltaire's Fault/La faute à Voltaire (Abdellatif Kechiche)
      Women's Expectations/L'attente des femmes (Naguel Belouad)

Morocco   *Ali, Rabia and the Others/Ali, Rabia et les autres* (Ahmed Boulane)
      Braids/Tresses (Jillali Ferhati)
      The Closed Door/La porte close/Bâb al-nasdûd (Abdelkader Lagtaâ)
      From Heaven to Hell/Du paradis à l'enfer (Saïd Souda)
      The Man Who Embroidered Secrets/L'homme qui brodait des secrets (Omar Chraïbi)
      She Is Diabetic and Hypertensive and She Refuses to Die/Elle est diabétique et hypertendue et elle refuse de crever (Hakim Noury)
      The Story of a Rose/L'histoire d'une rose (Abdelmajid Rchich)
      Thirst/Soif (Saâd Chraïbi)
      A Woman's Judgement/Jugement d'une femme (Hassan Benjelloun)
      Yacout (Jamal Belmejdoub)

Tunisia   *Be My Friend/Sois mon amie/Hlou morr* (Naceur Ktari)
      The Men's Season/La saison des hommes (Moufida Tlatli)
      No Man's Love (Nidhal Chatta)

2001

Algeria   *The Other World/L'autre monde* (Merzak Allouache)

Immigrant Cinema   *Beyond Gibraltar/Au delà de Gibraltar* (Mourad Boucif, with Taylan Barman, in Belgium)

Control of Origin/Origine contrôlée (Ahmed and Zakia
　　Bouchaâla)
Gilded Youth/Jeunesse dorée (Zaâda Ghorab-Volta)
Inch'Allah Sunday/Inch'Allah dimanche (Yamina Benguigui)
Little Senegal/Little Sénégal (Rachid Bouchareb)
Marie-Line (Mehdi Charef)
*The Mistress in a Swimming Costume/La maîtresse en maillot
　　de bain* (Lyèce Boukhitine)
17 rue Bleue (Chad Chenouga)

Morocco　　*The Lips of Silence/Les lèvres du silence* (Hassan Benjelloun)
A Love Story/Une histoire d'amour (Hakim Noury)
Love without a Visa/Amour sans visa (Najib Sefrioui)
*The Loves of Hadj Mokhtar Soldi/Les amours de Hadj Mokhtar
　　Soldi* (Mostapha Derkaoui)
Mona Saber (Abdelhaï Laraki)
The Wind Horse/Le cheval de vent (Daoud Aoulad Syad)

Tunisia　　*Fatma* (Khaled Ghorbal)
A Thousand and One Voices/Les mille et une voix (Mahmoud
　　Ben Mahmoud)

2002

Algeria　　*The Neighbor/La voisine/Al jara* (Ghaouti Bendeddouche)
Rachida (Yamina Bachir-Chouikh)

Immigrant　　*Keltoum's Daughter/La fille de Keltoum/Bint Keltoum* (Mehdi
Cinema　　　　Charef)
Letters from Algeria/Lettres d'Algérie (Azize Kabouche)
*Wesh Wesh—What's Happening?/Wesh Wesh, Qu'est-ce qui se
　　passe?* (Rabah Ameur-Zaïmèche)

Morocco　　*And Afterwards . . . /Et après . . .* (Mohamed Ismaïl)
The Lovers of Mogador/Les amants de Mogador (Souheil
　　Benbarka)
A Minute of Sunshine Less/Une minute de soleil en moins
　　(Nabil Ayouch)
The Pal/Le pote (Hassan Benjelloun)
The Paradise of the Poor/Paradis des pauvres (Imane Mesbahi)
Taif Nizar (Kamal Kamal)
The Years of Exile/Les années de l'exil (Nabyl Lahlou)

Tunisia　　*Bedwin Hacker* (Nadia El Fani)
The Bookstore/La librairie/El-Kotbia (Nawfel Saheb-Ettaba)
Clay Dolls/Poupées d'argile (Nouri Bouzid)
Khorma: Stupidity/Khorma, la bêtise/Khorma (Jilani Saadi)
The Magic Box/La boîte magique (Ridha Behi)
The Noria's Song/Le chant de la noria (Abdellatif Ben
　　Ammar)
Red Satin/Satin rouge (Raja Amari)

Notes

Introduction

1. Moumen Smihi, "Moroccan Society as Mythology," in John D. H. Downing, ed., *Film and Politics in the Third World* (New York: Praeger, 1987), 82.

2. Edward Said, *Culture and Imperialism* (London: Vintage, 1994), 84.

3. Ibid., 82.

4. Ibid., 83.

5. Ibid., 107.

6. Ibid., 122.

7. Richard Maltby, *Harmless Entertainment: Hollywood and the Ideology of Consensus* (Metuchen, N.J: Scarecrow Press, 1983), 80.

8. David Ellwood and Rob Kroes, eds., *Hollywood in Europe: Experiences of Cultural Hegemony* (Amsterdam: VU University Press, 1994), 8.

9. Thomas Guback, *The International Film Industry: Western Europe and America Since 1945* (Bloomington: Indiana University Press, 1969), 199–200.

10. Ellwood and Kroes, 9.

11. Peter Brooks, *Reading for the Plot: Design and Intention in Narrative* (Cambridge, Mass.: Harvard University Press, 1984), 5.

12. Roy Armes, "Readings and Viewings," in Roy Armes, *Action and Image: Dramatic Structure in Cinema* (Manchester: Manchester University Press, 1994), 3–17.

13. Brooks, 12.

14. Brooks, 23.

15. David Mamet, *On Directing Films* (London: Faber & Faber, 1992), xv.

16. Brooks, 38.

17. Ibid., 39–40.

18. Ibid., 39.

19. Ibid., 173.

20. Ibid., 287.

21. Translated from the French: "la vision du monde explicite des colonisateurs. . . . En ce qui concerne ces films (une cinquantaine environ), la société coloniale n'avait aucunement besoin de certaines interprétations conscientes ou subconscientes pour faire coïncider le réel vécu quotidiennement et la fiction de l'image.

La correspondance entre les deux est brute, brutale, continue, totale. Conformément à la logique implacable de la colonisation, l'Algérien est quasi absent partout. Que ce soit au sein du public de cinéma, ou au sein de la profession elle-même.

Partout, si on parvient à l'entrevoir, c'est sous une forme fantômatique, fugace, représenté par une silhouette à deux dimensions, sans aucune épaisseur, tel un palmier de carte postale, soit par une ombre menaçante, brandissant un coutelas ou un fusil." Abdelghani Megherbi, *Les algériens au miroir du cinéma colonial* (Algiers: SNED, 1982), 12–13.

22.   David Henry Slavin, *Colonial Cinema and Imperial France, 1919–1939* (Baltimore: Johns Hopkins University Press, 2001), vi.

23.   Ibid., 16.

24.   Ibid., 83.

25.   Ibid., 183.

26.   Ginette Vincendeau, *Pépé le Moko* (London: BFI, 1998), 59.

27.   Wimal Dissanayake, ed., *Colonialism and Nationalism in Asian Cinema* (Bloomington: Indiana University Press, 1994), ix.

28.   See Pierre Boulanger, *Le cinéma colonial* (Paris: Seghers, 1975), 22–23, for a listing.

29.   For Samama's multifarious career, see Guillemette Mansour, *Samama Chikly: Un tunisien à la rencontre du XXième siècle* (Tunis: Simpact Editions, 2000).

30.   Translated from the French: "Et quand on parle de ce fameux cinéma colonial, on ne sait pas du tout de quoi il s'agit. On sait que des réalisateurs importants sont venus filmer en Algérie. Qu'il y a eu toutes sortes de films, du plus raciste au plus élaboré, au plus paternaliste. . . . Le problème, c'est qu'on n'a pas vu ces films. On en a vu en tout cas très peu." Merzak Allouache, interview with Fanny Colonna, in Fanny Colonna and Zakya Daoud, eds., *Etre marginal au Maghreb* (Paris: CNRS Editions, 1993), 225–226.

31.   See *Cinémaroc* 8 (1998).

32.   Translated from the French: "Contrer l'influence croissante du cinéma égyptien dans les pays du Maghreb, en cherchant à poser les premiers jalons d'une production locale contrôlée par le pouvoir colonial." Abdelkader Benali, *Le cinéma colonial au Maghreb* (Paris: Editions du Cerf, 1998), 337.

33.   Translated from the French: "de grosses machines de production . . . balayer les structures classiques du cinéma. . . . Une équipe en liberté, caméra à l'épaule si nécessaire. Avec bien sûr la liberté du point de vue d'expression." Merzak Allouache, interview with Hubert Corbin and Monique Carcaud-Macaire, in *Actes du Septième Festival International* (Montpellier, 1985): 73.

34.   Translated from the French: "Pourquoi notre cinématographie n'a pas été capable jusqu'à présent, après des décennies d'existence, de communiquer avec les publics étrangers et de susciter leur intérêt." Abdelkader Lagtaâ, "Présentation: La dialectique du national et de l'universel," in *Catalogue du Quatrième Festival National du Film* (Rabat, 1995), 11.

35.   Smihi, 80.

36.   Abdellatif Ben Ammar, "Putting Forward a Clear View of Life," in Downing, 110.

37. Thomas Elsaesser, *New German Cinema: A History* (London: Macmillan, 1989), 74.

38. See Seán Allan and John Sandford, eds., *DEFA: East German Cinema, 1946–1992* (New York and Oxford: Berghahn Books, 1999).

39. Kevin Dwyer, "'Hidden, Unsaid, Taboo' in Moroccan Cinema: Abdelkader Lagtaâ's Challenge to Authority," *Framework* 43, no. 2 (Detroit, 2002): 132.

40. René Prédal, *Le jeune cinéma français* (Paris: Nathan, 2002), 1.

41. See Khalid El Khodari, *Guide des réalisateurs marocains* (Rabat: El Maarif Al Jadida, 2000).

42. Smihi, 78.

43. Nouri Bouzid, "New Realism in Arab Cinema: The Defeat-Conscious Cinema," in Ferial J. Ghazoul, ed., *Arab Cinematics: Toward the New and the Alternative, Alif* 15 (Cairo, 1995): 246–247.

1. Beginnings in the 1960s

1. Sabry Hafez, "Shifting Identities in Maghribi Cinema: The Algerian Paradigm," in Ferial J. Ghazoul, ed., *Arab Cinemematics: Toward the New and the Alternative, Alif* 15 (Cairo, 1995): 43.

2. Lotfi Maherzi, *Le cinéma algérien: Institutions, imaginaire, idéologie* (Algiers: SNED, 1980), 62.

3. Mouny Berrah, "Algerian Cinema and National Identity," in Alia Arasoughly, ed., *Screens of Life: Critical Film Writing from the Arab World* (Quebec: World Heritage Press, 1996), 64.

4. Merzak Allouache, interview with Hadani Ditmars, in *African Conversations* (London: BFI, 1995), n.p.

5. Ali Akika, "Les coulisses du cinéma," in Georges Châtillon and Edwige Lambert, eds., *Algérie,* 2nd ed. (Paris: Autrement, 1991), 271–277.

6. Berrah, 65.

7. Ibid., 66.

8. Rachid Boudjedra, "The Birth of Algerian Cinema," in Ghazoul, 265–266.

9. Berrah, 66–67.

10. Boudjedra, 264.

11. Hafez, 55.

12. Translated from the French: "Les films réalisés répondaient aux exigences des différents Ministères commanditaires en plus des bandes d'actualités destinées à la 'propagande' étatique." Moulay Driss Jaïdi, *Le cinéma au Maroc* (Rabat: Collection al majal, 1991), 112.

13. Translated from the French: "Les longs métrages (co)produits par le C.C.M. et réalisés par ses techniciens entendaient prolonger cette tradition folklorisante qui a été propre au film de court métrage de commande touristique." Moulay Driss Jaïdi, *Diffusion et audience des médias audiovisuels* (Rabat: Collection al majal, 2000), 31.

14. Moulay Driss Jaïdi, *Vision(s) de la société marocaine à travers le court métrage* (Rabat: Collection al majal, 1994), 107.

15. Tahar Chikhaoui, "Le cinéma tunisien de la maladroite euphorie au juste désarroi," in Abdelmajid Cherfi et al., eds., *Aspects de la civilisation tunisienne* (Tunis: Faculté de Lettres de Manouba, 1998), 18.

16. Translated from the French: "Les années 60 ont été celles de la construction, de la mise en place. Il s'agissait avant tout de mettre la Tunisie en image." Ibid., 6.

17. Translated from the French: "La production nationale est plutôt complexe. Elle est trop diversifiée pour permettre justement de dégager des lignes de force." Cited in Victor Bachy, *Le cinéma en Tunisie* (Tunis: Société Tunisienne de Diffusion, 1978), 54.

18. Translated from the French: "Les films tunisiens offrent une image de la Tunisie indépendante, pas encore libérée de toutes les sequelles du colonialisme, confrontée à tous les problèmes du développement économique et culturel." In Bachy, 55.

19. Khalid El Khodari, *Guide des réalisateurs marocains* (Rabat: El Maarif Al Jadida, 2000), 199.

2. The 1970s

1. Mouny Berrah, "Algerian Cinema and National Identity," in Alia Arasoughly, ed., *Screens of Life: Critical Film Writing from the Arab World* (Quebec: World Heritage Press, 1996), 67.

2. Sabry Hafez, "Shifting Identities in Maghribi Cinema: The Algerian Paradigm," in Ferial J. Ghazoul, ed., *Arab Cinemematics: Toward the New and the Alternative, Alif* 15 (Cairo, 1995): 55.

3. Berrah, 74.

4. Ibid., 63.

5. Moulay Driss Jaïdi, *Le cinéma au Maroc* (Rabat: Collection al majal, 1991), 118.

6. Translated from the French: "western, Zorro, Robin des bois, Karaté, mélos hindous et égyptiens." Ferid Boughedir, "Les quatres voies du cinéma marocain," in Mouny Berrah, Victor Bachy, Mohand Ben Salama, and Ferid Boughedir, eds., *Cinémas du Maghreb* (Paris: Editions Papyrus, 1981), 208.

7. Translated from the French: "pour plusieurs motifs: d'abord nos films sont assez médiocres. *Les mille et une mains* ou *La guerre du pétrole n'aura pas lieu*, si vous les avez vus, sont, je trouve exécrablement mauvais et ils sont considérés comme faisant partie des meilleurs au Maroc. . . . " Souheil Benbarka, interview, in *Actes du Douzième Festival International* (Montpellier, 1990): 50.

8. Translated from the French: "pour la simple raison qu'il n'était pas en couleurs et qu'il ne comportait pas d'action." In Jaïdi, 124.

9. Fouad Souiba and Fatima Zahra el Alaoui, *Un siècle de cinéma au Maroc* (Rabat: World Design Communication, 1995), 8.

10. Translated from the French: "Ces films s'élèvent contre le blocage d'une société traditionaliste figée dans ses rites et ses dogmes en adoptant une forme extêmement novatrice, d'une grande force d'expression, mais parfois peu accessible aux non-initiés." In Ferid Boughedir, ed., *Jeune Afrique Plus: Le cinéma en Afrique et dans le monde* (special issue, 1984), 75.

11. Translated from the French: "Le regard devient nettement plus critique dans les années 70, l'accent étant mis sur les problèmes sociaux de l'époque; en même temps, le cinéma acquiert plus de maturité technique." Tahar Chikhaoui, "Le cinéma tunisien de la maladroite euphorie au juste désarroi," in Abdelmajid Cherfi et al., eds., *Aspects de la civilisation tunisienne* (Tunis: Faculté de Lettres de Manouba, 1998), 6.

12. Mohamed Benayat, interview, in Guy Hennebelle and Roland Schneider, eds., *Cinémas métis: De Hollywood aux films beurs* (Paris: Corlet/Télérama, 1990), 164.

13. Translated from the French: "Il s'agit moins d'un film 'contestataire' que d'utiliser une fiction cinématographique à seule fin de provoquer une exacte prise de conscience des données sociales, donc une réflexion politique." Claude Michel Cluny, *Dictionnaire des nouveaux cinémas arabes* (Paris: Sindbad, 1978), 179.

14. Mohamed Jibril, "Cinéma marocain, l'improbable image de soi," in Nicole De Poncharra and Maati Kabbal, eds., *Le Maroc en mouvement: Créations contemporaines* (Paris: Maisonneuve & Larose, 2000), 180.

3. The 1980s

1. Translated from the French: "les chasseurs de primes." Fouad Souiba and Fatima Zahra el Alaoui, *Un siècle de cinéma au Maroc* (Rabat: World Design Communication, 1995), 33.

2. Translated from the French: "Cette autobiographie doublée d'un auto-portrait convainquent enfin de cette quête permanente et constante de l'identité du cinéaste marocain, de son rôle socio-culturel." Ibid., 81.

3. Translated from the French: "Les studios . . . les plus importants construits en Afrique depuis les indépendances." Ferid Boughedir, "Le cinéma en Tunisie," in *La semaine du cinéma arabe* (Paris: Institut du Monde Arabe, 1987), 97.

4. Translated from the French: "Aux cours des années 80, l'individu prend le dessus avec une tendance autobiographique et un notable retour sur les lieux de mémoire." Tahar Chikhaoui, "Le cinéma tunisien de la maladroite euphorie au juste désarroi," in Abdelmajid Cherfi et al., eds., *Aspects de la civilisation tunisienne* (Tunis: Faculté de Lettres de Manouba, 1998), 6.

5. Mouny Berrah, "Algerian Cinema and National Identity," in Alia Arasoughly, ed., *Screens of Life: Critical Film Writing from the Arab World* (Quebec: World Heritage Press, 1996), 82.

6. Translated from the French: "Azzedine Meddour, en rompant avec les commentaires ronronnants des 'films de guerre', inaugure, incontestiblement, une nouvelle école du documentaire et réconcilie le public avec un genre tombé en

disgrâce précisément à cause de son aspect triomphaliste." Mouny Berrah, in Mouny Berrah, Victor Bachy, Mohand Ben Salama and Ferid Boughedir, eds., *Cinémas du Maghreb* (Paris: Editions Papyrus, 1981), 71.

4. The 1990s

1. Jacques Mandelbaum, "Alger renaît au cinéma," *Le Monde* (Paris, 17 October 2000): 16.

2. Translated from the French: "Ce qui frappe avant tout avec ces quelques films, dans une période si grise, c'est la volonté de survie. Comme si les cinéastes avaient pris la décision collective d'aller à la rencontre d'un monde qui, visiblement, ne les attendait plus." Benjamin Stora, *La guerre invisible: Algérie années 90* (Paris: Presses de sciences PO, 2001), 90.

3. Translated from the French: "la figure de proue." Ahmed Araib and Eric de Hullessen, *Il était une fois . . . Le cinéma au Maroc* (Rabat: EDH, 1999), 66.

4. Lagtaâ, cited in Kevin Dwyer, "'Hidden, Unsaid, Taboo' in Moroccan Cinema: Abdelkader Lagtaâ's Challenge to Authority," *Framework* 43, no. 2 (Detroit, 2002): 122.

5. Translated from the French: "Affrontant des sujets encore largement 'tabous,' Lagtaâ est attentif aux effets troubles de normes 'traditionelles' qui ne sont plus exprimées que sous forme coercitive ou castratrice par des parents ou d'autres autorités morales, discrédités par leur propre incohérence." Mohamed Jibril, "Cinéma marocain, l'improbable image de soi," in Nicole De Poncharra and Maati Kabbal, eds., *Le Maroc en mouvement: Créations contemporaines* (Paris: Maisonneuve & Larose, 2000), 183.

6. Translated from the French: "Une série de situations où il est difficile de savoir ce que font des gens ou ce qu'ils se disent. . . . " Cited in *Les cinémas d'Afrique: Dictionnaire* (Paris: Editions Karthala and Editions ATM, 2000), 127.

7. For a detailed analysis of Dhouib's three principal short films, see Andrea Flores Khalil, "Images That Come Out at Night: A Film Trilogy by Moncef Dhouib," in Ida Kummer, ed., *Cinéma Maghrébin,* special issue of *Celaan* 1, no. 1–2 (Saratoga Springs, N.Y., 2002): 71–80.

8. Translated from the French: "qui semble le plus en prise avec la réalité sociale du Maroc moderne . . . le septième art a certainement joué un rôle important dans l'évolution et le mûrissement de la société." Pierre Vermeren, *Le Maroc en transition* (Paris: La Découverte, 2001), 144–145.

5. Into the Present

1. Neïla Gharbi, "Production en hausse, salles en baisse," *SeptièmArt* 98 (Tunis, 2002): 1.

2. Translated from the French: "Si le cinéma algérien a surtout été un cinéma politique, et si le cinéma marocain a plutôt été un cinéma culturel, le cinéma tunisien est dans sa majeure partie un cinéma social." Tahar Chikhaoui, "Le cinéma tunisien des années 90: permanences et spécifités," *Horizons Maghrébins— Le Droit à la Mémoire* 46 (Toulouse, 2002): 114–115.

3. Translated from the French: "cette volonté de remuer les consciences, de jouer un rôle dans le développement des mentalités." Ibid., 114.

4. Translated from the French: "témoigner des problématiques sociales, politiques, économiques, des tensions et des contradictions dont les sociétés de référence sont l'objet." Michel Serceau, "Les cinémas du Maghreb: Un imaginaire par défaut," in Ida Kummer, ed., *Cinéma Maghrébin,* special issue of *Celaan* 1, no. 1–2 (Saratoga Springs, N.Y., 2002): 18.

5. Translated from the French: "à une catégorie socio-culturelle qui n'est guère plus en prise sur la culture populaire (arabo-berbère) de leurs pays que la culture arabo-musulmane classique." Ibid., 25.

6. Translated from the French: "il ne serait pas exagéré d'y déceler autant de courants que de cinéastes." Chikhaoui, 114.

7. Translated from the French: "l'expression d'un souci de recherche, la manifestation d'une cinématographie en quête d'identité." Ibid.

8. Translated from the French: "Des personnages en quête d'auteurs. Et des auteurs en quête de sens." Raphaël Millet, *Cinémas de la Méditerranée: Cinémas de la mélancolie* (Paris: L'Harmattan, 2002), 82.

9. Translated from the French: "le lieu des paradoxes. L'expérience du vide y densifie celle de la vie même." Millet, 89.

10. Translated from the French: "Même si parfois il ont un peu tourné à vide." Ibid., 33.

11. Translated from the French: "c'est tout simplement qu'il fait secrètement le deuil de lui-même. Comme s'il ne croyait pas tout à fait à ce qu'il fait, à ce qu'il vit, à ce qu'il voit." Ibid., 43.

12. Translated from the French: "Les nouvelles fictions abordent directement les va-et-vient entre les frontières, les désirs d'exil, les émotions du retour, via le regard des créateurs attentifs aux évolutions de l'âme arabe." Michel Amarger, "Ruptures de l'espace identitaire," *Qantara* 44 (Paris, 2002): 22.

13. Translated from the French: "elles le sont encore. Et pourtant, le mouvement s'amorce depuis une douzaine d'années et surtout depuis trois ou quatres ans." Millet, 97.

14. Translated from the French: "une foule de nouveaux talents, montrant que cette 'nouvelle vague' a de la profondeur, que c'est presque une lame de fond." Ibid., 99–100.

15. Translated from the French: "sont loin d'être les plus mauvais de la décennie." Chikhaoui, 117.

16. Translated from the French: "est effectivement devenu à certains égards un cinéma féministe." Michel Serceau, "Questions de genre, questions de sexe: les femmes dans le cinéma maghrébin," in Françoise Puaux, ed., *Le machisme à l'écran* (Paris: Corlet/Télérama, 2001), 116.

6. An Indigenous Film Culture: *El Chergui*

1. Translated from the French: "le cinéma d'auteur, ou d'expression, est majoritaire au Maghreb. Car les Etats subventionnent plus volontiers un cinéma

d'expression, qui peut dignement les représenter à l'étranger. A l'intérieur de
ce cinéma subventionné il y a de la place aussi bien pour les oeuvres de haute
qualité artistique que pour les films de propagande.

Liés à l'Etat, les films des pays du Maghreb voient dès lors souvent leurs
thèmes, leur style, leur degré de liberté, liés au passé politique ou à l'économie
du cinéma propre à chaque pays." Ferid Boughedir, "Panorama des cinémas
maghrébins," in Mouny Berrah, Jacques Lévy, and Claude-Michel Cluny, eds.,
Les cinémas arabes (Paris: Cerf/IMA, 1987), 67.

2. Albert Memmi, *The Colonizer and the Colonized* (New York: Souvenir Press,
1974), 114.

3. Translated from the French: "Il faut montrer que le cinéma est capable de tout
dire et qu'il faut briser les anciennes formes pour inventer le nouveau cinéma
arabe." Nouri Bouzid, interview, in *Actes du Onzième Festival International*
(Montpellier, 1989): 181.

4. Moumen Smihi, "Moroccan Society as Mythology" in John D. H. Downing,
ed., *Film and Politics in the Third World* (New York: Praeger, 1987), 81.

5. Ibid., 79.

6. Ibid., 82.

7. Ibid., 83.

8. Ibid., 80.

9. Ibid., 82.

10. Translated from the French: "*Wechma* fut une véritable révolution dans le
cinéma maghrébin. Pour la première fois, un cinéaste avait réfléchi murement
au langage cinématographique qu'il allait utiliser, plan par plan, avait cherché
et trouvé une forme d'expression originale qui s'éloignait totalement des
clichés du cinéma occidentale, qu'il soit d'auteur ou de consommation, et
puisait directement ses sources dans l'imaginaire collectif marocain." Fouad
Souiba and Fatima Zahra el Alaoui, *Un siècle de cinéma au Maroc* (Rabat:
World Design Communication, 1995), 80.

11. Translated from the French: "Cinéma élytique par excellence, celui de
Derkaoui constitue un genre sans grande appréciation publique, mais qui
pousse à la réflexion permanente." Ahmed Araib and Eric de Hullessen, *Il
était une fois . . . Le cinéma au Maroc* (Rabat: EDH, 1999), 56.

12. Translated from the French: "un grand moment dans l'évolution du langage
cinématographique national." Souiba and el Alaoui, 86.

13. Smihi, 80.

14. Ibid., 85.

15. Moulay Driss Jaïdi, *Le cinéma au Maroc* (Rabat: Collection al majal, 1991),
124.

16. Smihi, 82.

17. Ibid., 80.

18. Ibid.

19. Ibid., 83.

20. Ibid.

21. Ibid., 84.

22. Translated from the French: "le chergui et le Gharbi sont les deux vents qui règnent à Tanger qui, au demeurant, est le lieu de la rencontre de l'Atlantique et de la Méditerranée." Moulay Driss Jaïdi, *Cinégraphiques* (Rabat: Collection al majal, 1995), 111.

23. Translated from the French: "une ville lézardée par l'injustice, l'exploitation et l'oppression." Ibid., 128.

24. Translated from the French: "Beaucoup de choses s'y sont décidées concernant la décolonisation officielle du pays. Des choses finissaient, d'autres commençaient à voir le jour." Moumen Smihi, interview, *Cinéma 76* 205 (Paris, 1976): 98.

25. Smihi, "Moroccan Society," 81.

26. Translated from the French: "un Gnaoui, population noire du Maroc originaire de Guinée." Smihi, interview, 94.

27. Ibid., 96–98.

28. Smihi, "Moroccan Society," 83.

29. Ibid., 82–83.

30. Translated from the French: "un film-phare. Son auteur y révèle une maîtrise stylistique et un tempérament de cinéaste authentique." Noureddine Ghali, "*El chergui ou le silence violent:* Une interrogation sur la société marocaine," *Cinéma 76* 205 (Paris, 1976): 131.

31. Translated from the French: "ont pour projet d'affirmer une liberté d'expression qui a été sans cesse revendiquée par les cinéastes-producteurs marocains." Moulay Driss Jaïdi, *Vision(s) de la société marocaine à travers le court métrage* (Rabat: Collection al majal, 1994), 108.

32. Translated from the French: "réside aussi dans son oscillement constant entre la réalité et la mythologie marocaines." Souiba and el Alaoui, 83.

33. Translated from the French: "Moumen Smihi hisse d'un cran le niveau du cinéma marocain . . . s'apparente au cinéma expérimental indissociable de son environnement social et philosophique." Araib and Hullessen, 44.

7. History as Myth: *Chronicle of the Years of Embers*

1. Philip Dine, "Thinking the Unthinkable: The Generation of Meaning in French Literary and Cinema Images of the Algerian War," *Maghreb Review* 19, no. 1–2 (London, 1994): 124.

2. Translated from the French: "Le F.L.N. n'est pas arrivé à l'indépendance avec un programme politique bien précis. C'est encore plus vrai pour la culture. On est resté dans ce domaine au niveau du slogan tout en pensant la subordination du culturel au politique comme allant de soi." Monique Gadant, "L'apolitique culturelle," in Georges Châtillon and Edwige Lambert, eds., *Algérie*, 2nd ed. (Paris: Autrement, 1991), 249.

3. Translated from the French: "les productions sont destinées à la défense et à

l'illustration de la vision officielle des événements." Mouny Berrah, "Histoire et idéologie du cinéma algérien sur la guerre," in Guy Hennebelle, Mouny Berrah, and Benjamin Stora, eds., *La guerre d'Algérie à l'écran* (Paris: Corlet-Télérama, 1997), 149–150.

4. Ibid., 146.

5. Benjamin Stora, *Histoire de l'Algérie depuis l'indépendance* (Paris: Editions La Découverte, 1994), 27.

6. Translated from the French: "Pour les militaires algériens qui prennent le pouvoir en 1965, il s'agit de refaire l'histoire algérienne en faisant oublier le rôle des maquis de l'intérieur. Il s'agit aussi de faire oublier, par cette histoire-fiction où les militaires jouent un rôle central, certains moments de l'histoire partisane du nationalisme algérien." Ibid., 57.

7. Translated from the French: "projetant l'image mythique d'un univers manichéen où les rôles sont clairement définis entre les héros et les traîtres, les libérateurs et les oppresseurs." Ibid., 57–58.

8. Translated from the French: "un nationalisme idéal . . . mettent l'accent sur les contradictions internes de la société algérienne de la même période." Mouny Berrah, "La guerre, la terre, la vie quotidien," in Mouny Berrah, Victor Bachy, Mohand Ben Salama, and Ferid Boughedir, eds., *Cinémas du Maghreb* (Paris: Editions Papyrus, 1981), 46.

9. Translated from the French: "Dans la période 1965–1980, paradoxalement, jamais l'histoire de 'la révolution algérienne' n'a été tant célébrée, commémorée. Mais de quelle histoire s'agissait-il?" Stora, 58.

10. Translated from the French: "comme l'expression achevée du code de bonne conduite prévalant pour le sujet." Berrah, "Histoire et idéologie," 162.

11. Sabry Hafez, "Shifting Identities in Maghribi Cinema: The Algerian Paradigm," in Ferial J. Ghazoul, ed., *Arab Cinematics: Toward the New and the Alternative, Alif* 15 (Cairo, 1995): 66.

12. Translated from the French: "J'ai dit et je répète, je n'ai pas fait oeuvre historique. Mon film ne donne qu'une vision personnelle, même s'il s'appuie sur des faits précis. Je n'ai jamais eu la prétention de fournir une vision d'ensemble de toute l'Algérie dans cette période historique, d'autant que j'ai vécu dans un petit village." Mohamed Lakhdar Hamina, interview, in Berrah et al., *Cinémas du Maghreb,* 70.

13. Translated from the French: "Un tel film historico-politique ne pourra jamais être fait avec toute la rigueur et l'objectivité voulue, puisqu'on ne peut réaliser ce genre de cinéma qu'avec la plus grande subjectivité passionelle." Ibid.

14. Wassyla Tamzali, *En attendant Omar Gatlato* (Algiers: Editions EnAP, 1979), 139.

15. Mostefa Lacheraf, "*Du Voleur de Bagdad* à *Omar Gatlato,*" in Berrah et al., *Cinémas du Maghreb,* 37.

16. Translated from the French: "Sur le plan sociologique, il reste un document incontournable en ceci qu'il a le mérite d'organiser et de synthétiser . . . une période de l'histoire déterminante de l'histoire moderne de l'Algérie." Berrah, "Histoire et idéologie," 218.

17. Hafez, 66.

18. Translated from the French: "vont définitivement creuser le fossé entre les deux communautés et convaincre nombre de nationalistes algériens que seule l'action armée peut arracher des concessions à la France." Benjamin Stora and Akram Ellyas, *Les 100 portes du Maghreb* (Paris: Les Editions de l'Atelier/ Editions Ouvrières, 1999), 217.

19. Translated from the French: "nous n'en voyons que de rares indications presque allusives." Lacheraf, 37.

20. Translated from the French: "le prélude à une véritable prise de conscience nationale orientée vers d'autres moyens de lutte." Ibid.

21. Translated from the French: "dans la grande tradition du cinéma soviétique." Berrah, "Histoire et idéologie," 218.

22. Translated from the French: "cimenté artibrairement par la prise de conscience d'un paysan-héros, devenu subitement un surhomme, tel que généralement conçu par le cinéma américain." Hassan Bouabdallah, "Entre le 'monumentalisme' et le réalisme," in Berrah et al., *Cinémas du Maghreb*, 63.

23. Translated from the French: "le fermier pacifique est soudain appelé à se transformer en vengeur. Il est montré, au début, en train de s'entrainer au tir; au milieu, en train de se battre dans un duel à forces égales; puis, il est seul contre deux, pour venir, enfin, à bout d'une quinzaine de bandits." Ibid.

24. Stora and Ellyas, 230.

25. Hafez, 66.

26. Translated from the French: "est représenté comme un élément pratiquement extérieur du conflit, au risque de faire croire au spectateur non averti, que la contradiction principale à cette période était entre le peuple et une couche d'Algériens complices de l'autorité coloniale." Lotfi Maherzi, *Le cinéma algérien: Institutions, imaginaire, idéologie* (Algiers: SNED, 1980), 282.

27. Ibid., 283.

8. A Fragile Masculinity: *Omar Gatlato*

1. Lotfi Maherzi, *Le cinéma algérien: Institutions, imaginaire, idéologie* (Algiers: SNED, 1980), 211–112.

2. Translated from the French: "le degré zéro de la sexualité vue ou dite." Abdou B., "Le dernier tabou?" in Jean-Pierre Brossard, ed., *L'Algérie vue par son cinéma* (Locarno: Festival International du Film de Locarno, 1981), 106.

3. Merzak Allouache, interview, in *African Conversations* (London: BFI, 1995), n.p.

4. Jerry Palmer, *The Logic of the Absurd: On Film and Television Comedy* (London: BFI, 1987).

5. Sarah Kozloff, *Invisible Storytellers: Voice-Over Narration in American Fiction Film* (Berkeley: University of California Press, 1988), 41.

6. Translated from the French: "le premier film algérien qui nous trace un portrait de cette culture que véhicule une partie importante de la population des

grandes villes." Wassyla Tamzali, *En attendant Omar Gatlato* (Algiers: Editions EnAP, 1979), 90.

7. Sanjeev Prakash, "Music, Dance and Popular Film," in Aruna Vasudev and Philippe Lenglet, eds., *Indian Cinema Superbazaar* (New Delhi: Vikas Publishing House, 1983), 114.

8. Ibid.

9. Tamzali, 89.

10. Translated from the French: "un monde fermé qui développera son langage, son code d'honneur, sa morale, en dehors des règles de la société." Tamzali, 90.

11. Translated from the French: "ce ne sont pas des marginaux. Ils ont un travail, une famille." Merzak Allouache, interview, in Tamzali, 94.

12. Translated from the French: "le mot homosexualité n'est pas très juste car il recouvre des notions différentes de ce qui se passe ici . . . des amitiés masculines très fortes, exclusives . . . de véritables scènes de jalouise." Ibid., 94–95.

13. Fatima Mernissi, *Beyond the Veil: Male-Female Dynamics in Muslim Society,* rev. ed. (London: Al Saqi Books, 1985), 41.

14. Ibid., 31.

15. Translated from the French: "Ce qui le tue, dans la réalité quotidienne, c'est sa nervosité, or en outre il s'agit d'une caracteristique 'féminine' que les hommes ont jusqu'ici utilisée pour souligner l'infériorité des femmes!" Maryse Léon, "L'image de la femme dans la littérature et le cinéma algérien," in Brossard, 143.

16. Mernissi, 173.

9. Memory Is a Woman's Voice: *La Nouba*

1. Georges Gusdorf, cited in Dwight F. Reynolds, ed., *Interpreting the Self: Autobiography in the Arab Literary Tradition* (Berkeley: University of California Press, 2001), 17.

2. Reynolds, 241.

3. Ibid., 242–243.

4. Ibid., 247.

5. Ibid., 251.

6. Hilary Kilpatrick, "Introduction," in Roger Allen, Hilary Kilpatrick, and Ed de Moor, eds., *Love and Sexuality in Modern Arabic Literature* (London: Saqi Books, 1995), 11.

7. Fedwa Malti-Douglas, *Woman's Body, Woman's World: Gender and Discourse in Arabo-Islâmic Writing* (Princeton, N.J.: Princeton University Press, 1991), 9.

8. Nadja Odeh, "Coded Emotions: The Description of Nature in Arab Women's Autobiographies," in Robin Ostle, Ed de Moor, and Stefan Wild, eds., *Writing the Self: Autobiographical Writing in Modern Arabic Literature* (London: Saqi Books, 1998), 264.

9. Malti-Douglas, 4–5.

10. Dinah Manisty, "Negotiating the Space between Private and Public: Women's Autobiographical Writing in Egypt," in Ostle et al., 273.

11. Ibrahim Fawal, *Youssef Chahine* (London: BFI, 2001), 117.

12. Translated from the French: "Ecoute! J'ai parlé de la société égyptienne et arabe durant toute ma vie, qu'on me laisse une fois parler de moi-même." Youssef Chahine, cited in Khémais Khayati, *Cinémas arabes: Topographie d'une image éclatée* (Paris and Montreal: L'Harmattan, 1996), 207.

13. Translated from the French: "en réalité, c'est le fait que Chahine parle à la première personne de lui-même, de sa famille, de ses rêves, de ses déboires et aussi de sa société. Bref Chahine s'est dénudé devant son public. Et quel choc!" Khayati, 207.

14. Nouri Bouzid, "New Realism in Arab Cinema: The Defeat-Conscious Cinema," in Ferial J. Ghazoul, ed., *Arab Cinematics: Toward the New and the Alternative, Alif* 15 (Cairo, 1995): 248–249.

15. Translated from the French: "petite fille sortant dans la rue avec une dame (ma mère), citadine enveloppée de son voile de soie blanc . . . qui se rendait, chaque jeudi, au hammam." Assia Djebar, *Ces voix qui m'assiègent* (Paris: Albin Michel, 1999), 43.

16. Translated from the French: "fillette arabe allant pour la première fois à l'école, un matin d'automne, main dans la main du père." Ibid., 45.

17. Translated from the French: "une pure joie d'inventer." Ibid., 18.

18. Translated from the French: "j'écrivais tout en restant voilée, je dirais même que j'y tenais: de l'écriture comme voile!" Ibid., 97.

19. Translated from the French: "dévoilement." Ibid., 64.

20. Translated from the French: "c'était une langue du discours politique . . . et, en même temps, de plus en plus une langue du masculin." Ibid., 177.

21. Assia Djebar, *So Vast the Prison* (New York: Seven Stories Press, 1999), 180.

22. Djebar, *Ces voix,* 178.

23. Translated from the French: "appréhender les mots dans l'espace." Ibid., 100.

24. Translated from the French: "écrire pour le cinéma . . . à partir d'un son enregistré, d'un son écouté, réécouté." Ibid., 37.

25. Ibid., 105.

26. Translated from the French: "elle trouve dans la tradition orale des femmes l'expression authentique de la culture algérienne." Mildred Mortimer, "Nouveau regard, nouvelle parole: le cinéma d'Assia Djebar," in Kenneth W. Harrow, ed., *With Open Eyes: Women and African Cinema* (Amsterdam and Atlanta, Ga.: Rodopi, 1997), 97.

27. Translated from the French: "pour le son et pour la parole féminine, que je voulais quêter si possible à la source." Djebar, *Ces voix,* 182.

28. Translated from the French: "un cinéma de recherche, et non de la consommation." Ibid., 169.

29. Mireille Calle-Gruber, *Assia Djebar, ou la résistance de l'écriture* (Paris: Maisonneuve & Larose, 2001), 267–277.

30. Assia Djebar, interview, in Mouny Berrah, Victor Bachy, Mohand Ben Salama, and Ferid Boughedir, eds., *Cinémas du Maghreb* (Paris: Editions Papyrus, 1981), 107.

31. Djebar, *Ces voix,* 36.

32. Translated from the French: "Filmer ainsi les lieux—en conservant en moi la litanie des mots murmurés de la langue maternelle—c'était autant un 'journal' de moi et des miens que j'allais commencer, qu'un retour aux lieux que les destructions de la guerre, pourtant si terrible, avaient épargnés." Ibid., 100–101.

33. Robin Ostle, "Introduction," in Ostle et al., 22.

34. Translated from the French: "une femme d'éducation française . . . et de sensibilité algérienne, ou arabo-berbère, ou même musulman." Djebar, *Ces voix,* 26.

35. Calle-Gruber, 9.

10. Imag(in)ing Europe: *Miss Mona*

1. Benjamin Stora and Akram Ellyas, *Les 100 portes du Maghreb* (Paris: Les Editions de l'Atelier/Editions Ouvrières, 1999), 153–155.

2. Winifred Woodhall, "Exile," in Françoise Lionnet and Ronnie Scharfman, eds., *Post/Colonial Conditions: Exiles, Migrations and Nomadisms,* Yale French Studies, no. 81 (New Haven, Conn.: Yale University Press, 1993), 7.

3. Leïla Sebbar, "The Richness of Diversity," in Eric Sellin and Hédi Abdel-Jaouad, eds., *North Africa: Literary Crossroads,* special issue of *The Literary Review* 41, no. 3 (Madison, Wis., 1998): 237.

4. Alec G. Hargreaves, *Immigration and Identity in Beur Fiction* (Oxford and New York: Berg, 1991), 171.

5. Ibid.

6. Ibid., 16.

7. Translated from the French: "Si j'étais resté en Algérie, j'aurais été peut-être bien, je n'aurais peut-être eu besoin de m'exprimer." Cited ibid., 26.

8. Ibid., 15.

9. Translated from the French: "A la maison, c'est tout le temps: 'Attention, ne fais pas ci, parce que tu es Arabe . . . Ne fais pas ça . . . N'oublie pas que tu es musulman!' Dans la rue, le gosse se retrouve carrément dans un autre monde que les parents ignorent." Cited ibid., 20.

10. Translated from the French: "Toujours tiraillés entre deux sociétés qui, en même temps, nous oublient—mais qu'est-ce que l'Algérie a fait pour nous, les jeunes?—et veulent nous enrôler, peu tentés par le retour en Algérie, poussés, au contraire, je dirais même condamnés à vivre en France, écorchés vifs, les jeunes de la migration pensent que maintenant le meilleur moyen de s'affirmer, c'est de vivre tels qu'ils sont, de se poser en fils de migrants vivant en France, en mettant en valeur ce qui a pu être sauvé de la culture d'origine, mais en affirmant aussi qu'ils appartiennent déjà et de plus en plus à la société française." Cited ibid., 27.

11. Ibid., 33–34.

12. Christian Bosséno, "Immigrant Cinema: National Cinema—The Case of Beur Film," in Richard Dyer and Ginette Vincendeau, eds., *Popular European Cinema* (London and New York: Routledge, 1992), 52.

13. Translated from the French: "Si l'on en croit le cinéma, c'est donc par le bas—misère pour misère—que le processus d'intégration a le plus de chance de s'enclencher." René Prédal, "Problèmes d'identité, droit à la différence et couples mixtes dans le cinéma français des années 90," in Abderrahim Lamchichi and Dominique Baillet, eds., *Maghrébins de France: Regards sur les dynamiques de l'intégration* (Paris: L'Harmattan, 2001), 181.

14. Abbas Fahdel, "Une esthétique beur?" in Guy Hennebelle and Roland Schneider, eds., *Cinémas métis: De Hollywood aux films beurs* (Paris: Corlet/Télérama, 1990), 150.

15. Carrie Tarr, "Questions of Identity in Beur Cinema: From *Tea in the Harem* to *Cheb*," *Screen* 32, no. 4 (Glasgow, 1993), 337.

16. Ibid.

17. Translated from the French: "Il y a un peu de Dostoïevski chez Charef à travers sa grande compassion pour les humbles." Fahdel, 151.

18. Bosséno, 51.

19. Translated from the French: "Indiscutiblement le cinéma ne les montre pas du côté des vainqueurs ou des gâtés par l'existence et s'ils sont toujours mis en scène avec chaleur sans misérabilisme, ils ne sauraient donner envie ni constituer des héros susceptibles de faire rêver le spectateur." Prédal, 185.

20. Translated from the French: "Construire un film autour d'un personnage beur conduit donc le cinéaste à modifier sa pratique comme son esthétique car ce nouveau 'héros' fait éclater les cadres du récit au même titre que les conventions psychologiques." Ibid.

11. Defeat as Destiny: *Golden Horseshoes*

1. Translated from the French: "Itinéraires de l'échec." Moulay Driss Jaïdi, *Cinégraphiques* (Rabat: Collection al majal, 1995), 79.

2. Translated from the French: "cette image de l'échec." Ibid., 81.

3. Translated from the French: "réflètent une vision pessimiste. Presque tous les personnages principaux subissent un échec." Ibid., 84.

4. Nouri Bouzid, "*Sources of Inspiration*" Lecture: *22 June 1994, Villepreux* (Amsterdam: Sources, 1994), 64.

5. Nouri Bouzid, "New Realism in Arab Cinema: The Defeat-Conscious Cinema," in Ferial J. Ghazoul, ed., *Arab Cinematics: Toward the New and the Alternative, Alif* 15 (Cairo, 1995): 249.

6. Bouzid, "*Sources*," 58.

7. Nouri Bouzid, "Mission Unaccomplished," *Index on Censorship* 6 (London, 1995): 104.

8. Martin Stollery, "Masculinities, Generations, and Cultural Transformation in Contemporary Tunisian Cinema," *Screen* 42, no. 1 (Glasgow, 2001): 53.

9. Translated from the French: "C'est le film le plus proche de mon coeur, de mon existence et de ma vie." Nouri Bouzid, "Propos de Nouri Bouzid," in Hédi Khelil, *Résistances et utopies: Essais sur le cinéma arabe et africain* (Tunis: Edition Sahar, 1994), 24.

10. Bouzid, "Mission," 102.

11. Bouzid, "*Sources*," 51.

12. For fuller details, see the Nouri Bouzid and Hichem Rostom interviews in *Actes du Onzième Festival International* (Montpellier, 1989): 175–178, and Bouzid's interview with Ferid Boughedir in the pressbook of the *Festival de Cannes 1989*, n.p.

13. Translated from the French: "bien que parfois bouleversant, n'est pas totalement sympathique et ne fait rien pour l'être. On peut juger que son destin est tragique, mais on ne se sent pas pour autant tout à fait à l'aise effectivement à son égard." Denise Brahimi, "Critique-éloge de l'intellectuel tunisien: A propos des *Sabots en or*, de Nouri Bouzid," *Ifriquiya* 1 (Paris and Montreal, 1997): 37.

14. Translated from the French: "l'intellectuel ex-révolutionnaire, avec toutes ses défaillances et toutes ses failles, est un personnage beaucoup moins négatif ou voué à la négativité qu'il ne semblait d'abord." Ibid., 39.

15. Translated from the French: "c'est Tunis en hiver, une ville où l'on grelotte, où tout est humide et froid. Le personnage principal, Youssef Soltane, porte symboliquement un grand manteau noir et une écharpe, tenue qui l'isole d'une ville où il revient après six ans en prison, mais qui ne parvient pas à lui redonner la moindre chaleur intérieure." Denise Brahimi, *Cinémas d'Afrique francophone et du Maghreb* (Paris: Nathan, 1997), 106.

16. Bouzid, "Mission," 103.

17. Bouzid, "*Sources*," 65.

18. Ibid., 49–50.

19. Bouzid, "Mission," 103.

20. Ibid.

21. Ibid., 102.

22. Ibid., 102–103.

23. Ibid., 102.

12. Sexuality and Gendered Space: *Halfaouine*

1. Judith Mayne, *Private Novels, Public Films* (Athens: University of Georgia Press, 1988), 16.

2. Ibid., 27.

3. Ibid., 29.

4. Fatima Mernissi, *Beyond the Veil: Male-Female Dynamics in Muslim Society,* rev. ed. (London: Al Saqi Books, 1985), 138.

5. Ibid.

6. Ibid., 139–140.

7. Translated from the French: "Espace et sexualité sont deux expressions privilégiées que la société utilise pour exprimer son identité profonde." Abdessamad Dialmy, *Logement, sexualité et Islam* (Casablanca: Eddif, 1995), 13.

8. Translated from the French: "la même logique binaire, manichéenne." Ibid., 27.

9. Translated from the French: "C'est une logique manichéenne qui semble régir l'univers traditionel patriarchal dans sa totalité, une logique dont le point de départ est le corps humain lui-même." Ibid., 28.

10. Translated from the French:

Schèmes binaires	Sexualité	Espace
Pur-impur	+	+
Propre-sale	+	+
Sec-humide	+	+
Clair-obscur	+	+
Central-périphérique	+	+
Haut-bas	+	+
Vertical-horizontal	+	+
Manifeste-caché	+	+
Extérieur-intérieur	+	+
Carré-circulaire	+	+
Droit-courbe	+	+
Masculin-féminin.	+	+

Ibid.

11. Serge Santelli, *Medinas: Traditional Architecture of Tunisia/Médinas: L'architecture traditionnelle en Tunisie* (Tunis: Dar Ashraf Editions, 1992), 13.

12. Translated from the French: "le lieu d'un secret intérieur, caché et protégé . . . une forme de l'utérus." Dialmy, 60.

13. Ibid.

14. Translated from the French: "cette ascension horizontale vers Allah." Ibid., 59.

15. Translated from the French: "Tiraillée entre ses signes phalliques et ses formes féminines, entre le vertical et le rond, la cité arabo-islamique fait preuve d'une bisexualité, à l'image du corps dont elle est la transposition architecturale et urbanistique." Ibid., 60–61.

16. See Lizbeth Malkmus and Roy Armes, *Arab and African Film Making* (London: Zed Books, 1991), 185–200.

17. A similar approach is adopted by Rachida Triki, "La symbolique des lieux dans le cinéma de Férid Boughedir," in Ida Kummer, ed., *Cinéma Maghrébin*, special issue of *Celaan* 1, no. 1–2 (Saratoga Springs, N.Y., 2002): 41–48.

18. Translated from the French: "vu par les yeux d'un enfant essayant de trouver sa voie vers l'univers des adultes, au sein d'une société conservatrice où règne la stricte séparation des sexes." Ferid Boughedir, "Un été à La Goulette," in Frédéric Mitterand and Soraya Elses-Ferchichi, eds., *Une Saison Tunisienne* (Arles: Actes Sud/AFAA, 1995), 123.

19. Translated from the French: "peut-être le film maghrébin à la fois le plus mûr

et le plus intelligent." Michel Serceau, "Questions de genre, questions de sexe: les femmes dans le cinéma maghrébin," in Françoise Puaux, ed., *Le machisme à l'écran* (Paris: Corlet/Télérama, 2001), 126.

20. Translated from the French: "un des films, sinon le film, maghrébins qui traite le plus, non seulement du corps des femmes, mais de la vision et des fantasmes du corps, dans un sexe et dans l'autre." Ibid.

21. Translated from the French: "Le cinéma maghrébin n'a jamais peut-être si bien parlé des femmes que dans ces comédies qui traitent de l'immaturité des hommes." Ibid.

22. Translated from the French: "d'une part tout et tous autour de lui le renvoient à cette obsession, parce qu'il vit dans un monde où la sexualité est omniprésente et exhibée alors que d'autre part, cette sexualité est tenue hors d'attente par un système d'interdits complexes et pervers." Denise Brahimi, *Cinémas d'Afrique francophone et du Maghreb* (Paris: Nathan, 1997), 103.

23. Cited in Mernissi, 141.

24. Afsanej Najmabadi, "Reading 'Wiles of Women' Stories as Fictions of Masculinity," in Mai Ghoussoub and Emma Sinclair-Webb, eds., *Imagined Masculinities: Male Identity and Culture in the Modern Middle East* (London: Saqi Books, 2000), 150.

25. Translated from the French: "une chasteté à toute épreuve." Abdou B., "Ni Dieu, ni sexe . . . ," in Mouny Berrah, Jacques Lévy, and Claude-Michel Cluny, eds., *Les cinémas arabes* (Paris: Cerf/IMA, 1987), 131.

26. Ferid Boughedir, "Cinémas et libertés en Afrique," in FEPACI, ed., *L'Afrique et le centenaire du cinéma/Africa and the Centenary of Cinema* (Paris: Présence Africaine, 1995), 39.

27. For a selection of memories by Tunisian artists, writers, and filmmakers, see Lizbeth Pelinq and Anne Thuaudet, *Le Hammam d'Othman Khadraoui* (Tunis: Cérès Productions, 1992).

28. Nouri Bouzid, *"Sources of Inspiration" Lecture: 22 June 1994, Villepreux* (Amsterdam: Sources, 1994), 59.

29. Martin Stollery, "Masculinities, Generations, and Cultural Transformation in Contemporary Tunisian Cinema," *Screen* 42, no. 1 (Glasgow, 2001): 56.

30. Lieve Spass, *The Francophone Film: A Struggle for Identity* (Manchester: Manchester University Press, 2000), 158.

31. Translated from the French: "très largement inspiré par des faits que j'ai personnellement vécus, enfant, dans le vieux quartier populaire d'Halfaouine, à Tunis." Boughedir, "Un été," 121.

32. Bouzid, 59.

33. Translated from the French: "procède à l'accouchement sans douleur de notre inconscient collectif . . . l'Homme arabe, avec ses blessures, ses frustrations et ses désirs." Houria Zourgane, cited in Touti Moumen, *Films tunisiens: Longs métrages 1967–98* (Tunis: Touti Moumen, 1998), 152.

34. Translated from the French: "pour un film sur l'éveil du désir, 'Halfaouine' manque de force, de ce qu'il y a de destructeur et de régénérateur dans le

désir, la mort, la vie, ce qui est au travail dans cette société." Tahar Chikhaoui, cited in Moumen, 153.

35. Mernissi, 140.

36. Ibid.

37. Ibid.

13. A Timeless World: *Looking for My Wife's Husband*

1. Frantz Fanon, *The Wretched of the Earth* (Harmondsworth: Penguin Books, 1967), 30.

2. Translated from the French: "comme un inéluctable parcours 'rituel,' et un instrument herméneutique, devant conduire à explorer tantôt le passé nostalgique, tantôt le présent désenchanté." Kamel Ben Ouanès, "La médina-mémoire dans le cinéma tunisien," *Cinécrits* 5 (Tunis, 1994): 8.

3. Translated from the French: "il transforme la mémoire en un miroir, et la vague impression d'une filiation identitaire et affective en une expression iconographique, soumise à la curiosité—ou peut-être à l'examen—du public." Ibid.

4. Translated from the French: "à quel moment précis se joue le film?" Cited in Touti Moumen, *Films tunisiens: Longs métrages 1967–98* (Tunis: Touti Moumen, 1988), 153.

5. Unpublished interviews with Kevin Dwyer (Rabat, 1999–2000).

6. Ibid.

7. Translated from the French: "quand on est à l'intérieur des murailles, dans la médina, on peut imaginer que nous sommes dans les années 50. . . . Mais quand on passe de l'autre côté des murailles, on est carrément en 1993." Mohamed Abderrahman Tazi, interview with Henri Talvat, in *Actes du Quinzième Festival International* (Montpellier, 1993): 23.

8. Interviews with Dwyer.

9. Ibid.

10. Ibid.

11. Ibid.

12. Ibid.

13. Ibid.

14. Ibid.

15. Translated from the French: "débats houleux entre fondamentalistes et modernistes." Abderrahmane Koudjil, "Polygamnie au Maghreb: Controverses autour d'un droit en mouvement," in Abderrahim Lamchichi, ed., *Sexualité et sociétés arabes*, Confluences Méditerranée, no. 41 (Paris: L'Harmattan, 2002): 84.

16. Tazi, 23.

17. Translated from the French: "les enfants vivaient avec les femmes et les servantes, dans cette communication qui existe entre eux et les mères, les concubines." Ibid., 25.

18. Translated from the French: "La problématique de la polygamie dans le contexte maghrébin est très complexe. Cet acte est marqué, d'une part, par les traditions ancestrales et coutumières, et, d'autre part, par la superposition de deux droits: le droit musulman et le droit positif hérité du système juridique français. Cette dialectique récurrente entre la tradition et la modernité, le particulier et l'universel rejoint une autre dialectique, celle des droits de l'homme et de la diversité culturelle." Koudjil, 25.

19. Fatima Mernissi, *Beyond the Veil: Male-Female Dynamics in Muslim Society,* rev. ed. (London: Al Saqi Books, 1985), 144.

20. Ibid., 49.

21. Tazi, 25.

22. W. Stephens, cited in Mernissi, 116.

23. Mernissi, 119.

24. Ibid., 54.

25. Interviews with Dwyer.

26. Ibid.

27. Ibid.

14. A New Future Begins: *Silences of the Palace*

1. Abdelkrim Gabous, *Silence, elles tournent!—Les femmes et le cinéma en Tunisie* (Tunis: Cérès Éditions/CREDIF, 1998), 198–210.

2. Translated from the French: "Aucune femme cinéaste tunisienne ne vit de la réalisation. Si elle n'est pas monteuse ou productrice, elle exerce un autre métier que le cinéma ou vit des revenus de son mari." Ibid., 33.

3. Translated from the French: "aider à ouvrir un dialogue entre les femmes et donner des éléments de discussion aux femmes." Selma Baccar, cited in Touti Moumen, *Films tunisiens: Longs métrages 1967–98* (Tunis: Touti Moumen, 1998), 72.

4. Translated from the French: "La femme artiste a du mal à trouver sa place dans notre société." Moufida Tlatli, interview, in Gabous, 157.

5. Translated from the French: "Pour expliquer les silences qui nous entourènt dans notre vie quotidienne, j'ai voulu remonter dans les temps et en trouver les causes lointaines, l'origine." Ibid., 156.

6. Translated from the French: "un témoignage, un cri, une oeuvre de femme pour les femmes, qu'elles soient tunisiennes ou autres. . . . Il faut changer, secouer les mentalités. De mon poste de cinéaste, j'essaie de le faire." Ibid., 161.

7. Moufida Tlatli, interview, *Ecrans d'Afrique/African Screen* 8 (Milan, 1994): 8.

8. Ibid., 11.

9. Moufida Tlatli, interview, *Sight and Sound* n.s., 5, no. 3 (London, 1995): 18.

10. Dinah Manisty, "Negotiating the Space between Private and Public: Women's Autobiographical Writing in Egypt," in Robin Ostle, Ed de Moor, and Stefan Wild, eds., *Writing the Self: Autobiographical Writing in Modern Arabic Literature* (London: Saqi Books, 1998), 274.

11. Fatima Mernissi, *Beyond the Veil: Male-Female Dynamics in Muslim Society*, rev. ed. (London: Al Saqi Books, 1985), 137.

12. Tlatli 1995, 19.

13. Ibid.

14. Ibid., 18.

15. Nawal el Saadawi, *The Hidden Face of Eve: Women in the Arab World* (London and New Jersey: Zed Books, 1980), 13.

16. Ibid.

17. Tlatli 1994, 8.

18. Karin van Nieuwkerk, *"A Trade Like Any Other": Female Singers and Dancers in Egypt* (Austin: University of Texas Press, 1995), 12.

19. Tlatli 1995, 18.

20. Marnia Lazreg, *The Eloquence of Silence: Algerian Women in Question* (London and New York: Routledge, 1994), 140–141.

21. Ibid., 141.

22. Tlatli 1995, 18.

23. See Hélé Béji, *Désenchantement national* (Paris: François Maspero, 1982).

15. A New Realism? *Ali Zaoua*

1. Nouri Bouzid, "New Realism in Arab Cinema: The Defeat-Conscious Cinema," in Ferial J. Ghazoul, ed., *Arab Cinematics: Toward the New and the Alternative, Alif* 15 (Cairo, 1995): 247.

2. Ibid.

3. Ibid., 249.

4. Ibid.

5. Ibid., 248–249.

6. Ibid., 248.

7. Ibid., 250.

8. Translated from the French: "J'ai voulu montrer le plus possible, une réalité que je vis moi aussi, même si c'est un film de femmes . . . dire que le problème de la femme n'est pas chose exceptionnelle et que c'est un combat qui nous concerne tous." Jilalli Ferhati, interview with Abdou B. and Moulay Brahimi, *Les Deux Ecrans* 47–48 (Algiers, 1982): 27.

9. Translated from the French: "un cinéma-vérité où l'effort du cinéaste consiste à refléter fidèlement cette réalité dont le principal témoin est le spectateur. . . . ses films dérangent parfois par l'amertume qui se dégage de cette réalité basée sur l'injustice et l'inégalité que Noury dénonce courageusement." Ahmed Araib and Eric de Hullessen, *Il était une fois . . . Le cinéma au Maroc* (Rabat: EDH, 1999), 67.

10. Translated from the French: "Les gosses se sont immédiatement mis en scène, me racontant n'importe quoi. . . . Ils savent donner à la société exactement ce

qu'elle attend d'eux en termes de misérabilisme. Le film avait envie d'aller ailleurs." Nabil Ayouch, interview, *La Libération* (Paris, 21 March 2001), 42.

11.   Translated from the French: "Il ne fallait absolument pas qu'ils envisagent ce film comme une planche de salut, mais comme une phase de transition dont on ne mesurera les conséquences que dans deux ans." Dr. Najat M'Djid, cited in Philippe Azoury, "Ne jamais se mentir, ni leur mentir," *La Libération* (Paris, 21 March 2001), 42.

12.   Translated from the French: "Je savais qu'il me fallait fonctionner avec cet univers déstructuré en bâtissant une fiction. Ça revenait à emmener ces enfants dans une structure." Ayouch, 42.

13.   Translated from the French: "cachent derrière leurs imposants édifices des foyers de misère abritant des enfants mal nourris, sans hygiène, sans école, pépinières de futurs délinquants. La société essaie de guérir cette plaie sociale, mais le résultat de ses efforts est très limité . . . C'est pour cela que ce film s'inspire de faits réels. Il n'est pas optimiste et laisse la solution du problème aux forces progressistes de la société." Luis Buñuel, "*Los Olvidados,*" *L'Avant-Scène du Cinéma* 137 (Paris, 1973): 7.

14.   Translated from the French: "Avec *l'Age d'or,* Buñuel découvrait la réalité quotidienne dans le surréel . . . la surréalité apparaît sous le réel." Ado Kyrou, *Luis Buñuel* (Paris: Editions Seghers, 1962), 43.

15.   Luis Buñuel, *My Last Breath* (London: Jonathan Cape, 1984), 199–200.

16.   Translated from the French: "l'onirisme tient aussi de la réalité. . . . Ils ont des rêves d'appartenance à la réalité matérielle: avoir une voiture, un foyer, une maison, un bateau. Ils rêvent au réel, à une promesse de réel . . . ils fixent les antennes paraboliques et se racontent des films. Il faut admettre qu'il n'y a que la violence dans leur vie." Ayouch, 42.

17.   Translated from the French: "Ne jamais se mentir, ni leur mentir." Ibid.

Conclusion

1.   Hamid Naficy, *An Accented Cinema: Exilic and Diasporic Filmmaking* (Princeton, N.J.: Princeton University Press, 2001), 8.

2.   Lotfi Maherzi, *Le cinéma algérien: Institutions, imaginaire, idéologie* (Algiers: SNED, 1980), 74.

3.   Ibid., 83.

4.   Translated from the French:
Le cinéma algérien, ou la dignité de l'humilié: "Nous fûmes un grand peuple. Ayons confiance en nous et nous bâtirons des montagnes. Dans mon film je redis ce que dit mon gouvernement, insiste chaque cinéaste algérien, car j'entends le pousser à être encore plus progressiste, si possible."
-Le cinéma marocain, ou la plainte silencieuse: "J'étouffe, j'étouffe, c'est le Moyen Age, proteste le cinéaste marocain. Comment écarter ces murailles? De l'air, de l'air! Ah, si je pouvais parler. Mais en attendant, déchiffrez déjà ce que j'ai à vous dire."
-Le cinéma tunisien, ou l'exigence de la vérité: "Ce n'est pas vrai, ce n'est pas vrai. La vérité, la voici, oui la voici la vraie vérité sur l'émigration, sur le tour-

isme, sur l'exode rural, sur la lutte nationale, sur la condition de la femme. Je démysifie, dit le cinéaste tunisien, je fais de la contre-information. J'ai un peu de liberté d'expression et je parle. Ah, si je pouvais en dire plus. Mais qui suis-je? Un orphelin qui cherche son visage. Lequel? Il y a trop de visages. Attendez, je cherche." Ferid Boughedir, cited in Mouny Berrah, Victor Bachy, Mohand Ben Salama, and Ferid Boughedir, eds., *Cinémas du Maghreb* (Paris: Editions Papyrus, 1981), 7.

5. Nouri Bouzid, "Mission Unaccomplished," *Index on Censorship* 6 (London, 1995): 102.

6. Translated from the French: "Après une année de lutte infructueuse, je me résigne, la mort dans l'âme, à le sortir mutilé en avril 2000 et là, plusieurs salles refusent de le programmer pour ne pas choquer leur public familial." Abdelkader Lagtaâ, "Un film non soutenu est enterré," *Cahiers du cinéma* 557 (Paris, 2001): 68.

7. Wimal Dissanayake, ed., *Colonialism and Nationalism in Asian Cinema* (Bloomington: Indiana University Press, 1994), xv–xvi.

8. Translated from the French: "Un projet de film qui ne réussit pas à bénéficier de l'aide est pratiquement enterré, étant donné qu'il n'y a pas d'autres structures d'acueil pour lui permettre de voir le jour." Lagtaâ, 68.

9. See Roy Armes, *Omar Gatlato* (Trowbridge: Flicks Books, 1998), 3–8.

10. Dissanayake, xiii.

11. Kevin Robins and Asu Aksoy, "Deep Nation: The National Question and Turkish Cinema Culture," in Mette Hjort and Scott Mackenzie, eds., *Cinema and Nation* (London and New York: Routledge, 2000), 210.

12. Ibid., 211.

13. Translated from the French: "Le drame algérien se nourrit en partie des mythes forgés dans la guerre de l'indépendance. Ce trop-plein d'une mémoire falsifiée apparaît comme un obstacle à une véritable réappropriation du passé, la construction d'un nationalisme à base d'esprit républicain et d'islam tolérant." Benjamin Stora, *Histoire de l'Algérie depuis l'indépendance* (Paris: Editions La Découverte, 1994), 102–103.

14. Philip Schlesinger, "The Sociological Scope of 'National Cinema,'" in Hjort and Mackenzie, 30.

15. Kevin Dwyer, "'Hidden, Unsaid, Taboo' in Moroccan Cinema: Adelkader Lagtaâ's Challenge to Authority," *Framework* 43, no. 2 (Detroit, 2002): 132.

16. Ibid.

17. Translated from the French: "Pour réaliser mes films, j'ai obtenu une subvention attribuée par la Commission d'aide à la production du ministère de la Culture, qui siège trois fois par an. Cette aide correspond à peu près à 15% du budget du film et on bénéficie par ailleurs d'aides ou plutôt de prestations du ministère du Tourisme, de la télévision tunisienne, une aide 'avance distributeur' et une aide de Canal+ Horizons. Toutes ces aides peuvent parvenir à boucler la moitié du budget d'un film d'auteur normal." Moufida Tlatli, "Si le film est bon, le public tunisien suit," *Cahiers du cinéma* 557 (Paris, 2001): 74.

18. Translated from the French: "une exigence d'exotisme: se cantonner à un terri-toire à la fois géographique (le lieu de tournage doit être l'Afrique . . .) et idéologique (l'Afrique magique, immémoriale, légendaire, mythique, etc) . . . une exigence de réalité: documenter l'Afrique actuelle à travers ses problèmes, en général ramenés à ceux du milieu urbain." Olivier Barlet, "Les nouvelles stratégies des cinéastes africains," *Africultures* 41 (Paris, 2001): 69.

19. Translated from the French: "Il y a des films marocains mais pas un cinéma marocain." Mohamed Abderrahman Tazi, interview, in *Actes du Quinzième Festival International* (Montpellier, 1993): 25.

20. Translated from the French: "Je n'existe qu'en tant que partie infime du cinéma tunisien (même si cela n'a pas de sens)." Nouri Bouzid, "Les cafés abonnés à Canal+ Horizons concurrent les salles," *Cahiers du cinéma* 557 (Paris, 2001): 75.

21. Translated from the French: "cette déterritorialisation cinématographique." Raphaël Millet, "(In)dépendance des cinémas du Sud &/vs France," *Théorème* 5 (Paris, 1998): 141–142.

22. Translated from the French: "à forte identité culturelle." Ibid., 144.

23. Translated from the French: "contribuant à instaurer, ne serait ce que partielle-ment et involontairement, un ordre cinématographique international occiden-talisé où l'indépendance est une valeur non seulement recherchée mais aussi et surtout bien relative." Ibid., 142.

24. Translated from the French: "C'est moins la politique française de soutien qui est au service des films du Sud que ces derniers qui sont mis au service de la politique culturelle française." Ibid., 163.

25. Translated from the French: "Nous pouvons *in fine* replacer le discours *médi-terranéiste* des Européens dans toute une tradition d'analse *orientaliste*." Isabel Schäfer, "Le dialogue des images entre l'Europe et la Méditerranée: Entre méditerranéisme et réalités," *EurOrient* 10 (Paris, 2001): 109.

26. Sheldon Hsiao-peng Lu, ed., *Transnational Chinese Cinemas: Identity, Nation-hood, Gender* (Honolulu: University of Hawaii Press, 1997), 1.

27. Ibid., 105.

28. Ibid., 107.

29. Translated from the French: "Nous le disons toute de suite à l'opinion publique internationale que ce film n'a rien de tunisien, il n'est même pas goulettois . . . La Tunisie d'aujourd'hui est autre que cette idiotie." Mustapha Nagbou, "*Un été à la Goulette:* Arrête ton opportunisme, Ferid!" *SeptièmArt* 83–84 (Tunis, 1996): 35–36.

30. Lu, 107.

31. Translated from the French: "je revendique mon oeuvre comme appartenant à la fois à une cinéma nationale (tunisienne), régionale (Maghreb et monde arabe), continentale (africaine) et bien entendu universelle (l'humanité)." Ferid Boughedir, "Le protectionnisme français nous nuit," *Cahiers du cinéma* 557 (Paris, 2001): 72–73.

32. Lu, 107.

33. Winifred Woodhull, "Exile," in Françoise Lionnet and Ronnie Scharfman, eds., *Post/Colonial Conditions: Exiles, Migrations and Nomadisms*, Yale French Studies, no. 81 (New Haven, Conn.: Yale University Press, 1993), 11.

34. Ann Marie Stock, ed., *Framing Latin American Cinema: Contemporary Critical Perspectives* (Minneapolis: University of Minnesota Press, 1997), xxiv.

35. Néstor Garcia Canclini, "Will There Be Latin American Cinema in the Year 2000? Visual Culture in a Postnational Era," in Stock, 247.

36. Ferid Boughedir agues that the film is not Tunisian in an interview with Pierre and Benoîte Pitiot, *Actes du Vingt-deuxième et du Vingt-troisième Festival International* (Montpellier, 2002): 77–78.

37. Translated from the French: "Aujourd'hui, je parlerai plutôt de films faits par des Marocains. J'entends par là qu'il n y a pas de véritable réflexion sur ce que signifie faire du cinéma au Maroc." Hassan Legzouli, interview, *Cinéma-roc* 12 (Rabat, 1999): n.p.

38. Translated from the French: "l'absense des hommes partis à la guerre, dans les champs pétroliers ou en France, l'absense de l'Algérie réelle (le film a été tourné au Maroc), l'absense des engagements idéologiques, l'absense du sang de la guerre." Benjamin Stora, *La guerre invisible: Algérie années 90* (Paris: Presses de sciences PO, 2001), 91.

39. Translated from the French: "Il m'a fallu me libérer du poids de la culture de mes parents, mais en même temps composer avec, car cette culture fait tout de même partie de moi . . . j'avais envie d'aller ailleurs, ne plus entendre parler d'immigration. Il me semblait que mon éducation m'empêchait de travailler librement." Cited in Najett Maatougui, "Mehdi Charef: S'exprimer autrement," *Salama* 20 (Algiers, 2001): 8.

40. Hamid Naficy, *An Accented Cinema: Exilic and Diasporic Filmmaking* (Princeton, N.J.: Princeton University Press, 2001), 3.

41. Ibid., 98.

42. Ibid.

43. Susan Hayward, "State, Culture and the Cinema: Jack Lang's Strategies for the French Film Industry 1981–93," *Screen* 34, no. 4 (Glasgow, 1993): 380.

44. Christian Bosséno, "Immigrant Cinema: National Cinema—The Case of Beur Film," in Richard Dyer and Ginette Vincendeau, eds., *Popular European Cinema* (London and New York: Routledge, 1992), 51.

45. Translated from the French: "Les Maghrébins deviennent-ils français au cinéma?" René Prédal, "Problèmes d'identité, droit à la différence et couples mixtes dans le cinéma français des années 90," in Abderrahim Lamchichi and Dominique Baillet, eds., *Maghrébins de France: Regards sur les dynamiques de l'intégration* (Paris: L'Harmattan, 2001), 171.

46. Translated from the French: "le cinéma d'auteur destiné à un vaste public: fiction, acteurs professionnels et problèmes de société susceptible d'intéresser les deux communautés." Ibid., 172.

47. Translated from the French: "la noirceur métaphysique et la grisaille sociologique." Ibid., 185.

48.   Translated from the French: "Les Maghrébins deviennent-ils français? Peut-être, mais ils sont en train d'abord de changer le sens des deux adjectifs qui en ont besoin." Ibid., 186.

49.   Translated from the French: "le courant beur a maintenant vingt ans et ne constitue plus un ensemble à part du reste du cinéma." René Prédal, *Le jeune cinéma français* (Paris: Nathan, 2002), 136.

Bibliography

Abdou B. "Ni Dieu, ni sexe. . . . " In Berrah et al. 1987, 131–134.

Actes du Festival International de Montpellier. 26 issues, Montpellier, 1979 to date.

Allen, Roger, Hilary Kilpatrick, and Ed de Moor, eds. *Love and Sexuality in Modern Arabic Literature.* London: Saqi Books, 1995.

Allouache, Merzak. *Omar Gatlato* (script). Algiers: Cinémathèque Algérienne/Editions LAPHOMIC, 1987.

———. *Bab el-Oued* (novel). Paris: Editions du Seuil; Casablanca: Editions le Fennec, 1996.

———. *Salut Cousin!* (script). Paris: L'Avant-Scène du Cinéma, 1996.

Amarger, Michel. "Ruptures de l'espace identitaire." *Qantara* 44 (2002): 22–25.

Aoulad-Syad, Daoud. *Marocains* (photographs). Paris: Contrejour; Agadir: Belvisi, 1989.

———. *Boujaâd, Espace et mémoire* (photographs). Paris: Edition Data Press, 1996.

Aoulad-Syad, Daoud, and Ahmed Bouanani. *Territoires de l'instant* (photographs and poems). Paris: Editions de l'Oeil & La Croisée des Chemins, 2000.

Arab Cinema and Culture: Round Table Conferences. 3 vols. Beirut: Arab Film and Television Center, 1965.

Araib, Ahmed, and Eric de Hullessen. *Il était une fois . . . Le cinéma au Maroc.* Rabat: EDH, 1999.

Arasoughly, Alia, ed. *Screens of Life: Critical Film Writing from the Arab World.* Quebec: World Heritage Press, 1996.

Armes, Roy. *Third World Film Making and the West.* Berkeley: University of California Press, 1987.

———. *Action and Image: Dramatic Structure in Cinema.* Manchester: Manchester University Press, 1994.

———. "Cinema." In Esposito 1995, 286–290.

———. "The Arab World." In Nowell-Smith 1996, 661–667.

———. *Dictionary of North African Film Makers/Dictionnaire des cinéastes du Maghreb.* Paris: Editions ATM, 1996.

———. *Omar Gatlato.* Trowbridge: Flicks Books, 1998. French translation: *Omar Gatlato de Merzak Allouache: Un regard nouveau sur l'Algérie.* Paris: Editions L'Harmattan, 1999.

———. "Reinterpreting the Tunisian Past: *Les silences du palais.*" In Lacey and Coury 2000, 203–214.

———. "Cinema in the Maghreb." In Leaman 2001, 429–517.

———. "History or Myth: *Chronique des années de braise.*" In Kummer 2002, 7–17.

Ashcroft, Bill. *Post-Colonial Transformation.* London and New York: Routledge, 2001.

Ashcroft, Bill, Gareth Griffiths, and Helen Tiffin. *The Empire Writes Back.* 2nd ed. London and New York: Routledge, 2002.

Ayouch, Nabil. Interview. *La Libération,* Paris, 21 March 2001, 42.

Aziza, Mohamed, ed. *Patrimonie culturel et création contemporaine en Afrique et dans le monde Arabe.* Dakar: Les Nouvelles Editions d'Afrique, 1977.

Bachy, Victor. *Le cinéma de Tunisie*. Tunis: Société Tunisienne de Diffusion, 1978.

Barlet, Olivier. *Les cinémas d'Afrique noire: Le regard en question*. Paris: L'Harmattan, 1996. English translation: *African Cinemas: Decolonizing the Gaze*. London and New York: Zed Books, 2000.

Bataille, Maurice-Robert, and Claude Veillot. *Caméras sous le soleil: Le cinéma en Afrique du nord*. Algiers, 1956.

Beaugé, G., and J.-F. Clément, eds. *L'image dans le monde arabe*. Paris: CNRS Editions, 1995.

Behi, Ridha. "La boîte magnifique." Interview with Mustapha Nagbou. *SeptièmArt* 100 (Tunis, 2003): 3–5.

Béji, Hélé. *Désenchantement national*. Paris: François Maspero, 1982.

Belfquih, Mohamed. *C'est mon écran après tout! Réflexions sur la situation de l'audiovisuel au Maroc*. Rabat: Infolive, 1995.

Ben Aissa, Anouar, ed. *Tunisie: Trente ans de cinéma*. Tunis: EDICOP, 1996.

Ben Aissa, Khelfa. *Tu vivras, Zinet! Tahia ya Zinet!* Paris: L'Harmattan, 1990.

Benali, Abdelkader. *Le cinéma colonial au Maghreb*. Paris: Editions du Cerf, 1998.

Ben el Haj, Bahri. *Une politique africaine du cinéma*. Paris: Editions Dadci, 1980.

Benguigui, Yasmina. *Femmes d'Islam* (script). Paris: Albin Michel, 1996.

——. *Mémoires d'immigrés: L'héritage maghrébin* (script). Paris: Albin Michel, 1997.

——. *Inch'allah dimanche* (novel). Paris: Albin Michel, 2001.

Benlyazid, Farida. "Image and Experience: Why Cinema?" In Zuhur 1998, 205–209.

Bensmaïa, Réda. *Experimental Nations; or, The Invention of the Maghreb*. Princeton, N.J.: Princeton University Press, 2003.

Bernstein, Matthew, and Gaylyn Studlar. *Visions of the East: Orientalism in Film*. London and New York: I. B. Tauris, 1997.

Berrah, Mouny. "Algerian Cinema and National Identity." In Arasoughly 1989, 63–83.

——. "Histoire et idéologie du cinéma algérien sur la guerre." In Hennebelle, Berrah, and Stora 1997, 144–183.

Berrah, Mouny, Victor Bachy, Mohand Ben Salama, and Ferid Boughedir, eds. *Cinémas du Maghreb*. CinémAction, no. 14. Paris: Editions Papyrus, 1981.

Berrah, Mouny, Jacques Lévy, and Claude-Michel Cluny, eds. *Les cinémas arabes*. CinémAction, no. 43. Paris: Cerf/Institut du Monde Arabe, 1987.

Bonn, Charles, ed. *Littératures des immigrations*. 2 vols. Paris: L'Harmattan, 1995.

Bossaerts, Marc, and Catherine Van Geel, eds. *Cinéma d'en Francophonie*. Brussels: Solibel Edition, 1995.

Bosséno, Christian. "Des maquis d'hier aux luttes d'aujourd'hui: Thématique du cinéma algérien." *La revue du cinéma—Image et son* 340 (Paris, 1979): 27–52.

——. "Le cinéma tunisien." *La revue du cinéma* 382 (Paris, 1983): 49–62.

——. "Immigrant Cinema: National Cinema—The Case of Beur Film." In Dyer and Vincendeau 1992, 47–57.

Bosséno, Christian, ed. *Cinémas de l'Emigration 3*. CinémAction, no. 24. Paris: L'Harmattan, 1983.

Boudjedra, Rachid. *Naissance du cinéma algérien*. Paris: François Maspéro, 1971.

Boughedir, Ferid. *Le cinéma africain de A à Z*. Brussels: OCIC, 1987.

——. "Panorama général du cinéma tunisien: La rencontre de l'orient et de l'occident," "Les films tunisiens (1982–1987)," and "Le cinéma en Tunisie." *La semaine du cinéma arabe* (1987): 85–88, 89–92, and 94–97.

——. "Cinémas et libertés en Afrique." In FEPACI 1995, 34–46.

——. "Un été à La Goulette." In Mitterand and Elses-Ferchichi 1995, 121–28.

——. "Le cinéma tunisien: des films qui ont une âme." *Vie Culturelle,* special issue "Tunisie Capitale Culturelle 1997" (Tunis, 1997): 51–56.

——. *Halfaouine: L'enfant des terrasses* (script). Paris: L'Avant-Scène du Cinéma, 1999.

——. "Vingt ans de cinéma tunisien." Interview with Pierre and Benoîte Pitiot. *Actes du Vingt-deuxième et du Vingt-troisième Festival International* (Montpellier, 2002): 77–81.

Boughedir, Ferid, ed. *Jeune Afrique Plus: Le cinéma en Afrique et dans le monde. Jeune Afrique* 1941 (special issue; Paris, 1984).

Boulanger, Pierre. *Le cinéma colonial.* Paris: Seghers, 1975.

Bourehla, Hédia. "La tradition orale: Source d'inspiration de la création cinématographique arabe." Ph.D. thesis, Université de Paris I, 1996.

Bouzid, Nouri. Interview with Ferid Boughedir. Cannes Festival Pressbook, 1989.

——. "*Sources of Inspiration*" Lecture: *22 June 1994, Villepreux.* Amsterdam: Sources, 1994.

——. "New Realism in Arab Cinema: The Defeat-Conscious Cinema." In Ghazoul 1995, 242–250.

Brahimi, Denise. *Cinémas d'Afrique francophone et du Maghreb.* Paris: Nathan, 1997.

——. "A propos de Tala ou *L'opium et le bâton* du roman au film." *Awal: Cahiers d'Etudes Berbères* 15 (Paris, 1997): 65–73.

——. "Critique-éloge de l'intellectuel tunisien: A propos des *Sabots en or,* de Nouri Bouzid." *Ifriquiya* 1 (Paris and Montreal, 1997): 35–51.

Brossard, Jean-Pierre, ed. *L'Algérie vue par son cinéma.* Locarno: Festival International du Film de Locarno, 1981.

Calle-Gruber, Mireille. *Assia Djebar, ou la résistance de l'écriture.* Paris: Maisonneuve & Larose, 2001.

Carter, Sandra. "Moroccan Cinema: What Moroccan Cinema?" Ph.D. thesis, University of Texas at Austin, 1999.

Castle, Gregory, ed. *Postcolonial Discourse: An Anthology.* Oxford: Blackwell, 2001.

Chagnollaud, Jean-Paul, ed. *Sexualité et sociétés arabes.* Confluences Méditerranée, no. 41. Paris: L'Harmattan, 2002.

Challouf, Mohamed, Giuseppe Gariazzo, and Alessandra Speciale, eds. *Un posto sulla terra: Cinema per (r)esistere.* Milan: Editrice il Castoro, 2002.

Charef, Mehdi. *Le thé au harem d'Archi Ahmed* (novel). Paris: Mecure de France, 1983. English translation: *Tea in the Harem.* London: Serpent's Tail, 1989.

——. *Le harki de Meriem* (novel). Paris: Mercure de France, 1989.

——. *La maison d'Alexina* (novel). Paris: Mercure de France, 1999.

Châtillon, Georges, and Edwige Lambert, eds. *Algérie.* 2nd ed. Paris: Autrement, 1991.

Cherfi, Abdelmajid, et al., eds. *Aspects de la civilisation tunisienne.* Tunis: Faculté de Lettres de Manouba, 1998.

Cheriaa, Tahar. *Cinéma et culture en Tunisie.* Beirut: UNESCO, 1964.

——. *Ecrans d'abondance . . . ou cinémas de libération en Afrique?* Tunis: Société Tunisienne de Diffusion, 1979.

Chikhaoui, Tahar. "Le cinéma tunisien de la maladroite euphorie au juste désarroi." In Cherfi et al. 1998, 5–33.

——. "Le cinéma tunisien des années 90: permanences et spécifités." *Horizons Maghrébins—Le Droit à la Mémoire* 46 (Toulouse, 2002): 113–119.

Cinéma arabe, cinéma dans le tiers monde, cinéma militant. . . . Dérives 3–4 (special issue; Montreal, 1976).

Cinéma et monde musulman. EurOrient 10 (Neuilly, 2001).

Cinéma: Production cinématographique 1957–1973. Algiers: Ministère de l'Information et de la Culture, 1974.

Cinémas des pays arabes: Le cinéma algérien. Algiers: Cinémathèque Algérienne/ Cinémathèque Française, 1977. (Bound photocopy.)

Cinémas des pays arabes: Les cinémas marocain, tunisien, mauritanien. Algiers: Cinémathèque Algérienne/Cinémathèque Française, 1977. (Bound photocopy.)

Cinquante ans de courts métrages marocains 1947–1997. Rabat: CCM, 1998.

Clap ou à la connaissance des cinéastes africains et de la diaspora, Le. Ouagadougou: Sykif, 2001.

Clerc, Jeanne-Marie. *Assia Djebar: Ecrire, Transgresser, Résister.* Paris and Montreal: L'Harmattan, 1997.

Cluny, Claude-Michel. *Dictionnaire des nouveaux cinémas arabes.* Paris: Sindbad, 1978.

Colonna, Fanny, and Zakya Daoud, eds. *Etre marginal au Maghreb.* Paris: CNRS Editions, 1993.

Dadci, Younès. *Dialogues Algérie-cinéma: Première histoire du cinéma algérien.* Paris: Editions Dadci, 1970.

———. *Première histoire du cinéma algérien, 1896–1979.* Paris: Editions Dadci, 1980.

Dahane, Mohamed, ed. *Cinéma: Histoire et société.* Rabat: Publications de la Faculté des Lettres, 1995.

De Arabische film. Amsterdam: Cinemathema, 1979.

De Poncharra, Nicole, and Maati Kabbal, eds. *Le Maroc en mouvement: Créations contemporaines.* Paris: Maisonneuve & Larose, 2000.

Deuxième biennale des cinémas arabes à Paris. Paris: Institut du Monde Arabe, 1994.

Dialmy, Abdessamad. *Logement, sexualité et Islam.* Casablanca: Eddif, 1995.

Di Martino, Anna, Andrea Morini, and Michele Capasso, eds. *Il cinema dei paesi arabi, quarta edizione/Arab Film Festival,* 4th ed. Naples: Edizioni Magma, 1997.

Dine, Philip. "Thinking the Unthinkable: The Generation of Meaning in French Literary and Cinema Images of the Algerian War." *Maghreb Review* 19, no. 1–2 (London, 1994): 123–132.

Djebar, Assia. *La soif* (novel). Paris: Julliard, 1957. Translated into English: *The Mischief.* New York: Simon & Schuster, 1958.

———. *Les Impatients* (novel). Paris: Julliard, 1958.

———. *Les enfants du nouveau monde* (novel). Paris: Julliard, 1962.

———. *Les alouettes naïves* (novel). Paris: Julliard, 1967.

———. *Femmes d'Alger dans leur appartement* (short stories). Paris: Editions des Femmes, 1980. Translated into English: *Women of Algiers in Their Apartment.* Charlottesville and London: University of Virginia Press, 1992.

———. *L'amour, la fantasia* (novel). Paris: Albin Michel, 1985. English translation: *Fantasia: An Algerian Cavalcade.* London: Quartet Books, 1989.

———. *Ombre sultane* (novel). Paris: Lattès, 1987. Translated into English: *A Sister to Scheherazade.* London: Quartet Books, 1988.

———. *Loin de Médine* (novel). Paris: Albin Michel, 1991. English translation: *Far from Madina.* London Quartet Books, 1994.

———. *Chronique d'un été algérien.* Paris: Plume, 1993.

———. *Vaste est la prison* (novel). Paris: Albin Michel, 1995. English translation: *So Vast the Prison.* New York: Seven Stories Press, 1999.

———. *Le Blanc de l'Algérie* (story). Paris: Albin Michel, 1996. English translation: *Algerian White.* New York: Seven Sisters Press, 2001.

——. *Les nuits de Strasbourg* (novel). Le Méjan: Actes Sud, 1997.

——. *Oran, langue morte* (short stories). Le Méjan: Actes Sud, 1997.

——. *Ces voix qui m'assiègent* (essays). Paris: Albin Michel, 1999.

——. *La femme sans sépulture* (novel). Paris: Albin Michel, 2002.

Dourari, Abderrezak, ed. *Cultures populaires et culture nationale en Algérie.* Paris, Budapest, and Turin: L'Harmattan, 2002.

Downing, John D. H. "Post-Tricolor African Cinema." In Sherzer 1996, 188–288.

Downing, John D. H., ed. *Film and Politics in the Third World.* New York: Praeger, 1987.

Dwyer, Kevin. "'Hidden, Unsaid, Taboo' in Moroccan Cinema: Adelkader Lagtaâ's Challenge to Authority." *Framework* 43, no. 2 (Detroit, 2002): 117–133.

Dyer, Richard, and Ginette Vincendeau, eds. *Popular European Cinema.* London and New York: Routledge, 1992.

Eke, Maureen N., Kenneth W. Harrow, and Emmanuel Yewah, eds. *African Images: Recent Studies and Text in Cinema.* Trenton, N.J., and Asmara: Africa World Press, 2000.

Elena, Alberto. *El cine del tercer mundo: diccionario de realizadores.* Madrid: Ediciones Turfan, 1993.

El Khodari, Khalid. "Le Maghreb entre le récit littéraire et l'adaptation cinématographique." *Deuxième biennale* (1994): 72–83.

——. *Guide des réalisateurs marocains.* Rabat: El Maarif Al Jadida, 2000.

Ellwood, David, and Rob Kroes, eds. *Hollywood in Europe: Experiences of a Cultural Hegemony.* Amsterdam: VU University Press, 1994.

El Saadawi, Nawal. *The Hidden Face of Eve: Women in the Arab World.* London and New Jersey: Zed Books, 1980.

El Yamlahi, Sidi Mohamed. *Bachir Skiredj: Biographie d'un rire.* Casablanca: Najah el Jadida, 1997.

Esposito, John, ed. *The Oxford Encyclopedia of the Modern Islamic World.* New York and Oxford: Oxford University Press, 1995.

Fahdel, Abbas. "Une esthétique beur?" In Hennebelle and Schneider 1990, 140–151.

FEPACI, ed. *L'Afrique et le centenaire du cinéma/Africa and the Centenary of Cinema.* Paris: Présence Africaine, 1995.

Ferhati, Jilali. Interview with Abdou B. and Moulay Brahimi. *Les Deux Ecrans* 47–48 (Algiers, 1982): 25–27.

——. "Universaliser plutôt que mondialiser." *Cahiers du cinéma* 557 (Paris, 2001): 67–68.

Fertat, Ahmed. *Une passion nommée cinéma: Vie et oeuvre de Mohamed Osfour.* Tangier: Altopress, 2000.

Film in Algerien ab 1970. Kinemathek 57 (special issue; Berlin, 1979).

Gabous, Abdelkrim. *Silence, elles tournent!—Les femmes et le cinéma en Tunisie.* Tunis: Cérès Editions/Centre de Recherches, d'Etudes, de Documentation et d'Information sur la Femme, 1998.

Gabriel, Teshome H. *Third Cinema in the Third World.* Ann Arbor: UMI Research Press, 1982.

Gariazzo, Giuseppe. *Poetiche del cinema africano.* Turin: Lindau, 1998.

——. *Breve storia del cinema africano.* Turin: Lindau, 2001.

Genini, Izza. *Maroc.* With photographs by Jean du Boisberranger. Paris: Editions Xavier Richer and Hoa-Qui Editions, 1995.

——. *Maroc: Royaume des mille et une fêtes.* With photographs by Jacques Bravo and Xavier Richer. Paris: Editions Plume, 1998.

Ghalem, Ali. *Une femme pour mon fils* (novel). Paris: Editions Syros, 1979.

Gharbi, Neïla. "Cinéma tunisien: La relance." *SeptièmArt* 100 (Tunis, 2003): 6–8.

Ghazoul, Ferial J., ed. *Arab Cinematics: Toward the New and the Alternative. Alif: Journal of Comparative Poetics* 15 (Cairo, 1995).

Ghoussoub, Mai, and Emma Sinclair-Webb, eds. *Imagined Masculinities: Male Identity and Culture in the Modern Middle East.* London: Saqi Books, 2000.

Givanni, June, ed. *Symbolic Narratives/African Cinema: Audiences, Theory and the Moving Image.* London: British Film Institute, 2000.

Gutberlet, Marie-Hélène, and Hans-Peter Metzler, eds. *Afrikanisches Kino.* Bad Honnef: Horlemann/ARTE, 1997.

Gutmann, Marie-Pierre, ed. *Le partenariat euro-méditerranéen dans le domaine de l'image.* Morocco: Service de Coopération et d'Action Culturelle de l'Ambassade de France au Maroc, 1999.

Hadj-Moussa, Rahiba. *Le corps, l'histoire, le territoire: Les rapports de genre dans le cinéma algérien.* Paris/Montreal: Publisud & Edition Balzac, 1994.

———. "The Locus of Tension: Gender in Algerian Cinema." In Harrow 1997, 45–66.

Hafez, Sabry. "Shifting Identities in Maghribi Cinema: The Algerian Paradigm." In Ghazoul 1995, 39–80.

Hargreaves, Alec G. *Immigration and Identity in Beur Fiction.* Oxford and New York: Berg, 1991.

Hargreaves, Alec G., and Mark McKinney, eds. *Postcolonial Cultures in France.* London and New York: Routledge, 1997.

Harrow, Kenneth W., ed. *The Marabout and the Muse.* Portsmouth, N.H.: Heinemann; London: James Currey, 1996.

———. *With Open Eyes: Women and African Cinema. Matatu: Journal for African Culture and Society* 19 (Amsterdam and Atlanta, Ga., 1997).

———. *African Cinema: Post-Colonial and Feminist Readings.* Trenton, N.J., and Asmara: Africa World Press, 1999.

Hayes, Jarrold. *Queer Nations: Marginal Sexualities in the Maghreb.* Chicago: University of Chicago Press, 2000.

Hennebelle, Guy, ed. *Les cinémas africains en 1972.* Paris: Société Africaine d'Edition, 1972.

———. *Cinémas de l'émigration.* CinémAction, no. 8. Paris: Filméditions, 1979.

Hennebelle, Guy, and Roland Schneider, eds. *Cinémas métis: De Hollywood aux films beurs.* CinémAction, no. 56, Hommes et Migrations. Paris: Corlet/Télérama, 1990.

Hennebelle, Guy, and Chantal Soyer, eds. *Cinéma contre racisme.* CinémAction, Tumulte, Numéro spécial hors série, Supplément à Tumulte no. 7. Paris: SET, 1980.

Hennebelle, Guy, Mouny Berrah, and Benjamin Stora, eds. *La guerre d'Algérie à l'écran.* CinémAction, no. 85. Paris: Corlet/Télérama, 1997.

Hill, John, and Pamela Church Gibson, eds. *World Cinema: Critical Approaches.* Oxford: Oxford University Press, 2000.

Hjort, Mette, and Scott Mackenzie, eds. *Cinema and Nation.* London and New York: Routledge, 2000.

Hurley, E. Anthony, Renée Larrier, and Joseph McLaren, eds. *Migrating Words and Worlds: Pan-Africanism Updated.* Trenton, N.J., and Asmara: Africa World Press, 1999.

Huughe, Laurence, ed. *Ecrits sous le voile: Romancières algériennes francophones écriture et identité.* Paris: Publisud, 2001.

Image(s) du Maghrébin dans le cinéma français. Grand Maghreb 47 (special issue; Paris, 1989).

Images et visages du cinéma Algérien. Algiers: ONCIC, Ministry of Culture and Tourism, 1984.

Jaïdi, Moulay Driss. *Le cinéma au Maroc.* Rabat: Collection al majal, 1991.

———. *Public(s) et cinéma.* Rabat: Collection al majal, 1992.

———. *Vision(s) de la société marocaine à travers le court métrage.* Rabat: Collection al majal, 1994.

———. *Cinégraphiques.* Rabat: Collection al majal, 1995.

———. *Diffusion et audience des médias audiovisuels.* Rabat: Collection al majal, 2000.

Jibril, Mohamed. "Cinéma marocain, l'improbable image de soi." In De Poncharra and Kabbal 2000, 179–184.

Khalil, Andrea Flores. "Images That Come Out at Night: A Film Trilogy by Moncef Dhouib." In Kummer 2002, 71–80.

Khannous, Touria. "The Subaltern Speaks: Re-Making/Her/Story in Assia Djebar's *La nouba des femmes du mont Chenoua.*" In Eke et al. 2000, 51–71.

Khayati, Khémais. "La problématique de la liberté individuelle dans le cinéma arabe." In Beaugé and Clément 1995, 305–310.

———. *Cinémas arabes: Topographie d'une image éclatée.* Paris and Montreal: L'Harmattan, 1996.

Khelil, Hédi. "La tradition orale: produit médiatique de consommation et oeuvre d'art." *Tradition orale et nouveaux médias* (1989): 231–238.

———. *Résistances et utopies: Essais sur le cinéma arabe et africain.* Tunis: Edition Sahar, 1994.

Khemir, Nacer. *Le soleil emmuré.* Paris: Editions la Découverte, 1981.

———. *Le conte des conteurs* (stories). Paris: Editions la Découverte, 1984. New French-language-only edition for children: Paris: Syros Jeunesse, 2001.

———. *Grand-père est né.* Bordeaux: Le Mascaret, 1985.

———. *L'ogresse* (stories). Paris: Editions la Découverte, 1991.

———. *Das Verlorene Halsband der Taube.* Baden: Lars Müller, 1992.

———. *Paroles d'Islam.* Paris: Albin Michel, 1995. Translated into English: *The Wisdom of Islam.* New York and London: Abbeville, 1996.

———. *L'alphabet des sables* (children's story). Paris: Editions la Découverte & Syros, 1998.

———. *J'avale le bébé du voisin* (children's story). Paris: Editions la Découverte & Syros, 2000.

———. *Le juge, la mouche et la grand-mère* (children's story). Paris: Editions la Découverte & Syros, 2000.

———. *Le chant des génies* (children's story). Arles: Actes Sud Junior, 2001.

———. *Le livres des djinns.* Paris: Syros Jeunesse, 2002.

Khemir, Nacer, and Oum el Khir. *Chahrazade* (stories). Bordeaux: Le Mascaret, 1988.

Khlifi, Omar. *L'histoire du cinéma en Tunisie.* Tunis: Société de Diffusion, 1970.

Khuri, Fuad I. *The Body in Islamic Culture.* London: Saqi Books, 2001.

King, John, Ana M. López, and Manuel Alvarado, eds. *Mediating Two Worlds.* London: British Film Institute, 1993.

Koudjil, Abderrahmane. "Polygamnie au Maghreb: Controverses autour d'un droit en mouvement." In Lamchichi 2002, 77–88.

Kummer, Ida, ed. *Cinéma Maghrébin.* Special issue of *Celaan* 1, no. 1–2 (Saratoga Springs, N.Y., 2002).

Lacey, Kevin R., and Ralph M. Coury, eds. *The Arab-African and Islamic Worlds: Interdisciplinary Studies.* New York: Peter Lang, 2000.

Lamchichi, Abderrahim, ed. *Sexualité et sociétés arabes*. Confluences Méditerranée, no. 41. Paris: L'Harmattan, 2002.

Lamchichi, Abderrahim, and Dominique Baillet, eds. *Maghrébins de France: Regards sur les dynamiques de l'intégration*. Confluences Méditerranée, no. 39. Paris: L'Harmattan, 2001.

Landau, Jacob M. *Etudes sur le théâtre et le cinéma arabes*. Paris: G-P Maisonneuve et Larosé, 1965.

Lanza, Federica. *La donna nel cinema maghrebino*. Rome: Bulzoni Editore, 1999.

La semaine du cinéma arabe. Paris: Institut du Monde Arabe, 1987.

La Tunisie: Annuaire 1995 (Etats des lieux du cinéma en Afrique). Paris: Association des Trois Mondes/FEPACI, 1995.

Lazreg, Marnia. *The Eloquence of Silence: Algerian Women in Question*. London and New York: Routledge, 1994.

Leaman, Oliver, ed. *Companion Encyclopedia of Middle Eastern and North African Film*. London and New York: Routledge, 2001.

Lequin, Lucie, and Maïr Verthuy, eds. *Multi-culture, multi-écriture: La voix migrante au féminin en France et au Canada*. Paris and Montreal: L'Harmattan, 1996.

Le rôle du cinéaste africain dans l'éveil d'une conscience de civilisation noire. Présence Africaine 90 (special issue; Paris, 1974).

Les cinémas d'Afrique: Dictionnaire. Paris: Editions Karthala and Editions ATM, 2000.

Lionnet, Françoise, and Ronnie Scharfman, eds. *Post/Colonial Conditions: Exiles, Migrations and Nomadisms*. 2 vols. Yale French Studies, nos. 81 and 82. New Haven, Conn.: Yale University Press, 1993.

Maherzi, Lotfi. *Le cinéma algérien: Institutions, imaginaire, idéologie*. Algiers: SNED, 1980.

Malkmus, Lizbeth, and Roy Armes. *Arab and African Film Making*. London: Zed Books, 1991.

Malti-Douglas, Fedwa. *Woman's Body, Woman's World: Gender and Discourse in Arabo-Islamic Writing*. Princeton, N.J.: Princeton University Press, 1991.

Mansour, Guillemette. *Samama Chikly: Un tunisien à la rencontre du XXième siècle*. Tunis: Simpact Editions, 2000.

Mansouri, Hassouna. *De l'identité ou pour une certaine tendance du cinéma africain*. Tunis: Editions Sahar, 2000.

Martineau, Monique, ed. *Le cinéma au féminisme*. CinémAction, no. 9. Paris: CinémAction, 1979.

Mayne, Judith. *Private Novels, Public Films*. Athens: University of Georgia Press, 1988.

McDougall, James, ed. *Nation, Society and Culture in North Africa*. London and Portland, Ore.: Frank Cass, 2003.

Mdarhri-Alaoui, Abdallah. "La place de la littérature 'beur' dans la production franco-maghrébine." In Bonn 1995, 1:41–50.

Meddour, Azzedine. *La montagne de Baya, ou la 'diya'* (novel). Algeria: Editions Marinoor, 1999.

Megherbi, Abdelghani. *Les algériens au miroir du cinéma colonial*. Algiers: SNED, 1982.

———. *Le miroir apprivoisé*. Algiers: ENAL, 1985.

———. *Le miroir aux alouettes*. Algiers and Brussels: ENAL, UPU, GAM, 1985.

Memmi, Albert. *Portrait du colonisé précédé du portrait du colonisateur*. New ed. Paris: Gallimard, 1985. English translation: *The Colonizer and the Colonized*. New York: Souvenir Press, 1974.

Mernissi, Fatima. *Sexe, idéologie et Islam*. Rev. ed. Paris: Edition Tierce, 1983. English translation: *Beyond the Veil: Male-Female Dynamics in Muslim Society*. Rev. ed. London: Al Saqi Books, 1985.

———. *La peur-modernité: Islam et démocracie*. Paris: Albin Michel, 1992. English translation: *Islam and Democracy: Fear of the Modern World*. London: Virago Press, 1993.

———. *Dreams of Trespass: Tales of a Harem Girlhood*. New York, Doubleday, 1994. Published as *The Harem Within: Tales of a Moroccan Girlhood*. London: Bantam Books, 1995. French translation: *Rêves de femmes: Une enfance au harem*. Paris: Albin Michel; Casablanca: Le Fennec, 1997.

———. *Women's Rebellion and Islamic Memory*. London and New Jersey: Zed Books, 1996.

———. *Etes-vous vacciné contre le harem?* Casablanca: Editions Le Fennec, 1998. Rev. ed., *Le harem et l'occident*. Paris: Albin Michel, 2001. English translation: *Scheherazade Goes West*. New York: Washington Square Press, 2001.

Miller, Christopher L. *Nationalists and Nomads: Essays on Francophone African Literature and Culture*. Chicago: University of Chicago Press, 1998.

Millet, Raphaël. "(In)dépendance des cinémas du Sud &/vs France." *Théorème* 5 (Paris, 1998): 141–177.

———. *Cinemas de la Méditerranée: Cinémas de la mélancolie*. Paris: L'Harmattan, 2002.

Mimoun, Mouloud, ed. *France-Algérie: Images d'une guerre*. Paris: Institut du Monde Arabe, 1992.

Mitterand, Frédéric, and Soraya Elses-Ferchichi, eds. *Une Saison Tunisienne*. Arles: Actes Sud/Association Française d'Action Artistique, 1995.

Morini, Andrea, Erfan Rashid, Anna Di Martino, and Adriano Aprà. *Il cinema dei paesi arabi*. Venice: Marsilio Editori, 1993.

Mortimer, Mildred. "Nouveau regard, nouvelle parole: le cinéma d'Assia Djebar." In Harrow 1997, 111–124.

Moumen, Touti. *Films tunisiens: Longs métrages 1967–98*. Tunis: Touti Moumen, 1998.

Naficy, Hamid. *An Accented Cinema: Exilic and Diasporic Filmmaking*. Princeton, N.J.: Princeton University Press, 2001.

Nagbou, Mustapha. "*Un été à la Goulette*: Arrête ton opportunisme, Ferid!" *SeptièmArt* 83–84 (Tunis, 1996): 35–36.

Ngansop, Guy Jérémie. *Le cinéma camerounais en crise*. Paris: L'Harmattan, 1987.

Niang, Sada, ed. *Littérature et cinéma en Afrique francophone: Ousmane Sembene et Assia Djebar*. Paris: L'Harmattan, 1996.

Nicollier, Valérie. *Der Offene Bruch: Das Kino der Pieds Noirs*. Revue CICIM, no. 34. Munich: Institut français de Munich, Centre d'information cinématographique, 1991.

Nieuwkerk, Karin van. "*A Trade Like Any Other*": Female Singers and Dancers in Egypt. Austin: University of Texas Press, 1995.

Nowell-Smith, Geoffrey, ed. *The Oxford History of World Cinema*. Oxford: Oxford University Press, 1996.

Ostle, Robin, Ed de Moor, and Stefan Wild, eds. *Writing the Self: Autobiographical Writing in Modern Arabic Literature*. London: Saqi Books, 1998.

Où va le cinéma algérien? Cahiers du cinéma, Hors-série. Paris: Cahiers du cinéma, 2003.

Paquet, André. *Cinéma en Tunisie*. Montreal: Bibliothèque Nationale de Québec, 1974.

Pelinq, Lizbeth, and Anne Thuaudet. *Le Hammam d'Othman Khadraoui*. Tunis: Cérès Productions, 1992.

Pines, Jim, and Paul Willemen, eds. *Questions of Third Cinema*. London: British Film Institute, 1989.

Pour une promotion du cinéma national. Rabat: CCM, 1993.

Prédal, René. "Problèmes d'identité, droit à la différence et couples mixtes dans le cinéma français des années 90." In Lamchichi and Baillet 2001, 171–186.

———. *Le jeune cinéma français*. Paris: Nathan, 2002.

Puaux, Françoise, ed. *Le machisme à l'écran*. CinémAction, no. 99. Paris: Corlet/Télérama, 2001.

Regard sur le cinéma au Maroc. Rabat: CCM, 1995.

Reynolds, Dwight F., ed. *Interpreting the Self: Autobiography in the Arab Literary Tradition*. Berkeley: University of California Press, 2001.

Sadoul, Georges. *The Cinema in the Arab Countries*. Beirut: Interarab Center for Cinema and Television/UNESCO, 1966.

Said, Edward. *Culture and Imperialism*. London: Vintage, 1994.

Salah, Rassa Mohamed. *35 ans de cinéma tunisien*. Tunis: Editions Sahar, 1992.

Salmane, Hala, Simon Hartog, and David Wilson. *Algerian Cinema*. London: British Film Institute, 1976.

Sandrini, Luca, ed. *Luminescenze: Panoramiche sui cinema d'Africa*. Verona: Cierre Edizoni, 1998.

Santelli, Serge. *Medinas: Traditional Architecture of Tunisia/Médinas: L'architecture traditionnelle en Tunisie*. Tunis: Dar Ashraf Editions, 1992.

Schäfer, Isabel. "Le dialogue des images entre l'Europe et la Méditerranée: Entre méditerranéisme et réalités." *EurOrient* 10 (Paris, 2001): 89–109.

Schlesinger, Philip. "The Sociological Scope of 'National Cinema.'" In Hjort and Mackenzie 2000, 19–30.

Seguin, Jean-Claude, *Alexandre Promio ou les énigmes de la lumière*. Paris: L'Harmattan, 1999.

Serceau, Michel. "Questions de genre, questions de sexe: les femmes dans le cinéma maghrébin." In Puaux 2001, 115–126.

Shafik, Viola. *Der arabische Film: Geschichte und kulturelle Identität*. Bielefeld: Aisthesis Verlag, 1996. Revised and expanded in English: *Arab Cinema: History and Cultural Identity*. Cairo: American University in Cairo Press, 1998.

Sherzer, Dina, ed. *Cinema, Colonialism, Postcolonialism: Perspectives from the French and Francophone Worlds*. Austin: University of Texas Press, 1996.

Shiri, Keith, ed. *Directory of African Film-Makers and Films*. London: Flicks Books, 1992.

———. *Africa at the Pictures*. London: National Film Theatre, 1993.

Shohat, Ella, and Robert Stam. *Unthinking Eurocentrism: Multiculturalism and the Media*. London and New York: Routledge, 1994.

Slavin, David Henry. *Colonial Cinema and Imperial France, 1919–1939*. Baltimore: Johns Hopkins University Press, 2001.

Souiba, Fouad, and Fatima Zahra el Alaoui. *Un siècle de cinéma au Maroc*. Rabat: World Design Communication, 1995.

Spagnoletti, Giovanni, ed. *Il cinema europeo del métissage*. Milan: Editrice Il Castoro, 2000.

Spass, Lieve. *The Francophone Film: A Struggle for Identity*. Manchester: Manchester University Press, 2000.

Stollery, Martin. "Masculinities, Generations, and Cultural Transformation in Contemporary Tunisian Cinema." *Screen* 42, no. 1 (Glasgow, 2001): 49–63.

Stora, Benjamin. *Histoire de l'Algérie depuis l'indépendence.* Paris: Editions la Découverte, 1994.

———. *La guerre invisible: Algérie années 90.* Paris: Presses de sciences PO, 2001.

Stora, Benjamin, and Akram Ellyas. *Les 100 portes du Maghreb.* Paris: Les Editions de l'Atelier/Editions Ouvrières, 1999.

Taboulay, Camille. *Mohamed Chouikh* (long interview plus script of *L'arche du désert*). Paris: K Films Editions, 1997.

Tamzali, Wassyla. *En attendant Omar Gatlato.* Algiers: Editions EnAP, 1979.

Tarr, Carrie. "Questions of Identity in Beur Cinema: From *Tea in the Harem* to *Cheb.*" *Screen* 32, no. 4 (Glasgow, 1993): 321–342.

———. "Beurz n the Hood: The Articulation of Beur and French Identities in *Le thé au harem d'Archimède* and *Hexagone.*" *Modern and Contemporary France* 3–4 (1995): 415–425.

———. "French Cinema and Post-Colonial Minorities." In Hargreaves and McKinney 1997, 59–81.

Tazi, Mohamed Abderrahman. "Le paradis est sous les pas des mères." Interview with Henri Talvat. *Actes du Quinzième Festival International* (Montpellier, 1993): 23–26.

Teulie, Gilles, ed. *Afrique, musiques et écritures.* Montpellier: Université Paul-Valéry, 2001.

Tlatli, Moufida. Interview with Nabiha Jerad and Ida Kummer. In Kummer 2002, 56–59.

———. Interview with Pierre Pitiot. *Actes du Vingt-deuxième et du Vingt-troisième Festival International* (Montpellier, 2002): 81–85.

Tradition orale et nouveaux médias. Brussels: OCIC, 1989.

Triki, Rachida. "La symbolique des lieux dans le cinéma de Férid Boughedir." In Kummer 2002, 41–48.

Vautier, René. *Caméra citroyenne: Mémoires.* Rennes: Editions Apogée, 1998.

———. *Afrique 50* (script). Paris: Editions Paris Expérimental, 2001.

Vermeren, Pierre. *Le Maroc en transition.* Paris: Editions la Découverte, 2001.

Videau, André, ed. *Mélanges culturelles. Hommes et Migrations* 1231 (special issue; Paris, 2001).

Vieyra, Paulin Soumanou. *Le cinéma africain des origines à 1973.* Paris: Présence Africaine, 1975.

Wayne, Mike. *Political Film: The Dialectics of Third Cinema.* London: Pluto Press, 2001.

Zinaï-Koudil, Hafsa. *La fin d'un rêve* (novel). Algiers: ENAL, 1984.

———. *Le pari perdu* (novel). Algiers: ENAL, 1986.

———. *Le papillon ne volera plus* (novel). Algiers: ENAL, 1990.

———. *Le passé décomposé* (novel). Algiers: ENAL, 1992.

———. *Sans voix* (novel). Paris: Plon, 1997.

Zuhur, Sherifa, ed. *Images of Enchantment: Visual and Performing Arts of the Middle East.* Cairo: American University in Cairo Press, 1998.

Index

Numbers in italic type indicate illustrations; those in bold type refer to whole chapters devoted to the particular film or filmmaker.

17 rue Bleue (Chenouga), 80, 81
100% Arabica (Zemmouri), 60
A la recherche du mari de ma femme (M. A. Tazi), 62
Abbas or Jouha Is Not Dead (M. B. A. Tazi), 44
Abbas ou Jouha n'est pas mort (M. B. A. Tazi), 44
Abbazi, Mohamed, 46–47, 53, 63, 71
Abdel Salem, Chadi, 8
Abdelwahab, Ali, 33, 36
Abdou B., 105, 145
Abidi, Ali, 68, 71
Abou Seif, Salah, 162
Aboulouakar, Mohamed, 10, 47, 53, 64
About Some Meaningless Events (M. Derkaoui), 31, 88
Achouba, Abdou, 47, 53
Adieu forain (Aoulad Syad), 65
Adventures of a Hero, The (Allouache), 28, 79
African Camera (Boughedir), 49
After the Gulf? (collective), 65
Âge d'or, L' (Buñuel), 175, 176
Al Kanfoudi (N. Lahlou), 29
Akdi, Ahmed Kacem, 45, 53
Akika, Ali, 16, 35, 38, 50–51, 125
Aksoy, Asu, 181
Alawiya, Borhan, 48
Albero dei destini sospesi, L' (Benhdj), 60
Alerte à la drogue (Zanchin), 178
Alexandria Again and Again (Chahine), 115
Alexandria . . . Why? (Chahine), 23, 115
Alexandrie pourquoi? (Chahine), 23
Alger-Beyrouth, pour mémoire (Allouache), 60
Alger insolite (Zinet), 27–28
Algeria in Flames (collective), 15
Algérie en flammes (collective), 15
Algiers-Beirut: In Remembrance (Allouache), 60
Ali au pays des mirages (Rachedi), 27
Ali in Wonderland (Rachedi), 27, 35, 38, 124
Ali, Rabia and the Others (Boulane), 77
Ali, Rabia et les autres (Boulane), 77
Ali Zaoua (Ayouch), 65, 73, 75, 77, **169–177**, *172, 176*

Al-kanfoudi (N. Lahlou), 29
Allouache, Merzak, 6, 7, 9, 10, 16, 28, 36, 40, 53, 58, 59–60, 72, 73, 79, 81, 89, **105–113**, *107, 113*, 116–117, 126, 132, 160, 180, 184
Alloula, Malek, 116
Almodóvar, Pedro, 79
Amants de Mogador, Les (Benbarka), 76
Amarger, Michel, 82
Amari, Raja, 10, 79, 159
Ambassadeurs, Les (Ktari), 34, 78
Ambassadors, The (Ktari), 34, 38, 123–124
Âme qui braît, L' (N. Lahlou), 44
Ameur-Zaïmèche, Rabah, 80, 82
Amina (M. B. A. Tazi), 44
Amis d'hier, Les (Benjelloun), 64
Amok (Benbarka), 44, 53
Amour interdit (Fettar), 56
Amour sans visa (Sefrioui), 76–77
Amours de Hadj Mokhtar Soldi, Les (M. Derkaoui), 77
And Afterward . . . (Ismaîl), 77, 81
And Tomorrow? (Babaï), 35, 38, 68
Angels, The (Behi), 49
Anges, Les (Behi), 49
Anh, Duyen, 69
Années de l'exil, Les (N. Lahlou), 76
Antonioni, Michelangelo, 11
Aouchtam (Ismaîl), 65, 77
Aoulad Syad, Daoud, 65, 71, 76, 77, 132
Arab (Jaïbi & Jaziri), 49, 53, 89
Arab Camera (Boughedir), 49
Araib, Ahmed, 61, 89, 95, 171
Arche du désert, L' (Chouikh), 59
Aristarain, Adolfo, 184
Arizona Stallion (Benayat), 51
Arms of Aphrodite, The (Dragan), 29
Arrabal, Francisco, 32
Arthuys, Philippe, 97, 99
Attente des femmes, L' (Belouad), 81
Attia, Ahmed, 48, 6
Au delà de Gibraltar (Boucif & Barman), 80
Au pays des juliets (Charef), 69

Au pays des Tararani (collective), 33
Aube, L' (Khlifi), 8, 21
Aube des damnés, L' (Rachedi), 8, 16, 18
Auprès du peuplier (Haddad), 25
Austen, Jane, 1–2
Autissier, Anne-Marie, 35, 50–51
Automne '86 (Ferhati), 68
Automne—octobre à Alger (Malek Lakhdar Hamina), 57
Autopsie d'un complot (Riad), 27
Autopsy of a Plot (Riad), 27, 28
Autre Algérie: Regards intérieurs (collective), 60
Autre France, L' (Ghalem), 35
Autre monde, L' (Allouache), 74
Autumn '86 (Ferhati), 68
Autumn—October in Algiers (Malek Lakhdar Hamina), 57, 73
Autumn Song (Yala), 41, 53
Aventures d'un héros, Les (Allouache), 28
Ayouch, Amal, 175
Ayouch, Nabil, 65, 71, 73, 75, 76, 77, **169–177**, *172, 176*
Aziri, Nadir, 25, 36
Aziz and Itto: A Moroccan Wedding (Ktiri Idrissa), 64
Aziz et Itto: Un mariage marocain (Ktiri Idrissa), 64
Aziza (Ben Ammar), 23, 48–49, 54, 160, 180

Bab el-oued City (Allouache), 58, 72
Babaï, Brahim, 34–35, 36, 38, 68, 72
Baccar, Jalili, 89
Baccar, Selma, 10, 23, 33, 36, 38, 55, 66, 159, 160
Bachir-Chouikh, Yamina, 10, 74, 75
Bachy, Victor, 21
Bad Weather for a Crook (Hakkar), 69
Badie, Mustapha, 16, 24, 36
Badis (M. A. Tazi), 46, 46, 153, 171
Bahloul, Abdelkrim, 52, 54, 69, 125, 185
Bakir, Myriam, 76
Bakti, Benamar, 57, 71
Baliseurs du désert, Les (Khemir), 49
Ball and Some Dreams, A (El Okbi), 34
Ballad of Mamelouk, The (Bouassida), 50
Ballade de Mamelouk, La (Bouassida), 50
Balzac, Honoré de, 135
Bamou (Mrini), 48
Baratier, Jacques, 21
Barber of the Poor Quarter, The (Reggab), 47
Barg ellil (Abidi), 68
Baricades sauvages (Benayat), 36
Barlet, Olivier, 182
Barman, Taylan, 80

Barrières (Lallem), 25
Barriers (Lallem), 25
Barthes, Roland, 4, 90
Bartók, Bela, 117, 118
Bataille d'Alger, La (Pontecorvo), 6
Bâton Rouge (Bouchareb), 52, 125
Battle of Algiers, The (Pontecorvo), 6, 16, 96
Baya's Mountain (Meddour), 59, 72
Be My Friend (Ktari), 78
Beach of Lost Children, The (Ferhati), 63
Beautiful Days of Sheherazade, The (M. Derkaoui), 44–45, 53, 89
Beaux jours de Charazade, Les (M. Derkaoui), 44–45
Bedwin Hacker (El Fani), 79, 81, 159, 160
Behi, Ridha, 10, 33, 36, 37, 49, 68, 72, 78, 132
Beirut the Meeting (Alawiya), 48
Belhachmi, Ahmed, 9
Belhiba, Fitouri, 49, 68, 72
Belmejdoub, Jamal, 77
Belouad, Naguel, 81
Beloufa, Frank, 24, 28, 36, 37, 89, 160
Ben Aïcha, Sadok, 21, 22, 32–33, 36
Ben Ammar, Abdellatif, 8, 9, 23, 33, 34, 36, 38, 48–49, 54, 78, 180
Ben Ammar, Tarek, 48
Ben Bella, Ahmed, 96
Ben Brahim, Rachid, 57, 60
Ben Halima, Hamouda, 21, 22, 33, 36, 68
Ben Jelloun, Tahar, 63
Ben Khalifa, Hedy, 33
Ben Mabrouk, Neija, 10, 39, 49, 51, 53, 54, 159, 160
Ben Mahmoud, Mahmoud, 10, 49–50, 50, 53, 54, 67, 78, 125, 160
Ben Moktar, Rabie, 57, 71
Ben Ouanès, Kamel, 150
Ben Salah, Mohamed, 35, 38
Ben Smaïl, Mohamed, 68, 71, 128, 132
Benali, Abdelkader, 7
Benallal, Rachid, 10, 57
Benani, Hamid, 9, 30, 36, 37, 63, 71, 88, 132, 180
Benayat, Mohamed, 36, 51
Benbarka, Souheil, 10, 29, 30, 31, 36, 37, 43, 53, 62, 76, 88, 170–171, 179, 180
Benchrif, Hamid, 48, 53
Bendeddouche, Ghaouti, 24, 25, 36, 39, 53, 55, 74
Benevolent, The (Laskri), 25
Benguigui, Yamina, 80–81
Benhadj, Mohamed Rachid, 42–43, 53, 58, 60, 73, 74, 126, 184
Benjelloun, Hassan, 64–65, 71, 76

Benlyazid, Farida, 10, 39, 47, 53, 54, 55, 62, 77, 145, 158, 160
Bennani, Larbi, 20, 22, 29, 63, 71
Bensaïd, Hamid, 47–48, 53
Bensaidi, Faouzi, 76
Bent familia (Bouzid), 66
Berrah, Mouny, 15, 16, 23, 27, 48, 53, 97, 99, 100
Beside the Poplar Tree (Haddad), 25
Beyond Gibraltar (Boucif & Barman), 80, 81
Beyrouth la rencontre (Alawiya), 48
Bezness (Bouzid), 66, 133, 160
Big Trip, The (M. A. Tazi), 45–46, 124, 153, 171
Bird of Paradise, The (Bensaïd), 47–48
Bitter Champagne (Behi), 49
Black Sun (Patellière), 16
Black Sweat (Mazif), 24
Blood Wedding (Benbarka), 30
Blue Stones of the Desert, The (Ayouch), 170
Blue Wedding (Gounajjar), 64
Boisset, Yves, 27, 35, 125
Boîte magique, La (Behi), 78
Bonnes familles, Les (Damardjji), 27
Bookstore, The (Saheb-Ettaba), 79
Bornaz, Kalthoum, 10, 11, 55, 66, 71, 159
Bosséno, Christian, 128, 131, 187
Bouamari, Mohamed, 10, 25, 26, 36, 37, 40, 53, 89
Bouanani, Ahmed, 29, 30, 31, 36, 37, 77, 88, 89, 132
Bouassida, Abdelhafidh, 50, 53
Bouberras, Rabah, 57, 71
Bouchaâla, Ahmed, 70, 81, 186
Bouchaâla, Zakia, 81, 186
Bouchareb, Rachid, 52, 69, 81, 125, 185, 186
Bouchemha, Rabah, 43
Boucif, Mourad, 80, 82
Boudjedra, Rachid, 17, 27, 99
Boughedir, Ferid, 10, 32, 33, 36, 48, 49, 65–66, 73, 85, 115, 134, **141–149**, *144, 148,* 151, 154, 160, 162, 178, 182, 183–184
Bouguermouh, Abderrahmane, 41, 52, 53, 59, 72, 132
Boukhitine, Lyèce, 81
Boulane, Ahmed, 77
Boulanger, Pierre, 6
Boumediene, Houari, 96
Bourguiba, Habib, 146
Bourquia, Farida, 10, 39, 47, 54
Bouzid, Nouri, 10, 11, 50, 53, 54, 65, 66, 72, 78, 87, 115, **132–140**, *135, 137,* 145, 146, 147, 150, 162, 169, 170, 176, 177, 179, 182
Brahim qui? (N. Lahlou), 44
Brahim Who? (N. Lahlou), 44

Brahimi, Denise, 134, 145
Braids (Ferhati), 76, 81
Braise, La (Bourquia), 47
Bras d'Aphrodite, Les (Dragan), 29
Breakdown (Chouikh), 43
Brecht, Bertolt, 35
Brooks, Peter, 3, 4
Bye Bye (Dridi), 70
Bye Bye Souirty (Aoulad Syad), 65, 76, 132

Caftan d'amour (Smihi), 45
Caftan of Love (Smihi), 45
Cairo Street (M. A. Derkaoui), 61–62
Calle-Gruber, Mireille, 121
Caméra arabe (Boughedir), 49
Caméra d'Afrique (Boughedir), 49
Camomile (Charef), 52
Camoumille (Charef), 52
Camus, Albert, 6
Canclini, Néstor García, 184–185
Cardinale, Claudia, 151
Carmet, Jean, 128
Casablancais, Les (Lagtaâ), 64
Casablancans, The (Lagtaâ), 64
Cauchmar (Yala), 47
Cavaliers de la gloire (Benbarka), 62
Ce que les vents ont emporté (Akti), 45
Cendres du clos, Les (collective), 31
Chahine, Youssef, 8, 23, 115, 162, 169, 180
Challenge, The (Khlifi), 49
Champagne amer (Behi), 49
Chams (Sefrioui), 46
Chaplin, Charlie, 89
Chant d'Amour (Yala), 41
Chant de la noria, Le (Ben Ammar), 78
Charbonnier, Le (Bouamari), 25
Charby, Jacques, 15, 22, 178
Charcoal Burner, The (Bouamari), 25, 37, 89
Charef, Abed, 60
Charef, Mehdi, 52, 69, 81, **123–131**, *127, 130,* 185, 186
Chatta, Nidhal, 78–79
Cheb (Bouchareb), 69
Check and Mate (Ferhati), 68
Chenouga, Chad, 80
Cheriaa, Tahar, 20
Cheval de vent (Aoulad Syad), 77
Chevaux de fortune (Ferhati), 63
Chibane, Malek, 69–70
Chikhaoui, Tahar, 21, 32, 48, 82, 83, 148, 151
Chikly [Albert Samama], 6
Chikly, Haydée, 6
Child of the Stars (Benayat), 51
Children of Boredom, The (Ferchiou), 35

Children of the Wind, The (Tsaki), 41, 54
Chouika, Driss, 65, 71
Chouikh, Mohamed, 42, 43, 53, 58, 59, 72, 82, 132
Chraïbi, Omar, 76, 77
Chraïbi, Saâd, 31, 64, 71, 76, 77
Chrigui, Tijani, 64, 72
Chronicle of a Normal Life (S. Chraïbi), 64
Chronicle of the Years of Embers (Lakhdar Hamina), 24, 37, **96–104**, *89, 103*
Chronique des années de braise (Lakhdar Hamina), 24, **96–104**, *89, 103*
Chronique d'une vie normale (S. Chraïbi), 64
Chroniques marocaines (Smihi), 62
Cinders of the Vineyard (collective), 31, 47, 63
Citadel, The (Chouikh), *42, 43,* 53
Clandestin, Le (Bakhti), 57
Clay Dolls (Bouzid), 78
Closed Door, The (Lagtaâ), 63–64, 179
Cluny, Claude Michel, 37
Coeur nomade (Belhiba), 68
Coiffeur du quartier des pauvres, Le (Reggab), 47
Collier perdu de la colombe, Le (Khemir), 66, *67*
Colline oubliée, La (Bouguermouh), 59
Compromise, The (L. Lahlou), 45
Compromission, La (L. Lahlou), 45
Conquer to Live (Tazi & Mesnaoui), 20, 29
Control of Origin (Bouchaâla & Bouchaâla), 81, 186
Copains du jour, Les (Zerouali), 45
Costa-Gavras, 6, 16, 27, 126
Coupe, La (Damak), 50
Crazy Years of the Twist, The (Zemmouri), 41, 53
Cri de pierre (Bouguermouh), 41
Cri des hommes, Le (Touita), 56
Crossing Over (Ben Mahmoud), 49–50, 54, 125, 132, 160
Cry of Men, The (Touita), 56
Cry of Stone (Bouguermouh), 41
Cup, The (Damak), 50

Dàc, Trân, 56
Damak, Mohamed, 50, 52, 53
Damardjji, Djafar, 9, 27, 36, 37, 56
Dame du Caire, La (Smihi), 62
D'Anna, Claude, 33
Danse du feu, La (Baccar), 66
Dawn, The (Khlifi), 8, 21
Dawn of the Damned (Rachedi), 8, 16, 17, *18*
Days, The Days, The (El Maânouni), 30, *37,* 38, 45, 124, 171
De Hollywood à Tamanrasset (Zemmouri), 56

De l'autre côté du fleuve (Abbazi), 46–47
De quelques événements sans signification (M. Derkaoui), 31
Dead End (Khayat), 48
Dead the Long Night (Riad & Bendeddouche), 24
Debboub, Yahia, 57, 71
December (Lakhdar Hamina), 23, 97
Décembre (Lakhdar Hamina), 23
Défi, Le (Khlifi), 49
Dehane, Kamal, 117
Delannoy, Jean, 71
Demain je brûle (Ben Smaïl), 68
Demain la terre ne changera pas (Mesbahi), 29
Démon au féminin, Le (Zinaï-Koudil), 58
Denial, The (Bouamari), 40, 53, 89
Depardieu, Gérard, 74
Déracinés, Les (Merbah), 26–27
Derkaoui, Mohamed Abdelkrim, 31, 46, 53, 61–62
Derkaoui, Mostafa, 9, 31, 36, 44–45, 53, 54, 61, 63, 72, 76, 77, 88
Dernière image, La (Lakhdar Hamina), 40
Des années déchirées (Bouchareb), 69
Des pas dans le brouillard (Benchrif), 48
Desert Ark, The (Chouikh), 59, 72
Desert Rose (Benhadj), 42–43
Destin de femme (Noury), 61
Deux larrons en folie (Mansour), 50
Devil's Treasure, The (Osfour), 29
Dhouib, Moncef, 65, 66, 71, 151
Dialmy, Abdssamad, 142, 143
Dietrich, Marlene, 129
Dine, Philip, 96
Diseurs de vérité, Les (Traïdia), 79
Dissanayake, Wimal, 5, 179, 180
Djadjam, Mostéfa, 79
Djebar, Assia, 10, 23, 36, 38, 39, 40, 54, **114–122**, *117, 120*
Djemaï, Ahmed, 68
Doigt dans l'engrenage, Le (Rachedi), 27
Dostoyevsky, Fyodor, 129
Douce France (Chibane), 70
Dove's Lost Necklace, The (Khemir), 66–67, 89
Drach, Michel, 35, 125
Dragan, Mircea, 29
Drama of the 40,000 (Akti), 45
Drame des 40,000, Le (Akti), 45
Dream Thief, The (Noury), 60
Dridi, Karim, 70
Driss, Mohamed, 89
Drug Alert (Zanchin), 178
Drums of Fire (Benbarka), 62
Du paradis à l'enfer (Souda), 76
Dust of Diamonds (Ben Mahmoud & Jaïbi), 67

Duvivier, Julien, 5
Dwyer, Kevin, 9, 156

Echec et mat (Ferhati), 68
Éclair nocturne (Abidi), 68
Egyptian Story, An, 115
El Alaoui, Fatima Zahra, 43, 45, 88, 95
El Chergui (Smihi), 8, 31, 37, 38, **87–95**
El chergui ou le silence violent (Smihi), 30,
   87–95, *91, 93*
El Fani, Nadia, 10, 79, 159
El Ghoula (Kateb), 24
El Kotbia (Saheb-Ettaba), 79, 81
Elle est diabétique et hypertendue et elle refuse
   de crever (Noury), 76
El Maânouni, Ahmed, 30, *31,* 36, 38, 45,
   124, 171
El moufid (Laskri), 25
El Okbi, Mohamed, 34, 36, 67
El ouelf essaib (Hilmi), 57
El Saadawi, Nawal, 164
Ellwood, David W., 2
Elsaesser, Thomas, 8
Embers, The (Bouquia), 47
Empire des rêves, L' (Lledo), 41
Empire of Dreams, The (Lledo), 41
Enfance volée (Noury), 60, 78
Enfant des étoiles, L' (Benayat), 51
Enfants de l'ennui, Les (Ferchiou), 35
Enfants des néons, Les (Tsaki), 56
Enfants du vent, Les (Tsaki), 41
Enfer à dix ans, L' (collective), 17
Ensaad, Abdelkader, 60
Errances (Damardjji), 56
Essaïda (Zran), 68
Essid, Lotfi, 50, 52, 53, 124
Et après (Ismaïl), 77
Et demain? (Babaï), 34–35
Étranger, L' (Visconti), 6
Évasion de Hassan Terro, L' (Badie), 24

Facteur, Le (Noury), 47
Fadel, Youssef, 173
Fanon, Frantz, 150
Fares, Nadia, 159, 185
Fares, Tewfik, 17
Fatma (Ghorbal), 79, 81
Fatma 75 (Baccar), 33, 159, 160
Faucon, Philippe, 187
Faute à Voltaire, La (Kechiche), 79–80
Fawal, Ibrahim, 115
Fazaî Melliti, Ezzedine, 68, 71
Fellagas, Les (Khlifi), 32
Fellagas, The (Khlifi), 32

Fellini, Federico, 11, 89
Female Demon, The (Zinaï-Koudil), 58, 73
Femmes d'Islam (Benguigui), 80
Femmes en mouvement (Allouache & Djebar),
   116–117
Femmes . . . et femmes (S. Chraïbi), 64
Ferchiou, Rachid, 35, 37, 67–68, 72
Ferhati, Jillali, 10, 30, 36, 45, 47, 54, 63, 65, 72,
   76, 78, 124, 132, 169, 171
Ferroukhi, Ismaïl, 76
Fertile Memory (Kheifi), 160
Fête des autres, La (Benjelloun), 64
Fettar, Sid Ali, 41, 53, 55, 56
Feu vert (Mesbahi), 29
Fiancée polonaise, La (Traïdia), 70
Fiction première (M. Derkaoui), 61
Fille de Carthage, La (Chikly), 6
Fille de Keltoum, La (Charef), 81
Finger in the Works, A (Rachedi), 27
Fire Dance, The (Baccar), 66, 159, 160
First Fiction (M. Derkaoui), 61
First Step (Bouamari), 25, 37, 40
Fishermen, The (Bendeddouche), 25
Fleur de lotus (Laskri), 55
Folles années du twist, Les (Zemmouri), 41
Forbidden Love (Fettar), 56
Forbidden Zone (Lallem), 24
Forgotten Hillside, The (Bouguermouh), 59, 72
Forty-Four, or Tales of the Night (Smihi), 45
From Heaven to Hell (Souda), 76
From Hollywood to Tamanrasset (Zemmouri), 56
From the Other Side of the River (Abbazi),
   46–47
Frontières (Djadjam), 79, 81
Frontiers (Djadjam), 79

Gabous, Abdelkrim, 159
Gadant, Monique, 96
(Ga)me in the Past (M. Derkaoui), 61
Garcia Lorca, Federico, 30
Gates of Silence, The (Laskri), 40, 53
Gateway to Heaven, A (Benlyazid), 47, 160
Ghalem, Ali, 35, 38, 43, 53, 54, 125
Ghali, Noureddine, 95
Ghanem, Ali. See Ghalem, Ali
Ghorab-Volta, Zaïda, 55, 70, 81
Ghorbal, Khaled, 79
Gilded Youth (Ghorab-Volta), 81
Girl from Carthage, The (Chikly), 6
Girls from Good Families (Bouzid), 66
Goha (Baratier), 21
Golden Horseshoes (Bouzid), 50, 54, **132–140,**
   135, 137, 146, 150, 169, 179
Good Families, The (Damardjji), 27, 37

Gounajjar, Nour Eddine, 10, 31, 64, 71, 72
Gouverneur-général de Chakerbakerbane, Le (N. Lahlou), 44
Governor-General of Chakerbakerbane, The (N. Lahlou), 44
Gramsci, Antonio, 136
Grand voyage, Le (M. A. Tazi), 45–46
Grande allégorie, La (M. Derkaoui), 61
Great Allegory, The (M. Derkaoui), 61
Green Fire (Mesbahi), 29
Guback, Thomas H., 2
Guerdjou, Bourlem, 70, 73, 80
Guerre de libération, La (collective), 24
Guerre du Golfe . . . et après?, La (collective), 65
Guerre du pétrole n'aura pas lieu, La (Benbarka), 30
Guerre sans images (Soudani), 185
Gusdorf, Georges, 114

Hadda (Aboulouakar), 47, 64
Haddad, Moussa, 24, 25, 28, 36
Hadhra (Jaziri), 78
Hadj, Messali, 102
Hadjadj, Belkacem, 58, *59*, 71, 72, 132
Hafez, Sabry, 24, 97, 100, 102
Haine, La (Kassowitz), 173
Hakkar, Amor, 69
Halfaouine (Boughedir), 65, 66, 73, **141–149**, *144, 148*, 153, 160, 162, 182
Halfaouine—l'enfant des terrasses (Boughedir), 65
Hamlet Sisters, The (Bahloul), 69
Hammami, Abderrazak, 33, 36
Hammami, Mohamed, 35, 37
Hammer and the Anvil, The (Noury), 60
Harem de Mme Osmane, Le (Moknèche), 79
Hargreaves, Alec, 126, 127
Harvests of Steel (Bendeddouche), 39, 53
Hassan Terro (Lakhdar Hamina), 17, 97
Hassan Terro au maquis (Haddad), 24
Hassan Terro in the Resistance (Haddad), 24
Hassan Terro's Escape (Badie), 24
Hassan-niya (Bendeddouche), 39
Hassan-Taxi (Riad), 39
Hayward, Susan, 187
Hell for a 10 Year Old (collective), 17
Hellal, Abderrazak, 57, 72
Hello Cousin! (Allouache), 59–60
Hennebelle, Guy, 87
Héritage, Le (Bouamari), 25
Hexagon (Chibane), 70
Hexagone (Chibane), 70
Hilmi, Mohamed, 57, 71

Hirondelles ne meurent pas à Jérusalem, Les (Behi), 68
Histoires de la révolution (collective), 17
Histoire d'une rencontre (Tsaki), 41
Histoire d'une rose, L' (Rchich), 77
H'mida (Michaud-Mailland), 21, 178
Hole in the Wall, A (Ferhati), 30, 47
Homme de cendres, L' (Bouzid), 50
Homme qui brodait des secrets, L' (O. Chraïbi), 77
Homme qui regardait les fenêtres, L' (Allouache), 40
Honey and Ashes (N. Fares), 159, 185
Honneur de ma famille, L' (Bouchareb), 69
Honneur du tribu, L' (Zemmouri), 58
Honor of the Tribe, The (Zemmouri), 58
Hors jeu (Dridi), 70
Hors-la-loi, Les (Fares), 17
Horsemen of Glory (Benbarka), 62
Houria (Mazif), 40, 53
Hurlement (Laloui), 55
Hurlements (Khlifi), 32
Hyena's Sun (Behi), 33, 37, 132

I Exist (Mazif), 40
I Shall Write Your Name in the Sand (Mesbahi), 63
If Moh, No Hope (Smihi), 87
I'm the Artist (Zerouali), 45, 63
Immigrants' Memories (Benguigui), 80
Impasse, L' (Khayat), 48
In het Huis van mijn Vader (Jebli Ouazzani), 70
In My Father's House (Jebli Ouazzani), 70, 73, 75
In the Land of the Juliets (Charef), 69
In the Land of the Tararani (collective), 33
Inch'Allah dimanche (Benguigui), 80–81
Inch'Allah Sunday (Benguigui), 80–81, 81
Inheritance, The (Bouamari), 25, *26*
Inspector Tahar's Holiday (Haddad), 28, 37
Ismaïl, Mohamed, 65, 72, 77

Jaïbi, Fadhel, 25, 49, 53, 67, 89
Jaïdi, Moulay Driss, 95, 132
Jancsó, Miklos, 11
Jaziri, Fadhel, 35, 49, 53, 78, 89
Jebli Ouazzani, Fatima, 55, 70, 73, 75
J'écrirai ton nom dans le sable (Mesbahi), 63
Je(u) au passé (M. Derkaoui), 61
Jeunesse dorée (Ghorab-Volta), 81
J'existe (Mazif), 40
Jibril, Mohamed, 37, 64
Jour du forain, Le (M. A. Derkaoui & Kettani), 46

Journey to the Capital (Akika & Autissier), 35
Jugement d'une femme (Benjelloun), 76

Kabouche, Azize, 80
Kalsoum, Oum, 167
Kamal, Kamal, 77
Kamel, Boualem, 60
Kassari, Yasmine, 76
Kassowitz, Mathieu, 173
Kateb, Mustapha, 24, 36
Kechiche, Abdellatif, 79–80
Keid ensa (Benlyazid), 62
Keltoum's Daughter (Charef), 81
Keswa—le fil perdu (Bornaz), 66
Keswa—The Lost Thread (Bornaz), 66,
    159, 160
Kettani, Driss, 46, 53, 61
Khafaya (Yachfine), 62
Khayat, Mustapha, 48
Khayati, Khémais, 115
Khéchine, Ahmed, 33, 36
Khemir, Nacer, 49, 53, 66–67, *67*, 72, 89, 160
Khleifi, Michel, 145
Khlifa le teigneux (Ben Halima), 21
Khlifa Ringworm (Ben Halima), 21, 68
Khlifi, Omar, 8, 21, 22, 32, 33, 36, 38, 49, 132
Khorma, la bêtise (Saadi), 79
Khorma: Stupidity (Saadi), 79
Khraief, Béchir, 68
Kif Road, The (Zanchin), 178
Kilpatrick, Hilary, 11
Komany (N. Lahlou), 44
Koudjil, Abderrahmane, 154
Kouyate, Sotigui, 81
Krim (Bouchaâla), 70, 81
Krim, Rachida, 55, 70, 80
Kroes, Rob, 2
Ktari, Naceur, 33–34, 38, 78, 123–124
Ktiri Idrissa, Naguib, 64, 71
Kyrou, Ado, 175

Lacheraf, Mostefa, 99, 100, 101
Lady from Cairo, The (Smihi), 62
Lagtaâ, Abdelkader, 7, 31, 63–64, 65, 71, 73,
    179, 180
Lahlou, Latif, 20, 22, 36, 45, 170
Lahlou, Nabyl, 29, 36, 44, 62, 76
Laisse un peu d'amour (Ghorab-Volta), 70
Lakhdar Hamina, Malek, 57, 71, 71–72, 73
Lakhdar Hamina, Mohamed, 8, 15, 17, *19*, 22,
    23, 24, 36, 37, 40, 53, 54, 57, 71, **96–104**, *98*,
    103, 179
Lalla chafia (M. B. A. Tazi), 44

Lalla Hobby (M. A. Tazi), 62–63
Lallem, Ahmed, 24, 25, 36
Laloui, Abderrahim, 55
Lamblin, Philippe, 173
Land in Ashes (Damardjji), 56
Land of Challenge (Mesbahi), 44, 63
Laradji, Rabah, 40, 53, 54
Laraki, Abdelhaï, 77
Larmes de sang (Akika & Autissier), 50–51
Larmes du regret, Les (Moufti), 48
Laskri, Amar, 24, 25, 37, 40, 53, 55, 56–57, 72
Last Image, The (Lakhdar Hamina), 40, 54
Layla ma raison (Louhichi), 50
Lazreg, Marnia, 167
Leave a Little Love (Ghorab-Volta), 70
Legzouli, Hassan, 76, 185
Leïla and the Others (Mazif), 27, 28
Leïla et les autres (Mazif), 27, 38
Leïla My Reason (Louhichi), 50, 132, 160
Léon, Maryse, 112
Letters from Algeria (Kabouche), 80, 81
Lettres d'Algérie (Kabouche), 80
Lèvres du silence, Les (Benjelloun), 76
Life Dust (Bouchareb), 69, 186
Lights (Lledo), 56
Lips of Silence, The (Benjelloun), 76
Little Senegal (Bouchareb), 81, 186
Little Sénégal (Bouchareb), 81, 186
Living in Paradise (Guerdjou), 70, 73
Lledo, Jean-Pierre, 41, 53, 56, 72
Looking for My Wife's Husband (M. A. Tazi),
    62, 72, 132, 145, **150–158**, *152, 158*, 170, 181
Lotfi, Mohamed, 63, 71
Lotus Flower (Laskri), 55, 56–57, 72
Louhichi, Taïeb, 50, 53, 67, 125, 132, 160
Love Affair in Casablanca, A (Lagtaâ), 63, 73
Love Story, A (Noury), 76
Love without a Visa (Sefrioui), 76–77
Lovers of Mogador, The (Benbarka), 76
Loves of Hadj Mokhtar Soldi, The (M. Der-
    kaoui), 77
Lu, Sheldon Hsiao-peng, 183–184
Lumière, Louis, 6
Lumières (Lledo), 56

Mabrouk (Chouika), 65
Machaho (Hadjadj), 58, *59*, 72
Madam Osmane's Harem (Moknèche), 79, 186
Magic Box, The (Fazaî Melliti), 68
Magique, Le (Fazaî Melliti), 68
Maherzi, Lotfi, 100, 103–104, 178
Maîtresse en maillot de bain, La (Bouktitine), 81
Make-Believe Horses (Ferhati), 63, 124, 132

Maltby, Richard, 2
Malt-Douglas, Farwa, 114
Mamet, David, 3
Mammeri, Mouloud, 17
Man of Ashes (Bouzid), 50, 54, 132, 162
Man Who Embroidered Secrets, The
 (O. Chraïbi), 77
Man Who Looked at Windows, The
 (Allouache), 40
Manisty, Dinah, 114, 162
Mannequin, Le (Ben Aïcha), 33
Mannequin, The (Ben Aïcha), 33
Mansour, Ali, 50, 53
Marathon Tam (Ben Moktar), 57
Marceau, Marcel, 129
Mariage de Moussa, Le (Mefti), 43
Marie de Nazareth (Delannoy), 71
Marie-Line (Charef), 81, 131, 186
Marteau et l'enclume, Le (Noury), 60
Masque d'une éclaircie, Le (Benayat), 36
Mask of an Enlightened Woman, The
 (Benayat), 36
Masrouki, Habib, 89
Maura, Carmen, 186
Mayne, Judith, 141
Mazif, Sid Ali, 24, 25, 27, 28, 36, 38, 40, 55
M'Djid, Dr. Najat, 171, 172
Meddour, Azzedine, 10, 53, 59, 60, 71, 72
Medicine Woman (M. B. A. Tazi), 44
Mefti, Tayeb, 43, 53
Megherbi, Abdelghani, 4
Mektoub (Ayouch), 65, 170, 173
Mektoub? (Ghalem), 35
Memmi, Albert, 87
Mémoire bleue (Gounajjar), 64
Mémoire fertile, La (Khleifi), 160
Mémoires d'immigrés (Benguigui), 80
Mengouchi, Mustapha, 43
Men's Season, The (Tlatli), 78, 151, 159, 160
Merbah, Lamine, 26–27, 28, 36, 56
Meriem (Fettar), 55
Mernissi, Fatima, 112, 141, 142, 149, 156,
 157, 162
Mesbahi, Addellah, 29, 36, 44, 63, 77
Mesbahi, Imane, 77
Mesguich, Félix, 6
Mesnaoui, Ahmed, 20, 22, 29
Michaud-Mailland, Jean, 20, 178
Miel et cendres (N. Fares), 159, 185
Mille et une mains (Benbarka), 30
Mille et une voix, Les (Ben Mahmoud), 78
Millet, Raphaël, 82, 83, 182–183
Mimouna (Mazif), 55
Mint Tea (Bahloul), 52, 54, 125

Minute of Sunshine, A (Ayouch), 77
Miquel, André, 50
Mirage (Bouanani), 29, 31, 37, 89
Mirka (Benhadj), 74, 184
Miss Mona (Charef), 52, **123–131**, *127, 130*
Mistress in a Swimming Costume, The (Boukti-
 hine), 81
Moi l'artiste (Zerouali), 45, 63
Moineau, Le (Chahine), 23
Moissons d'acier (Bendeddouche), 39
Mokhtar (Ben Aïcha), 21
Moknèche, Nadir, 79, 186
Mon village (M. Hammami), 35
Mona Saber (Laraki), 77, 81
Monroe, Marilyn, 129
Monsieur Fabre's Mill (Rachedi), 39, 53
Montagne de Baya, La (Meddour), 59
Moon Wedding (Louhichi), 67
Moonlighting (Bakhti), 57
Moroccan Chronicles (Smihi), 62
Mort trouble, La (Boughedir & d'Anna), 33
Morte la longue nuit (Riad & Bendeddouche), 24
Mortimer, Mildred, 116
Moufti, Hassan, 48, 53
Moulin de Monsieur Fabre, Le (Rachedi), 39
Moussa's Wedding (Mefti), 43
Mrini, Driss, 48, 53
Mselmani, Habib, 50, 53
Murky Death (Boughedir & d'Anna), 33
My Family's Honor (Bouchareb), 69
My Village (M. Hammami), 35, 37

Naficy, 178, 186, 187
Nagbou, Mustapha, 183
Nahla (Beloufa), 28, 37, 89, 160
Najmabadi, Afsanej, 145
Neighbor, The (Bendeddouche), 55, 74
Neon Children, The (Tsaki), 56
Nieuwkerk, Karin van, 165
Night is Afraid of the Sun, The (Badie), 17
Night of Destiny, The (Bahloul), 69
Night of the Crime, The (N. Lahlou), 62
Night of the Decade, The (Babaï), 68
Nightmare (Yala), 47
No Man's Love (Chatta), 78–79, 81
Noce, La (collective), 35
Noces de lune (Louhichi), 67
Noces de sang (Benbarka), 30
Nomades, Les (Mazif), 25
Nomads, The (Mazif), 25
Noria's Song, The (Ben Ammar), 78, 81
Noua (Tolbi), 26, 28
Nouba des femmes du Mont Chenoua, La
 (Djebar), 28, **114–122**, *117, 120*

Nouba of the Women of Mount Chenoa, The (Djebar), 28
Noury, Hakim, 9, 47, 53, 60–61, *61*, 65, 72, 76, 78, 170, 171
Nous irons sur la montagne (Mengouchi & Bouchemha), 43
Noweir, Sawan, 120
Nuit a peur du soleil, La (Badie), 16
Nuit de la décennie, La (Babaï), 68
Nuit du crime, La (N. Lahlou), 62
Nuit du destin, La (Bahloul), 69

O les jours (El Maânouni), 30
Oil War Will Not Happen, The (Benbarka), 30, 160–161
Oiseau du paradis, L' (Bensaïd), 47–48
Old Lady and the Child, The (Debboub), 57
Olive Tree of Boul'Hilet, The (Azizi), 25
Olivier de Boul'Hilet, L' (Azizi), 25
Olvidados, Los (Buñuel), 175
Om Abbes (Abdelwahab), 33
Omar Gatlato (Allouache), 28, 58, 89, **105–113**, *107*, *113*, 132, 145, 153, 160, 180
Ombre de la terre, L' (Louhichi), 50
Ombre du gardien, L' (Souda), 46
Ombre du pharaon, L' (Benbarka), 62
Ombres blanches (Ould Khelifa), 57
Omi Traki (A. Hammami), 33
Once Upon a Time (Hadjadj), 58
One Summer at La Goulette (Boughedir), 65–66, 151
Opium and the Stick (Rachedi), 17, 24, 37
Opium et le bâton, L' (Rachedi), 17, 37
Origine contrôlée (Bouchaâla & Bouchaâla), 81
Osfour, Mohamed, 29, 36
Other France, The (Ghalem), 35
Other People's Celebrations (Benjelloun), 64
Other World, The (Allouache), 74, 81
Où cachez-vous le soleil? (Mesbahi), 29
Ould Khelifa, Saïd, 57, 72
Out of Play (Dridi), 70
Outlaws, The (Fares), 17

Pal, The (Benjelloun), 76
Pals for the Day (Zerouali), 45
Pappas, Irene, 30
Paradis des pauvres (I. Mesbahi), 77
Paradise of the Poor (I. Mesbahi), 77
Parisian Love Story, A (Allouache), 40, 53
Pasolini, Pier Paolo, 11, 30
Patellière, Denys de la, 16
Patrol in the East, 24
Patrouille à l'est (Laskri), 24
Pêcheurs, Les (Bendeddouche), 25

Pépé le Moko (Duvivier), 5
People on the March, A (collective), 22
People's Victory, A (Babaï), 35
Petri, Elio, 30
Peuple en marche (collective), 22
Picnic (Boughedir), 33
Pierres bleues du désert, Les (Ayouch), 170
Pigalle (Dridi), 70
Pique-nique, Le (Boughedir), 33
Plage des enfants perdus, La (Ferhati), 63
Plunderers, The (Merbah), 26, 28,
Polish Bride, The (Traïdia), 70
Pomegranate Siesta, The (Ben Mahmoud), 67
Pontecorvo, Gillo, 6, 16, 96
Porte Close, La (Lagtaâ), 63–64
Portes du silence, Les (Laskri), 40
Portrait, Le (Rahim), 57
Portrait, The (Rahim), 57
Postman, The (Noury), 47
Pote, Le (Benjelloun), 76
Poupées d'argile (Bouzid), 78
Poupées de roseau (Ferhati), 45, 78
Pour que vive l'Algérie (collective), 27
Poussière de diamants (Ben Mahmoud & Jaïbi), 67
Poussières de vie (Bouchareb), 69
Prayer for the Absent, A (Benani), 63
Prédal, René, 128, 131, 187
Premier pas (Bouamari), 25
Prends dix milles balles et casses-toi (Zemmouri), 41
Prière de l'absent, La (Benani), 63
Provisional Title (M. Derkaoui), 45, 53

Quand murissent les dattes (Ramdani & Bennani), 20
Quarante-quatre, ou les récits de la nuit (Smihi), 45
Que fait-on ce dimanche? (Essid), 50
Question d'honneur (Hellal), 57
Question of Honor (Hellal), 57

Rachedi, Ahmed, 8, 15, 16, 17, *18*, 22, 23, 24, 27, 35, 36, 38, 39, 53, 124
Rachida (Bachir-Chouikh), 74, *75*, 81
Radhia (Merbah), 56
Rahim, Hadj, 57, 72
Rai (Fettar), 41
Ramdani, Abdelaziz, 20, 22, 29
Rchich, Abdelmajid, 10, 77, 82
Rebel, The (Khlifi), 21
Rebelle, Le (Khlifi), 21
Red Satin (Amari), 79, 159, 160
Redeyef 54 (Abidi), 68

Redgrave, Vanessa, 74
Reed Dolls (Ferhati), 45, 47, 54, 171
Refus, Le (Bouamari), 40
Reggab, Mohamed, 31, 47, 53, 63
Renaissance (Ruspoli), 20
Rescapé, Le, (Touita), 41
Resistance Fighters, The (Debboub), 57
Résistant inconnu, Le (Bennani), 63
Résistants, Les (Debboub), 57
Retour du fils prodigue, Le (Chahine), 23
Return of the Prodigal Son, The (Chahine), 23
Reynolds, Dwight, 114
Rhesus or Another Person's Blood (Lotfi), 63
Rhésus ou le sang d'un autre (Lotfi), 63
Riad, Mohamed Slim, 17, 22, 23, 24, 25, 27,
    28, 36, 37, 39
Richardson, Samuel, 1
Roberts, Kevin, 181
Rose des sables (Benhadj), 42
Rosi, Francesco, 30
Rouiched, 17, 24, 97
Route du Kif, La (Zanchin), 178
Rue le Caire (M. A. Derkaoui), 61–62
Rupture (Tlili), 159, 185
Rupture, La (Chouikh), 43
Ruspoli, Mario, 20

Saadi, Jilani, 79
Saadi, Yacef, 16
Sabots en or, Les (Bouzid), 50
Sabra and the Monster from the Forest (Msel-
    mani), 50
Sabra et le monstre de la forêt (Mselmani), 50
Sacrificed, The (Touita), 41, 53
Sacrifiés, Les (Touita), 41
Saddiki, Tayeb, 47, 53
Sahara Blues (Boubarras), 57
Sahed-Ettaba, Nawfel, 79
Said, Edward, 1, 2, 4, 88
Saison des hommes, La (Tlatli), 78
Sale temps pour un voyou (Hakkar), 69
Saleh, Tewfik, 169
Salle d'attente, La (Gounajjar), 64
Salut cousin! (Allouache), 59–60
Samia (Faucon), 187
Sana'oud (Riad), 24, 36
Sand Storm (Lakhdar Hamina), 40, 53, 99
Satin rouge (Amari), 79
Saugeon, Nathalie, 173
Sauve-moi (Vincent), 187
Savage Barricades (Benayat), 36
Save Me (Vincent), 187
Schäfer, Isabel, 183
Schlesinger, Philip, 181

Scream (Lalouï), 55
Screams (Khlifi), 32, 38
Searchers of the Desert, The (Khemir), 49, 53,
    66, 89, 160
Sebbar, Leïla, 126
Sefioui, Najib, 46, 53, 77
Segou (Bouchareb), 69
Sejnane (Ben Ammar), 8, 33, 34, 38, 160
Sembene, Ousmane, 154–155
Sept portes de la nuit, Les (M. Derkaoui), 61
Seqqat, Med, 30
Serceau, Michel, 82, 83, 144
Seven Gates of the Night, The (M. Derkaoui), 61
Shadow of the Earth, The (Louhichi), 50, 53,
    125, 132, 160
Shadow of the Guardian, The (Souda), 46
Shadow of the Pharaoh (Benbarka), 62
Sharif, Omar, 21
Shattered Years (Bouchareb), 69
She is Diabetic and Hypertensive and She Re-
    fuses to Die (Noury), 76
Shenna, Leïla, 90
Si Moh pas de chance (Smihi), 87
Siestes grenadine, Les (Ben Mahmoud), 67
Silence, No Entry (Mesbahi), 29
Silence, sens interdit (Mesbahi), 29
Silences du palais, Les (Tlatli), 66
Silences of the Palace (Tlatli), 66, 73, 77, **159–
    168**, 161, 166
Simple News Item, A (Noury), 60–61
Skirej, Bachir, 77, 154
Slavin, David Henry, 5
Smihi, Moumen, 1, 8, 9, 30–31, 36, 37, 38, 45,
    62, 72, **87–95**, 91, 93, 180
Smith-Rosenberg, Caroll, 141
So That Algeria May Live (collective), 27
Soeurs Hamlet, Les (Bahloul), 69
Soif (S. Chraïbi), 76
Sois mon amie (Ktari), 77
Soleil de printemps (L. Lahlou), 20
Soleil des hyènes (Behi), 33
Soleil noir (Patellière), 16
Soltane el Madina! (Dhouib), 66
Some People and Others (Ben Salah), 35
Souda, Saïd, 46, 53, 76
Soudani, Mohamed, 185
Souiba, Fouad, 43, 45, 88, 95
Soul That Brays, The (N. Lahlou), 44
Sous la pluie d'automne (Khéchine), 33
Sous les pieds des femmes (Krim), 70
Sparrow, The (Chahine), 23
Spoliateurs, Les (Merbah), 26
Spring Sunshine (L. Lahlou), 20, 45, 170
Steps in the Mist (Benchrif), 48

Stock, Ann Marie, 184
Stolen Childhood (Noury), 60, *61*, 171
Stollery, Martin, 133, 146
Stora, Benjamin, 58, 96, 97, 181, 186
Storaro, Vittorio, 74
Stories of the Revolution (collective), 17
Story of a Meeting (Tsaki), 41, 54, 89
Story of a Rose (Rchich), 77
Such a Simple Story (Ben Ammar), 33
Such a Young Peace (Charby), 15, 178
Sueur noire (Mazif), 24
Sultan of the Medina, The (Dhouib), 66, 151
Survivor, The (Touita), 41
Swallows Don't Die in Jerusalem (Behi), 68, 72
Sweet France (Chibane), 70

Taghmaouï, Saïd, 173
Taghounja (Achouba), 47
Tahia ya Didou (Zinet), 27–28
Taif Nizar (Kamal), 77
Take a Thousand Quid and Get Lost (Zemmouri), 41, 54
Tambours du feu (Benbarka), 62
Tamzali, Wassyla, 99, 100, 108, 110
Tarounja (Achouba), 47
Tarr, Carrie, 129
Tazi, Mohamed Abderrahman, 30, 45–46, *46*, 53, 54, 62–63, 72, 88, 124, 132, **150–158**, *152*, *158*, 170, 171, 182
Tazi, Mohamed B. A., 20, 22, 29, 178
Tea at Archimedes' Harem (Charef), 52, 125–126
Tears of Blood (Akika & Autissier), 50–51
Tears of Regret (Moufti), 48
Teddy Boys, The (El Okbi), 67
Terre du défi, La (Mesbahi), 44, 63
Terre en cendres (Damardjji), 56
Terzieff, Laurent, 30
Thé à la menthe, Le (Bahloul), 52
Thé au harem d'Archimède, Le (Charef), 52
Third Act, The (Ben Brahim), 57
Thirst (S. Chraïbi), 76, 81
Thousand and One Hands, A (Benbarka), 30, 31, 37, 170
Thousand and One Voices, A (Ben Mahmoud), 78
Titre provisoire (M. Derkaoui), 45
Tlatli, Moufida, 10, 55, 65, 66, 71, 73, 78, 134, 151, **159–168**, *161*, *166*, 159, 181
Tlili, Najwa, 159, 185
Tolbi, Addelaziz, 26, 28, 36
Tomorrow I Burn (Ben Smaïl), 68, 132
Tomorrow the Land Will Not Change (Mesbahi), 29

Touchia (Benhadj), 58
Touita, Okacha, 41, 53, 56, 72
Tourbillon, Le (Zerouali), 29, 45
Trace, La (Ben Mabrouk), 49
Trace, The (Ben Mabrouk), 49, *51*, 159, 160
Traces (Benani), 30, 63
Traïdia, Karim, 70, 79, *80*, 186
Trances (El Maânouni), 45
Transes (El Maânouni), 45
Travelling Showman, The (M. A. Derkaoui & Kettani), 46, 61
Traversées (Ben Mahmoud), 49
Treasures of the Atlas, The (Abbazi), 63
Tree of Suspended Fates, The (Benhadj), 60
Trésor infernal, Le (Osfour), 29
Trésors de l'Atlas, Les (Abbazi), 63
Tresses (Ferhati), 76
Troisième acte, Le (Ben Brahim), 57
Truth Tellers, The (Traïdia), 79, *80*, 186
Tsaki, Brahim, 10, 41–42, 53, 56, 72, 90
Tunisiennes (Bouzid), 66
Two Thieves in Madness (Mansour), 50

Uland Mohand, Mohamed, 76
Un amour à Casablanca (Lagtaâ), 63
Un amour à Paris (Allouache), 40
Un ballon et des rêves (El Okbi), 34
Un été à la Goulette (Boughedir), 65–66
Un simple fait-divers (Noury), 60–61
Un toit, une famille (Laradji), 40–41
Un vampire au paradis (Bahloul), 69
Under the Autumn Rain (Khéchine), 33
Under Women's Feet (Krim), 70
Une brèche dans le mur (Ferhati), 30
Une femme pour mon fils (Ghalem), 43
Une histoire d'amour (Noury), 76
Une minute de soleil (Ayouch), 77
Une porte sur le ciel (Benlyazid), 47
Une si jeune paix (Charby), 15
Une si simple histoire (Ben Ammar), 33
Unknown Resistance Fighter, The (Bennani), 63
Uns, les autres, Les (Ben Salah), 35
Uprooted, The (Merbah), 26–27

Vacances de l'Inspecteur Tahas, Les (Haddad), 28
Vaincre pour vivre (Tazi & Mesnaoui), 20
Vampire in Paradise, A (Bahloul), 69
Vautier, René, 15, 22
Vent de sable (Lakhdar Hamina), 40
Vent des Aurès, Le (Lakhdar Hamina), 8, 17, *19*
Vent des destins (Djemaï), 68
Vent du sud (Riad), 25
Vermeren, Pierre, 72

Victoire d'un peuple (Babaï), 35
Vieille dame et l'enfant, La (Debboub), 57
Vincendeau, Ginette, 5
Vincent, Christian, 187
Visconti, Luchino, 6
Viva la muerte (Arrabal), 32
Vivre au paradis (Guerdjou), 70
Voie, La (Riad), 17
Voisine, La (Bendeddouche), 55, 74
Voleur de rêves, Le (Noury), 60
Voltaire's Fault (Kechiche), 79–80, 81
Voyage en capital (Akika & Autissier), 35

Waalo fengo (Soudani), 185
Waiting Room, The (Gounajjar), 64
Wandering Heart (Belhiba), 49, 68
Wanderings (Damardjji), 56
War of Liberation, The (collective), 24
War without Images (Soudani), 185
Way, The (Riad), 17)
We Shall Go onto the Mountain (Mengouchi &
    Bouchemha), 43, 53
Wechma (Benani), 30, 31, 37, 88
Wedding, The (collective), 35, 37, 49, 89
Wedding in Galilee (Khleifi), 145
Wesh-Wesh, qu'est-ce qui se passe? (Ameur-
    Zaïmèche), 80
Wesh Wesh—What's Happening? (Ameur-
    Zaïmèche), 80, 81
What Are We Doing This Sunday? (Essid),
    50, 124
What the Winds Have Carried Away (Akti), 45
When the Dates Ripen (Ramdani & Mes-
    naoui), 20, 29
Where Are You Hiding the Sun? (Mesbahi), 29
Whirlpool, The (Zerouali), 29, 45, 63
White Shadows (Ould Khelifa), 57
Wife for my Son, A (Ghalem), 43, 54
Wind from the Aurès, The (Lakhdar Hamina),
    8, 17, 19, 97
Wind from the South (Riad), 25
Wind Horse, The (Aoulad Syad), 77
Wind of Destinies (Djemaï), 68
Woman's Fate, A (Noury), 61

Woman's Judgment, A (Benjelloun), 76
Women . . . and Women (S. Chraïbi), 64
Women of Islam (Benguigui), 80
Women on the Move (Allouache & Djebar), 117
Women's Expectations (Belouad), 81
Women's Wiles (Benlyazid), 62, 145
Woodhall, Winifred, 123

Xala (Sembene), 155

Ya ouled (Benallal), 57
Yachfine, Ahmed, 47, 52, 62
Yacout (Belmejdoub), 77
Yala, Mohamed Meziane, 41, 52, 53
Yarit (Benjelloun), 64
Years of Exile, The (N. Lahlou), 76
Yesterday's Friends (Benjelloun), 64
Yimou, Zhang, 183–184
Ymer or The Flowering Thistles (Chrigui), 64
Ymer ou les chardons florifères (Chrigui), 64
Youcef: la légende du septième dormant
    (Chouikh), 58
Youssef: The Legend of the Seventh Sleeper
    (Choukh), 58, 72
Yusra (Ferchiou), 35

Z (Costa-Gavras), 6, 16
Zalila, Tijani, 21
Zanchin, N., 178
Zazous de la vague, Les (El Okbi), 67
Zeft (Saddiki), 47
Zemmouri, Mahmoud, 41, 53, 54, 56, 58, 60,
    72, 73
Zerda, La (Djebar), 40, 54, 116
Zerda, ou les chants de l'oubli, La (Djebar),
    40, 116
Zerouali, Abdallah, 29, 45, 53, 63, 71
Zinaï-Koudil, Hafsa, 10, 55, 58, 72, 73
Zinet, Mohamed, 27–28, 36
Zohra (Chikly), 6
Zone interdite (Lallem), 24
Zougane, Houria, 148
Zran, Mohamed, 68, 71

ROY ARMES is Emeritus Professor of Film at Middlesex University in London. His recent books include *Third World Film Making and the West, Arab and African Film Making, Dictionary of North African Film Makers,* and *Omar Gatlato.* He is preparing a new study of African filmmaking north and south of the Sahara.